THE MIGHTY
REVOLUTION: Negro Emancipation
in Maryland, 1862–1864

THE MIGHTY REVOLUTION: Negro Emancipation in Maryland, 1862–1864

By CHARLES LEWIS WAGANDT

Baltimore · Maryland Historical Society

Library of Congress Cataloging-in-Publication Data

Wagandt, Charles.
  The mighty revolution : Negro emancipation in Maryland,
1862-1864 / by Charles Lewis Wagandt.
     p. cm.
  Reprint. Originally published: Baltimore : Johns Hopkins
University Press, 1964.
  Includes bibliographical references and index.
  ISBN 0-938420-91-7 (alk. paper)
  1. Maryland—Politics and government—1861-1865. 2.
Slaves—Emancipation—Maryland. 3. Slavery—Maryland—
History. 4. Maryland—Race relations. 5. United States. President
(1861-1865 : Lincoln). Emancipation Proclamation. 6. Slaves—
Emancipation—United States. I. Maryland Historical Society. II.
Title.

   E512.W2 2004
   973.7'14—dc22   2004019464

124389

The paper used in this publication meets the minimum require-
ments of the American National Standard for Information Sciences
Permanence of Paper or Printed Library Materials
ANSI Z39.48-1984

Cover: Painting by James F. Brisson.
Slave shackles courtesy Ms. Vivian M. Rigby.

*To my Mother
and the memory of my Father*

FOREWORD

IN 1861 MARYLAND teetered briefly on the brink of secession but quickly righted itself on the side of the Union. Out of that decision arose another issue, which dominated the political arena until the end of 1864. That issue had been a strong force behind the disruption of the nation. Now it too must be fought openly.

Slavery went on the politicians' block, to be damned and praised, harried and protected until only a skeleton remained for the abolitionists to bury. This is our subject—the political movement of 1862 to 1864 to free the slaves of Maryland, a struggle that ranged from the White House and Congress into the military camps throughout the state. It built and destroyed political careers, ravaged the Unionists with faction, incited them to a battle for power, and resulted in the expropriation of large amounts of property without compensation. It inflamed the conflict for control of the state between the static, agricultural society of the tidewater counties and the growing commercial, industrial, and farm interests of the north and west. It witnessed the exercise of arbitrary power and rapid shifts in public sentiment. This was a revolution reflecting the larger struggle throughout America for freedom not only from slavery but also from an outmoded social and economic order.

Never before has this story received more than brief attention. And yet it is one of the most dramatic and significant events in the history of the state.

ACKNOWLEDGMENT

THIRTEEN YEARS AGO I began research for this book. The quest for correspondence, periodicals, and documents led me to many historical societies, libraries, and individual holders of private papers. I am indebted to so many people for their help that it is impossible to name all of them.

But I would like to note a few. First, I recall Jeter A. Isley, an able scholar, stimulating lecturer, and challenging teacher, who introduced me to the trials and tribulations of historical research while I was an undergraduate at Princeton. He died in 1954, while still a comparatively young man.

Mr. A. D. Emmart and that outstanding historian, Dr. Roy F. Nichols, Dean of the Graduate School of Arts and Sciences at the University of Pennsylvania, read some of my work and gave me encouragement when I most needed it. Certainly Professor Nichols' provocative lectures have influenced my studies. Professor C. Van Woodward, though I was a stranger to him, very kindly put me on the trail of the Henry Winter Davis correspondence in the Samuel Francis DuPont Papers, uncovered by Rear Admiral John D. Hayes, U.S.N. Ret. The latter most generously made the Davis letters available to me.

Colonel Henry Page, now deceased, proved helpful. He vividly recalled conversations with his grandfather, Congressman John W. Crisfield, to whose surviving papers I was guided. Gerard H. Borstel produced old issues of the *Cecil Democrat* for examination in his office.

Research aid was granted at times in various libraries. Mrs. Beatrice I. Pugh finished my investigations into the consular papers in the Public Record Office in London. Dr. Robert V. Bruce did an exceptional job in the National Archives in addition to some work at the

Library of Congress. Mrs. Llewellyn W. Lord, Jr. accomplished some fine art work in the maps and line drawing.

I presumed upon the facilities of numerous depositories, spending the largest amounts of time at the Library of Congress, the Hall of Records in Annapolis, the Enoch Pratt Library in Baltimore, the Maryland Historical Society, and the Peabody Institute Library. I am indebted to the staffs of these institutions for their assistance and shall also fondly recall the work of such people as Miss Betty Adler and Miss Lillian O'Brien. Through many years and drafts, Mrs. Betty M. Weigand gave of her talents in typing most of my manuscript, and her work was completed by Mrs. David R. Sanderson. To those I have not named, I am also deeply grateful.

CHARLES L. WAGANDT

Baltimore, Maryland
March, 1964

CONTENTS

FOREWORD vii

ACKNOWLEDGMENT ix

PART I

UNION AND SLAVERY INDIVISIBLE

I   Maryland a Divided State 1

II   The Union Victorious in Maryland 15

III   A New State Government 29

IV   The Tarnished Idol of Slavery 41

PART II

THE RISING ASSAULT ON SLAVERY

V   Lincoln's Offer of Compensation 55

VI   Lincoln's Emancipation Proclamations 71

VII   The Emergence of Maryland Emancipationists 84

VIII   The Disruption of the Union Party 95

IX   The Flight and Enlistment of Slaves 116

X   The Political Campaign of 1863 133

PART III

THE WINNING OF EMANCIPATION

XI   Election by Sword and Ballot 155

XII   The Shifting Struggle for Political Power 185

XIII   Another Victory at the Polls 197

XIV   The Constitutional Convention of 1864 221

XV   Fusion of the Presidential and Constitutional Campaigns 231
XVI   Maryland Free 246

BIBLIOGRAPHY 269

INDEX 285

LIST OF TABLES

Table A   Results of Congressional Election June 13, 1861 18
Table B   List of Elections in Which Baltimore Unionists
           Were Entitled to Vote, May–November, 1863 138
Table C   Somerset County Election Results 170
Table D   Election Statistics, November 4, 1863 182
Table E   Vote on Constitutional Convention, 1864 219
Table F   Allocation of Seats in the Maryland General Assembly 229
Table G   Vote on Constitution, October 12–13, 1864 262

LIST OF ILLUSTRATIONS

1. Map of Maryland 3
2. Map of Somerset County Showing Results of
    November 4, 1863, Election 169
3. Map of Maryland Showing Results of November 4, 1863, Election ... 179
4. Map of Maryland Showing Results of April 6, 1864, Election 218
5. Ballots Used by the Soldiers in the
    Constitutional Election of October, 1864 259

PART I

UNION AND
SLAVERY
INDIVISIBLE

CHAPTER I

MARYLAND
A DIVIDED STATE

"SIR, THE STATE of Maryland has been sectionalized, just as the whole country has been sectionalized. . . . the northern and western counties . . . are wantonly waging an aggressive war upon the institutions of Southern Maryland."[1]

The year was 1864; the orator, a member of the Constitutional Convention sitting in Annapolis. Speaking on behalf of a hopeless minority of delegates, he stood in the path of the flood tide of immediate emancipation. Stripped of the power that only two years ago had been theirs to wield, the proponents of slavery doggedly clung to each vanishing hope as the irresistible majority pressed forward. As the speaker bewailed the course history had taken, he struck at the stronghold of his antagonists, the north and west of Maryland. When he said the state had been sectionalized, he was thinking of the struggle for political ascendancy, which was in many ways predetermined by geography.

From the broken terrain of the mountainous west, Maryland stretched eastward, fanning out to the Chesapeake Bay and then narrowing once again to claim a short beach on the Atlantic Ocean. Below the Patapsco River, with its metropolis of Baltimore, spread the seven counties of southern Maryland. It was from this section that Eli J. Henkle had come to cry out his protest from the floor of the old state capitol on that June day. His region, shaped like a foot, pointed southeastward, its heel washed by the Potomac River and its instep bathed by the Chesapeake. Except for the two westernmost counties, the countryside lay within the coastal plain, close to navigable water. In the five tidewater counties lived nearly half of

[1] *The Debates of the Constitutional Convention of the State of Maryland* (Annapolis, 1864), I, 624.

Maryland's 87,000 slaves and some 11,000 free Negroes. Together they far outnumbered the white residents,[2] who comprised only 7.4 per cent of Maryland's Caucasians but more than 27 per cent of the slaveholders. These demographic facts permeated the psychology of southern Marylanders and made them the most reactionary people within the state. Nowhere else in Maryland did the counterrevolution of the Confederacy find such strong support.

Immigrants shunned the area, most of which counted fewer white residents in 1860 than in 1790. These people formed an unchanging agricultural society that grew the nation's third largest tobacco crop in 1860.[3] Only in Howard County, on the outer fringes of the region, did manufacturing assume any importance.

An even more homogeneous white population looking with even less concern on industry lived on the Eastern Shore. Not one of its seven counties could produce enough industrial manufactures to report sales of $200,000 annually.[4] Cut off from the rest of the state by the long arm of the Chesapeake, the shore had the shape of an extremely ragged "L." No one lived more than twenty miles from either the sandy beaches of the Atlantic Ocean or the deeply serrated shoreline of the bay, with its abundant rivers and inlets. Seafood abounded, but farming dominated—wheat, corn, and oats were the principal crops. Tobacco was unimportant, and so slavery did not assume the prominence it held in southern Maryland. Nonetheless, these were called slave counties, for one fifth of their people lived in bondage. A slightly larger number of Negroes (20.9 per cent) were free.

To the north of the two slave regions sprawled another group of seven counties and Baltimore City. Tidewater Cecil,[5] tucked away into the northeastern corner of Maryland, looked westward across the mighty Susquehanna into a countryside of beautiful, rolling terrain. Beyond lay mountains and fertile valleys cutting across the state. Squeezed at one point to a two-mile width, the long arm of

---

[2] Total white population for the five counties was 37,945. Slaves numbered 40,622 and free blacks 10,837. *Population of the United States in 1860* . . . (Washington, 1864), p. 214.

[3] *Agriculture of the United States in 1860* . . . (Washington, 1864), Vol. 73, pp. 184–85.

[4] *Manufacturers of the United States in 1860* . . . (Washington, 1865), p. 228.

[5] Cecil County is often considered part of the Eastern Shore, but much of its territory lies north of the Chesapeake Bay. Economically and politically the county bore a closer kinship to Maryland's northern counties. It has been included as part of that group for the purpose of this work.

Maryland broadened as it reached westward into the highlands of the Allegheny Plateau and there gave birth to rivers that nourished the Mississippi Valley.

A heterogeneous people enriched this northern land with growing towns, fertile farms, bustling industry, and vigorous commerce that strongly contrasted with the static life of the Eastern Shore and southern Maryland. Onto this land by 1860 settled all but a small fraction of Maryland's 77,436 foreign-born white people. Lured by

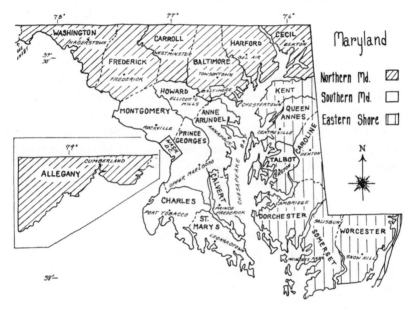

the vision of freedom and opportunity for better life, some 32,000 Germans established themselves in Baltimore alone. The Irish numbered almost half that many and boosted the proportion of the alien-born to one-fourth of the city's residents.[6]

Thousands more came into the northern counties from other states, the population spurting three and three quarter times from 1790 to 1860. In the same seventy years southern Maryland and the Eastern Shore crept along at a 20 per cent rate. The proportion of slaves was small, 3.2 per cent; so these northern lands were known as the free counties.

[6] The four largest immigrant groups in Baltimore City were: German—32, 613; Irish—15, 536; English—2, 154; Scots—524; Kennedy, *Population, 1860*, p. 611.

Unlike much of the Chesapeake Bay region, the white settler usually tilled his own soil. He harvested corn, oats, and wheat and around Baltimore engaged in truck farming and dairying. Though the size of his homestead averaged only seventy per cent of those in the slave counties, its value per acre soared to 170 per cent more.[7]

By the War of 1812 the din of new factories echoed through the deep, winding valley of the Patapsco River. Between 1840 and 1860 the worth of Maryland industrial products more than tripled. In 1850 the state led the South in value of industrial products produced. Though Virginia and Missouri later edged her out, the value of Maryland manufactures was estimated by the time of the Civil War as twice that of her agricultural production.[8]

Flour and cotton mills predominated just outside of Baltimore, while boots and shoes, clothing, packed oysters, refined sugar, and the products of foundries and furnaces flowed in such abundance from within the city that they accounted for the value of over half of Maryland's manufactures. Coal arrived from the mines of western Maryland to feed the city's furnaces and to provide a valuable export. Through the harbor passed shiploads of guano on their way to fertilize the farms of America. From New York came wholesale dry goods for Baltimore jobbers, who resold them to the South.[9]

Baltimore stood fourth among the nation's ports in the value of foreign commerce and ranked as America's third largest city, growing from 13,503 in 1790 to 212,418 in 1860. Her shipbuilders made the famous Clippers and earned enough business to give Maryland the lead in shipbuilding in the South.[10] The city also boasted three railroads. Part of the Baltimore and Ohio route roughly paralleled the Chesapeake and Ohio Canal from the District of Columbia to the town of Cumberland. This railroad, in which Maryland invested far more than in slaves, proved vital for strategic and eco-

[7]*Agriculture 1860*, p. 72. The assessed worth of the free counties and Baltimore, including industry, was three times the rest of the state.

[8]Anthony Kennedy in U.S. Senate on February 28, 1863, *Congressional Globe* (now *Congressional Record*) 37th Cong., 3rd Sess., Part 2, p. 1375. The census of 1860 listed $41,735,157 as the annual value of Maryland manufactures.

[9] Report of Frederick Bernal, British Consul, on trade of Baltimore for 1861, Foreign Office Papers (F. O. 5/847, Public Record Office 874), London, England.

[10] Charles Branch Clark, *Politics in Maryland During the Civil War* (Chestertown, Md., 1952), p. 17. The chapters from this book appeared in various issues of the *Maryland Historical Magazine* between 1941 and 1946.

nomic reasons. Thirty-six million dollars worth of trade yearly traveled westward out of Baltimore by B&O in 1860.[11] The city's largest trade, however, was directly to the southwest and south.

With a disparity of peoples and interests, Maryland suffered from internal friction. In many ways her struggles were typical of the larger conflicts within the nation as a whole. Between 1750 and 1850 the hinterland and the tidewater struggled for political control as ties with Pennsylvania developed more rapidly than the already strong bonds with Virginia. The desire of the growing free counties to expand commercially and industrially clashed with the wishes of the static slave counties. Internal improvements spelled progress to one area but only an added tax burden to the other.

In 1851 Maryland framed a new constitution. It yielded to the more energetic north and west a larger voice in the legislature, but the slave counties retained ample power for vetoing any measure deemed inimical to their interests. They based representation not only on the white population but also on every Negro, slave and free, even though the colored man had no rights that the white man was bound to respect. In fact, the slave was alternately considered as person or property, depending on which classification benefited the planter.

The late eighteenth century reflected a more enlightened attitude. The state Constitution of 1776 gave some free Negroes the right to vote (later rescinded), and in 1789 Marylanders organized the world's sixth anti-slavery association.[12] This movement flourished for a time, only to wither by 1830. Its remnants were absorbed by the unsuccessful attempt to colonize Negroes in Africa.[13]

Economics speeded the decline of southern emancipationists. The profitableness of cotton cultivation sent prices for slaves soaring. That gave the institution status as a money-maker, which in turn created respectability and powerful political backing. Though Maryland grew very little cotton, slavery linked her to southern culture and customs. The institution exerted a strong influence even on the leaders

[11] U.S. Senator Anthony Kennedy, February 28, 1862, *Congressional Globe*, 37th Cong., 3rd Sess., Vol. 33, Part 2, 1374.

[12] William Frederick Poole, *Anti-Slavery Opinions before the Year 1800* (Cincinnati, 1873), p. 50; John T. Scharf, *History of Maryland* (Baltimore, 1897), III, 306.

[13] Despite state support, only some 1,450 Negroes sailed to Liberia from 1833 to 1859. James M. Wright, *The Free Negro in Maryland: 1643–1860* (New York, 1921), p. 337.

of the free counties, a fact that tended to dampen a freer expression of the needs of northern Maryland.

As a new wave of emancipation sentiment emerged in the north, Maryland and its sister states to the south showed none of their earlier enlightenment.[14] Instead, they looked anxiously at their relative decline in wealth and numbers. Fearing the loss of their ability to block unfriendly national legislation, they devised a stout defense for their weakest link—slavery. Men, government, and religion were forced into obeisance while a counteroffensive sought to extend slavery westward.

Fear of the Negro, both real and imaginary, stiffened the southern position. For instance, Nat Turner's gory uprising of slaves in Virginia in 1831 spurred reactionary legislation. The Maryland General Assembly that year ordered the expulsion of slaves thereafter freed (though this law was not enforced).

Under the impact of sectional differences, two new political parties emerged—the Republican and the American. The latter mushroomed out of the nativistic Know-Nothings.[15] In 1855 the American party abolished the policy of secrecy that had lured many people to its fold. When the majority refused to adopt a hard-fought plank against slavery, the American Party splintered.[16]

That left the dominant forces within the Know-Nothings free to straddle the slavery question in such a way as to favor the South. This dovetailed nicely with the prejudice against immigrants, many of whom were German political refugees with anti-slavery sentiments. Marylanders could therefore pay homage to slavery and strike against sectional strife, aliens, and Roman Catholicism by adopting Know-Nothing "Americanism." The party sprouted at an opportune time, for the Democrats were squabbling among themselves while the Whigs were on the road to extinction.

---

[14] A spirit of reform was on the march at home and abroad. By 1848 the American Anti-Slavery Society counted 2,000 auxiliary groups. Albert Bushnell Hart, *Slavery and Abolition 1831–1841* (New York, 1906), pp. 183–84.

[15] Originating as a secret society, its members replied upon interrogation that they knew nothing; hence the name.

[16] Lawrence Frederick Schmeckebier, *History of the Know Nothing Party in Maryland* (Baltimore, 1899), p. 22.

The election of a mayor in Baltimore highlighted a succession of local victories for the Know-Nothings in 1854. The party placed a national ticket in the field for 1856, with ex-President Millard Fillmore at the helm, but only in Maryland did it muster enough support to win any electoral votes. Thomas Holliday Hicks completed the Know-Nothing sweep in this state by his election as governor in 1857.

A one time Democrat and former Whig, Hicks grew up in a plain but respectable family on the Eastern Shore. Average in height, thick set, and sporting side-whiskers, he possessed only a rudimentary education but held public office most of his life.[17] Although not a very talented man, Hicks won fame because he favored the union and occupied the governorship during that critical period when the South was splitting the nation.

In an area when rioting was not uncommon in American cities and policing was inadequate, Baltimore endured elections during the Know-Nothing ascendancy that were marked with such violence that she more than warranted her old nickname of "Mobtown." The autumn of 1856 was one of the bloodiest periods.

Reaction in 1859 thrust the Democratic Party back into a legislative majority. Baltimore soon thereafter fell to a reform ticket. George William Brown won the mayoralty as the entire City Council ticket swept into office. The election put an end to the power of the Know-Nothings throughout the nation, for the party was now only a memory outside of Maryland.

The brief but turbulent era died unmourned, but the divisive threat of political parties regrouping along sectional lines continued to plague the United States. As many Americans looked to new political alignments to answer needs denied by the old order, the nation experienced the greatest decade of material progress it had yet known, and this despite the financial panic of 1857. The rewards of this burgeoning economy fell far more to the expanding North than to the agricultural South, which resisted the blandishments of Yankee entrepreneurs. These financial and political cycles

[17] *Cambridge Herald*, January 28, 1863. A biographical sketch of Thomas Holliday Hicks appears in Allen Johnson and Dumas Malone (eds.), *Dictionary of American Biography* (New York, 1928–1936), IX, 8–9. See also George L. Radcliffe, *Governor Thomas H. Hicks of Maryland and the Civil War* (Baltimore, 1901).

climaxed in a period of religious revival and romanticism.[18] When into this volatile mixture was injected fear, an emotional atmosphere arose in which grave issues resisted settlement and threatened the life of Maryland and the nation.

Upon this troubled land descended John Brown. With the financial backing of northern abolitionists, he set out from his Maryland rendezvous in the autumn of 1859 upon one of the most quixotic ventures in American history. He sought the creation of a free state within the Appalachian Mountains and a great rising of the South's slave population. His band of eighteen men seized the federal arsenal and armory at Harpers Ferry but failed to arouse the Negroes. The two-day insurrection quickly collapsed when, on October 18, a marine detachment under Colonel Robert E. Lee's command stormed the fire-engine house in which the embattled abolitionists had barricaded themselves.

Some weeks later John Brown coolly met death on the gallows, but the agitation swirling out of his act did not die. Many in the North hailed John Brown as a martyr, struck down by barbarous slaveholders, while in the South some saw in this wild foray the precariousness of their security if a Republican administration were elected. One firebrand secessionist, Edmund Ruffin, gratefully acknowledged John Brown's raid as "a godsend 'to stir the sluggish blood of the South.'"[19]

Rumors of slave uprisings swept Maryland in the wake of the Harpers Ferry incident. As had similar reports in 1855 and 1857, they proved groundless,[20] but the uneasiness affected the 1859 election and propelled the Maryland legislature into passing acts further restricting the Negro population. Manumission was henceforth prohibited by the act of the 1860 General Assembly. This prevented a slave-holder from freeing his Negro even if he wished to do so. Such a ruthless attack upon human rights became necessary because the insidious doubt as to the basic right of one man to own the body of another gnawed at more than a few consciences. So many Marylanders had emancipated their slaves by 1860 that more free Negroes

[18] For an interesting analysis of the attitudes and forces at work within America prior to the Civil War, see Roy F. Nichols' *The Disruption of American Democracy* (New York, 1948).

[19] Alfred Steinberg, "Fire-eating Farmer of the Confederacy," *American Heritage*, IX, No. 1 (December, 1957), 115.

[20] Jeffrey R. Brackett, *The Negro in Maryland. A Study of the Institution of Slavery* (Baltimore, 1889), pp. 97–99.

could be found in Maryland than in any other state of the Union. They nearly equaled the slaves in numbers.[21]

The year 1860 saw Americans divide their votes between four major adversaries for the presidency of the United States. Old line Whigs and Know-Nothings rallied around the new Constitutional Union Party. It organized in the old First Presbyterian Church in Baltimore with a short platform that avoided controversy by simply supporting the Union, the Constitution, and the enforcement of the laws. John Bell of Tennessee, former Untied States Congressman and Senator, got the presidential nod.

But it was too late. Much as the border states may have wished for peace, they could no longer solve the nation's problems by ignoring them and speaking in platitudes. The Republicans, on the other hand, were ready to take a stand. At their convention they designed a platform calling for internal improvements and other measures to help an expanding nation. They opposed slavery in the territories and denounced efforts to reopen the slave trade. On May 18, in a Chicago swarming with an estimated 40,000 visitors, the delegates chose Abraham Lincoln of Illinois as their candidate for President.

The Democrats split their forces, the fire-eaters backing John C. Breckinridge, a Kentuckian and Vice-President of the United States, for the nation's top office, while the more moderate faction rallied to "the Little Giant," Stephen A. Douglas. As leader of a divided party, he faced an impossible task. His campaign nonetheless earned him a popular vote second to the victorious Lincoln but electoral votes in only Missouri and New Jersey. John Bell took three states, while Breckinridge carried eleven, including Maryland. In this state Breckinridge's 42,482 votes squeezed Bell out by only 722. Douglas picked up just 5,966 votes, with Lincoln's 2,294 a poor fourth. Breckinridge thus failed of a popular majority.

South Carolina, with its tradition of hostility to federal power, would have none of Republican rule. On December 20 it seceded. By February 1, 1861, six more states followed. Southern firebrands charged the North with attacking their domestic institutions and refused to submit to a President and party hostile to their interests.

Late in February of 1861, Lincoln slipped secretly through Baltimore on his way to Washington. On March 4, a day that dawned

---

[21] It is also of interest to note that from 1830 to 1860 the proportion of colored people to the total population dropped from 35 per cent to 25 per cent.

pleasant only to turn bleak and chilly, Lincoln assumed office. In his inaugural address he assured the American people he had no intention of interfering with slavery in the states where it existed. He reminded his "dissatisfied fellow countrymen" that they bore no pledge to destroy the government, while he had solemnly sworn to preserve it. In his final words Lincoln stirred the mystic ties of Union and said, "We are not enemies, but friends. We must not be enemies. Though passion may have strained, it must not break our bonds of affection."[22]

But passion had strained and broken the bonds uniting North and South. Neither the Peace Convention in Washington nor the passage by Congress of a proposed constitutional amendment to forbid forever any federal intervention in slavery in the states where it existed could preserve the Union. A workable compromise failed, for the secessionists could envision no plan assuring their old dominance, and the Republicans could find no settlement that would not destroy the power they had just gained.[23]

A cautious Lincoln planned no rash, punitive expedition into the South, but he did not intend to surrender federal fortifications. He determined to replenish the dwindling provisions of Fort Sumter by ship-borne supplies. Upon this news President Jefferson Davis ordered an attack on the rock-walled island defenses, just three miles outside of Charleston, South Carolina. On April 12 rebel batteries opened fire. The siege exploded the peaceful attempts to solve the greatest crisis in American history. Now the sword was to strike at the impasse.

On April 15 Abraham Lincoln called for 75,000 militiamen to suppress the insurrection. The North responded. The chaos and uncertainty of preceding months resolved into action. Abolitionists, once ready to let the South go, now jumped into the fray, eager to assault the bastions of slavery. Thousands of others rushed to defend the flag.

Vigorously opposed to coercion, Virginia dissolved her allegiance to the United States just two days after Lincoln summoned troops. In the following month Arkansas, Tennessee, and North Carolina seceded from the Union. While decisive action followed hardening sentiments in most states, the border regions of Missouri, Kentucky, and Maryland suffered tumult.

---

[22] Roy P. Basler (ed.), *The Collected Works of Abraham Lincoln* (New Brunswick, 1953), IV, 262–71. Hereafter cited as *Lincoln Works*.

[23] Nichols, *The Disruption of American Democracy*, p. 491.

So intense was the excitement in Maryland that Mayor Brown of Baltimore and Governor Hicks issued proclamations calling for calm. Passions, however, did not respond to pacific words. Crowds of Union and southern sympathizers thronged the city streets on April 18. A group of Pennsylvania volunteer troops got safely through the city,[24] but the Sixth Massachusetts Regiment was not so fortunate when it tried the following day. A secessionist mob attacked the soldiers. Many so-called respectable persons joined the town rowdies.[25] As the riot swirled through the streets of "Mobtown," four soldiers and three times as many citizens suffered mortal wounds, while scores were injured.[26] Thus died the first Union soldiers killed by enemy action in the Civil War. Ironically, that date marked the eighty-sixth anniversary of the skirmish at Lexington, beginning the American Revolution.

To prevent further bloodshed, the authorities ordered the railroad bridges to the north burned, thus blocking the passage of more troops. Prominent Marylanders hurried to Washington to implore Lincoln not to send any additional soldiers through Baltimore.

The mob action seemed to tear the state from its national moorings. Unionism, which appeared dominant on April 18, collapsed. Distorted reports circulated through the state of civilians shot down on the streets of Baltimore by Yankee troops on their way to subjugate the South. At no time in the history of the Civil War did Maryland sentiment come so close to being swept into the Confederacy. Staunch Unionist John Pendleton Kennedy, author and statesman, wrote Secretary of the Treasury Salmon P. Chase that the Union was severed. "Maryland," he said "has found herself impelled into opposition by a popular sentiment no man can withstand."[27]

---

[24] A Negro, accompanying the Pennsylvania soldiers, was, however, struck in the face by a stone thrown during the march through Baltimore. See the *Baltimore American* of April 19, 1861, and Benjamin Quarles, *The Negro in the Civil War* (Boston, 1953), pp. 24–25.

[25] Radcliffe, *Governor Hicks*, p. 54.

[26] *Lincoln Works*, IV, 341; Baltimore *Sun*, March 30, 1958. Casualty figures differed. Frederick H. Dyer, *A Compendium of the War of the Rebellion* (Des Moines, 1908), p. 759, listed the Union loss as four killed and twenty wounded. For an eyewitness account of the riot, see George W. Brown, *Baltimore and the 19th of April, 1861* (Baltimore, 1887). The author was then mayor of Baltimore.

[27] John P. Kennedy to S[almon] P. Chase, April 24, 1861, Salmon P. Chase Papers, Historical Society of Pennsylvania, Philadelphia, Pa. John Pendleton Kennedy (1795–1870) served in the War of 1812, the profession of law, the House of Representatives,

Another of Chase's correspondents spoke of "revolution here and all over Maryland."[28] Even Governor Hicks shifted. Before a dramatic public meeting in Baltimore on the afternoon of April 19, a "badly frightened" governor tempered his love of the Union with the claim that he would suffer the loss of his right arm before he would "raise it to strike a sister state."[29] The governor would have been killed, believed one observer, if he had not responded favorably to the people's fiery feelings.[30]

For a day or two the secessionists controlled Baltimore and seemed to be in possession of the state. The upheaval forced Hicks to act. For many months he had been subjected to heavy pressure both for and against summoning the legislature. He had stalled, fearing that these legislators who had ridden into office on a wave of revulsion against the Know-Nothings and John Brown's uprising might take the state into secession. Now he could hold back no longer. To do so would risk an illegal convening of the General Assembly.[31] On April 22 he summoned the legislature to meet four days later in Frederick.

The General Assembly organized under the control of the Democrats, the party which gave the South its strongest support. The governor sought to steer the legislators along the middle way. His message called for "Union and peace" and said Maryland's safety lay in "preserving a neutral position between . . . North and South."[32] To this policy the lawmakers responded by denouncing the Lincoln administration, yet they disclaimed any power to carry the state out of the Union.

An undeterred Lincoln suspended the writ of habeas corpus along the Philadelphia to Washington railroad. The suspension was to take effect only when required by public safety but, of course, led to

<hr/>

speakership of the Maryland House of Delegates, and secretaryship of the navy under President Fillmore. He was a writer of note and patron of Edgar Allan Poe.

[28] Wm. Prescott Smith to S. P. Chase, April 21, 1861, Chase Papers.

[29] Baltimore *Sun*, April 20, 1861. See also H. Winter Davis to Samuel F. DuPont, April 19, 1861, Samuel F. DuPont Papers, Eleutherian Mills Historical Library, Wilmington, Del.

[30] Frederick Bernal to Lord Richard Lyons, April 20, 1861, F. O. 5/784, Public Record Office 874.

[31] For Hicks' explanation of his action, see "Message of the Governor of Maryland to the General Assembly" in the special session of December, 1861, Document A, 4–5 of *Maryland House Documents Dec., 1861; Jan., 1862 Sessions; Congressional Globe,* 37th Cong., 3rd Sess., Vol. 33, Part 2, p. 1376. See also Radcliffe, *Governor Hicks,* pp. 27, 55, 62–63.

[32] *Baltimore American,* April 29, 1861.

arrests. The General Assembly reacted with growing hostility to the government in Washington and increased friendliness for the Confederacy.[33] In so doing the legislators failed to reflect the attitude of a large body of Marylanders.

It was only a week after the riots of April 19 when Union sentiment began reasserting itself.[34] April 26, the day the southern sympathizing legislature convened, saw the Stars and Stripes flying from a dozen different points in Baltimore. On April 28 Henry Winter Davis wrote Secretary of State William H. Seward, "A great reaction has set in. If we now act promptly the day is ours and the city is safe."[35] Three days later Lincoln's secretary heard that the new Union officeholders had quietly taken over their jobs in Baltimore. An encouraged President said he believed that if Baltimore remained quiet a while longer, Maryland might become "the first of the redeemed."[36]

By early in May many a lapsed patriot regained his Union bearings. Reason extinguished the passions sparked by the April 19 riots. The United States still stood, its capital defended by thousands of troops who had traveled around Baltimore. No border state confederacy had formed. The streets of Baltimore were free of secession mobs that gave a false impression of Maryland's position.

On the night of May 13, during a violent thunderstorm, Brigadier General Benjamin Butler and his troops entered the city and

---

[33] Radcliffe, *Governor Hicks*, p. 105.

[34] Frederick Bernal wrote Lord John Russell on April 29, 1861 (F.O. 5/784, Public Record Office 874) that the "state of feverish excitement . . . has diminished, & the public mind has become more calm, & reasonable. The character of the people of Baltimore is decidedly impulsive, & many who a week ago advocated the most violent measures, now confess it would be madness on the part of Maryland to precipitate herself into a combat with the North. The Union men have begun to raise their heads again. . . . I believe if nothing occurs to rekindle the excitement here that a reaction will take place in favor of the Union, but much depends on the North's acting in a conciliatory manner."

[35] Bernard C. Steiner, *Life of Henry Winter Davis* (Baltimore, 1916), p. 195.

[36] Tyler Dennett (ed.), *Lincoln and the Civil War in the Diaries and Letters of John Hay* (New York, 1939), p. 216. Large majorities were cast in Washington and Cecil Counties in May for pro-Union, pro-coercion candidates seeking to fill legislative vacancies. See Francis Thomas in United States House of Representatives, February 18, 1863 (*Congressional Globe*, 37th Cong., 3rd Sess., Vol. 33, Part 2, p. 1082) and Radcliffe, *Governor Hicks*, pp. 93–94.

[37] Union troops had passed through Baltimore unmolested a few days before. Benjamin Butler, a controversial political leader, gave his version of entering Baltimore in *Butler's Book* (Boston, 1892), pp. 225–33.

occupied Federal Hill.[37] No resistance was offered. Three weeks earlier such a move would have been violently fought.

The fate of the nation's capital, perhaps of the United States, had for many days laid at the mercy of the state of Maryland. Its citizens did not strike. Now Washington was safe. The presence of Yankee soldiers and the remarkable resurgence of Union sentiment in Maryland assured it.

CHAPTER II

THE UNION
VICTORIOUS
IN MARYLAND

"YOUR MARYLANDER is very tenacious about being a gentle-man, and what he does not consider gentlemanly is simply unfit for anything."[1] So observed that talented correspondent of the *London Times*, William Howard Russell. Obviously, most of the fashionable world clung to the South and regarded loyalty to the Union as nothing less than vulgar. Lincoln seemed to epitomize this boorishness. This reaction had a curious result. It enabled the socially ambitious to grease their way into the inner circle of the elite by fervent devotion to secession.[2]

The appeal of the snob had its attraction, but actually Maryland could ill afford the dismemberment of the Union. Joined to a northern federation, her ships sailing out of the Chesapeake Bay into the Atlantic would be at the mercy of alien guns. Maryland's trade with the South would be lost[3] and her trade with the West hampered. The Baltimore and Ohio would enter foreign soil at Harpers Ferry.

Should the state ally its fortunes with the South, the railroad would tap Midwestern markets loyal to the shrunken United States. Trade might well be diverted from the foreign port of Baltimore. As one writer has expressed it, "the Union needed Baltimore and Baltimore needed the Union and both needed the Baltimore and Ohio."[4] Per-

[1] William Howard Russell, *My Diary North and South* (London, 1863), I, 114.

[2] John P. Kennedy to Robert C. Winthrop, January 21, 1862, John P. Kennedy Papers, Peabody Institute Library, Baltimore, Md.

[3] In his letter of January 2, 1861 to his constituents in the 4th Congressional District, Henry Winter Davis forcefully recounted the dire effects of a divided land upon Maryland. *Speeches and Addresses . . . by Henry Winter Davis, of Maryland* (New York, 1867), pp. 190–91. Hereafter cited as *Davis Speeches*.

[4] Hamilton Owens, *Baltimore on the Chesapeake* (Garden City, New York, 1941), p. 286.

haps President John W. Garrett's realization that secession would cripple his railroad influenced him to operate it so effectively on behalf of a united America despite rebel sympathy within his family.

Confederate enthusiasts envisioned Baltimore as the New York of the South, but the disenchanted pointed to the Virginia cities. They, not the frontier town of Baltimore, would reap this distinction.[5] Then there were the textile mills, iron foundries, and other industries of Maryland's growing economy. What could they expect from a South ruled by an oligarchy enamored with free trade? Not surprisingly, many manufacturers and businessmen did not share the sympathy of the landed gentry for the Confederacy. Their occupations were being strangled by political uncertainty even before the outbreak of the war.

The tobacco planters and other slaveholders faced an ominous future. Slavery could not survive in a land hostile to its presence. That ruled out alliance with the North, but paradoxically, a dismal future also awaited membership in the Confederacy. No fugitive slave law could then retrieve Negroes fleeing across the Pennsylvania border. Furthermore, if rebel agitation for a reopening of the slave trade succeeded, the market value of slaves would drop.

Whichever side Maryland joined, the state promised to be a battleground. Understandably Unionists cried out, "Our people are the people of all sections. Our institutions are the institutions of all sections."[6] Yet thousands of citizens opposed coercing the South.[7] However deplorable they considered secession, they believed a Union maintained by force of arms was not worth preserving and could not survive anyway. War would only destroy hopes for some kind of loose confederation of the two regions. Besides, claimed the Baltimore *Sun*, at least one beneficial result would redound from secession. It would remove slavery from northern concern. As the paper expressed it, "It may be fatal to certain politicians, sensation preach-

[5] *Address of the Union State Central Committee of Maryland* (Baltimore, [1861]), p. 2; John P. Kennedy, "The Great Drama. An Appeal to Maryland," *Political and Official Papers* (New York, 1872), pp. 597–98; *Davis Speeches,* p. 190.

[6] *Address of the Union State Central Committee,* p. 2. To the plea that the South wanted peace, the *Address* (p. 7) retorted that "WE, TOO, ARE FOR PEACE; *but we* [believe] *. . . there can be no enduring peace without Union."*

[7] For example, the *Port Tobacco Times,* a southern Maryland newspaper, said on June 20, 1861, "We have been strong Union men . . . but for war, coercion, and bloodshed— never." Yet many of these advocates of "peace" were ready to fight those who would use force to preserve the Union.

ers and newspapers, but it will be out of society, out of Congress, and out of the country."[8]

Many Marylanders would not so readily accept division. Once they had joined in deploring radicals north and south. Now they clung to the Union while divided loyalties split families and friends, sowing a harvest of heartache and bitterness. In August of 1861 one agitated citizen confided to his diary that politics "is undermining and destroying our whole social life, and with it our happiness and peace."[9]

In the pandemonium the old political parties fell apart. The Constitutional Union Party disappeared, and the Democratic organization collapsed. The Republicans failed to attract any significant support. Into the political vacuum were drawn fresh aggregates of power to give expression to the debate over Maryland's position and whether Confederate recognition was preferable to war.

On May 23 pro-Union delegates from throughout the state gathered at the Maryland Institute in Baltimore. Ignoring old party lines, the delegates set up a State Central Committee and called for an August convention to pick state-wide candidates for the fall election. Resolutions thundered at secession and charged that revolutionary leaders were seeking the destruction of the nation, not the redress of alleged wrongs to slavery. But the Unionists did not want a vindictive war nor an abolitionists' crusade. They pleaded for "a spirit of fraternal kindness" and warned against any attempt by the Lincoln Administration to mix its views on slavery with the defense of the government.[10]

The first state-wide test of union strength brought out the Maryland voters the very next month. They went to the polls on June 13, 1861, to choose congressmen who would sit in the special session opening July 4 (see Table A). No charges of corrupt or prejudicial practices marred the results.[11] This was particularly significant because southern sympathizers have tried ever since to discount loyal sentiment in Maryland by pointing to various irregularities in later elections.

---

[8] Baltimore *Sun*, June 14, 1861.

[9] Journal of Dr. Samuel A. Harrison, August 4, 1861, Maryland Historical Society. Hereafter cited as Harrison Journal.

[10] An account of the convention was published in the *Baltimore American*, May 24, 1861.

[11] For example, the Baltimore *Sun*, an independent journal with southern leanings, on June 14, 1861, said, "The Congressional election . . . proved in every respect worthy of the people of Baltimore. . . . It was conducted . . . without interferences from any quarter, and the very best order was observed. . . ."

How did the untrammeled voice of Maryland speak on that day in June? A surprising result flashed across the state. All but five of the twenty-one counties recorded Union majorities.[12] Only in one district in Baltimore City was there some doubt as to the position of the victor, a so-called independent Unionist.

TABLE A. RESULTS OF CONGRESSIONAL ELECTION JUNE 13, 1861

Candidates	Votes	Candidates	Votes
1st District		*5th District*	
John W. Crisfield	7,181	Francis Thomas	10,582
Daniel M. Henry	5,331	Scattered votes	320
2nd District		*6th District*	
Edwin H. Webster	7,251	Charles B. Calvert	4,467
Scattered votes	126	Benjamin G. Harris	4,305
3rd District			
Cornelius L. L. Leary	6,702	Total for regular Union	
William P. Preston	6,200	candidates	42,395
4th District *			
H. Winter Davis	6.212	Opponents	24,702
Henry May	8,420	Total votes	67,097

*The *Baltimore American,* June 14,1861, listed 6,287 for Winter Davis and 8,335 for Henry May.

The district votes were taken from the *Report on Military Interference at Elections,* pp. 28–29, by the Committee on Military Affairs and the Militia, Senate Reports No. 14, 38th Cong., 1st Sess. This report inexplicably gave the total votes cast as 63,597 with 43,750 going to the Unionists.

On the Eastern Shore John Woodland Crisfield rolled up a strong majority over his State Rights opponent. A native of the Shore, born in 1808, he served as a Whig in the state legislature before joining Abraham Lincoln as a member of the Thirtieth Congress. There the two men became friends. Declining renomination, Crisfield did not quit public life. He sat in the Maryland Constitutional Convention of 1850–51 and on the Peace Commission of 1861. In returning to Congress, Crisfield assumed a role of leadership for the border state

[12] The five were Talbot and Worcester on the Eastern Shore and St. Mary's, Charles, and Calvert in southern Maryland.

delegations. An amiable man, he achieved the reputation of being one of the best lawyers in the House of Representatives. His views were conservative.[13]

The Second Congressional District sent Harford Countian Edwin Hanson Webster to Washington unopposed. Like Crisfield, Webster was a member of the bar. Although only 32 in 1861, Webster had already achieved the distinction of being president of the state senate. During the war he saw active duty as an officer in the Union Army.

Cornelius L. L. Leary, a former Know-Nothing of prominence, was not so easily blessed with success as Webster. In the Eighth Ward, stronghold of Baltimore's Irish, he was swamped by a vote of 2 ½ to 1.[14] Many of the Irish swung blindly toward Confederate support when they saw the hated leaders of the now defunct American Party gain the confidence and much of the patronage of Lincoln's administration. The Germans, on the other hand, swallowed their old hostility and gave Leary strong support in the lower city wards.[15] Leary was thus able to come out of Baltimore City only slightly behind his State Rights opponent, William P. Preston. The county districts overcame the deficit and carried the forty-seven-year-old lawyer to his first congressional triumph.

In western Maryland former Governor Francis Thomas emerged from his political retirement to capture the Fifth District seat unopposed. He polled two-thirds of the region's vote.[16] A notable and at times tempestuous career preceded his new triumph. One of the leading lawyers in western Maryland, the 62-year-old Thomas in his younger years served several terms in the state legislature before moving to Congress for ten years. There he befriended and defended Andrew Jackson. In 1841 Maryland bestowed the governorship upon

[13] For information on John W. Crisfield see Maryland Historical Society vertical file; *The Biographical Cyclopedia of Representative Men of Maryland and District of Columbia* (Baltimore, 1879), pp. 297–98; Albert Gallatin Riddle, *Recollections of War Time: Reminiscences of Men and Events in Washington 1860–1865* (New York, 1895), p. 115; and Ward Hill Lamon, *Recollections of Abraham Lincoln* (Washington, 1911), p. 290. Winter Davis, who differed with Crisfield politically, called him "the ablest man of the Eastern Shore." *Davis Speeches*, pp. 387–88.

[14] *Port Tobacco Times*, June 20, 1861. the vote was 866 to 337, without which Preston would have lost the Baltimore wards.

[15] Baltimore *Sun*, June 14, 1861. Those Irishmen who remained loyal refused to vote. See the remarks of Patrick McLaughlin, an Irish leader, in the *Baltimore Republican*, July 30, 1862.

[16] *Daily National Intelligencer* (Washington, D.C.), June 17, 1861.

him, only to have his triumph marred by an unsuccessful marriage to the young daughter of Virginia's Governor James McDowell. Thomas' public airing of his domestic difficulties created a furor and culminated in divorce.[17]

The Sixth Congressional District enveloped all of southern Maryland, notorious for its sympathy with the South. A State Rights Convention there denounced the "unholy war" against the South and called for recognition of the Confederacy, with Maryland's joining it.[18] Its candidate, Benjamin Gwinn Harris, swept the lower end of the peninsula but suffered defeat in the other four counties. This enabled Unionist Charles Benedict Calvert to squeeze through to a surprise victory.[19] Many observers considered this the most significant triumph of all.

Unlike the other five men elected, Calvert was not an attorney. He devoted his life to farming and helped found the Maryland Agricultural College.[20] A direct descendant of Charles, fifth Lord Baltimore, he was, like Leary, entering Congress for the first time.

The sole district to lie entirely within Baltimore City was the turbulent Fourth. It chose between two old antagonists, each with previous congressional service. Running as an independent Unionist on a platform "shrouded in a mist,"[21] Henry May picked up State Rights votes when the candidate on that ticket withdrew. The secessionists did not care for May, but in their determination to beat Congressman Henry Winter Davis they did not dare risk defeat by a

[17] *Dictionary of American Biography*, XVIII, 429–30 gives a biographical sketch of the life of Francis Thomas (1799–1876).

[18] The resolutions claimed sovereignty for the states and charged the North with seeking commercial supremacy by subjugating the South. Opponents of this view were accused of supporting "not the Union of *all* the States, which we advocate, but of Maryland with the Northern. . . ." *Port Tobacco Times,* June 13, 1861.

[19] Modern smear tactics have not surpassed the scurrilous attacks of the Civil War period. In the *Montgomery County Sentinel*, August 2, 1861, Calvert was accused of a willingness to have Maryland citizens imprisoned, Annapolis occupied, and Baltimore denied self-government; "What can be Mr. Calvert's motive? It cannot be an abolition love for his mulatto half brothers and sisters, and their children, for they charge him with keeping money due them. It must be his instinctive love of arbitrary, monarchical power, and . . . love of the National Hotel in Washington, of which he is the owner, and which might lose somewhat of its value, if the South succeed in maintaining their [sic] rights."

[20] *Dictionary of American Biography*, III, 427–28.

[21] Harrison Journal, June 6, 1861.

divided opposition.[22] With secessionists, peace Unionists, and personal enemies united against Davis, May won.[23] His sympathies then turned more to the South, and he proposed an armistice. May was arrested and imprisoned in September of 1861 but was later allowed to resume his congressional duties.

While some of May's supporters cried for peace as if this were not the same as dissolving the government, Henry Winter Davis boldly called for coercing the South back into the Union. A self-willed genius, Davis' contentious past foreshadowed a turbulent career as a Civil War politician of national renown.

Born in Annapolis in 1817, he displayed considerable precociousness, reading before he was four.[24] As a youth he entered Kenyon College in Ohio and there was impressed by the oratory of Bishop Charles P. McIlvaine, the one time counselor of Robert E. Lee's spiritual life at West Point.[25] After leaving Kenyon, Davis procured with difficulty funds necessary to study law at the University of Virginia.[26] His choice of profession was limited because trade was then considered beneath the dignity of a gentleman. Large profits eventually eroded this practice.[27]

In 1840 Winter Davis began practicing law in Alexandria, Virginia, but moved his office to Baltimore in the latter half of that decade. Yielding to the lures of public life, he joined the Know-Nothing Party and in 1855 won his first term in Congress through a victory tarnished by violence.

Four years later he shocked the state by voting for Republican William Pennington of New Jersey, whose compromise candidacy broke the deadlock over the speakership of the House of Representatives. Maryland's General Assembly rebuked this independent course, but Davis lashed back. He charged the Democrats with seeking to retain power by exploiting the fears of the people for either slavery or the Union.[28]

[22] *The South* (Baltimore), June 13, 1861.

[23] H. Winter Davis to Samuel F. DuPont, June 14, 1861, S. F. DuPont Papers.

[24] Bernard Steiner, *Life of Henry Winter Davis* (Baltimore, 1916), p. 11 or the Henry Winter Davis Papers in the Maryland Historical Society. Henry Winter Davis' father was Rev. Henry Lyon Davis, pastor of St. Ann's parish and president of St. Johns College.

[25] Steiner, *Davis*, p. 7, and Douglas Southall Freeman, *R. E. Lee* (New York, 1949), I, 59–60.

[26] *Dictionary of American Biography*, V, 119.

[27] Steiner, *Davis*, p. 42, or see Davis papers.

[28] Davis *Speeches*, p. 133.

In 1859 David sought a fusion of the Know-Nothings and the Republicans. The attempt failed at the outset. Davis, who was more northern than southern in his political and economic views, turned aside from further flirtations with the Republicans and even rejected a proposal to become Lincoln's running mate. He realized the hopelessness of that party in Maryland. Anyway, the main enemy was the same, the Democratic Party, which he attacked as he stumped for the Constitutional Union ticket of Bell and Everett in 1860.

Independent, fiery, and bold, Davis cared not whom he assailed. Even his friends could not sway him once he had embarked on a course of action, regardless of its unpopularity. A temperamental, vindictive genius, Davis never suffered from humility. One political associate said of him, "There never was a prouder or more intolerant man. We think he is *great*—our greatest man in power and ability by long odds: but no constituency ever had so much trouble with their pet."[29]

Justifiable as some of the bitter condemnation of Davis might seem, he merited on occasion the applause of his admirers. In many ways this intensely partisan and enigmatic leader, steeped in the religious heritage of the Episcopal Church, was a fighter for constitutional justice. He blasted arbitrary arrests and the presidential suspension of the writ of habeas corpus as illegal acts[30] and defended congressional power against the usurpations of the President. Though admitting that any one who would not compromise a political measure was a fool, he denounced all compromisers of moral principle as scoundrels.[31] He often saw clearly where others walked in darkness. It was said of him he "has great power with the multitude as an orator, and if he throws away the scabbard of expediency and draws the sword of principle, he may put to rout all the enemies of the Union, whether open or secret."[32]

In the wartime struggle to free the slaves, Davis shifted rapidly from advocating silence on the Negro question to leadership in the

[29] Peter G. Sauerwein to Edward McPherson, October 8, 1864, Edward McPherson Papers, Box 8, Library of Congress. Sauerwein, a flour merchant, noted that "Davis's element is agitation and he is never comfortable unless fighting somebody." Though "Perverse and hardheaded . . . he has wonderful power with the people. They admire him for his very insolence. . . ."

[30] *Davis Speeches*, p. 258, and H. Winter Davis to Mrs. Samuel F. DuPont, December 4, 1861, S. F. DuPont Papers.

[31] Carl Sandburg, *Abraham Lincoln: the War Years* (New York, 1939), III, 126.

[32] *New York Daily Tribune*, May 22, 1861.

abolition campaign. Dropping his conservative approach, he raced ahead, too fast for men unwilling to slough off old ways and prejudices. He castigated all who failed to meet his standards. Expediency he generally scorned. True, abolition gave him a handy weapon to strike at his old enemies, but he believed in the essential rightness of the cause.[33]

Rising to the forefront of American orators, Winter Davis commanded the attention of his colleagues on the floor of Congress as few others have done before or since.[34] A slender six-footer, handsome in appearance, gentlemanly in manners, and scholarly in attainments, he possessed an eloquence that was "clear and cold, like starlight."[35] Davis spoke in a high voice, notable for its sharpness and firmness.[36] He used reiteration with great force but did not always avoid demagoguery. Nor did he fail to exert his genius in humiliating an opponent with keen-edged sarcasm.[37] Humorous anecdotes and jokes did not intrigue him, though he could stir his listeners to laughter. In so doing, he did not seek merely to amuse but rather to instruct and persuade.

Both friend and foe attested to Henry Winter Davis' restless, fiery brilliance. Nobody denied his great ability. He was one of the most talented and controversial men ever to enter political life in Maryland.

Davis was one of two Marylanders who gained strong backing for a cabinet office. Lincoln talked to his various sponsors, including

[33] On February 25, 1864 Davis etched his philosophy of the races in these terms: "The folly of our ancestors and the wisdom of the Almighty, in its inscrutable purposes, having allowed them [Negroes] to come here . . . , they have a right to remain here. . . . And whether they become our equals or our superiors, whether they blend or remain a distinct race, your posterity will know. . . . These are things which we cannot control. Laws do not make, laws cannot unmake them." *Davis Speeches,* p. 363; *Congressional Globe,* 38th Cong., 1st Sess., Vol. 34, Part 4, Appendix, p. 46.

[34] Yet in 1865 he wrote, "The glories of the world have passed before me, but have not lighted on my head. I have lived during great events in which I have not been permitted to be an actor." (Steiner, *Davis,* p. 7, or Davis MSS.) No doubt the consuming fire of ambition, then suffering from lack of sustenance, spurred this remark. Ironically, he said of his youth, "I would have been idle if I could, for I had no ambition." (Steiner, *Davis,* p. 41, or Davis MSS.)

[35] Noah Brooks, *Washington in Lincoln's Time* (New York, 1958), p. 28. Brooks was quoting James A. Garfield.

[36] *Ibid.*

[37] See for example *Congressional Globe,* 38th Cong., 1st Sess., Vol. 34, Part 3, p. 2189.

cousin Judge David Davis, a staunch friend of the President. Thurlow Weed, the New York political leader, also urged Lincoln to appoint him, all to no avail. Davis had "Davis on the brain," Lincoln told Weed.[38]

Lincoln's selection of a cabinet provided one of the earliest and most difficult tasks of his presidency. Composed of "mutually suspicious groups,"[39] the new Republican Party required imaginative and diplomatic leadership. Lincoln gave it by recognizing not only the various political factions but also geographical and pivotal areas. His seven cabinet members, four of whom had been unsuccessful candidates for the presidency, had only one principle in common—maintenance of the Union.

The man chosen for Postmaster General was a Marylander who bore a name that bespoke hostility to Davis and his allies. He was Montgomery Blair, ex-Democrat, a citizen of the Old Line State by adoption, and member of a controversial but influential family. His father, Francis P. Blair, Sr., served in Andrew Jackson's "Kitchen cabinet" and acted as a confidential adviser to Lincoln during the Civil War. The President frequently tried out important plans upon the wise old politician.[40]

Blair cherished great ambitions for his sons, Francis, Jr. and Montgomery. Francis, Jr. helped save Missouri for the Union, while Montgomery assumed leadership of Marylander's small Republican Party. Although Lincoln harbored no illusions about the clannish Blairs, he valued their support and the strength they could wield in the border states. To appoint one of the trio was the same thing, as one writer has pointed out, "as naming all three."[41]

Born in 1813, Montgomery grew up in Kentucky and went to West Point under an appointment from Andrew Jackson. Following graduation, he served in the Seminole War, but his military career quickly yielded to the lure of law and politics. He settled in Missouri as the protégé of Thomas Hart Benton and held successively the

[38] Paul M. Angle (ed.), *Herndon's Life of Lincoln* (Cleveland and New York, 1949), p. 383 or William E. Smith, *The Francis Preston Blair Family in Politics* (New York, 1933), I, 515.

[39] Harry J. Carman and Reinhard H. Luthin, *Lincoln and the Patronage* (New York, 1943), p. 52.

[40] Ward Hill Lamon, *Recollections of Abraham Lincoln 1847–1865* (Washington, 1911), p. 205.

[41] Burton J. Hendrick, *Lincoln's War Cabinet* (Boston, 1946), p. 70.

offices of United States district attorney, mayor of St. Louis, and judge of the Court of Common Pleas. After the death of his first wife, Montgomery married the daughter of New Hampshire's Judge Levi Woodbury, a prominent political figure and old friend of the family. In 1853 Montgomery abdicated his political future in Missouri for a similar career in Maryland.[42]

Seven years later he presided over the state convention of Maryland Republicans and acted as a delegate to the Chicago convention that nominated Lincoln. Assuming the forlorn task of infusing strength and enthusiasm into the Republican Party of Maryland, he organized open air meetings, appeared with his father and brother, but failed to gain much support. Most of the Democratic opposition rallied around Bell and Everett.

For the first two years of Lincoln's Administration the Blairs exercised a strong influence at the White House. Waning in 1863, it continued effective for another year[43] despite dissension within and without the Cabinet.

Always strict constitutionalists, the Blair family fought abolition in the 1830s, only to yield to the conviction that slavery was morally wrong. In 1856 Montgomery championed the cause of free soil before the Supreme Court. One of the nation's foremost constitutional lawyers, Reverdy Johnson, challenged Blair's position in this, the famous Dred Scott case. Chief Justice Roger B. Taney's decision pleased the South but enraged the abolitionists. All three of these men were Marylanders.

Although an advocate even before the Civil War of gradual, compensated emancipation, Montgomery Blair rejected the radicalism of the abolitionists. In writing to the Cooper Institute Meeting of March 6, 1862, he blamed the rebellion on the political interest in slavery and called it "a vain attempt to stem the tide of civilization and progress." On the other hand, he supported "jealousy of caste" and believed the Negro could not exist in the temperate zone, except as a slave. The solution, Blair felt, lay in sending the Negroes to colonies in the tropics. With only the white race living in America's temperate regions, secession would no longer be a threat.[44]

[42] For biographical material on Montgomery Blair, see *Dictionary of American Biography*, II, 339–40 and Smith, *Blair Family in Politics*.

[43] Smith, *Blair Family in Politics*, II, 189.

[44] Montgomery Blair, "M. Blair to Cooper Institute Meeting of March 6, 1862,"

Montgomery was not without strong prejudices and could be temperamentally obstinate when convinced he was right. He engaged at times in personal feuding and mischief-making. Both the Secretary of War, Edwin M. Stanton, and Secretary of the Treasury, Salmon P. Chase, incurred his hostility. Yet Blair was courteous and genial, frank and honest.[45] He loved art and good books and was said to be the "best read man" in the cabinet.[46] Religion appealed to him though ritual did not. His speeches, however, presented a poor contrast to Winter Davis'. Court reporters could hardly hear his "thin fine voice."[47] In a day when so many men wore beards, Montgomery Blair presented a clean-shaven face and close-cropped hair. Tall and lean, he had sharp, deeply set eyes. His "hard, Scotch, practical-looking head" gave the impression of "an anvil for ideas to be hammered on."[48]

Blair and Winter Davis were obstinate, pugnacious, and determined. Each knew that the path to political preferment lay, to a considerable degree, in the destruction of the other's ambitions. Winter Davis, darling of the radicals, and Montgomery Blair, leader of the moderate Unionists, found Maryland too small a state to sustain both. Their battle bubbled over the borders, engaged differing factions throughout the Union, and plagued Lincoln with its bitter rivalry. The President's try at a just distribution of Maryland patronage inevitably satisfied neither.

Job seekers so harassed the President during the secession crisis that he said his position was getting to be much like the man who was so busy renting rooms at one end of his house that he did not have time to put out the fire at the other end.[49] In dispensing the patronage, Lincoln followed the time-honored practice of consulting governors, congressmen, senators, and political leaders. He tried as well to heed the wishes of his cabinet members.[50]

William H. Purnell, comptroller of the treasury in Hicks' administration, became postmaster of Baltimore. The post of navy agent in the same city went to Wm. Pinkney Ewing, a Blair supporter and

Comments on the Policy Inaugurated by the President, in a Letter and Two Speeches (New York, 1863); Frederick *Examiner*, March 26, 1862.

[45] *Dictionary of American Biography*, II, 340.

[46] Brooks, *Washington in Lincoln's Time*, p. 41.

[47] Smith, *Blair Family in Politics*, I, 212.

[48] Russell, *Diary*, I, 63.

[49] Noah Brooks, *Abraham Lincoln* (New York, 1888), p. 423.

[50] Carman and Luthin, *Lincoln and the Patronage*, pp. 113, 333.

member of the Republican electoral ticket in 1856 and 1860.[51] Maryland won representation in foreign office as well. Republican Edward Wiss went to Rotterdam as consul, while James R. Partridge, a Davis man, left for Honduras to become minister-resident.[52] Other job seekers harassed the new Administration with pleas for numerous positions such as appraisers, provost marshals, and later, collectors of internal revenue.

Although initially Montgomery Blair and Winter Davis seemed willing to accommodate one another,[53] the peace did not last long. Montgomery Blair soon complained about appointments. Failing to get his choices accepted, he consented to the chief ones going to Winter Davis' friends. But "Davis did not keep faith with me." Instead of new and acceptable men getting the smaller jobs, they too often fell into the hands of "the most obnoxious plugs in Baltimore." Blair accused Davis of being "impracticable and selfish and not likely to be of much service."[54]

Blair's rancor about appointments was readily reciprocated by Winter Davis, who in vain urged Blair to replace U.S. Marshal Washington Bonifant with a more suitable officer.[55] The President even became involved in disputes concerning some of the lesser offices.

[51] *United States Official Register Sept. 30, 1861* (Washington, 1862), p. 182; Wm. Pinkney Ewing to Lincoln, Elkton, Md., Feb. 2, 1861, Robert Todd Lincoln Collection of Abraham Lincoln Papers XXXI, Library of Congress. Hereafter cited as Lincoln Collection.

[52] Reinhard H. Luthin, "A discordant Chapter in Lincoln's Administration: the Davis-Blair Controversy," *Maryland Historical Magazine,* XXXIX (1944), 30. See also H. Winter Davis to Charles Sumner, January 17, 1862, Charles Sumner Papers, Harvard College Library, Cambridge, Mass.

[53] Winter Davis to Samuel F. DuPont, March 20, 1861, S. F. DuPont Papers. In this letter Davis claimed a lack of disappointment over not being named to the Cabinet.

[54] Unaddressed and undated draft or copy of a letter in the handwriting of Montgomery Blair, Blair Family Papers, Gist Blair Collection, Box 7, Library of Congress. Blair was no doubt dismayed to find his Republican colleague, Judge William L. Marshall, replaced as Surveyor of the Port by the American Party journalist John F. McJilton. Blair tried unsuccessfully to oust him in favor of William Wales, writing editor of the *Baltimore American.* Though that newspaper was "coming up to the work very well . . . ," Blair wanted to assure a continuing favorable press by using the surveyor's office as a political plum. McJilton made himself expendable when he severed his ties with the *Patriot.*

[55] Henry Winter Davis to Montgomery Blair [1861?], Blair-Lee Papers, Princeton University. Washington Bonifant was a Republican in Maryland and served as a delegate to the Chicago Convention in 1860.

He indignantly wrote Republican Corkran, whom he had just appointed Naval Officer,

> I am quite sure you are not aware how much I am disobliged by the refusal to give Mr. F. S. Evans a place in the Custom House. I had no thought that the men to whom I had given the higher officers [sic] would be so ready to disoblige me. I still wish you would give Mr. Evans the place of Deputy Naval Officer.[56]

Corkran finally agreed and granted the job to French S. Evans, a former newspaper editor who had been forced to flee the city because of his Union sentiments.[57]

Federal patronage helped build a new party in Maryland—a party named for the nation's war aim—the Union. Republicans, war Democrats, and loyalists of all backgrounds became members of the new organization. Victorious in the congressional race of June, 1861, it faced a contest for control of the state government in November of the same year.

---

[56] A. Lincoln to F. S. Corkran, Washington, May 6, 1861, *Lincoln Works*, IV, 357.

[57] *Lincoln Works*, IV, 357. A letter from Secretary of the Treasury Salmon P. Chase to John P. Kennedy, dated March 26, 1861, indicated a source of the pressure exerted by Lincoln upon Corkran.

Mr. Chase wrote: "I shall be much disappointed should any circumstances not now understood by me prevent the appointment of Mr. Evans to the office you so kindly ask for him." (John P. Kennedy Collection, III, Letters to). It is interesting to note that Kennedy and Blair seemed to share similar political views, yet Kennedy turned to Blair's more radical antagonist, Chase, for help. This aid in turn was obstructed by Blair's ally, Corkran. Such incongruities should not prove troublesome, for it is important not to compartmentalize political figures too closely. Though not necessarily the case here, many politicians have friends among the opposition and often feel a greater personal antipathy for some members of their own group.

CHAPTER III

A NEW STATE
GOVERNMENT

WHILE CONNIVING POLITICIANS scrambled for federal offices, Lincoln turned to planning an attack on General Beauregard's 21,000 Confederates at Manassas, Virginia. The public demanded action, and it was not to be denied. Unbelievable though it may seem, even the date and location of the impending battle were announced. Crowds of spectators, including members of Congress, gathered at the site. Picnic luncheons were brought. It was to be a real Sunday outing, but it turned into a bloody tragedy. Before that sweltering day of July 21 was ended, Union troops plunged toward Washington in a disorganized retreat. A victory almost within grasp evaporated into agonizing defeat. The Battle of Bull Run was lost.

A chastened, worried House of Representatives took heed. The next day they hustled through a resolution, proposed by John J. Crittenden of Kentucky, to reassure border state conservatives, whose support Congress could now ill afford to lose. The resolution blamed the hostilities on southern disunionists and proclaimed the war a struggle not to subjugate the South nor to interfere with any established institutions but rather to uphold the Constitution and preserve the Union.[1] On July 25 the Senate passed a similar statement of policy. Only two congressmen and five senators voted against the resolutions. Such unanimity was misleading. It apparently stemmed from fear-driven expediency. When the resolution again came before Congress in December, 1861, it was not reaffirmed.[2]

A resolution similar in tone passed the Maryland State Union Convention in August. The delegates denounced secession as a "fatal heresy" and ripped into the General Assembly for misrepresent-

[1] *Congressional Globe*, 37th Cong., 1st Sess., Vol. 31, pp. 222–23.
[2] *Ibid.*, 37th Cong., 2nd Sess., Vol. 32, Part 1, p. 15.

ing Maryland.[3] Then came the selection of candidates for state-wide office in the November general election. Samuel S. Maffit, a Democratic supporter of Stephen A. Douglas in the 1860 campaign, got the nod for comptroller.

The gubernatorial post went to Augustus W. Braford after only one ballot. A native of Harford County, born in 1806, Bradford graduated from St. Mary's College in Baltimore in 1824 at the top of his class. Returning to his home town of Bel Air, he studied law, was admitted to the bar, and in 1835 was married. In 1838 he left Bel Air to seek greater opportunity in Baltimore. As with so many other members of his profession, Bradford dabbled in politics. He championed the cause of Henry Clay in the campaign of 1844 and ran as one of his electors. Clay's defeat dampened Bradford's political ardor. He slid into relative obscurity and did not emerge until 1861.[4]

Sent by Governor Hicks to the Peace Conference in Washington during the spring of 1861, Bradford spoke strongly in favor of an indivisible nation. During the troublesome months that followed, many Union leaders looked upon him with increasing favor. On the rostrum Bradford spoke well. A respectable though not distinguished lawyer, he possessed, as one supporter expressed it, "every qualification for a Candidate. Loyalty, ability, availability."[5] Furthermore, Bradford had not been embroiled in the bitter political fights of recent years. Here was a man for whom hostile factions within the Union Party could campaign.[6]

Not until October did the southern sympathizers field a candidate. The selection went to Benjamin C. Howard of Baltimore County. His advocates assumed various names in different parts of the state. However acceptable "States Rights" might be to Charles County in southern Maryland, it apparently sounded too suspicious in loyal Cecil. There the ticket called itself National Democratic. Other designations sprouted throughout Maryland. On election day five kinds

[3] *Baltimore American*, August 16, 1861.

[4] Bradford did, however, hold the Clerkship of the Baltimore County Court, 1845 to 1851.

[5] Harrison Journal, August 1, 1861.

[6] Biographical information on Augustus W. Bradford can be found in Harrison Journal, Heinrich E. Buchholz, *Governors of Maryland* (Baltimore, 1908), pp. 178–83; *Dictionary of American Biography*, II, 553–55; and the *Biographical Cyclopedia of Maryland and District of Columbia*, pp. 32–37. It is of interest to note that a son of Governor Bradford fought in the Confederate Army.

of tickets appeared in a Frederick polling place, each with a different heading but all with the same Peace Party candidates.[7]

Rebel sympathizers campaigned by attacking the arbitrary action of the Lincoln Administration. They talked about the Baltimoreans murdered on Pratt Street last April by federal troops, even though the soldiers were only defending themselves. A more rational charge criticized the military for seizing control of the Baltimore police force and arresting its chief and four man board.[8] The mayor and the city council protested, but the United States did not release all connected with the Baltimore police until March of 1862.

During 1861 many Marylanders were thrown into federal prisons. John Merryman of Baltimore County, arrested on May 25 on charges of being an officer in a secessionist company, tried unsuccessfully to invoke the writ of habeas corpus. Chief Justice Taney entered the case and refuted the President's right to suspend the writ, but Lincoln refused to heed.[9] High public office offered no bar to imprisonment. Baltimore's Mayor George W. Brown, who, umbrella in hand, had courageously tried to quell the April 19 riots, heard a violent rapping at his door one September evening. Arising from bed, he confronted a detachment of police and soldiers waiting to arrest him.[10]

Maryland legislators suspected of Confederate sympathies suffered a comparable fate before the General Assembly reconvened in Frederick on September 17. Fear that the legislators might pass an act of secession prompted the act. The news provoked not "the smallest effect" in Washington, arbitrary power having become such an accepted instrument.[11]

---

[7] The following were the captions: *"Peace Ticket!' 'Southern Rights!' 'State Rights!' 'Constitution & Law!' and 'Democratic!'" The Maryland Union* (Frederick, Md.), November 14, 1861.

[8] *War of the Rebellion: A Compilation of the Official Records of the Union and Confederate Armies* (Washington, 1880–1901), Series I, II, 138–39. Cited hereafter as *Official Records.*

[9] Carl Brent Swisher, *Roger B. Taney* (New York, 1935), pp. 550–53; Edward McPherson, *The Political History of the United States of America, During the Great Rebellion* (Washington, 1865), pp. 154–62

[10] George W. Brown, *Baltimore and the 19th of April, 1861* (Baltimore, 1887), pp. 102–4.

[11] William Howard Russell, *My Diary North and South* (London, 1863), II, 346. Entry of September 11, 1861. Though Lincoln issued a statement that no capricious arrests were made (*Lincoln Works*, IV, 523), it is hard to justify Mayor George William Brown's apprehension. From his prison Brown wrote the prominent Union lawyer, Thomas Donaldson, to thank him for "the very handsome and manly defence which you made of

The British consul in Baltimore, Frederic Bernal, said no one was safe. Denunciation "by some nameless 'Tom,' 'Dick,' or 'Harry'" spelled arrest and imprisonment. In Baltimore a nurse and two children were held for hours in a station house because she refused to remove the red bows from the youngsters' white frocks—red and white were the southern colors.[12] Even Winter Davis complained. He believed the government was making itself look ridiculous.[13]

In the November election Major General George B. McClellan dispatched troops to protect Union voters and ordered all secessionists returning from Virginia and appearing at the polls held prisoners until after the election.[14] In obeying these instructions, Major General John A. Dix called for the prevention of "treasonable votes" but refused requests to authorize a loyalty oath for all persons of doubtful allegiance. He recognized that he had no right to interfere with state law.[15] Besides, he wanted to show that Maryland could be controlled by a freely expressed public opinion.[16] Obstruction of the suffrage would render victory meaningless. Dix chose, however, to overlook the fact that any act of the federal government in a state election could be interpreted as intervention.

Election day in Baltimore was raw and dismal. The voter braved rain and wind overhead and muddy streets and sidewalks underfoot. Great care was taken to avoid illegal voting. A number of arrests occurred, but most were released that evening, the charges being

---

me. . . . You did me justice in denying absolutely all implications whatever on my part in the Southern movement. . . ." This letter dated March 11, 1862, was in the possession of Mrs. James M. Hemphill of Elkridge, Md., now deceased. See also unaddressed statement by John Lee Chapman from Mayor's Office, Baltimore, April 4, 1862, Blair Family Papers, Gist Blair Collection, Box 5.

[12] Frederic Bernal to Earl Russell, September 10, 1861 F. O. 5/784, Public Record Office 874.

[13] H. Winter Davis to Samuel F. DuPont, September 9, 1861, S. F. DuPont Papers. Davis said, "It is impossible to beat into their heads that the people of Maryland are loyal & that it is all nonsense to disgust loyal men by acting as if it were not so."

[14] Major General George B. McClellan issued the order on October 29, 1861. Among the places where this order can be read is *Congressional Globe*, 38th Cong., 1st Sess., Vol. 34, Part 4, p. 3194.

[15] John A. Dix to Daniel Engel and William Ecker, November 1, 1861, McPherson, *Political History*, p. 308. There s a copy of this letter in the Augustus W. Bradford Papers, Maryland Historical Society. See also John A. Dix to A. W. Bradford, November 7, 1863, Morgan Dix, *Memoirs of John Adams Dix* (New York, 1883), II, 340.

[16] John A. Dix to Provost Marshal Dodge, November 1 & 5, 1861; McPherson, *Political History*, pp. 308–9; Dix, *Memoirs Dix*, II, 339–40.

unsubstantiated. Rumors circulating about eleven o'clock that the Democratic candidates had withdrawn curtailed balloting, as probably did the presence of soldiers. Not surprisingly, the election proceeded peaceably.[17]

Bradford overwhelmed Howard by a vote of 17,922 to 3,347 and would have won by a decided margin even if those who stayed away from the polls had marked their ballots for the loser. Unfortunately, the intimidation of voters tarnished the moral impact of the victory and disgusted some Unionists.[18]

The counties offered a far better opportunity for the electorate to express its will freely. The soldiers conducted themselves well and did not intervene.[19] A remarkably large number of voters turned out despite the bad weather; the total number was only 53 short of 1860. Bradford swept every county except St. Marys, Charles, and Calvert in southern Maryland and Talbot on the Eastern Shore, which he lost by one vote. The state, including Baltimore City, gave Bradford a thumping majority, 57,502 to 26,070, better than two to one.

The landslide overwhelmed rebel enthusiasts in the House of Delegates, the new membership voicing their Union sentiments by 68 to 6. Distinguished men rode the legislative tide, foremost of whom was Reverdy Johnson, ex-U.S. Senator and cabinet officer. The state senate reacted less violently to the deluge because nearly

[17] The election was reported in the November 7, 1861 issues of *Baltimore Clipper, Sun,* and *Baltimore American.* The election judges possessed a proclamation that requested the pointing out of all who helped the rebels or engaged in the riots against the Union troops on April 19.

[18] See Harrison Journal, November 7, 1861. The total vote of 21,069 compared with 24,944 in the Congressional election earlier that year, 30,146 in the presidential election of 1860, and 26,061 in the gubernatorial election of 1857. See *Baltimore American,* November 7 and 14, 1861, and Baltimore *Sun,* November 20, 1857.

[19] There was a minimum of disorder but some charges of illegality from disgruntled secessionists. For varied reports on election see the Baltimore dailies and county weeklies; Frederic Bernal to Earl Russell, November 8, 1861 (F. O. 5/784, Public Record Office 874); *Secret Correspondence Illustrating the Condition of Affairs in Maryland,* pp. 37–38, bound with Maryland Pamphlets, Peabody Institute Library, Baltimore; and Charles Branch Clark, *Politics in Maryland during the Civil War* (Chestertown, Md., 1952), pp. 78–81. John T. Scharf's *History of Maryland* (Baltimore, 1879), copied (III, 457–60) verbatim, without acknowledgment, most of its account from an anonymous, pro-South pamphlet, *The "Southern Rights" and "Union" Parties in Maryland Contrasted* (Baltimore, 1863). Scharf fought for the Confederacy during the Civil War.

half of its membership were holdovers. The Unionists had to content themselves with a 12 to 10 edge in the upper house.[20]

Regardless of some intimidation, it was a great victory, one that greatly relieved federal authorities. Lincoln looked upon it as a sign of returning loyalty in the rebel states. He was so pleased that he prepared a proclamation to release all Maryland political prisoners who took an oath of allegiance and agreed not to reclaim any offices. Reverdy Johnson and others urged its promulgation, but the President did not comply.[21]

As Bradford prepared to assume his new office, job seekers clamored for his favor. At the governor's command were such jobs as notary public, wood corder, and inspectors of fish, guano, grain, and lumber. Letters of recommendation flooded his desk.[22] Unlike the federal offices in Maryland, the state patronage did not generate a heated conflict between factions. Many Unionists who later divided into opposing camps now supported the same men for minor offices. Of course it must be remembered that Bradford went into the gubernatorial campaign backed by all elements within his party.

The essential requirement for any applicant was his devotion to the Union. One successful supplicant told how his life had been threatened as he tried to reason with the people during the April 19 riots in Baltimore, and modestly added, "but nothing could waver me."[23] Another applicant, John Frazier, Jr., claimed his business suffered severely because of his loyalty. A former Whig and Know-Nothing and a frequent delegate to political conventions, he enlisted the active backing of prominent conservative Unionists James B. Ricaud and George Vickers, both of whom lived, as did Frazier,

[20] Baltimore *Sun*, November 15, 1861.

[21] Clark, *Politics in Maryland*, p. 82. By November 27, 1862, all political prisoners had nonetheless been released. *Lincoln Works*, IV, 523. After the election, according to John P. Kennedy, "All the malice, treasonable wish, and mischievous ambition [of the secessionists] remain—but curbed, and cribbed from public demonstration." See J. P. Kennedy to R. [Robert] C. [Charles] Winthrop, December 16, 1861, John P. Kennedy Papers, Peabody Institute Library, Baltimore, Md.

[22] Many letters of recommendation and application for office can be found in the Executive Papers of Governor Bradford in the Hall of Records, Annapolis.

[23] Thomas R. Rich to Governor Bradford, December 28, 1861, Executive Papers. Rich claimed his secessionist employer reduced his salary to a point where he could not even pay his family's board. Southern sympathizers also claimed they suffered from job discrimination. See Edward A. Pollard, *Observations in the North: Eight Months in Prison and on Parole* (Richmond, 1865), p. 99.

in Kent County. Frazier won the appointment of assistant grain inspector.[24] No doubt these conservative leaders deeply regretted their action when, less than two years later, Frazier became embroiled in a violent political storm centering upon his highly questionable acts on behalf of the radical cause.

Like the federal government, the state tried to care for its newspaper supporters. For example, the office of notary public was urged for the proprietor and editor of the *Eastern Gazette*, William H. Councill. He had, according to his sponsors, labored well for the government and at personal sacrifice.[25]

While Bradford prepared to assume office, a special session of the new legislature convened. It met in Annapolis in December and exacted homage to union and slavery. This worship continued through the regular session, which convened at noon on January 1, 1862.

The next day Governor Thomas H. Hick's message was read to each house of the General Assembly. It was the last communication he transmitted as governor to the General Assembly.[26] Although more distinguished men have held that high office and for a longer period of time, no Marylander has ever sat in the gubernatorial chair during so critical a period of state history. Despite his momentary wavering in April of 1861, Thomas Holliday Hicks must be credited as having played an important role in preserving Maryland for the Union.

On Wednesday, January 8, Augustus Williamson Bradford walked, amid much pomp and ceremony, into the Senate chamber of the old state house. In that same building George Washington had resigned his military commission, thereby assuring the nation of a republican government, with an army subservient to the will of the people.

[24] See letters of John Frazier, Jr. to Augustus W. Bradford: December 14, 1861; January 23, 1862; April 7 1862; April 10, 1862. Also see James B. Ricaud to Augustus W. Bradford, December 16, 1861; Samuel S. Maffit and H. Morton [?] to Augustus W. Bradford, January 28, 1862; and George Vickers to Augustus W. Bradford, December 18, 1861. All these letters are in the Executive Papers.

[25] Chris C. Cox and L. Dodson [?] to Augustus W. Bradford, January 13, 1862, Executive Papers. The *Baltimore American* was Maryland's leading daily. Its publisher, Charles Carroll Fulton, kept contact with various federal officials, including Lincoln, and supported the Republican administration. Like other favored papers, the *Baltimore American* received government printing orders.

[26] Document B, 10, *Maryland House Documents: Special Session December 1861; January Session 1862* (Annapolis, 1861 and 1862). In this address Hicks avoided any discussion of slavery.

Now it filled with military bands both houses of the General Assembly, as well as many ladies and army officers. They had come to Bradford's inauguration to hear his address, which was frequently interrupted by applause.[27]

The new governor declared his love for the Union and the Constitution and re-enforced it by the practical observation that for Maryland nationality was a necessity. But he injected a veiled threat. This was the way Bradford put it: "So long as the Federal administration shall continue to devote . . . the power at its command faithfully to . . . the single and sacred purpose of sustaining the supremacy of the Constitution, so long will Maryland . . . unite . . . in upholding the Union of which she is proud to be the heart." The phrase, "So long as," implied conditions, conditions that required the national government to resist any attempt to misapply federal power. This obviously referred to slavery. In other words the attitude seemed to be that Maryland would remain loyal as long as the slaves were left alone.

Bradford looked upon the emancipation movement swirling out of the North as a "treason" that would, if not suppressed, inflict upon the Union its greatest blow. Taking heart, however, from Lincoln's affirmation that he would not interfere with slavery in the states, Bradford lulled his audience with a magnificent illusion that the renewed abolitionism "seems rather a sort of dying struggle of a desperate minority, the last spasm of an expiring faction."[28]

The General Assembly in its December, 1861, and January, 1862, sessions endorsed Bradford's views and passed the proposed United States constitutional amendment prohibiting federal interference in the domestic institutions of any state. The lawmakers protested against any plans that might incite a slave insurrection and warned that Maryland loyalty was untouched by "servility."[29] Praise for Lincoln's current policy softened the strident notes.

[27] *Port Tobacco Times*, January 16, 1862; *Baltimore American*, January 9, 1862.

[28] Bradford's inaugural address appeared in Document F, *Maryland House Documents 1861–1862; Port Tobacco Times*, January 16, 1862; and other newspapers.

[29] The resolutions sustaining the war effort were diluted by a "so long as" clause restricting the struggle to upholding the Union, with the constitutional right of the state unimpaired. On George Washington's birthday the House of Delegates fired another salvo at "the useless and wicked agitation of the slavery question," blaming it for furnishing a pretext to break up the government. It therefore appealed to the North to resist all attempts to stir up the subject. *Baltimore American*, February 24, 1862.

The *Baltimore American* had nothing but applause for these declarations.[30] *The Easton Star*, a not so loyal journal, pointed out a seeming incongruity, the impression given by Bradford and the legislature that under certain circumstances, "Maryland will neither be with the Administration or the Union." These contingencies presumably were abolition and arming the slaves to fight against their masters. The *Star* doubted the sincerity of such expressions, for if issue were to be taken with Washington, certainly the people would be placed in a position to defend themselves.

Instead, the legislature passed a treason bill that "irrevocably sold [Maryland] to the Yankees," and, should it be forthcoming, abolition rule.[31] The act prescribed death or imprisonment for those citizens who waged war against the state or gave aid or comfort to its enemies. The enforcement of such a vindictive measure could have caused a savage bloodletting in Maryland. Fortunately, the state was spared such ravages as the law lay dormant throughout the Civil War.

The attempt to push through the General Assembly a test oath of allegiance sputtered and died. Agitation for such measures prompted one southern Maryland journal to ask why one section of the state should act so pharisaically and adamantly toward fellow Marylanders?[32] His was a plaintive cry but one that would stimulate little compassion in the columns of the loyal *Cecil Whig*—which denounced the mal-apportionment of the General Assembly. A third of the state's population (one quarter of the white) took 34 of the 74 house seats and 14 of the 22 in the senate.

A bill to give more equitable representation was reported by Cecil County delegate John A. J. Creswell. It got through the House but was rejected by the Senate.[33] The defeat did not, however, kill the plan because it was part of the sectional strife so intimately linked with the coming movement for emancipation.

In the December session Senator John H. Bayne of Prince George's County called attention to severe losses in Negroes as slaves fled to the safety of army camps. Warning that an abolitionist war would annihilate the Union party in the loyal slave states, Bayne urged

[30] *Baltimore American*, December 24, 1861.
[31] *Easton Star*, February 4, 1862.
[32] *Port Tobacco Times*, March 6, 1862.
[33] *Ibid.*, February 6 and 27, 1862.

that Major General George B. McClellan be asked to stop letting his army accept fugitive slaves.[34]

The problem of runaways opened one of the rankest wounds cutting into Union support. It generated one of the fiercest quarrels in Maryland, involving not only slaves and slaveholders but also Governor Bradford, abolitionist generals, congressmen, and President Lincoln and his cabinet. Out of it evolved another of the important issues in the struggle to free the Maryland slaves.

Early in March the General Assembly adjourned. Its record rankled those who were already beginning to step out from Union conservatism. One journal, disappointed for lack of more stringent measures against the disloyal, concluded that the treason bill was as much as could be expected from a legislature composed of so many "used up politicians" tossed back into power by the political upheaval of November, 1861.[35] Winter Davis called the legislature "timid, irresolute," nor did Bradford's inaction escape his criticism.[36]

A test oath failed to be enacted, claimed one observer, because of "the lobbying, log rolling and shameful frauds,"[37] involved in electing a United States senator. The term of Anthony Kennedy, brother of John Pendleton Kennedy, was nearing an end. He did not seek re-election, nor would any attempt on his part probably have been successful. He and his colleague, James A. Pearce, hedged their support for the Union with too many qualifications to satisfy a number of Maryland legislators, one of whom introduced a resolution calling for their resignations.

Kennedy's successor had to be picked from the Western Shore, for under a peculiar provision of the state constitution each shore was entitled to one United States senator. Every other legislator seemed to be a candidate. Each one appeared paralyzed for fear of hurting his own chances.[38] Among the contestants in and out of the General Assembly were five lawyers: United States District Attorney William Price, Congressman Edwin H. Webster, Thomas Alexander, Thomas Donaldson, and Reverdy Johnson.[39] None of them gener-

---

[34] *Ibid.*, December 19, 1861.

[35] Fredrick *Examiner*, cited by *Cecil Whig*, March 29, 1862.

[36] H. Winter Davis to Samuel F. DuPont, February 8, 1862, S. F. DuPont Papers.

[37] Frederick Examiner, March 19, 1862.

[38] H. Winter Davis to Samuel F. DuPont, December 4, 1861, and March 10 or 11, 1862, S. F. DuPont Papers.

[39] *Cambridge Herald*, March 5, 1862; *Baltimore American*, February 28, 1862.

ated as much heated controversy as Henry Winter Davis. He gained the backing of the Frederick *Examiner* on the Western Shore and the *Cambridge Herald* on the Eastern Shore, which called him "the best abused man in the state; yet its most brilliant light."[40]

Davis' chances looked good as the General Assembly opened. He appeared to have a probable majority and managed to get John S. Berry elected Speaker.[41] An auspicious beginning, but the bright hopes quickly darkened. Berry turned aside from the Davis alignment by letting Davis' enemies control the organizing of the committees. Reverdy Johnson won the Committee of Federal Relations, a move which seemed to favor his claims on the United States Senate seat.[42]

The breaking of Berry destroyed Davis' confidence in his allies under fire. "I fully expect," said Davis, "a *Bull Run*—a shameful & causeless rout after a victory!"[43] He was right. In a caucus of Union legislators the real battle revolved around Price and Johnson, with Johnson winning on the tenth ballot. On March 5 the General Assembly legalized this action by electing Reverdy Johnson to the six year term beginning March 4, 1863.[44]

Johnson was no newcomer to politics. Born in 1796, he got elected to the upper house of the state legislature when only in his mid-twenties. In 1845 he went to the United States Senate for the first time, resigning four years later to become Attorney General in the short-lived cabinet of President Taylor. The latter's death precipi-

[40] *Cambridge Herald*, January 15, 1862. It reassured conservatives by saying that Davis had gone into Brooklyn, N.Y. and boldly denounced both abolitionists and Lincoln's unconstitutional acts. Another supporter charged Davis' sole crime as being his belief in the right of Congress to exclude or permit slavery in the territories.

[41] H. Winter Davis to Samuel F. DuPont, December 4, 1861, and March 10 or 11, 1862, S. F. DuPont Papers.

[42] H. Winter Davis to Samuel F. DuPont, December 18, 1861, S. F. DuPont Papers. Reverdy Johnson charged that Davis was being portrayed to the state legislators as the choice of Chase and the Lincoln Administration. Believing this action unauthorized, Johnson expressed hope that Chase would correct it. Reverdy Johnson to Salmon P. Chase, January 27, 1862, Salmon P. Chase Papers, Vol. 55, Library of Congress.

[43] H. Winter Davis to Samuel F. DuPont, December 18, 1861, S. F. DuPont Papers. In this letter Davis also noted, "This is the *old* story of my treatment by every one on whom I rely outside of the great mechanical class."

[44] Information on the caucus and the election can be found in such papers as the *National Intelligencer*, March 7, 1862; *Civilian and Telegraph*, March 6, 1862; *Baltimore American*, February 28, March 5 and 6, 1862; and *Cecil Democrat*, March 1, 1862.

tated Johnson's departure from public office. With the collapse of
the Whigs, he joined the Democrats and then turned to the Unionists as the rebellion erupted. In 1861 he returned to the Maryland
General Assembly as a member of the House of Delegates.

An effective speaker blessed with a "deep and impressive voice,"[45]
he achieved renown as one of the greatest lawyers of his time, particularly in constitutional cases. His quick, incisive mind, aided by
an excellent memory, enabled Johnson to gain an unequalled reputation in cross-examining witnesses. As might be expected, he was a
learned man, a quality nicely complemented by a good sense of humor and a courteous manner.

Upon being officially advised of his senatorial victory, Johnson
wrote John Summerfield Berry, Speaker of the House of Delegates,
and Henry H. Goldsborough, President of the Maryland Senate,
that he would do all he could "to arrest the causeless rebellion . . .
and to heal the dissensions."[46]

This would not be easy. The border state conservatives were battling more than an altruistic movement, for the flaming zeal of cru-
sading abolitionists mingled with less lofty motives. To many the
slave was no more than a pawn in a great revolution. The breaking
of his bonds simply became part of a package deal. What some radical republicans were after was power, power to execute a social, political, and economic revolution. Up to then southern politicians
had been largely able to frustrate the legislative will of the burgeoning North. Now that war had rendered this power impotent, the
radicals were able to act as the handmaiden of the rising capitalism,
opening the way for its unbridled surge.

Out of the ashes of a burned out social system they hoped to
build their victory. To assure lasting dominance, the South had to
be subjugated. The key to success, abolition, enlisted many moderate men who saw in slavery the cause of war and perpetual conflict.
Pressure intensified upon Congress and the President to constrict
and ultimately destroy slavery.

[45] Bernard C. Steiner, *Life of Reverdy Johnson* (Baltimore, 1914), p. 4. The *Dictionary of
American Biography*, X, 112–14, gives a biographical sketch of Johnson

[46] *Kent News* on March 15, 1862, quoted this letter. It can also be seen in the
Executive Papers in the Hall of Records.

CHAPTER IV

THE TARNISHED
IDOL OF SLAVERY

IN AUGUST OF 1861 William Howard Russell of the *London Times* boarded a Baltimore and Ohio passenger car in Baltimore. Up the hilly, picturesque Patapsco Valley, the train wound its way to the town of Ellicott's Mills in Howard County. Along the route smokeless factory chimneys and pleasant villas, many of which appeared deserted, caught his eye. When the train stopped, Russell alighted and got into Colonel Charles Carroll's carriage. The vehicle attracted the stares of local mechanics. Their eyes reflected no good will. Many were foreigners or former residents of the North, who did not sympathize with the state rights attitude of the Carrolls and the rest of the landed gentry.[1]

The drive from loyal Ellicott's Mills to the Carroll estate took more than an hour. Darkness had fallen by the time the carriage moved up the avenue of fine trees to old-fashioned Doughoregan Manor. If it had not been for the black faces of the servants, Russell could easily have fancied himself in an Irish country house. The land, gloriously wooded and well cultivated, recalled the hills of Gloucestershire. Tobacco and corn flourished in the large fields.

The Negroes on the estate lived in a village of brick and wood houses. Although windowless, the homes were more substantial than those in the South and could be considered palaces compared to the huts of Irish laborers. These slaves, however, were less servile, less civil, and less obliging than the field hands on the plantations of Louisiana. The local priest acknowledged to Russell that slavery was an evil and, in fact, not even profitable. But what were the landed gentry to do? The slaves had been inherited and with the right of property came obligations. The priest rejected emancipation as im-

---

[1] William Howard Russell, *My Diary North and South* (London, 1863), II, 284–85.

possible because the slaves would not work unless their master's land was confiscated and divided among them.[2] Carroll did hope, however, that on some distant day his Negroes could be freed and colonized in the West Indies or Africa.[3]

Unlike Colonel Carroll, some slaveholders energetically championed the Union cause. Congressman Crisfield prided Maryland on its loyalty despite "interests, attachments, and social relations" drawing it toward the South, but he joined Carroll in defending the institution of slavery against the "evil passions" of Yankee radicals. Nothing enraged these landed proprietors more than the abolitionist charge that they were slave-breeders and slave-dealers. Such an insult provoked the gentry to resolve never to yield to a party that attacked its institutions, its reputations, and its honor.

On March 25, 1862, Crisfield told the House of Representatives that the Negroes must be kept in servitude as long as they remained in the state. Otherwise "degradation, poverty . . . and ultimate extinction" would befall them. His words reflected the sentiments of many slaveholders:

> Sir, I am the owner of slaves; they are the descendants in a great degree of the woman who nursed me. They . . . look upon me as their protector. I am in truth their only friend. Am I to turn them off as outcasts on the world? I have been my whole life engaged in their protection. I have an affection for them, and have a duty to perform for them. . . . They have labored for me, it is true, but they have in turn received from me quite as much as they have given me.[4]

This view of slavery as a sort of benevolent patriarchy was quite popular. The *Easton Star* played upon this theme in reflecting on the death of Will Tolson, a 105-year-old Negro servant in Talbot County. The journal told its readers that his passing undoubtedly caused great sorrow in the master's family, for the respect offered these "old darkies" bordered on veneration. Had a "mammon-loving Yankee"

---

[2] *Ibid.*, 284–89. Colonel Carroll, the owner of the estate, was the grandson and namesake of a signer of the Declaration of Independence.

[3] So stated the will, dated March 12, 1861, of Charles Carroll of Doughoregan Manor, *Baltimore County Advocate*, February 28, 1863.

[4] *Congressional Globe*, 37th Cong., 2nd Sess., Vol. 32, Part 2, p. 1368. Crisfield claimed, however, that he was "not enamored of slavery."

family been responsible for him, he probably would have starved to death long ago or been "killed outright by brutal treatment."[5]

Nowhere on earth had the African achieved so good a life as in southern slavery, according to this viewpoint. One newspaperman wrote about the "cheerful, happy, sleek faces and generally neat attire" of the Negroes pouring into Chestertown, Kent County, for the Whitsuntide holidays.[6] Other people said that slavery had done more to elevate and Christianize the Negro than all the abolitionist societies put together. Maryland even taxed herself to find an asylum for the free Negroes in a foreign land.

Abundant food and clothing, comfortable shelter, and medical attention uplifted the lives of slaves. Ministers of God attended their suffering and performed slave marriages if the master consented. Only "pressing necessity" could make a slaveholder separate a family.[7] Some ladies even taught their servants how to read and write until the abolitionists tried to flood the slave states with incendiary printed matter. Inability to read was of no real importance anyway because the Scriptures could be expounded by the spoken word. What a healthy contrast slavery presented to the intolerable living conditions of northern and foreign wage earners!

Hailed as "the negro's kindest protector," the slave owners posed simultaneously as the poor whites' "best friend."[8] Virtue, justice, and a respect for the rights of individuals and property—all these things the gentry taught its less fortunate brethren. Then too, the affluent helped poor young men of promise to gain education and social position.[9] Under this system white laborers enjoyed a superiority that emancipation would wrench from them. Negro freedom raised the frightening specter of Negro equality. Rather than accept this calamity, a southerner, according to one Maryland congressman, would "strike though he may die immediately."[10]

Glorying in the "high and noble destiny"[11] of the master race, the

---

[5] *Easton Star* (Talbot County, Md.), January 7, 1862.

[6] *Chestertown Transcript* (Kent County, Md.), June 10, 1862.

[7] Samuel H. Berry of Prince George's County, *The Debates of the Constitutional Convention of the State of Maryland 1864* (Annapolis, 1864), I, 686.

[8] Daniel Clarke of Prince George's County, *Debates*, I, 664.

[9] Chapman Billingsley of St. Mary's County, *Debates*, I, 583.

[10] *Congressional Globe*, 38th Cong., 1st Sess., Vol. 34, Part 2, p. 1516. The speaker was Benjamin G. Harris, who served in Congress 1863–67.

[11] *Cambridge Herald*, January 8, 1862.

poor white found himself bound to this social structure. He heard that abolition would depress wages and overlooked the charge that slave competition stole from him. He listened to the political hucksters bolt the door against reason by hawking the wares of racial prejudice. Nightmarish portrayals of intermarriage and a mongrel people mingled with the fanatical speeches of men like Senator Anthony Kennedy, who conjured up visions of "blood and carnage" that would destroy one race or the other should slavery be abolished.[12]

So militant were some defenders of slavery that they spoke of it as "a divine institution. It is just as much sacred . . . as the rite of marriage."[13] Its worship attracted those who felt the government too popular in character and too lax in recognizing distinctions in society. Slavery spawned a privileged leisure class of educated gentlemen, statesmen, theologians, and lawyers, dedicated to high honor and exalted patriotism. The field of government provided a good example: the South, though less populous than the North, had filled a majority of the nation's top offices.

Other slaveholders shrugged off all attempts to justify their ownership of human beings by simply stating that their Negroes were as much their property as any other possession. To prove it, they pointed to the constitutions and laws of both the nation and the state. They considered any tampering with this property as nothing less than an atrocity. They reasoned that the North did away with slavery because it failed to be profitable, but they argued that Maryland tobacco growers required slave labor.

One of the chief troublemakers in the eyes of the Maryland slaveholders was the free Negro. Moving from bondage to freedom did not essentially change the occupations, abodes, and diversions of the Negroes, who continued to associate with slaves.[14] These "social monstrosities" blocked progress and prosperity. They drank too much[15] and achieved notoriety as vagabonds and thieves, prowling about at night like "wild beasts."[16] The further they got from slavery, the more worthless they became.[17]

[12] *Congressional Globe*, 37th Cong., 2nd Sess., Vol. 32, Part 2, p. 1356.

[13] S. H. Berry, *Debates*, I, 684.

[14] James M. Wright, *The Free Negro in Maryland: 1634–1860* (New York, 1921), p. 17.

[15] Eli J. Henkle of Anne Arundel County, Debates, I, 625.

[16] *Cambridge Herald*, January 8, 1862.

[17] Easton *Star*, May 6, 1862.

The lower counties of both shores bristled with complaints about being taxed for the support of improvident and idle free Negroes.[18] Planters feared that their evil influence might tempt the slaves to strike for liberty. On two occasions some Charles Countians proposed the eviction of the free Negroes, who were accused simultaneously of throwing white men out of work and lacking enterprise.[19] The free Negro thus provided a convenient, defenseless scapegoat for a stagnant economy run by a white population that had declined 38.6 per cent in fifty years.

Those who accepted this fallacious description of the free Negro apparently had short memories. Just prior to the Civil War a committee headed by United States Senator James A. Pearce, a Marylander sympathetic to southern ways, reported to a slaveholders' convention that most free Negroes were neither idle nor vicious. Baltimore City alone employed over 25,000 (estimated), mostly as servants and laborers. The planting and harvesting of Maryland's crops depended upon their help. Pearce's committee rejected the idea of expulsion or enslavement of the free Negroes.[20]

In this highly emotional period, logic seemed to boil away over the hot fires of passion. People did not stop to think how implausible it was to call the Negro unfit for freedom because he was degraded, when this degradation had been caused by his enslavement. They blindly believed any statement, no matter how conflicting, as long as it fitted their purposes and prejudices.

The social and political ramifications of slavery throughout Maryland were immense. Edward Dicey, English author and traveler, recalled a Baltimore lady who sat next to him on a train. Sympathetic to the South but not a secessionist, she lacked the wealth to own slaves. Nonetheless, she accepted without question the pro-slavery creed that had become part of her culture and spoke threateningly of abolitionist Wendell Phillips. The women of Baltimore, she said, would break every bone in his body if they could catch him. As in Great Britain where only a very few were of the peerage, so in America only a relatively small number were slaveholders, yet both systems

---

[18] The majority of the free Negroes lived in Baltimore and the northern counties, yet this area complained but little about the free Negroes.

[19] Wright, *The Free Negro in Maryland*, p. 304.

[20] William Daniel of Baltimore City quoted Pearce's report in *Debates*, I, 634.

generated interest and care on the part of those not immediately connected with either institution.[21]

This factor helped the proponents of slavery to wield a power far out of proportion to their numbers. Nearly all of Maryland's congressmen, United States senators, and governors were said to have owned slaves or sympathized with the institution.[22] Every one of the six representatives elected in June, 1861, were slaveholders—Charles B. Calvert and John W. Crisfield being two of the largest in the state.[23] In the Maryland legislature the slave counties exercised a veto over unfriendly measures, while the more populous north and west cowered before the false worship of servitude. Laws were enacted to hold the railroads responsible for any slave escaping by train. This bound as well the steamship lines plying the Chesapeake Bay and its tributaries.[24]

An example of justice as dispensed in Maryland at that time was compensation for the runaway slave. The sheriff could summon the only son of a dependent widow to help chase a fugitive slave. Should the son and the Negro be killed, the widow received nothing, while the slave owner was reimbursed. The master also received compensation if the state executed his Negro or sent him out of Maryland upon conviction for some crime. No such favor was offered the owner of a vicious bull, who was liable for any damages inflicted by the beast.[25]

To weld the chains of servitude more securely, the press was curbed, and a person could be imprisoned for possessing certain literature opposing slavery. In 1857 a free Negro was sentenced to a ten-year jail term for having a copy of *Uncle Tom's Cabin*.[26] The old cry of

[21] Edward Dicey, *Six Months in the Federal States* (London, 1863), II, 39–40.

[22] William T. Purnell of Worcester County, *Debates*, I, 719. A majority of the state legislators, according to Purnell, had also been slaveholders. His colleague, David Scott of Cecil County, commented upon the fear that free soil would produce free schools which would "excite free thoughts" and take the power out of the hands of those who had wielded it so long. *Debates*, I, 610.

[23] *The Maryland Union*, June 20, 1861. According to the 1860 census, Maryland's slaveholders numbered 13,783.

[24] John H. B. Latrobe to John W. Garrett, July 25, 1863, Salmon P. Chase Papers, Historical Society of Pennsylvania, Philadelphia.

[25] Unconditional Union Address, *Baltimore American*, September 16, 1863; Frederick *Examiner*, May 21, 1862; David Scott, *Debates*, I, 609.

[26] Jeffrey R. Brackett, *The Negro in Maryland* (Baltimore, 1889), pp. 225–26. *Uncle Tom's Cabin*, written by Mrs. Harriet Beecher Stowe and published in the early 1850s,

freedom for all men lay strangled, choked by abolitionist insults and fear that the slaveholder might lose his power to the emerging North.

Learned men such as John P. Kennedy and Reverdy Johnson could not justify slavery with the democratic principles of a sovereign people. Johnson considered the institution an affliction, and Kennedy said in the spring of 1861 that Maryland must become free.[27] Both men liberated their slaves. Yet these two leaders were too bound by southern mores to seek abolition. Kennedy went so far as to declare Negro servitude necessary to civilization where it already existed. He warned in December, 1860, that the old Union was impossible unless agitation over slavery ended.[28]

Kennedy's attempts at justification reflected the troubled hearts and sensitive nerves of many Marylanders upon the Negro question. Even in the North there were those who feared that the abolitionists would alienate the border state Unionists and destroy dormant loyalty within the South. One writer likened the southern dilemma on slavery to a man who had a wolf by the ears. He could not "hold on with comfort nor let go with safety, and it made them [him] extremely indignant to be goaded in the rear."[29]

Northern radicals feasted on southern discomfort. They stripped slavery of all adornments, revealing it as a heinous device to force labor without wages. Unlike anti-slavery men who simply hoped "to wall in" the system until it slowly suffocated to death, the abolitionists cast caution aside. Slavery must die and die speedily, "cost what it might, suffer who must, for the salvation of the souls of the

---

was a famous anti-slavery novel. Another interesting case involved the law that decreed all children of a slave mother to be slaves. Emanuel Mason, a Washington Negro, bought his freedom for $300 and then hired his wife. When their children, whom Mason raised with his own money, were large enough to be valuable, they were seized by the owner of Mason's wife. Only a little son, Ben, was left. Later Mason's wife was taken from him. Then an officer called to get Ben so that he might be sold. The father, failing to produce the boy, was arrested, convicted, and jailed until a fine should be paid. This story was recounted in *Daily National Republican* (Washington, D.C.), April 22, 1862, and *Congressional Globe*, 37th Cong. 2nd Sess., Vol. 32, Part 4, Appendix, p. 104.

[27] John Pendleton Kennedy, "The Great Drama: An Appeal to Maryland" (Baltimore, May 9, 1861), *Political and Official Papers* (New York, 1872), p. 603.

[28] Kennedy, "The Border States: Their Power and Duty in the Present Disordered Condition of the Country" (Baltimore, December 17, 1860), *Political and Official Papers*, pp. 578, 584.

[29] Ward Hill Lamon, *Recollections of Abraham Lincoln, 1847–1865* (Washington, 1911), p. 66.

masters, for the rights of man, for the love of Christ."[30] Even the Constitution and the Union were expendable if they seemed to stand in the way of human freedom.

Abolitionists had little patience for conservative Unionists from the border states. Owen Lovejoy's fiery tongue lashed at Maryland's John W. Crisfield from the floor of Congress. Lovejoy accused him of intimating that if the nation did not allow the perpetuation of

> . . . that system of concubinage and righteousness, they will dissolve this Union. I am tired of such talk. . . . How does it happen that these men appeal to our sympathies because they are loyal States? We never boast of our loyalty. It is because this system of slavery exists among them—a system of robbery; a system of rapine and outrage, . . . which is a stench in the nostrils of God, and which the whole universe is clamoring to have done away.[31]

Such remarks hardly endeared themselves to citizens in the border states. Many an incensed citizen questioned which was the greater threat to the nation: abolition or armed rebellion. Certainly Henry Garrett, a member of the prominent Maryland family, could not have been pleased when he received a letter early in 1862 from a "Presbyterian Elder" in New York. The writer bluntly said, "we must all go in for 'General emancipation,' right or wrong—This everlasting squabble about the 'Poor Slave,' will drive us all to the Devil, if we do not set him free!—What do you say—how many have you on hand, now burning your fingers, and searing your guilty Conscience?"[32]

One of America's leading abolitionists grew up in Maryland. Born of a slave mother and white father in a backward district of Talbot County, he is known to history as Frederick Douglass. Before he was seven, young Frederick was sent to the plantation of Colonel Edward Lloyd on the Wye River. This was one of the finest plantations in Maryland and, like those farther south, had its great house, cabins, children of all shades, venerable aunts and uncles, and overseers. Although public opinion supposedly restricted slavery in Maryland to its mildest forms, there were secluded places, like Lloyd's, where it developed all its evil traits without the danger of exposure.[33]

[30] Albert Bushnell Hart, *Slavery and Abolition 1831–1841* (New York, 1906), p. 174.

[31] *Congressional Globe*, 37th Cong., 2nd Sess., Vol. 32, Part 2, p. 1367.

[32] "Presbyterian Elder" (probably Jeremiah Wilson) to Henry S. Garrett, New York, January 14, 1862, Garrett Family Papers, Library of Congress.

[33] Frederick Douglass, *Life and Times of Frederick Douglass Written by Himself* (Hartford,

In this system a master could sell his own son or daughter without reproach if through the veins of that child coursed a drop of African blood. Mother and children were often separated and hired out. A white man could invariably kill a Negro, slave or free, with impunity. The murderer could say that his victim resisted him. No colored witness could legally deny it because a Negro was not allowed to testify against a white person.

Frederick Douglass wrote at length of the injustices of the system, a system devoid of any Negro rights that the white man had to respect. On one occasion he was rented for a year to a relatively poor man, Edward Covey. This Eastern Shoreman was a pious person, but he proved as unscrupulous as the worst of his neighbors in struggling to build his fortune. The ownership of a Negro bespoke respectability and wealth in a slave state; so he scraped enough together to buy a female "as a breeder."[34] To assure success he locked the woman up every night with a hired man and was overjoyed when she gave birth to twins.

The professedly Christian Mr. Covey overworked and brutally beat Douglass until the bloodied slave escaped to his master to plead his case. Douglass recalled seeing the man's inherent goodness rise against slavery, but tyranny extinguished this spark of humanity. Following the credo that the slave was always guilty, the master or overseer always innocent, the white man told Douglass he must have deserved the flogging. A desperate Douglass was at last driven to a grave and serious crime: he fought Covey. The gamble won him freedom from further abuse and a resurrection of Douglass' spirit.[35]

In 1835 Douglass was hired by a well-bred southern gentleman, from whom he received more humane treatment. But only freedom would now satisfy him. Douglass said of the slave: "Give him a *bad* master, and he aspires to a good master; give him a good master, and

---

Conn., 1883), Douglass, *Life and Times*, pp. 20, 26, 30, 40. Douglass believed that he was born in 1817.

[34] *Ibid.*, p. 151. This was not an unusual expression. Back in 1802 one of the Shrivers of Frederick County referred to a Negro woman who had been "turned out for breeding." Frederic Shriver Klein, "Union Mills, the Shriver Homestead," *Maryland Historical Magazine* (December, 1957), Vol. 52, p. 300.

Reverdy Johnson called the disregard of the marital relation one of "the horrible vices of the institution, . . . out of that, immorality of every description arises. . . ." Bernard C. Steiner, *Life of Reverdy Johnson* (Baltimore, 1914), p. 74.

[35] Douglass, *Life and Times*, pp. 161, 171.

he wishes to become his own master. Such is human nature."[36] A slaveowner, Dr. Samuel A. Harrison, confided to his diary much the same view. He observed during the Civil War that the Negroes belonging to "the most strict and severe masters" did not flee, while those subject to "the more lenient and kind" often took flight.[37]

To stop potential fugitives, owners sometimes locked them in Campbell's private jail on Pratt Street in Baltimore. Masters who had already lost Negroes went to the newspapers to advertise rewards for their return. The notice was usually headed by the drawing of a Negro carrying a bundle at the end of a stick perched over his shoulder. Such action prompted one newspaper to pluck the mask from those who talked pathetically about how they regretted the necessity of keeping slaves and the impossibility of being rid of them. "The mask is off," said this Washington daily, "when the world is imploringly offered so many dollars to 'lodge my boy Sambo in jail so that I can get him again.'"[38]

The men who trafficked in human flesh were despised not only by those hostile to slavery but also by Maryland gentlemen, who looked upon them as a necessary but detestable lot. One Marylander late in the Civil War called the "slave-trader, the most degraded, the most debased, the most ferocious and cruel of the human race."[39]

Yet otherwise kind and hospitable gentlemen made this trade possible. A Cecil Countian told about such a man, a Virginia friend, who sold his Negroes in Richmond. When asked how it felt to break up families and engage in this sort of business, he replied, "At first . . . it was just the hardest thing I ever went through, but I soon got used to their squalling, and latterly I did not notice it at all."[40]

A pious slave brought a premium price in the market place, the

---

[36] *Ibid.*, p. 185.

[37] Harrison Journal, September 25, 1863, pp. 553–54. Harrison said Miles River neck, near where Frederick Douglass lived as a boy, was owned mostly by large holders of land and slaves. These wealthy few were refined, proud, and exclusive. Their slaves had "no intercourse with their superiors, except thro' the overseer. In this their situation differs from that of the Negroes in other portions of the county, where they live in the family of the master. . . ." Such contact provided some civilizing influences.

Despite the riches of the few, "the aggregate wealth of this section is very far inferior to that of any similar section of the county of the same extent and fertility." Harrison Journal, April 20, 1863, Part 2, pp. 474–75.

[38] *National Republican*, March 7, 1862.

[39] David Scott, *Debates*, I, 615.

[40] Cited by Joseph B. Pugh of Cecil County, *Debates*, I, 676.

slave trader picking up an extra one or two hundred dollars.[41] Masters might have been confident of the piety of some of their slaves, but Douglass claimed that this was seldom reciprocated. Every slave believed that his owner could not "go to heaven without blood on his skirts."[42] Emancipation by the master was considered the best evidence of his acceptance by God.

Swept into the debate, many clergymen reflected the views of their congregations, while others stifled whatever anti-slavery sentiments they harbored. One pastor from the Eastern Shore confessed that he had not dared to speak against slavery for fear that he would lose his life or be thrown out of the community. He charged that restrictions upon Negro churches practically closed them for months at a time, an ironic twist to the praise of slavery as a Christianizing influence.

Southerners might proclaim its glories, but others criticized slavery for contributing to "intellectual demoralization." While America's centers of learning, charity, and industry flourished in the North, education in Maryland languished. White illiteracy was more than double that of more populous New Jersey. Yet the General Assembly invariably greeted all efforts to promote a "liberal common school education" by rebuffing them. Too much learning among the masses could prove dangerous to the control exercised by the oligarchy. At the same time the "useless drones" of society cultivated a distaste for labor, even though they did not hesitate to upbraid the Negro for laziness.[43]

So demoralizing did some people consider slavery that they viewed it as a greater wrong to the white man than to the Negro. One slave owner saw the ill effects, particularly on young men. Idleness, dissipation, and obstructions to progress and prosperity were induced by the system.[44] Slavery fostered as well an anti-democratic spirit among the upper classes and begot a servile obeisance to the gentry on the part of the non-slaveholders. It bred pride, arrogance, a sense of superiority, and a scorn for those who worked with their hands.

Only the German-language newspapers, with their restricted circulation, dared speak out against slavery before and during the early

---

[41] David Scott, Debates, I, 615.

[42] Douglass, *Life and* times, p. 133.

[43] Robert W. Todd, *Debates*, I, 554–55, 557–58.

[44] *New York Daily Tribune*, June 20, 1861. The dateline was Hagerstown, June 17, 1861.

stages of the Civil War. The *Wecker*, a daily published in Baltimore, supported the Republican presidential nominees in 1856 and 1860. Of course, privately some Marylanders unequivocally denounced slavery, but they were obviously a small minority. Judge William L. Marshall, a Republican, was one of them. He disagreed with a friend who said in the spring of 1861 that slavery must cease to be an issue and be left in "*God's hands*"; otherwise a "military Despotism [would be] established here." The judge fired back that he was fearful of throwing "upon '*God*' a great moral responsibility which he seemed . . . to have imposed upon me."[45]

Forebodings for the future appeared in the press. On January 14, 1862, the *Easton Star* wrote of "the increasing radicalism—as it would have been called once—of conservative leaders on slavery." Positions were shifting outside of Maryland. This so-called "increasing radicalism" referred to the feeling that if slavery stood in the way of the Union, it must be destroyed, the intimation being that it did pose such a threat.[46] The shifting tide hurled against border state Unionists the charge that they loved slavery more than the Union.

In the winter of 1861–62 those most hostile to secession could not yet wrench themselves free from the long years of indoctrination that damned the free Negro as worthless and labeled slavery a necessity. This carefully nurtured prejudice generated a greater fear of the emancipated than of emancipation.[47] It chained minds to the status quo, applied balm to the pricks of conscience, and assured a negative approach to any question pertaining to slavery.

These were the weapons exploited by the gentry and their political allies as they struggled to retain control of the state. Abolition summoned them to fight because through it "their social conventions were challenged, their privileges imperiled, their positions endangered."[48]

[45] William L. Marshall to Charles Sumner, February 20, 1862, Charles Sumner Papers, Harvard College Library.

[46] *Easton Star*, January 14, 1862.

[47] Brantz Mayer, *The Emancipation Problem in Maryland* (Baltimore, June 17, 1862). This pamphlet was based on an article appearing originally in the *Baltimore American*.

[48] Dr. Henry Pitney Van Dusen, president of Union Theological Seminary in New York, used these words to describe the forces that nailed Jesus Christ to a cross. Henry P. Van Dusen, *Life's Meaning: The Why and How of Christian Living* (New York, 1951), p. 76.

PART II

THE RISING ASSAULT ON SLAVERY

CHAPTER V

LINCOLN'S OFFER
OF COMPENSATION

LINCOLN DISPLAYED A considerable ingenuity as he guided the nation through its stormy political battles between the conservatives who would uphold the Union by saving slavery and the abolitionists who would rescue the nation by destroying the bonds of black servitude. He readily adjusted to shifting public opinion and rapidly changing events, but on one point he would not compromise. He expressed it simply and concisely in a letter to North Carolinian John A. Gilmer, "You think slavery is right and ought to be extended; we think it is wrong and ought to be restricted."[1] That he felt deeply on the issue could be seen in his fervent declaration that Senator Stephen A. "Douglas doesn't care whether slavery is voted up or voted down, but God cares, and humanity cares, and I care; and with God's help I shall not fail."[2] Lincoln suffered for the slave and hated the opportunity given the enemies of free institutions to charge America with hypocrisy. Nonetheless, he understood the torments of border state conservatives and harbored no prejudice against southerners. He believed they acted no differently than northerners would under the same circumstances.[3]

On assuming the presidency, Lincoln did not press his views on slavery upon the people. He considered it his duty neither to save nor destroy slavery but rather to preserve the Union. In order to achieve this goal, Lincoln usurped powers not expressly granted by the Constitution or by the laws of the nation. During the emergency in 1861 he called for troops, proclaimed a blockade of southern

---

[1] Abraham Lincoln to John A. Gilmer, December 15, 1860, *Lincoln Works*, IV, 152.
[2] Noah Brooks, *Abraham Lincoln* (New York, 1888), p. 309.
[3] Speech at Peoria, Illinois, October 16, 1854, *Lincoln Works*, II, 255.

ports, and suspended the writ of habeas corpus without congressional approval. Later in the war he permitted acts of dubious validity in a Maryland election. But Lincoln never tried to make himself a dictator, for he was at heart a faithful servant of the highest and best ideals in a free republic. In fact, he was sometimes attacked for not acting boldly enough.

During 1861 radicals urged Lincoln to free the slaves. The President listened but knew the country was not ready. Any interference with slavery might disturb the delicate balance of Union sentiment in the border states. Nevertheless, he considered ways of gradually eliminating the troublesome institution. He experimented with compensated emancipation for Delaware's 1798 slaves (1860 census), writing two proposed bills for the state legislature.[4] His efforts came to naught. The proposal failed to be introduced and spawned a hostilely worded resolution that missed passage only by a tie vote in one house.[5]

On December 3 Lincoln planted the seed of a similar idea in his annual message to Congress. Lincoln referred to the Confiscation Act of August 6, 1861, that declared forfeited all slaves used for hostile purposes against the United States. Suggesting that some states might pass similar laws, the President recommended that Congress accept such persons in return for some kind of compensation and urged that provision be made for colonizing the free Negroes.[6]

His allusions to emancipation were unproductive, but at least the *Baltimore American* was happy. It rejoiced that the message did not urge general emancipation or the arming of slaves. Lincoln's treatment of slavery was called "eminently conservative."[7]

The President, however, was not satisfied. He readied a more explicit plan for freeing the slaves. It closely resembled a proposal submitted by Secretary of the Treasury Chase toward the end of December, 1861.[8] With the hour of the announcement close at hand, Montgomery Blair tried to reach the President. He had left an evening conversation with Congressman George P. Fisher of Delaware con-

---

[4] *Lincoln Works*, V, 29–30.

[5] John G. Nicolay and John Hay, *Abraham Lincoln: a History* (New York, 1890), V, 206–8.

[6] Lincoln *Works*, V. 48.

[7] *Baltimore American*, December 4, 1861.

[8] David Donald (ed.), *Inside Lincoln's Cabinet, the Civil War Diaries of Salmon P. Chase* (New York, 1954), pp. 65–69.

vinced that the greatest obstacle to emancipation was the non-slaveholder. Believing the latter could be won if the freed Negroes were removed, Blair wrote Lincoln a note urging him to include colonization in his message.[9] The advice was not taken. Early the next morning Lincoln showed his proposal to Charles Sumner of Massachusetts. Though opposed to the gradual form of emancipation, Sumner welcomed the idea. It at least seemed a step along the road that could end only in complete abolition of slavery. Sumner objected, however, to one brief paragraph and tried to rewrite it. Lincoln interrupted, "Don't trouble yourself; I will strike it all out." But the senator continued to study the message. In a pleasant way the President stopped him "Enough; you must go, or the boys won't have time to copy it."[10]

Later that day, March 6, the message went to Congress. It began by recommending a joint resolution: "Resolved that the United States ought to co-operate with any state which may adopt gradual abolishment of slavery, giving to such state pecuniary aid, to be used by such state in its discretion, to compensate for the inconveniences public and private, produced by such change of system."[11]

Lincoln pleaded that "initiation of emancipation" in the loyal slave states would deprive the South of any hopes that the border region would join them. Such action would "substantially" end the war, but he wanted it understood that the proposal was a matter of "perfectly free choice." The federal government claimed no right to intervene. Then Lincoln shifted his attention to his annual message of the preceding December in which he said that every necessary means must be used in order to preserve the Union. Now he warned that if the war continued, it was impossible to foretell all the events and destruction that might result.[12]

The clerk in the House of Representatives read the message rapidly in a casual manner. The surprised legislators showed great interest. Some congressmen went to the clerk's desk to examine the document more closely.[13] Yet, in the days following, the border state representatives who visited the President avoided its mention. Be-

[9] Montgomery Blair to Abraham Lincoln, March 5, [1862]. Some one has incorrectly penciled "[1863]" on this letter. Lincoln Collection, Vol. 105.

[10] *The Works of Charles Sumner* (Boston, 1880), VI, 391–92.

[11] *Lincoln Works*, V, 144–45.

[12] *Ibid*, pp. 144–46.

[13] *Baltimore Clipper*, March 8, 1862.

lieving that they must have regarded the proposal as unfriendly, Lincoln determined to talk to them. He sent Montgomery Blair to see John W. Crisfield in order to invite him and his colleagues to a morning meeting at the White House.

In the conference the President spoke about the terrible war afflicting the nation and how inevitably slaves came to the army camps. One group pleaded for the military protection of such fugitives, while the slaveholders complained that their rights were being violated and their Negroes encouraged to run away. These conflicting charges were "numerous, loud and deep." They fed a spirit of hostility to the government in the border states.

The President's comments prompted Crisfield to ask what would happen if the proposal were rejected. Lincoln replied that he had no further plans. Crisfield probed further. He believed Maryland did not regard slavery as a permanent institution, but he wanted it known that the state disliked being forced into emancipation by either direct or indirect governmental action.

Lincoln countered that as long as he remained in the White House, Maryland institutions and interests "had nothing to fear" on these points. Crisfield quickly injected: "Mr. President, if what you now say could be heard by the people of Maryland they would consider your proposition with a much better feeling than I fear" they will otherwise do. Lincoln, however, was not willing to publish the comments because it would involve him in a quarrel with the abolitionists before the right time.[14]

On the very day of this conference, March 10, Roscoe Conkling of New York tried to introduce into the House of Representatives Lincoln's resolution. Crisfield protested; he wanted more time to think, but a vote of 86 to 35 suspended the rules, granting Conkling's wish. By the next day Crisfield had made up his mind. He rejected the resolution. Crisfield believed a firm offer should first come from the northern congressmen, and ample time should be allowed for deliberation.[15]

---

[14] The foregoing paragraphs are based on a memorandum by John W. Crisfield, who wrote it immediately after the meeting with Lincoln. His remarks were verified by three others present at the interview. The account, dated March 10, 1862, can be found in Edward B. McPherson, *The Political History of the United States of America During the Great Rebellion* (Washington, 1865), pp. 210–11 and various newspapers such as *Baltimore American*, October 31, 1862. Congressman Leary was the only other Marylander to attend the conference.

[15] *Congressional Globe*, 37th Cong., 2nd Sess., Vol. 32, Part 2, pp. 1149, 1152, 1169–70.

His border state allies joined in deploring the haste. They suspiciously eyed the plan as governmental interference and doubted the constitutionality of appropriating money for this purpose. Besides, the country was in no condition to bear the added expense. This position was supported by the entire Maryland delegation. Nevertheless, Lincoln's resolution easily passed the House on March 11 by a vote of 89–31.[16] Only when in later years it looked as though there would be neither slaves nor compensation did the slave owners forget their fussiness and plead for dollars to allay their losses.

Lincoln's proposal worried border state conservatives. Congressman John J. Crittenden of Kentucky rightly believed that those seeking the President's favor would inaugurate emancipation parties in the border states. United States Senator Willard Saulsbury of Delaware saw in the plan a similar threat. He brought up again various shop-worn doubts, attacked the vagueness of the resolution, and claimed that the war would be nearly over if its goal had been restricted to preserving the Union and constitutional rights.[17] Maryland's Kennedy sided with Saulsbury and eight other senators in voting against the proposal on April 2. It nonetheless was carried by a vote of 32–10, with Pearce's vote not recorded.[18] On April 10 Lincoln signed the joint resolution.

The talented radical from Pennsylvania, Thaddeus Stevens, called the measure "diluted milk and water gruel,"[19] but the brilliant orator and frequent critic of Lincoln, abolitionist Wendell Phillips, seemed satisfied. Phillips spoke of the plan as an entering wedge and told of the Negro preacher who said, "'If I found in the Testament a command to go through that stone wall, I should go at it. Going at it is my part; getting through it is the Lord's.' Well, now, I hold to this in some measure in regard to this emancipation. Going at it is the President's part, and getting through it is the people's part."[20]

Through his proposal, Lincoln seized leadership on the slavery issue from a host of lesser figures who were seeking it. His moderate

[16] *Congressional Globe*, 37th Cong., 2nd Sess., Vol. 32, Part 2, pp. 1179, 1197. Although May and Webster did not vote, their records showed they were opposed to such action.

[17] *The Southern Ægis and Harford County Intelligencer* (Bel Air, Md.), May 3, 1862.

[18] McPherson, *History of the Rebellion*, p. 210.

[19] *Congressional* Globe, 37th Cong., 2nd Sess., Vol. 32, Part 2, p. 1154.

[20] Wendell Phillips' address is recounted in Edward Dicey, *Six Months in the Federal States* (London, 1863), I, 157–89. The quotation is from p. 164.

policy temporarily hushed the mighty roar of the highly vocal radicals and quieted the fears of many loyal conservatives, who won assurances that their slaves were recognized as property, under the exclusive control of the states. The President threw his heart as well as the influence of his great office behind his policy. He got the *New York Times* to correct an intimation that the cost would destroy the plan. Lincoln pointed out that the expense of waging the war for eighty-seven days would pay for all of the slaves, at a rate of $400 each, in Kentucky, Maryland, Delaware, Missouri, and the District of Columbia. The President asked, "do you doubt that it would shorten the war more than eighty-seven days . . . [?]"[21] The plan, believed the President, opened a way out of the slavery dilemma with the least possible disturbance to social, economic, and political life.

The news of Lincoln's proposal must, however, have shaken many a slave owner in the Maryland General Assembly. A bill had passed the Senate by a 16–2 vote on February 14[22] to let the voters decide whether or not to call a constitutional convention. This action was required by the old Constitution of the first legislature after each census. On the evening of March 10 the bill came before the House of Delegates for final action. An amendment was accepted that delayed the election of delegates if the convention were approved. In this form the bill passed unanimously, 55–0.[23] It then went back to the Senate. There it died as the chief clerk of the House of Delegates requested in vain that the Senate extend its final session to give consideration to a number of important measures.[24] The Senate adjourned *sine die* at twelve that evening.

Apparently the fear of tampering with the organic law of the state during agitation for emancipation haunted the lawmakers, frightening one house into tacking on a restrictive amendment and the

[21] Abraham Lincoln to Henry J. Raymond, March 9, 1862, *Lincoln Works*, V, 152–53. Lincoln wrote Horace Greeley of the New York *Tribune* fifteen days later (*ibid.*, V, 169) to suggest that the measure be urged "*persuasively*, and not *menacingly*, upon the South."

[22] *Journal of the Proceedings of the Senate of Maryland, January Session, Eighteen Hundred and Sixty-Two* (Annapolis, 1862), p. 250. Hereafter cited as *Maryland Senate Proceedings 1862*.

[23] *Journal of the Proceedings of the House of Delegates, of the State of Maryland, January Session, Eighteen Hundred and Sixty-Two* (Annapolis, 1862), pp. 896–97. Hereafter cited as *Maryland House Proceedings 1862*.

[24] *Maryland Senate Proceedings 1862*, p. 525.

other into avoiding the revised bill altogether. A later Union political manifesto charged one of the senators with bottling up the bill.[25]

Locking the door on all legislative action for another two years did not quiet the impending storm; it simply gave it longer to brew. Marylanders could scorn and hate at leisure the fulminations and schemes of fiery abolitionists. They could not so easily ignore the policy of the President of the United States, as endorsed by the Congress. It "is startling—novel—but . . . must be met," said the influential *Baltimore American*.[26]

Secessionists greeted Lincoln's program as a vindication of their cause and a means of bolstering sagging fortunes. The charge went forth that the war for the Union was being "perverted into an abolitionist crusade . . . ,"[27] while down in the tobacco country the *St. Mary's Beacon* echoed with the refrain that the "diabolical and nefarious policy of Greeley and his cohorts" was taking over the national councils.[28] If the government could find no better cause than warring upon slavery, then it should let peace be restored. One extremist predicted emancipation by force as the next likely infringement of constitutional liberty, to be followed by the obliteration of state lines and the creation of a monarchy.[29] This fanciful propaganda appeared as a reprint from a Pennsylvania newspaper.

Some Maryland papers, sympathetic to the South, copied such material in order to express views they dared not adopt openly. Undoubtedly they feared suppression and arrest. The selection of letters to the editors by the newspapers also indicated political preferences. These communications, loyal as well as disloyal, were usually signed with a pseudonym or initial.

Union papers, of course, could write more freely. Many of them regretted the necessity for Lincoln's offer but defended him for defining his position. The *Kent News* conceded that if the question had to be raised, Lincoln's method of introducing it "was most appropri-

---

[25] *Address of the Unconditional Union State Central Committee to the People of Maryland*, September 16, 1863 (Baltimore, 1863), p. 14; *Baltimore American*, September 16, 1863, and other papers. According to this address, the bill also "contained a clause that the Convention . . . should 'not alter or abolish the relation of master and slave. . . .'"

[26] *Baltimore American*, March 8, 1862.

[27] *Montgomery County Sentinel*, May 23, 1862, State Rightist Charles Carroll, however, reportedly favored Lincoln's plan (Frederick *Examiner*, May 7, 1862).

[28] St. *Mary's Beacon* quoted in *Ægis*, April 12, 1862.

[29] Hanover (Pa.) *Citizen* quoted by *Ægis*, May 10, 1862.

ate."[30] Anyway, the rebels were to blame. They had done more damage to slavery in the last year *than the crazy fanatics of the North could
have done in one hundred years to come.*"[31] Another Eastern Shore paper
added, "We don't intend to let them [secessionists] ruin our slave
property, and then frighten us out of taking the money for it."[32]

The *Baltimore American*, which initially handled Lincoln's proposal
quite gingerly, adopted a more favorable attitude toward it and
printed a letter from "a gentleman at Washington, high in the confidence of the Government."[33] That screen concealed the identity of
Montgomery Blair, who said no thoughtful man believed slavery
could survive. To rid the nation of it, the President had embraced
the proposal of southern leaders so popular before slavery became "a
political hobby,"—that is, gradual, compensated emancipation "and
the separation of the races."[34]

Lincoln's March 6 message broke the bonds that gagged the press
and subserved every other interest to slavery. Newspapers and politicians spoke openly and favorably about freeing the Negroes. A
small minority of the Union press joined their rebel counterparts in
denouncing the action, but most moved toward some sort of approval
of Lincoln's program, swallowing whatever distaste they might have
felt or redirecting it at the rebels. That the Maryland press would meet
an emancipation proposal even halfway was a remarkable advance.

Newspaper policy stemmed largely from old party loyalties. Patronage and printing lured many an editor into an amenable position
and goaded rivals into slanderous charges. The *Cecil Whig* and *Cecil
Democrat*, both published in Elkton, demonstrated a particularly scath-
ing variety of mutual hostility, in which one editor accused his rival of
such offenses as "lying and forgery and advocating treason."[35] This
virulent form of personal journalism enlivened many a weekly.

The influence of the President upon papers which looked to him
for sustenance can well be shown by the Frederick *Examiner*. The day

[30] *Kent News* (Chestertown, Md.), March 15, 1862.

[31] *Ibid.*, April 19, 1862.

[32] *Cambridge Intelligencer* quoted in *Baltimore American*, May 7, 1862.

[33] *Baltimore American*, April 12, 1862.

[34] Montgomery Blair to Allen B. Davis, April 9, 1862, Blair Family Papers, Gist
Blair Collection, Box 5; *Baltimore American*, April 12, 1862.

[35] *Cecil Whig*, April 12, 1862. The *Whig* evolved into what was probably the most
radical journal in Maryland.

before the announcement of Lincoln's plan, that journal attacked Senator Henry Wilson's proposal for federal help in ridding Delaware and Maryland of slavery, flourishing such words as "unacceptable" and as "officious interference in our domestic affairs."[36] No amount of money could compensate for having such a large body of shiftless Negroes set loose upon the people. When Lincoln's proposal appeared, a remarkable thing happened. The *Examiner's* objections dissolved. The editor tried to rationalize his about face in the next issue by pointing to differences in the two plans, but most of these were non-existent.

As a supporter of the Administration, editor Frederick Schley was ready to give up the ancient clichés of the slave culture in order to follow Lincoln's lead. Schley was soon rewarded with an appointment as collector of internal revenue.

While the debate raged around Lincoln's March 6 proposal, most of Maryland cried "Foul" at the bill to abolish slavery in the District of Columbia. The Maryland House of Delegates assailed the act as a peril to state interests and said it would show Congress lacking in respect for Maryland's feelings, rights, and institutions.[37] Many men who sympathized with Lincoln's border state policy joined the chorus of dissent.

Senator-elect Reverdy Johnson reportedly called the measure "unconstitutional,"[38] while another respected Unionist labeled it "impolitic and ungracious."[39] The act allegedly violated Maryland's intentions when it ceded the territory to the federal government.[40] At a meeting in Rockville, near Washington, protestants expressed the fear that the District would become a refuge for runaway slaves and a focal point for inciting insurrection in the state.[41] Rebel sympa-

---

[36] Frederick *Examiner*, March 5, 1862.

[37] The resolution making these charges was passed by a vote of 61–0 in the House of Delegates on February 27, 1862. *Maryland House Proceedings 1862*, pp. 615–16.

[38] *Baltimore County Advocate*, May 3, 1862; Baltimore *Sun*, April 25, 1862.

[39] Harrison Journal, April 17, 1862.

[40] Minority Report from the committee for the District of Columbia, March 12, 1862, *Reports of Committees on the House of Representatives, Made During the Second Session of the Thirty-Seventh Congress* (Washington, 1862), Vol. 3, House Report No. 58.

[41] The April 7 resolution also claimed that private property could be appropriated only "*for public use*' and upon 'just compensation' . . . ," neither of which was fulfilled by the act. Such "unwise and illtimed" emancipation would be a blow to restoring the

thizers exclaimed that the cry of Union stood revealed as "a miserable cheat" and Lincoln as "something worse than a promise breaker."[42]

Lincoln, however, did not push the measure.[43] He feared it would upset the nervous sensitivity of Unionists and interfere with his hopes to coax, prod, and entice the border states into freeing their slaves. He talked to John W. Crisfield about the dilemma posed by the District bill, along with similar matters, and won his sympathy. The Maryland Congressman wrote his wife that the president was "surrounded with immense difficulties."[44] Lincoln said he objected to the timing as well as the terms of the legislation but believed its approval would cause less mischief than a veto. He hoped Maryland would understand.[45]

On April 16 Lincoln affixed his signature to the District bill, thereby incorporating into a law the only federal legislation that ever granted compensated emancipation. Only loyal masters were entitled to remuneration. Unwilling to accept the law, a number of Marylanders petitioned through Senator Kennedy for its repeal.[46] It was to no avail.

Although the Negro had no voice in the act, he was not unaware of its great significance. The day before Lincoln signed the bill, a friend of the English author and traveler, Edward Dicey, went out in a hired carriage, driven by an old Negro coachman "of long acquaintance." To the friend's astonishment, the Negro repeatedly took the wrong way. Angered, he asked the driver what was the trouble. "'Ah, massa,' the Negro answered; 'all this matter about the emancipation has got into my head somehow, and I feel stunned like.'"[47]

He was not the only one shaken by the changing status of the

Union. *Montgomery County Sentinel*, April 18, 1862; *National Intelligencer*, April 12, 1862; *Ægis*, April 26, 1862.

[42] *St. Mary's Beacon*, quoted by Baltimore *Republican*, May 2, 1862.

[43] Montgomery Blair suggested attaching to it an offer of compensated emancipation for Maryland, only to have the project collapse because of the state's opposition. Rough draft of letter, Montgomery Blair to ?, August 31, 1865, Blair Family Papers, Gist Blair Collection, Box 8. *Ibid.*

[44] John W. Crisfield to Mary [Crisfield], April 25, 1862, John W. Crisfield Papers, Maryland Historical Society.

[45] *Ibid.*

[46] *Congressional Globe*, 37th Cong., 2nd Sess. Vol. 32, Part 2, pp. 1979, 2274. Probably only 1,000 to 1,500 of the District's 3,000 slaves remained to be freed. Some had been moved to Maryland. See *National Intelligencer*, April 3, 1862.

[47] Dicey, *Six Months in the Federal States*, II, 34–35.

Negro. No doubt concerned by the growing political and military implications of Negroes, the Washington correspondent of the *Chicago Times* crudely wrote: "Negrophobia has seized the entire party of the Administration; they have nigger on the brain, nigger in the bowels, nigger in the eyes, nigger, nigger, everywhere."[48]

This attitude was one of many that made Lincoln's course of moderation difficult. He had to contend as well with insubordinate generals such as Major General David Hunter. As commander of the Department of the South, Hunter declared all slaves free in Georgia, Florida, and South Carolina. That was on May 9, 1862. Not until a week later did Lincoln hear of the proclamation, because mail to the North was restricted to sea transportation. The news stirred up a tempest.

The President reacted firmly. He told Salmon P. Chase, who wanted to let the order stand, "No commanding general shall do such a thing, upon *my* responsibility, without consulting me."[49] Lincoln revoked the order but hinted of possible future action. He used the opportunity for a forthright appeal to the border states. Urging them to consider his March 6 proposal, he said, "I do not argue. I beseech you to make the arguments for yourself. You can not . . . be blind to the signs of the time."[50]

Disgruntled abolitionists bemoaned Lincoln's revocation. Northern conservatives found satisfaction in it, while southern sympathizers pointed to the threatening overtones of the message. They accused Lincoln of trying to disregard the Constitution and laws in order to force emancipation upon the border states. One journal called Lincoln "blind, ignorant and deluded."[51] On the other hand, *Harper's Weekly* said the nation awaited Maryland's answer to Lincoln's plea.[52]

America would have to wait a long time if it relied on Maryland's elected officials to act. Like their counterparts in the other border states, they displayed a notorious immobility on the issue. They breathed defiance at the insidious doctrines from the North. Conservative Unionists demanded, urged, and prayed that all other issues

[48] *Chicago Times* quoted by *Baltimore Republican*, May 21, 1862.

[49] Abraham Lincoln to Salmon P. Chase [May 17, 1862], *Lincoln Works*, V, 219.

[50] Lincoln added that the change contemplated by his proposal "would come gently as the dews of heaven. . . ." Proclamation Revoking General Hunter's Order of Military Emancipation of May 9, 1862, May 19, 1862, *Lincoln Works*, V. 222–23.

[51] New York *Caucasian* as quoted by *Ægis*, June 7, 1862.

[52] *Harper's* Weekly, May 31, 1862.

other than the Union be set aside until the war was won. In so doing, they helped to incite the very turmoil they hoped to quell.

Keyed to the defense, striking at every offer of their opponents, these negativists exhibited an alarming incapacity for any constructive action that might have preserved the very leadership to which they clung. As apostles of the status quo, they looked with anguish upon divided families in a divided state in a divided nation and cried out, "No," to any change in the established order. Though they doubtlessly would not have admitted it, these people regarded an uprooting of time-honored customs as intolerable under any circumstances. Now they clung to all arguments, no matter how conflicting or facetious, to support their stand. Old shibboleths about inexpedience, "impolitic," and tending "to weaken the Union sentiment." flowed from their pens and mouths.[53] Though confessing the inevitability of slavery's destruction, they refused to heed. "What need," they asked, "for a movement to bring about a result which has already been obtained?"[54] They stalled for time and pleaded against tampering with the organic structure of society during a period of civil strife.

Conservatives saw in congressional offers of financial help ominous overtones of bribery and federal intervention, indignities insufferable to their pride. Yet some of them tried to give the impression that the state would abolish slavery if it stood in the way of the Union. The catch lay in the qualifications with which the conservatives encompassed the statement. Those debatable congressional funds must be provided for emancipation, deportation, and colonization before the border states would consider the proposal.

Stripped of rhetoric, what did this mean? As Lincoln's wartime secretaries pointed out, it meant inaction which was tantamount to resistance.[55] It was simply an empty position, a specious sop to self-justification. Why?—because Maryland legislators believed no choice was necessary between Union and slavery. The two were inseparable.

Comforted by presidential solicitude, conservative Unionists refused to be moved by Lincoln's earnest pleas and warnings, or by the obvious erosion of slavery. They foolishly hoped that the President would continue to act as a bulwark against rising sentiment hostile to slavery.

[53] *Cecil Whig*, April 26, 1862.
[54] Letter signed by "Anne Arundel," *Baltimore American*, June 18, 1862.
[55] Nicolay and Hay, *Lincoln*, VI, III.

Such negativism did not keep Congress from nibbling away at the institution. Less than a year had passed since the enactment of a comparatively tame Confiscation Act when Lincoln signed the controversial and far-reaching second Confiscation Act of July 17, 1862. It bestowed freedom upon the rebel's slave who came within the Union lines. It restricted the benefits of the Fugitive Slave Law to the loyal master and forbade any officer of the armed forces to surrender a runaway to his claimant. Of particular importance, it empowered the President to employ Negroes in any way he saw fit to suppress the rebellion. This could be interpreted as sanctioning the enlistment of Negro soldiers, a hotly contested issue. The bill passed the House by a vote of 82–54, with the Maryland delegation opposed.[56]

Anthony Kennedy in the Senate added his disapproval.[57] Senator James A. Pearce, ill and with only nine months to live when he entered the Senate for the last time on March 24, of course did not vote. Lincoln, who had intended to veto the legislation because of questionable points pertaining to the confiscation of property, signed it when Congress rushed through an explanatory resolution to obviate some of his objections.[58]

Congress in the same session outlawed slavery in the territories, despite previous Supreme Court decisions indicating such an act would be unconstitutional. This leftward swing deeply disturbed the conservatives. Some fifty senators and representatives, including John W. Crisfield and Edwin H. Webster, met on May 10, 1862, to devise ways of defeating abolitionists and secessionists.[59] Nothing permanent came out of the effort, nor did ex-Governor Hick's plea to stop the "mad doings" of northern "ultra men" have much effect.[60]

Some of these Yankees aroused ill will by tossing "taunts and low

[56] *Congressional Globe*, 37th Cong., 2nd Sess., Vol. 32, Part 3, p. 2793.

[57] *Ibid.*, Vol. 32, Part 4, p. 3276.

[58] *Baltimore American*, July 18, 1862. According to James G. Randall in *Constitutional Problems under Lincoln* (New York, 1926), p. 363, there was "no evidence of the actual enforcement of the emancipating clause of the act."

[59] *National Intelligncer*, May 12, 1862; *Baltimore American*, May 13, 1862. Throughout the second session of the 37th Congress the Maryland delegation fought a running battle against northern radicals. The slavery issue kept working its divisive way into congressional debate.

[60] Hicks worried over a revival of the "infernal Democratic Party." Thomas H. Hicks to Abraham Lincoln, May 26, 1862, Governor Thomas H. Hicks Papers, Maryland Historical Society.

flings" at Maryland loyalty. Congressman John Hickman of Pennsylvania, for instance, charged that the fear of force, not the love of freedom, held the border states in the Union. He tactlessly asserted, "I have never been able to discover a difference in views or feelings between a man from Maryland and a man from South Carolina or Alabama. I have found wherever the Negro is there is an undivided loyalty to slavery, and every day's proceedings here show it."[61]

The more diplomatic Lincoln shunned such tactics. He still clung to his March 6 policy as a way out of the slavery dilemma. "Oh, how I wish the border states would accept my proposition," Lincoln said to two Illinois Congressmen,[62] but he could not afford to appease the slave states much longer. Northerners were in no mood to pamper slaveholders, regardless of their loyalty. To do so would risk serious dissension in the North.

Four months had passed since Lincoln unveiled his plan on March 6. Now, with only a few days remaining in the second session of the 37th Congress, he once again called to the White House the border state delegations. With an earnestness that impressed his audience, Lincoln talked. He believed the war would be practically over if the men before him had voted for the resolution. If the fighting persisted, "mere friction and abrasion" would extinguish slavery. It would be gone, with nothing to show for it. As he had before, Lincoln spoke not "of emancipation *at once*, but of a *decision* at once to emancipate *gradually*." As to the freed Negroes, they could be colonized in South America, where land was cheap and abundant.

Then the President referred to his repudiation of Mayor General Hunter's proclamation. This action dissatisfied many people whose support he could not spare. Pressure was increasing and could be relieved by border state acceptance of the proposal. He beseeched the members of his audience to consider it before leaving Washington and asked them to commend it to the deliberation of their states.[63]

Before the delegation drafted a reply, Crisfield got together with Lincoln at the White House. The President asked, "Well, Crisfield, how are you getting along with your report, have you written it

---

[61] *Congressional Globe*, 37th Cong., 2nd Sess., Vol. 32, Part 2, pp. 1176–77.

[62] Cited by Carl Sandburg, *Abraham Lincoln: The War Years* (New York, 1939), I, 562.

[63] Lincoln's Appeal to the Border State Representatives on July 12, 1862 can be found in *Lincoln Works*, V, 317–19 and McPherson, *History of the Rebellion*, pp. 213–14.

yet?" Replying that he had not, Crisfield got some good advice from the President, who said, "You had better come to an agreement. Niggers will never be higher."[64]

Such counsel had little effect on the Eastern Shore Congressman. Apparently the author of the majority report,[65] signed by twenty of the conferees, he reaffirmed his attachment to the old order. The report reminded Lincoln that the signers had voted all the men, money, and supplies requested for the prosecution of the war and had done so despite distasteful measures injurious to their interests. This emancipation issue was an entirely different matter. The North could not be trusted to provide compensation. Other old arguments were repeated. As colonization was essential, the signers looked upon the scheme as nothing less than the substitution of a $1,600,000,000 debt for a deported labor force of the same value.[66] Even if only Maryland, Delaware, Virginia, Kentucky, Tennessee, and Missouri were included in the proposition, it would cost nearly half a billion. The report urged the President to wage war only for the restoration of the Constitution to its proper authority. For Maryland, Cornelius L. L. Leary, Charles B. Calvert, John W. Crisfield, Edwin H. Webster, and Francis Thomas signed.[67]

No Marylander put his signature to the minority report, whose authors displayed keen insight into a much befogged issue. They sloughed off the disputatious briefs about constitutional rights, burdensome finances, and proper war aims. They said it did not make any difference whether or not the many northerners who believed slavery the "lever-power of the rebellion" were right. The fact was the belief existed, and they had to deal with matters as they were. Certainly the border state delegations could urge their people to consider emancipation in order to save the Union.[68]

[64] Ward Hill Lamon, *Recollections of Abraham Lincoln: 1847–1865* (Washington, 1911), p. 290.

[65] *Ibid.; Cecil Democrat,* July 26, 1862.

[66] This was calculated on the average of $300 a slave, "greatly below their real worth," plus $100 for colonization.

[67] The Reply of the Majority, July 14, 1862, was reported in *Baltimore American,* July 19, 1862, and McPherson, *History of the Rebellion,* pp. 214–17. The majority believed that Border State emancipation would not appease the anti-slavery forces as long as 3,000,000 more Negroes remained in bondage in the South. As to the Union, the border states would remain loyal even if the Confederacy were recognized.

[68] The Reply of the Minority, July 15, 1862, was reported in McPherson, *History of*

Lincoln, who had remarked to the conferees on Saturday "that if no appropriation were made, then the bottom would be out of the tub,"[69] rushed the draft of a bill to Congress the following Monday. It was referred to the House select committee on emancipation, created by a resolution passed on April 7, 1862. Two days after receiving Lincoln's message, Representative Albert S. White of Indiana introduced a committee bill covering the loyal border states plus Virginia and Tennessee. To be eligible for compensation, a state had to abolish slavery within twenty years of passing the necessary legislation. The offer was good for only the next five years.[70]

Seven men signed the report, including Francis P. Blair, Jr. of Missouri. The only Marylander on the committee, C. L. L. Leary, excused himself from endorsing the work by explaining that he had no opportunity to read it. Without giving an opinion, he simply concurred in offering it to the House.[71] The bill got as far as a second reading, but Congress adjourned July 17 before it could reach a final vote.

The summer of 1862 saw Maryland's legislators standing immovable as the winds of change swirled about them. The president of the Union Central Committee of Maryland, the top governing body of that party in the state, joined the conservative chant. He characterized emancipation as the beginning "of a great social revolution of labor and representation, in the midst of a political revolution."[72] And indeed it was. To meet this revolution the border state delegations surrendered the opportunity not to stop emancipation but to direct it in such a way that it would disturb as little as possible their social, political, and economic life.

---

the Rebellion, pp. 217– 18. Much of the material on Lincoln's appeal and the replies to it can be seen in Nicolay and Hay, Lincoln, VI, 109–11, and various Maryland newspapers.

[69] Baltimore Evening Express, July 19, 1862, George W. Brown Scrapbook, 1862– 1864, Maryland Historical Society.

[70] Report of the Select Committee on Emancipation and Colonization, House of Representatives, 37th Congress, 2d Session, Report No. 148 (Washington, 1862). The bill provided each master who was not disloyal $300 maximum per slave, financed by $180,000,000 maximum in bonds bearing 5% annual interest. Out of unappropriated money in the treasury, $20,000,000 was made available to deport and colonize the freed slaves. An 83-page report accompanied and included the bill. The report called the greatest obstacle to emancipation the fear of Negro equality.

[71] Select Committee Report, p. 33.

[72] Brantz Mayer, The Emancipation Problem in Maryland, p. 3.

CHAPTER VI

LINCOLN'S EMANCIPATION PROCLAMATIONS

AS A REBEL column under Major General Stonewall Jackson waded across the Potomac River early in September of 1862, the voices of countless battle-hardened soldiers rang with the thunderous stanzas of "Maryland, My Maryland." The song summoned men to

> Avenge the patriotic gore
> That flecked the streets of Baltimore,
> And be the Battle-queen of yore,
> Maryland! my Maryland!1

Into the beautiful valleys bordered by Catoctin and South Mountains the Confederates marched. Their grimy, thread-bare appearance contrasted sharply with this land of milk and honey. To the Maryland secessionists, relatively untouched by the ravages of war, the rebels must have seemed a motley crew to bear the glorious title of "liberators." They wore the symbols of privation and hardship, shielding from public view a mighty fighting spirit.

On entering Maryland, General Robert E. Lee addressed its people by proclamation. He spoke of liberating them from the oppression of a "foreign yoke" and restoring "freedom of thought and speech."[2] lofty goal from a noble leader, but his phrases remained mere words. They ignited no sparks. The hope for a great outpouring of southern sympathy and support soon collapsed. Some residents, of course, did greet the invaders with joy, but only a few accepted the oppor-

---

[1] Alfred H. Guernsey and Henry M. Alden, *Harper's Pictorial History of the Civil War* (Chicago, 1866), p. 393.

[2] *Official Records*, Series I, Vol. 19, Part 2, pp. 601–2. The proclamation also appeared in various newspapers.

tunity to trade their civilian ease for the perils and discomforts of a
tattered army.

Most of the local inhabitants eagerly welcomed the return of the
American flag. Enthusiastic Unionists almost overwhelmed Major
General George B. McClellan as he retook Frederick. They wept,
shouted, and prayed as they crowded about the soldiers.[3] One Yankee on his way to fighting the invaders at South Mountain valued
the inspiration of the Frederick ovation as equal to a reinforcement
of a thousand fresh troops.[4]

That battle at South Mountain went to the Union army, but over
in Harpers Ferry a different drama unfolded. Stonewall Jackson
smashed at the federal defenders, compelling surrender of the town
along with 11,000 soldiers and large quantities of arms. This freed
Major General Ambrose P. Hill's division for a forced march to the
savage struggle erupting around Sharpsburg and Antietam Creek.

There the blood of the sacrificed etched the names of the Corn
Field, Bloody Lane, and Dunkard Church into American history.
Shot and shell ravaged the countryside, leveling cornfields and pil-
ing them high with bodies. Over a stone bridge stormed Major General
Ambrose E. Burnside's Union troops, but A. P. Hill's weary forces
slammed into the advance and saved Lee from a disastrous defeat.
Both sides suffered heavily. Some 23,500 soldiers lay dead or wounded.
The terrible slaughter won the infamous distinction of the bloodiest
day's battle of the Civil War.

Lee held his position the next day, and McClellan did not attack.
On the night of September 18 the battered and out-numbered Confederates withdrew across the Potomac River. McClellan, forever hesitant, let slip the opportunity to shatter the retiring rebels. As the
grey columns forded the Potomac below Shepherdstown, an occasional soldier struck up the tune "My Maryland," only to be cursed
by some comrade, who called back, "Damn my Maryland."[5]

That battle did more than spread grief in thousands of homes and
stop Lee's invasion. It provided Lincoln with a long awaited chance
to drop his border state policy in favor of a more progressive ap-

---

[3] George B. McClellan to his wife, September 14, 1862, cited by Warren W. Hassler,
Jr., "The Battle of South Mountain," *Maryland Historical Magazine* (Baltimore, 1957),
III, 45–46.

[4] George F. Noyes, *The Bivouac and the Battle-Field; or, Campaign Sketches in Virginia and
Maryland* (New York, 1864), pp. 165–66.

[5] Douglas Southall Freeman, *R. E. Lee* (New York, 1934), II, 406.

proach. Back in July Lincoln had begun to outline his new program. During that summer he felt affairs were going "from bad to
worse."[6] He was confronted by discouraging news from the war front
and the immobility clamped upon the border states by their leaders.
Radicals were pressuring him for a strike at slavery. Charles Sumner,
for instance, pleaded for a July 4 emancipation edict. Lincoln rejected it on grounds that half of his officers would quit, and three
additional states would rebel.[7] Nonetheless, he wrestled with the
same idea.

In the cipher room of the War Department telegraph office, freer
from interruptions than at the White House, Lincoln pondered over
the first draft of an Emancipation Proclamation.[8] On July 12 he
made his fruitless appeal to the border state delegations in Congress,
knowing there was little or no chance they would reconsider his
March 6 message. The very next day Lincoln invited Secretary of the
Navy Gideon Welles to join him in the carriage with Secretary of
State William H. Seward and Mrs. Frederick Seward. They were on
their way to the funeral of Secretary of War Edwin M. Stanton's in-
fant. As they rode, Lincoln talked earnestly. He had about decided it
was a military necessity to proclaim freedom for the slaves.[9] Once he
renounced any right to interfere with slavery until every other means
of restoring the Union had been exhausted. Now that time had come.
Like a surgeon bound to try to save a diseased limb, he would sacrifice it if that limb threatened the life of the patient.[10]

On July 22 the President presented to his cabinet a proclamation
affecting the rebellious region, but he did not forget the border
states. In spite of the disdain that greeted his earlier efforts, Lincoln
announced his intention of again recommending federal compensation for loyal states voluntarily abolishing slavery.[11]

Chase welcomed the proclamation despite some reservations.[12]
Montgomery Blair, who came in late, reacted differently. He did not

---

[6] Francis B. Carpenter, *Six Months at the White House with Abraham Lincoln* (New York, 1867), p. 20.

[7] Carl Sandburg, *Abraham Lincoln: The War Years* (New York, 1939), I, 566.

[8] David Homer Bates, *Lincoln in the Telegraph Office* (New York, 1907), pp. 138, 141.

[9] *Diary of Gideon Welles* (Boston, 1911), I, 70.

[10] Carpenter, *Six Months at the White House*, pp. 76–77.

[11] *Lincoln Works*, V, 336–37.

[12] *Chase Diaries*, p. 99.

like Lincoln's idea. It would lose the fall elections, he feared.[13] The next day Blair set his thoughts in writing. He found no public demand for the proclamation. Besides, the border states would see it as a fatal blow to their property in slaves. Such a move should be reserved for counteracting foreign intervention.[14]

Lincoln had already considered and decided in his mind all questions raised until Seward spoke. The Secretary of State approved but doubted the advisability of announcing it at this time. "It may be viewed as the last measure of an exhausted government," he said.[15] Seward suggested waiting until it could be backed by military success. In admitting the wisdom of this thought, Lincoln confessed he had overlooked it. Other influences also urged delay; so Lincoln put the document aside and waited, waited two months before a propitious circumstance furthered the Union cause.

During the interim, belief in emancipation as a military necessity grew. Even the Democrats would have difficulty opposing it under this guise. And the President feared the radicals would embarrass the war effort if he did not satisfy their clamor. It began to appear more serious to deny their impetuous desires than to continue the futile courtship of unresponsive border state conservatives. Then came the invasion of Maryland. Lincoln vowed to God that if the rebels were driven back from the state, he would issue the Emancipation Proclamation. He was at the Soldiers' Home, three miles from Washington, when the news came that cleared the way for the document. Lincoln finished a second draft and returned to the capital.

He called his cabinet together to announce his decision. Opening the meeting on the unlikely note of a reading from the humorist Artemus Ward, Lincoln did not win unanimous appreciation for this buffoonery. Stanton sat glumly, annoyed and angry. "Gentlemen, why don't you laugh?" asked Lincoln, "With the fearful strain that is upon me . . . if I did not laugh I should die, and you need this medicine as much as I do."[16]

---

[13] Carpenter, *Six Months at the White House*, p. 21.

[14] Blair believed as well that the proclamation should be effective at the moment of issue. Summary of a long letter from M. Blair to President Lincoln, July 23, 1863 (apparently not sent), Blair Family Papers, Gist Blair Collection, Box 5.

[15] Carpenter, *Six Months at the White House*, pp. 21–22. See comments on Carpenter's account in Benjamin P. Thomas and Harold M. Hyman, *Stanton: The Life and Times of Lincoln's Secretary of War* (New York, 1962), pp. 239–40.

[16] Don C. Seitz, *Lincoln the Politician* (New York, 1931), p. 336

Taking a paper from his tall hat on the table, he became solemn. While reading the document, he commented as he read. It began by a reaffirmation of the purpose of the war to restore the Union. One section supported compensated emancipation for non-rebellious states and combined it with an assurance that colonizing efforts would be continued. To this Seward had Lincoln insert "with their consent,"[17] which robbed the statement of any impression that compulsory deportation might be contemplated. The President also agreed to recommend financial assistance to loyal slave owners in rebel states.

None of these clauses, however, achieved historical immortality for Abraham Lincoln. The core of the proclamation lay elsewhere. It lay in the formal, prosaic language of the first five lines of the third paragraph: "That on the first day of January in the year of our Lord, one thousand eight hundred and sixty-three, all persons held as slaves within any state, or designated part of a state, the people whereof shall then be in rebellion against the United States shall be then, thenceforward, and forever free."[18] This was a preliminary Emancipation Proclamation, for it announced to the world what the final document would achieve on New Year's Day, exactly 100 days hence.

Blair still felt hesitant about the proclamation. He doubted its expediency, believing it might throw the border states to the secessionists and give a club to northern partisans with which to pummel the administration.[19] Lincoln admitted the seriousness of the first objection but believed there was at least as great a drawback in not acting. The second criticism carried but little weight with the President.

Stanton enthusiastically endorsed Lincoln's proclamation. As the Secretary of War was leaving, the president said, "Stanton, it would have been too early last spring."[20] The country was not ready for it. To the painter Francis B. Carpenter the President likened the process to a man watching his pear tree, awaiting the "ripening of the fruit." It cannot be forced, but with patience, "the ripe pear at length falls into his lap."[21]

[17] *Lincoln Works*, V, 434.

[18] *Ibid.*

[19] M. Blair to A. Lincoln, September 23, 1862, Lincoln Collection, Vol. 88; *Diary of Gideon Welles*, I, 143; Allen T. Rice (ed.), *Reminiscences of Abraham Lincoln by Distinguished Men of His Times* (New York, 1886), p. 535.

[20] Seitz, *Lincoln*, p. 336.

[21] Carpenter, *Six Months at the White House*, p. 77.

The Emancipation Proclamation stirred again controversy on the slavery question, which for a time seemed overshadowed by the draft and Lee's invasion. The document further solidified the South. Its effect "was profound and electrical," but the fears of its inciting servile insurrection failed to materialize.[22]

Secession sympathizers north of the Potomac raged. Many distraught conservative Unionists broke with the administration, while more moderate citizens muttered about the trouble-making potential of Lincoln's edict.[23] A soured John W. Crisfield, leader of Maryland's congressional delegation, felt cheated. A self-imposed rift severed his relations with Lincoln. In the following months Crisfield wrote his wife that he was "disgusted with the littleness of our [?] public men." As to the President, the conviction of his "incapacity is every day becoming more universal."[24]

To share his revulsion with the nation, the articulate Mr. Crisfield delivered a lengthy address to the House of Representatives on Friday, December 19. He deplored calling differences of opinion treasonous and blamed faction for secession, abolition, and the ruining of the country. How depressing the national scene! But then came Antietam. What joy it brought! The battle stripped "the argument of necessity" from the President's path. What, however, did he do? After struggling manfully and standing firmly in times of great danger, "he struggled and stood no longer."

Crisfield struck hard at the Emancipation Proclamation, denouncing its "utter contempt for the Constitution," and its "suddenness," which was apparently a great sin under any circumstances. "Every

---

[22] E. Merton Coulter, *The Confederate States of America 1861–1865* (Louisiana State Univ. Press, 1950), pp. 264–66.

[23] The British consul in Baltimore observed, "The President's Emancipation Proclamation has fallen like a thunder-bolt on the Union men here, who regard it with dismay as being in direct contradiction with what they were led to expect." Frederic Bernal to Lord Russell, September 23, 1862 (F. O. 5/847, Public Record Office).

[24] John W. Crisfield to wife Mary, January (?) 22, 1863, John W. Crisfield Papers. In an interview with this writer on April 21, 1953, Colonel Henry Page (1870–1954), a grandson of Crisfield, recalled long talks with the former congressman. Crisfield, a beautiful speaker and wonderful conversationalist, spoke to Page of frequent consultations with Lincoln. Page quoted Crisfield as saying, "Lincoln had promised me that he would not issue the proclamation freeing the Negroes without further consultation with me. I was in Philadelphia . . . and I heard a newsboy proclaiming the Emancipation Proclamation. I immediately returned to Washington."

patriotic heart," according to Crisfield, filled "with astonishment, terror and indignation." The old fear, an uprising of the Negro, gained support, for the proclamation said the federal government "will do no act or acts to repress such persons [slaves] . . . in any efforts they may make for their actual freedom." These words prompted Crisfield to speak of the slave in terms of "an ignorant and savage enemy" embarked upon "indiscriminate butchery." The South would "never make peace" confronted by such a sweeping pronouncement. To think that it would help preserve the Union was beyond Crisfield's comprehension. He conceded Lincoln's sincerity but not his rationality, saying, "it is hard to see how a sane mind can . . . arrive at such a conclusion."[25]

Congressman Calvert shared Crisfield's distaste for Lincoln's Emancipation Proclamation. He pointed to the *"hellish* designs" of the abolitionists, who hated the loyal border states.[26] Leary and Thomas joined Calvert and Crisfield in voting against a resolution that the House of Representatives passed in support of the Emancipation Proclamation.[27] Nor did Governor Bradford find Lincoln's proclamation to his liking.

Two days after its announcement, Bradford attended a governors' conference at Altoona, Pennsylvania. It had been called under the vastly different circumstances prevailing ten days earlier. Though the ostensible purpose was to devise better ways to support the government, some of the state executives had hoped to accomplish two things: to get Major General George B. McClellan removed from his command and to apply pressure for more positive action against slavery. In the closed sessions Bradford was elected chairman. No agreement could be reached on McClellan whose removal Bradford opposed, but enough of the governors approved the Emancipation proclamation to include its endorsement in an address to the President. Sixteen signed it, but the governors of New Jersey and the

[25] The quotations from Crisfield's speech, delivered on December 19, 1862, are taken from *Congressional Globe,* 37th Cong., 3rd Sess., Vol. 33, Part 1, pp. 147–51. Crisfield believed it absurd to advocate putting aside the constitution in order to preserve it.

[26] Charles B. Calvert to editors of the *Baltimore American,* October 1, 1862, *Chestertown Transcript,* October 14, 1862.

[27] *Congressional Globe,* 37th Cong., 3rd Sess., Vol. 33, Part 1, p. 92. The vote was 78–51 and the date, December 15, 1862.

border states of Kentucky, Missouri, Delaware, and Maryland held back.[28]

Most Marylanders probably shared Bradford's dislike for the proclamation. The majority of the newspapers registered distaste ranging from mild regret to bitter criticism. One writer scorned the value of the edict, calling it nothing more than a "paper manifesto," while another claimed it would have no influence in rebel areas but would exert a "crushing and withering" effect upon Maryland.[29] Lincoln's policy, commented one journal, seemed bent on freeing the Negroes and "virtually" enslaving the free.[30] But there was another danger. It was the idea "that this Federal Government was created to do about everything, instead of little or nothing."[31] This effort to destroy the old Union and erect a new one centralizing all control in Washington alarmed many conservatives.

Some Marylanders were not so smitten by fear of the proclamation. Though they might question its merit, they believed it demonstrated the importance of accepting Lincoln's proposal for compensated emancipation. These people emphasized that slavery, "the cause of the rebellion," would never be tolerated in Maryland after the war.[32] The radical-learning *Cecil Whig* went further. It berated those border state men who objected to the proclamation, calling them "depraved" and "traitors."[33]

Henry Winter Davis struck boldly too. He told a Newark, New Jersey audience that the proclamation must be given legal force in order to be effective. He suggested a constitutional amendment to abolish slavery and proposed the confiscation of the lands of the rebel leaders, the property to be distributed among Negro soldiers. As to colonization, he tossed it aside as a delusion. Even if practical, "it would not be desirable."[34] Southern soil needed to be cultivated.

[28] See John G. Nicolay and John Hay, *Abraham Lincoln: A History* (New York, 1890), pp. 166–67; *Baltimore American*, September 26 and 27, 1862; and Baltimore *Sun*, September 26, 1862.

[29] "Observer" to editor, *Baltimore American*, October 14, 1862. The *Maryland Union* of October 2, 1862 doubted if any man outside of Greeley and a few others had "given the rebels more *aid and comfort* than President Lincoln. . . ."

[30] *Chestertown Transcript*, October 7, 1862.

[31] New York *Express* as cited in Baltimore *Republican*, December 4, 1862.

[32] *Baltimore American*, October 6, 1862.

[33] *Cecil Whig*, October 18, 1862.

[34] *Davis Speeches*, p. 305. Speech was delivered on October 30, 1862. Though he wanted to abolish slavery, Davis did not approve Lincoln's methods. He wrote Mrs.

Twelve months ago that same fiery orator scoffed, "Only ignorant fanatics prate about decrees of emancipation."[35] Now he raced ahead, caught up in a revolution from which there would be no turning back. The past inflicted no paralysis upon him. He jumped in front of Blair and Lincoln in his dash toward radical leadership.

So many northern newspapers and distinguished persons applauded the Emancipation Proclamation that Lincoln confessed the praise was "all that a vain man could wish."[36] But he was disturbed. Six days had passed. During that time stocks declined, and recruiting ambled along at an even slower pace than before. Then came the Republican defeat in the fall elections. Some blamed the proclamation, while *Harper's Weekly* attributed the debacle to dissatisfaction with the slow progress of the war.[37] Others saw defeat arising from annoyance at conscription and interference with individual rights. Whatever the cause, the Democrats carried New York and Pennsylvania, both of which gave healthy majorities to Lincoln in 1860, and won in the Republican states of Indiana, Illinois, and Ohio. Democratic congressmen gained over thirty seats. Who would control the new Congress, to meet in December, 1863, would be determined by Maryland and eight states that had yet to hold elections.

The third and last session of the old Congress, the 37th, received Lincoln's annual message on the day it convened, December 1, 1862. The President used the opportunity to try to soothe the ruffled feelings of the border states. He proposed as a Union-saving device a constitutional amendment to grant United States bonds to those states freeing their slaves before 1900. Included was authorization to Congress to colonize, if it so chose, those free Negroes who were willing to emigrate. The plan left to each state the decision on how and when to abolish slavery.

Lincoln wanted to make one point clear. He was not changing his policy by this recommendation. He was simply supplementing it. Lincoln still adhered to the Emancipation Proclamation and the proposal for a Congressional appropriation to any state adopting emancipation prior to the amendment's approval.

Samuel F. DuPont on September 24, 1862 (S. F. DuPont Papers), "These proclamations are powerless but for mischief; and like all other violent acts they are the offspring of terror."

[35] *Davis Speeches*, p. 253. The date was October 16, 1861.

[36] A. Lincoln to Hannibal Hamlin, September 28, 1862, *Lincoln Works*, V. 44.

[37] *Harper's Weekly*, November 22, 1862.

In his peroration the President appealed to his fellow citizens, saying, "The fiery trial through which we pass; will light us down, in honor or dishonor, to the latest generation. . . . In *giving* freedom to the *slave*, we *assure* freedom to the *free*—honorable alike in what we give, and what we preserve. We shall nobly save, or meanly lose, the last best, hope of earth."[38]

Lincoln must have realized how time-consuming the adoption of a constitutional amendment would be, probably too long to help in shortening the war. Its offer, however, demonstrated the extent to which he was willing to go to overcome the objections of conservatives. Long had they complained that Lincoln's proposal of March 6 was unconstitutional and that the North could not be counted upon to appropriate the money. Now they were being offered a program that struck down these two arguments.

Lincoln's message evoked from journals like the *Baltimore American* the desired effect. The message "appeals to the hearts of men wherever opened to human sympathies." It revealed the author as a man of "discerning intellect, noble affections, and exalted patriotism."[39]

In the course of his message Lincoln touched upon one of his fondest hopes, colonization, saying he "strongly" favored it. But it was a hope hampered by crippling frustrations that spelled its eventual demise. Lincoln sincerely believed that both races would be better off with the Negroes in a more congenial land. Back on August 14, 1862, he told a group of Negroes at the White House that freedom did not bring equality and asked their support for colonizing Central America. The plan, however, eventually collapsed and forced abandonment of an initial colony of 500.[40]

Interest in colonization waned as emigration schemes collapsed, and the Negro gained greater acceptance by donning a military uniform.[41]

---

[38] Lincoln's annual message to Congress can be found in *Lincoln Works*, V, 530–37. No doubt, said Lincoln, some would object to the cost of his plan, but he believed southerners "not more responsible" for introducing slavery than were northerners. By extending the deadline for eligibility to 1900, the price would be much less, for Lincoln estimated the nation would have three times as many people to share the expense. The President believed emancipation would increase prosperity and warned against specious arguments about white and black labor.

[39] *Baltimore American*, December 11, 1862.

[40] *Lincoln Works*, pp. 370–75. See also Nicolay and Hay, *Lincoln*, VI, 358–59.

[41] Montgomery Blair and Attorney General Edward Bates urged deportation for the free Negroes, but Lincoln opposed compulsion. See *Diary of Gideon Welles*, I, 152.

Lincoln altered his approach, which was gratefully noted by his secretary John Hay on July 1, 1864, "I am happy the President has sloughed off that idea of colonization."[42]

Meanwhile contention ensnared the final Emancipation Proclamation. Border state congressmen met on the evening of December 17 and selected the 75-year-old John J. Crittenden of Kentucky, William A. Hall of Missouri, and John W. Crisfield of Maryland as a committee to urge the President to recede from his position.[43] Lincoln agreed to meet them at 10 o'clock the next morning. Their efforts were as fruitless as the opposition of old Francis P. Blair and Orville H. Browning, both of whom had been close to the President. Browning frankly admitted, "The President was fatally bent upon his course."[44]

Lincoln felt that a failure to issue the final proclamation would spark revolt in the North and set up a dictator.[45] On December 30 he presented a draft of his forthcoming document to the cabinet and asked for criticism. The next morning the cabinet met again, and various members suggested changes. With these in mind, Lincoln did some rewriting, though he made no significant alterations.[46]

The completed work, justified as "a fit and necessary war measure," listed those southern areas omitted from its sting as well as the regions affected. Unlike the preliminary proclamation, it urged the Negroes declared "free to abstain from all violence, unless in necessary self-defence." and recommended that they, whenever possible, "labor faithfully for reasonable wages." It announced that suitable persons would be accepted into the armed forces but said nothing about colonization, compensating the loyal, or pursuing the border state plan.[47]

---

[42] Tyler Dennett (ed.), *Lincoln and the Civil War in the Diaries and Letters of John Hay* (New York, 1939), p. 203.

[43] Baltimore *Republican*, December 18, 1862.

[44] Theodore C. Pease and James G. Randall, *The Diary of Orville Hickman Browning* (Springfield, Mass., 1925), I, 607.

[45] *Ibid.*

[46] Nicolay and Hay, *Lincoln*, VI, 405, 420–21.

[47] The proclamation is printed in *Lincoln Works*, VI, 28–30. The approach of January 1 stimulated some Marylanders to conjure up nightmarish fantasies of a slave uprising. An Anne Arundel County delegation beseeched Governor Bradford to prevent the catastrophe, which of course proved to be mere fiction. See Augustus W. Bradford Journals, I, December 16, 1862, Maryland Historical Society; Nathan Shipley, Jr. to

During the morning of January 1, 1863, Lincoln put the finishing touches on his document and hurried to the traditional White House reception for New Year's Day. For three hours he stood in the blue Room, shaking hands, chatting, and greeting visitors.[48] Then he walked upstairs to the President's room, where Secretary of State Seward and his son Frederick had brought the document. Laid out on the cabinet table, it awaited Lincoln's signature. Holding his pen momentarily above the paper, Lincoln looked around and said, "I never in my life felt more certain that I was doing right, than I do in signing this paper." Then, "slowly and carefully," he wrote, "Abraham Lincoln."[49] It came out clear and bold though the President called it "slightly tremulous."[50]

The deed gave him a deep sense of fulfillment. Twenty years before a dark cloud descended upon Lincoln. Afflicted by depression, he even considered ending his life. He brooded over his lack of accomplishments. But Lincoln "cast off the works of darkness, and . . . put on the armor of light."[51] He labored through trial and anguish, striving to fulfill his yearnings to link his life with events that would advance the cause of man. In the Emancipation Proclamation Lincoln believed his fondest hopes would be realized.[52] And so they were.

In Boston, Buffalo, and Pittsburgh one-hundred-gun salutes roared a welcome to a new birth of freedom. Anti-slavery crowds resounded with jubilation though some radicals felt the proclamation did not go far enough. Abroad English laborers displayed their sympathy. Critics reacted in much the same way they did to the proclamation of September 22. The loyal *Civilian and Telegraph* seemed doubtful as to its effect but willingly accepted it.[53] Private Richard I. Gist wrote from Company C of the 6th Maryland Regiment that the proclamation "has caused a great dissatisfaction in the army."[54] Some

---

Governor Bradford, December 2, 1862, Executive Papers; and A. W. Bradford to A. C. (?) Gibbs, December 17, 1862, Executive Letterbook, pp. 348–50.

[48] Nicolay and Hay, *Lincoln*, VI, 421, 429; Carpenter, *Six Months at the White House*, p. 87.

[49] Frederick W. Seward, *Reminiscences of a War-Time Statesman and Diplomat, 1830–1915* (New York, 1916), p. 227.

[50] Carpenter, *Six Months at the White House*, p. 87.

[51] Romans 13:12.

[52] Sandburg, *Lincoln War Years*, II, 24.

[53] *Civilian and Telegraph*, January 1, 1863.

[54] Richard I. Gist to Mary S. Gist (typed copy) January 7,1863, Gist Family Papers, Hall of Records.

officers of Maryland troops stationed at Frederick reportedly "refused to draw their swords in Virginia."[55]

Baltimoreans, if they felt any rancor, did not publicly show it.
New Year's Day saw that volatile city crowded but quiet, the occasion being observed as one of "festivity and enjoyment."[56] Perhaps
the people sensed that Lincoln's opponents were indulging in no
more than the usual political squawking. Certainly the President's
historic act caused far less turmoil in Maryland than might have
been expected, particularly when it was recognized that destruction
of slavery in the South would inevitably doom it in Maryland.

[55] William Kirkwood to Henry Wilson, February 21, 1863. See entry in Irregular
Book 3, RG 107 (Off. of Sec. War), National Archives.

[56] *Baltimore American*, January 2, 1863.

CHAPTER VII

THE EMERGENCE OF
MARYLAND EMANCIPATIONISTS

EVEN BEFORE LINCOLN'S Emancipation Proclamation, the first hesitant steps were being taken toward Negro freedom in Maryland. They took place in a far from favorable setting. Southern Maryland Unionists squawked so loudly about fugitive slaves that they lost their effectiveness as patriots. Some federal officials, instead of backing the Administration, labeled supporters of Lincoln's appeal to the border states as abolitionists and unworthy of a gentleman's confidence. Nor did the governor, the Union State Central Committee, or the congressional delegation help. They lessened prospects of emancipation by spurning Lincoln's offer of compensated emancipation.

But there was another side, a far brighter one in regard to Lincoln's goals. As long as the war lasted, Negroes would continue to undermine slavery by fleeing to friendly hands in the military. At the same time Congress stepped up its legal attacks. Then there was Montgomery Blair. He did his bit for emancipation. And even his ally, Francis S. Corkran, who complained about pro-slavery men in government, admitted he was not alone among local politicians in supporting the President's plan. In fact, Corkran worried about those "treacherous-and-deceitful" Winter Davis partisans who sought control of the emancipation movement and exploited it for political advancement.[1]

Into Corkran's office on the morning of May 20, 1862, walked Peter G. Sauerwein, a well-to-do flour merchant, later appointed a collector of internal revenue. Sauerwein carried some interesting news—prospects looked favorable for a bold espousal of emancipation at the forthcoming City Union Convention.[2] This would be a

[1] Francis S. Corkran to Montgomery Blair, June 6, 1862, Lincoln Collection.
[2] Francis S. Corkran to Montgomery Blair, May 20, 1862, Lincoln Collection.

remarkable step forward because the convention exercised general control over the Union Party in Baltimore

The Union Central Committee of Maryland, the top governing body at the state-wide level, looked on with anguish. Its city members met on May 6 and publicly expressed "surprise and regret" at the call for a new city convention. There was "no need" for it; Baltimore wanted rest from any political action at this time.[3] The plea to desist failed, forcing the Union State Central Committee to decide what to do next. The suggestion that the full State Central Committee be convened incurred the opposition of the president, Brantz Mayer. And Governor Bradford was inclined to agree. He believed it more discreet to avoid the possible controversy over slavery that might arise in such a meeting.[4]

This do-nothing position of the party hierarchy tossed the political initiative to Baltimore's "Unconditional Union men," who gathered in their wards to elect delegates to a one-year term in the new city convention. The successful candidates met on May 21. Present were men destined for prominent roles in the movement to free Maryland from slavery. They included those friendly to Winter Davis as well as others who preferred Blair. Archibald Stirling, Jr., a close friend of Davis, won the presidency, while Massachusetts-born attorney Henry Stockbridge assumed the vice presidency. A week later the convention reassembled amid "harmony and enthusiasm" and heard Peter G. Sauerwein report a series of unprecedented resolutions.[5]

These resolutions, unanimously adopted, gave Maryland emancipationists their first important political victory of the Civil War. Embodying the heart of the yet-to-be-born platform of 1863, the resolutions affirmed unconditional loyalty to the federal government and the Constitution and gave Lincoln's March 6 message unequivocal support. Both "duty" and "interest" dictated its acceptance, for the offer would rid the state of an unprofitable institution that proved harmful to political "interests, and dangerous to our peace and safety."[6] A call for colonization joined the entreaty.

The resolutions criticized the last legislature's failure to fulfill its

---

[3] *Baltimore American*, May 8, 1862.
[4] Augustus W. Bradford to Brantz Mayer, May 21, 1862, Simon Gratz Collection, Historical Society of Pennsylvania, Philadelphia, Pa.
[5] *Baltimore County Advocate*, June 14, 1862.
[6] *Baltimore American*, May 30, 1862.

legal obligation to provide for a state-wide vote on whether or not to convene a constitutional convention. But it was not just the peculiar institution of slavery that these politicians wished to erase through changes in the constitution. Their ambitions went beyond that. They determined to break the slave-ridden power of tidewater Maryland. The delegates pointed to the City of Baltimore as having fifteen less delegates in the General Assembly than she should be allotted.

The resolutions sparked varying responses. Some journals correctly assessed their importance. In Frederick the *Examiner* gleefully portrayed them as endorsing and vindicating its own "Platform," announced on April 16.[7] A more conservative journal on the Eastern Shore took a different tack. It rejected the plea for a more equitable distribution of legislative seats as "an old song." For the greater interest of the landed and agricultural group to submit itself to the lesser interest of the city would be "preposterous."[8] This discordant note of provincialism exposed the customary journalistic conformity to local self-interest.

The resolutions struck John S. Berry, speaker of the House of Delegates, as being "Very bold" and "exceedingly premature." He feared for the Union Party "if such spirits are to be our leaders."[9] Less worried was that prominent Easter Shoreman, George Vickers, who believed the party could not be abolitionized.[10] The *Kent News* agreed. It scoffingly asked, "Who gave to these [few] men the right to teach slaveholders their duty . . . ?"[11] How presumptuous, how imprudent this "rule or ruin faction [!]"[12] Did not the state constitution prohibit the overthrow of slavery?

But the security founded upon this constitution was like a house

---

[7] Frederick *Examiner*, June 4, 1862. This paper supported the convention's appeal for more equitable representation but brazenly twisted it so as to avoid equality for Baltimore. *Ibid.*, May 21, 1862.

[8] *Kent News* as cited by *Easton Gazette*, June 21, 1862. Another journal commented: "What cared the convention delegates if the war had become a struggle to free the Negro and enslave the white?" These "Old brazen-faced, political hacks" never lost "sight of the public skillet." *Montgomery County Sentinel*, July 4, 1862.

[9] John S. Berry to Augustus W. Bradford, May 30, 1862, Executive Papers. That same year Berry was appointed adjutant-general of Maryland.

[10] George Vickers to Augustus W. Bradford, June 4, 1862, Executive Letterbook, 305 and also in Executive Papers.

[11] *Kent News* as cited by *Easton Gazette*, June 21, 1862.

[12] *Worcester Shield* as cited by *Cecil Democrat*, June 21, 1862; *Montgomery County Sentinel*, June 27, 1862.

built upon sand, for as constitutions were framed by men so could they be changed by men. Those who then fought against emancipation and their descendants who today fight against equal rights for all enshrouded their platforms in the majesty of the Constitution as interpreted by themselves. The freedom they proclaimed was the freedom of a privileged group to rule as it chose. They did not stop to answer the question: Freedom for whom to do what?

Those who condoned slavery used God for the purpose of extolling the glories of Negro servitude. The Almighty, they said, designed the Negro as an inferior being. Woe unto the white man who would violate the laws of God by artificially thrusting the two races on an equal plane. Slavery could not be changed without inflicting injury on both races.

As God and American rights might seem better suited to Sunday services and July 4 celebrations, these partisans of slavery dwelt as well upon economic and social self-interest. They warned the slave owners not to expect Congress to abide by its unconstitutional pledge to compensate Maryland. They also cautioned the "poor white man" not to be deceived. Emancipation would not break down the distinction between the white laborer and the slave owner, who could hire help. Nor would the upper classes have to come in contact with the freed Negro. The poor white would be the one to be humbled if his rich neighbor happened to be a "pompous" Negro.[13]

Southern sympathizing Maryland papers delighted in talking about the laziness of Negroes on the one hand, and, on the other, reprinting stories of how competition from free Negroes drove wages down. Accounts came out of Chester County, Pennsylvania, of "ruinous competition," in which Negroes hired themselves for as little as 10 cents a day.[14] No debate in heated discussion over abolition became more grotesquely twisted than the economic effect of freeing the slaves.

The emancipationists shared this guilt. They dinned into the poorer citizenry a reverse set of claims that had one thing in common—the appeal to self-interest. While slavery excluded and degraded white labor, free Negro labor, according to the progressives, did not. One writer contended: "whenever the two races are placed in competition the black soon goes to the wall, and is crushed out."[15]

[13] "Maryland" in *Chestertown Transcript*, June 17, 1862.
[14] *Evening Journal*, as cited in *Montgomery County Sentinel*, July 4, 1862.
[15] *Cecil Whig*, March 22, 1862. It is interesting to compare this with the statement

Comparative land values got attention too. The free states boasted higher prices than Maryland. The same held true between the free and slave counties. One citizen envisioned prosperity as doubling within a few years by ridding the state of both slavery and the Negro.[16]

While the tempo of debate grew faster and the impact of war whittled away at slavery, politicians jockeyed for position. Baltimore engaged in an election during the fall of 1862. Its importance stretched beyond the immediate offices being contested, for the victors would inevitably play an important role in selecting congressional and legislative candidates in the following year.

To pick a mayoralty nominee, the executive committee of the City Union Convention called primary meetings for September 16 in each ward. At most of these gatherings the supporters of Acting Mayor John Lee Chapman gained control. Out of the 100 delegates chosen, 85 voted for him.[17] The selection was then made unanimous.

The City Council candidates, selected in the various ward meetings,[18] did not please quite a few Unionists. A disgusted observer charged political manipulators with controlling the primary meetings. What did this signify? To the *Baltimore American* it meant that winning a nomination in the dominant party required deals with ward bosses—"contracts and jobs for ballots and voters."[19]

Disgruntled Unionists conferred on September 29 and bestowed their mayoralty blessings upon Frederick Fickey, Jr., treasurer of the Union State Central Committee and one of three commissioners for Baltimore to superintend enrolling and drafting militia.

---

in the *Cecil Democrat* of May 24, 1862, which said that in the "irrepressible conflict" between white and colored labor, the whites would "be crushed out or reduced to a mere song." And yet in the preceding issues "Eno" implied that abolition would "overrun the country with idle vagrants and fill our alms houses with Negro paupers." Equally illogical was the demand of many slavocrats to deport the free Negro at the very time their fields were left fallow for want of labor.

[16] "A Native of B. M. House" to *Whig*, May 16, 1862, *Cecil Whig*, May 24, 1862.

[17] *Baltimore American*, September 18, 1862. Chapman, as president of the First Branch of the City Council, was acting mayor. The imprisoned Mayor George William Brown was not freed until shortly after his term of office expired.

[18] Each of the twenty ward leaders called a meeting of Union voters to nominate one candidate for the First Branch of the City Council. At the same time five delegates were chosen to meet a like number from the adjoining ward to pick a candidate for the ten-member Second Branch.

[19] *Baltimore American*, October 7, 1862.

One observer accused the "Fickey" movement of originating in resistance to emancipation.[20] Another tried to smear him for tempting
treason.[21]

Considerable feeling embittered rival partisans, but the election
was a quiet one. Only 10,000 citizens, much less than half of what
would be considered a full vote, bothered to cast their ballots. This,
of course, indicated a victory for the organized ticket. Job holders
and others controlled by the city administration would naturally
vote. Chapman swamped Fickey by a vote of 9,027 to 1,231 for a
two-year term.[22] Of fourteen independent Union candidates running for the two branches of the City Council, only one triumphed,
Sebastian F. Streeter.

Two months later another event occurred of significance to the
initial movement for emancipation. Conservative James Alfred Pearce,
the senior senator from Maryland, was dead. Four times he had gained
election to the United States Senate. A southern gentleman and a
slaveholder, he opposed Lincoln's Administration and many of its
acts, yet he longed to see the nation reunited.[23]

Who would replace him? Even before Pearce's death, Governor
Bradford heard from conservative Anna Ella Carroll, who liked also
to counsel Lincoln. She championed ex-Governor Hicks.[24] Bradford
agreed, making the interim appointment on December 29, 1862.[25]
Hicks took his seat on January 14.

Differences existed on where, if anywhere, the new senator stood.
Hicks appeared to gain "the confidence of the ultras," during his
first week in office, but this course reckoned without the astute Mr.
Crisfield. The latter watched, ready to steer his fellow Eastern
Shoreman back to a more conservative path. Crisfield, in fact, thought
of himself as "a sort of Senatorial balance wheel." As Hicks trod the
"slippery bank" of "the dirty-lake of abolition," Crisfield watched

[20] *N.Y Evening Post* as cited by *Baltimore Daily Gazette*, October 13, 1862.

[21] *Baltimore Clipper*, October 8, 1862.

[22] *Baltimore American*, October 9, 1862.

[23] See the following for information on Senator James A. Pearce: *Congressional Globe*,
37th Cong., 3rd Sess., Vol. 22, Part 1, pp. 292–93, 299–302; *Dictionary of American
Biography*, Vol. 14, 352–53; and obituaries in Maryland newspapers.

[24] Anna Ella Carroll to Governor Bradford, November 1, 1862, Anna Ella Carroll
Papers, Maryland Historical Society. The *Baltimore American* of December 25, 1862, also
suggested Hicks for senator.

[25] Augustus W. Bradford Journals, I, December 29, 1862.

him, encouraged by the feeling he had the senator's heart on his side.[26]

Perseverance paid off. On February 12 Hicks "paired" against the bill for Missouri emancipation.[27] This doubtlessly gratified Crisfield but not the *Civilian & Telegraph*. It accused Hicks of arraying himself "with the enemies of the Government against every leading measure" upon which he voted.[28] Hicks, said Winter Davis, showed an "extremely *'stampedy'* character."[29]

In this final session of the Thirty-seventh Congress Hicks expounded upon his beloved Union and how he was ready to die for it. This offering of a variety of physical sacrifices became almost a conditioned reflex with him. Back in 1861 Hicks expressed a readiness to endure the severing of his right arm rather than strike a sister state in the South. Less than two years later he was willing, if necessary, to sacrifice his "life on the altar of my country."[30] He would even give up his Negroes, but then he must have remembered Crisfield's preachings, for he qualified his statement. No unconstitutional force must be used to grab Maryland slaves. Rather than submit to it, he would "fight against that force until I die."[31] Yet he was not a bit fussy about arbitrary arrests without trial, and he would willingly have exonerated Lincoln had the President hung forty secessionists.[32]

Fortunately for Hicks, words were cheap. Otherwise, he would have needed the nine lives of a cat to survive. Innocent of logic and devoid of genius, Hicks veered from side to side until he reached a firmer position on behalf of all measures deemed necessary for the preservation of the Union.

On the last day of the Thirty-seventh Congress he presented a petition from radical Judge Hugh Lennox Bond and twenty-five others for a $10,000,000 appropriation for freeing Maryland's slaves. Like other similar proposals, benefits were to go only to the loyal.[33]

[26] Quotations from John W. Crisfield to wife Mary, January (?) 22, 1863, John W. Crisfield Papers.

[27] *Congressional Globe*, 37th Cong., 3rd Sess., Vol. 22, Part 1, p. 903.

[28] *Civilian & Telegraph*, February 26, 1863. Back on January 8, 1863, the *Civilian & Telegraph* had hailed Hicks, believing him a supporter of Lincoln's proclamation and compensated emancipation for Maryland.

[29] H. W. Davis to A. Lincoln, February 19, 1863, John G. Nicolay Papers, Library of Congress.

[30] *Congressional Globe*, 37th Cong., 3rd Sess., Vol. 33, Part 2, p. 1373.

[31] *Ibid.*, p. 1372.   [32] *Ibid.*, p. 1373.   [33] *Ibid.*, p. 1525.

This exclusion spurred partisans of slavery of questionable allegiance to fight emancipation. They clung to the battered hope that Jefferson Davis would triumph and save them.

This would never happen if Winter Davis could prevent it. He was already at work with his congressional contacts. As soon as the bill for compensated emancipation in Missouri passed the House of Representatives, he drafted a similar plan for his own state.[34] He took it to John A. Bingham, an Ohio Republican, because supposedly no Maryland congressman would introduce it. Bingham accepted the bill and on January 12, 1863, tried to get it before the House, only to be blocked by Congressman May. Francis Thomas successfully countered with a resolution instructing the Committee on Emancipation and Colonization "to inquire into the expediency of" appropriating money to help Maryland free and resettle her Negroes.[35]

The *Baltimore American* called the resolution extremely significant,[36] but the *Examiner* derided it and late that month accused Thomas of stalling a bill until he could show that more than $10,000,000 was needed.[37] A year ago twice that amount could have been obtained, believed the *Examiner*, while a year hence it doubted that Congress would appropriate so much as a dollar. By then Maryland emancipation would be "a matter of indifference to the nation."[38]

On January 19 Bingham finally succeeded in introducing his Maryland bill.[39] Five weeks later Albert S. White of Indiana reported it back from committee with amendments. The bill offered Maryland $10,000,000 in United States bonds if it adopted immediate emancipation by January 1, 1865. The federal government would at the same time obligate itself to help colonize all emancipated slaves willing to leave the country.[40]

Through the use of various parliamentary questions, Crisfield and then Clement L. Vallandigham of Ohio, fought the legislation. Both wanted to refer it to the Committee of the Whole, which, according

[34] See H. W. Davis' speech in Elkton on October 6, 1863, reported by the *Baltimore American* of October 9, 1863.

[35] *Congressional Globe*, 37th Cong., 3rd Sess., Vol. 33, Part 1, p. 283.

[36] *Baltimore American*, January 14, 1863.

[37] Frederick *Examiner*, January 28, 1863.

[38] *Ibid.*, January 14, 1863.

[39] *Congressional Globe*, 37th Cong., 3rd Sess., Vol. 33, Part 1, p. 381.

[40] *Congressional Globe*, 37th Cong, 3rd Sess., Vol. 33, Part 2, p. 1293. Compensation, which was to go only to the loyal, was to come indirectly from confiscated rebel property.

to Winter Davis, at that stage of Congress would have prevented its consideration.[41] White countered by moving to send the bill back to his committee; the motion won by a vote of 75 to 55. Calvert, Crisfield, May, and Webster voted in the negative, but Francis Thomas and Leary joined the majority.[42] The bill, however, did not come up again.

Significantly, the Maryland congressional delegation split on the question. No longer could Crisfield count on Thomas and Leary as he had in the First and Second Sessions of the Thirty-seventh Congress. They were beginning to heed the rising sentiment for emancipation in their districts.[43] Thomas demonstrated his shift by switching from opposition to the Missouri emancipation bill in December, 1862, to approval in early March of 1863.[44] That bill had already passed the Senate.[45]

Efforts to extend the benefits of the Missouri bill to Maryland, Delaware, and West Virginia failed, though Senator Henry Wilson said some of the first and best men in Maryland wished the state to be included. Senator Anthony Kennedy, John Pendleton Kennedy's immovable brother, retorted, "Not among the slaveholders, I presume."[46] But the Massachusetts senator refused to give ground. He assured his colleague that a number of Maryland's largest slaveholders were for the aid. Anthony Kennedy later commented, "my advice to my people is to spit upon your insult of $10,000,000."[47]

The same day Kennedy regaled his colleagues with a variety of demons. It was a sort of valedictory oration. Kennedy's senatorial career was within a few days of ending. A more dejected and morbid defeatist probably could not be found. Kennedy brooded over his love of the Union while opposing the coercion necessary to maintain it. Admittedly "a stricken-down man," he bemoaned the alleged

[41] *Baltimore American*, October 9, 1863.

[42] *Congressional Globe*, 37th Cong., 3rd Sess., Vol. 33, Part 2, p. 1294.

[43] John Pendleton Kennedy, for instance, talked at length with Leary as the two men traveled to Washington one January morning in 1863. Kennedy told Leary Maryland should accept the federal offer of help for emancipation as soon as possible. J. P. Kennedy's Journal, January 9–12, 1863, John Pendleton Kennedy Collection.

[44] See *Congressional Globe*, 37th Cong., 3rd Sess., Vol. 33, Part 1, p. 168 and Part 2, p. 1545 for Francis Thomas' votes on December 22, 1862, and March 3, 1863, respectively. The Missouri bill did not gain final passage.

[45] *Ibid.*, Part 1, p. 903. Senators Kennedy and Hicks opposed it, but the bill passed on February 12 by a 23–18 vote.

[46] *Ibid.*, p. 588.   [47] *Ibid.*, Part 2, p. 1374.

slights of his government and said that the introduction of the question of emancipation into Maryland meant "revolution."[48] No wonder one newspaper sarcastically referred to it as "Tony Kennedy's Last Boo-Hoo."[49]

His exit enabled Maryland to move one step further from its position of rigidly rejecting reality. Montgomery Blair must have been gratified, for he was trying to steer a course for emancipation in the state. In so doing he sought to avoid the political right and left.

Early in March, 1863, Blair gave his views in a letter to Richard Chambers of Caroline County. Unlike his published remarks in April of 1862, Blair's authorship was acknowledged in the newspapers. He told Chambers that it was useless to debate the merits of avoiding the emancipation issue because "The question is upon us and all that we can do is to say on which side we will range ourselves." Too many Unionists were terrified by the cry of abolitionists and suffered the delusion they could join in the cry without aiding the rebels. Blair slapped at this timidity and described the war as teaching that cowering before traitors was "inconsistent with patriotism and self respect."[50]

Chambers also wrote Secretary of the Treasury Chase asking him, in the event that emancipation was an issue, if a candidate should be run against Crisfield? How much aid would Chase give such a nominee? Defeat being probable, could the candidate "be patronized by the administration?"[51]

Men like Chambers, and there were many of them, were ready to move wherever political expediency led them. Money and patronage determined their support. Though the election was still seven or eight months away, it was not too soon to test the political currents. An early move with the right tide could gain a profitable position.

Ex-Mayor Thomas Swann, conservative weather vane par excellence, was just as assiduous in checking conditions. He protected his political future by moving into a fence-straddling position. Out of one side of his mouth he announced his favor of Lincoln's proposal for border state emancipation. He blamed slavery for smothering

---

[48] *Ibid.*

[49] *Cecil Whig*, March 7, 1863.

[50] Quotations in this paragraph are from Montgomery Blair to Richard Chambers, March 27, 1863, Blair Family Papers, Gist Blair Collection, Box 6.

[51] Richard Chambers to S. B. [sic] Chase, March 23, 1863, Salmon P. Chase Papers, Library of Congress.

the development of Maryland by keeping down land values, excluding population and capital, and cramping energies. Out of the other side he reiterated the hackneyed phrases of the reactionaries and rebels. He warned, "A war of races is no improbable contingency."[52]

Even Governor Bradford edged away from his earlier iron-bound policy of hands off slavery. In a speech on January 22, 1863, Bradford said that loyal Marylanders would save the Union "at all hazards."[53] He seemed to be hinting that he would now even be willing to give up slavery.

Thus by the spring of 1863 that amorphous party, known as the Union Party, demonstrated a wide spectrum of opinion on the issue of slavery. Some leaders still stood immovable upon the platform of 1861—men like John W. Crisfield and George Vickers on the Eastern Shore and Charles Calvert in southern Maryland. Others began to lean toward emancipation—men like Francis Thomas of western Maryland, and Thomas Hicks of the Eastern Shore. Then there were the Thomas Swanns, who tried to move in both directions at the same time. This shifting of positions was essential to Montgomery Blair's hopes for molding a moderate emancipation program. It was, however, still questionable whether his allies would bend fast enough and far enough.

Moderation did not trouble Winter Davis. He cared not for the sensitivities of conservative obstructionists. With his followers concentrated in Baltimore City and assisted by allies in the counties, he was ready to ram his radical faction to victory in November.

The outcome of the election would determine whether the landed gentry, with all its trappings of a static, agricultural society, could continue its rule of Maryland. Or would a new force, recognizing and accepting the revolutionary social, political, and economic changes in the nation and the state, gain control? If so, who would dominate the movement, moderates or Winter Davis radicals? These questions confronted Maryland in the critical year of 1863.

---

[52] Swann's remarks in this paragraph are from a speech he gave before the Union League of Philadelphia in March of 1863, cited in *Cecil Whig*, March 14, 1863.

[53] *Baltimore American*, January 24, 1863; *Chestertown Transcript*, February 3, 1863.

CHAPTER VIII

THE DISRUPTION
OF THE UNION PARTY

DURING THE CIVIL War Maryland experienced great changes, but at least one thing appeared constant. That was the unerring capacity of the military commander of the Middle Department, whomever he might be, to incur the hostility of one or another group of Marylanders. In various ways these disputes permeated state politics and affected the emancipation movement. The septuagenarian Major General John A. Dix ran afoul of many Unionists in 1861–62, but Major General John E. Wool, his successor, aroused even wider and more intense hostility. Wool's ultimate downfall perhaps can best be traced to the "Monster War Meeting," held, on July 28, 1862, in Baltimore. That rally drew a crowd of some 20,000, reputedly the largest public demonstration that had ever been held in Baltimore.[1] Out of the meeting came resolutions calling for army volunteers and the deportation of all men refusing to take a loyalty oath.

This reflected upon Wool, for he was accused of associating too closely with John W. Garrett, president of the railroad, and Colonel Moore N. Falls, president of the Bay Line Steamboat Co. The general rallied to their support, stoutly defending both men against denigration as secessionists. Wool said of John W. Garrett that he had not met a man "whose views on the great questions of the day are sounder."[2]

[1] *Baltimore American*, July 29, 1862. Most Marylanders lived within the jurisdiction of the Middle Department, whose headquarters were in Baltimore.

[2] John E. Wool expressed this view in identical letters on November 20, 1862, to *New York Express* and *Philadelphia Inquirer*. See *Baltimore American*, November 24, 1862, or *Baltimore County Advocate*, November 29, 1862.

This failed to mollify Wool's enemies. A committee, formed as a result of the July 28 rally, pressed charges of incompetence against the military administration of Maryland.[3] A petition was drawn up that charged Wool with "imbecility."[4] Mighty must have been the general's wrath when he heard of it. A Major Jones of his staff swooped down upon an anti-Wool conference, seized papers, and arrested four men, including one of the governor's aides. Pleas for their release sparked Wool's heated rejection.

What a furor this caused! An outraged governor demanded the prisoners' freedom and the return of the seized papers.[5] Congressman Leary asked the President to relieve Wool of his command, calling his conduct in this affair insulting and a "wicked exercise of military power."[6] Two Baltimoreans, Peter G. Sauerwein and Dr. James Armitage, went to see Lincoln, who hastily commented, "I know what you have come for, gentlemen, it is in reference to the arrests in Baltimore. I have settled that matter satisfactorily, and sent my decision to the War Department. I trust you will excuse me, as I am very busy."[7]

On November 15 the *Cecil Whig* spread upon its pages the glad tidings that "the imbecile old military fossil" was to be replaced. His successor, 53-year-old Major General Robert C. Schenck, had already achieved distinction as an Ohio politician, soldier, and diplomat. Fresh from beating Copperhead Clement L. Vallandigham out of a seat in the House of Representatives, Schenck had until December 1863 before he could assume office, for that was the date the next Congress would meet.

With his right hand aching[8] from a battle wound, Schenck arrived in Baltimore shortly before Christmas, 1862. A banquet was

---

[3] Baltimore committee of Thos. H. Gardner, Thos. R. Rich, Amos McConas, James H. Stimpson, and Alfred D. Evans to Lincoln. Someone has mistakenly dated it "Aug. 8 (?), 1863." Lincoln Collection, Vol. 119. On August 13 and 25 and September 20, 1862 the committee also met with the President.

[4] *Baltimore County Advocate*, November 1, 1862.

[5] Augustus W. Bradford to Lincoln, October 29, 1862, Executive Papers.

[6] C. L. L. Leary to Lincoln, October 29, 1862, Lincoln Collection, Vol. 91.

[7] *Baltimore Daily Gazette*, November 3, 1862. Governor Bradford, Henry W. Hoffman, William H. Purnell, and Judge Hugh L. Bond were among those who followed Sauerwein and Armitage to Washington for interviews with Lincoln and various Cabinet officers. The prisoners were released.

[8] John P. Kennedy Journal, December 20, 1862.

held in his honor, at which time Governor Bradford publicly welcomed him. Both men were former Whigs, but the time would come when they would not think well of each other's acts. Schenck clung to the more radical elements and generated an even greater storm than that which descended upon Wool.

Schenck inaugurated his regime with a resolute, uncompromising position. Proclaiming through his first general order that in this war, "there can be . . . no middle-ground on which any honest men or true patriot can stand,"[9] he warned against disloyal acts. No shelter would he allow under the cloak of religion or other subterfuge. Schenck believed it the army's duty to crush the Copperheads behind the lines.

Sharing his sympathies was a civilian organization of obscure origins. Like the Now-Nothings, it cherished certain secrets. Its beginnings have been variously credited to Ohio and Illinois in 1862 and to Washington, D.C. Similar organizations, however, sprouted in the border states early in the war.[10] Maryland was the home of a Union League by the spring of 1861.[11]

The League endeavored to open a way for Maryland Unionists to become acquainted and act together for the preservation of the nation.[12] By December, 1861, its membership reportedly numbered thousands.[13] The organization mushroomed. Before the spring of 1863 Baltimore City alone boasted nearly 10,000 members.[14] To oversee the system, representatives from the various subordinate leagues created the Grand League of Maryland.

Only ten men were needed to form each chapter. Its ritual pre-

[9] *Baltimore County Advocate*, December 27, 1862. Schenck assumed command on December 22, 1862.

[10] Guy James Gibson is his unpublished dissertation, "Lincoln's League: The Union League Movement during the Civil War," University of Illinois, 1957, p. 2, said, "The variety of origins attributed to the Union League suggests that it was a general movement including a group of organizations using one name rather than one society with a single origin."

[11] *Civilian and Telegraph*, April 23, 1862, called June "the second anniversary of the organization of Union Leagues in Maryland, and, we believe, in some other states." The preamble of resolutions passed at an April 20, 1863, meeting (see *Baltimore American*, April 21, 1863) said that the Union Leagues of Baltimore were organized in the spring of 1861.

[12] Jno. B. Seidenstricker to Augustus W. Bradford [1862], Adjutant General's Papers, Hall of Records, Annapolis, Maryland.

[13] Thomas R. Rich to Governor Bradford, December 28, 1861, Executive Papers.

[14] *Cambridge Herald*, March 18, 1863.

scribed the initiation and catechizing of prospective members. They swore to keep secret all "passwords—grips and rallying cries" and pledged to do everything in their power to prevent the dissolution of the Union "should it even require of me the sacrifice of life and fortune."[15]

During 1862 the Union Leagues in Maryland concentrated on military and patriotic work. For instance, the Baltimore City members joined with the Union City Convention in calling the massive meeting in Monument Square to help raise troops to meet the federal quota.[16] In the late winter and early spring of 1863 there seemed to be a heightened effort to organize branch leagues in the counties. The *Cecil Whig* asked an extension into the rural districts to save the credulous from entrapment by rebel lies.[17] About the same time a league was formed in Frederick.

In 1863 the Union Leagues extended their spheres of operations to the political arena. A number of elements seemed to thrust them into it. Preservation of the nation involved the fierce debate over slavery, a debate which found no sympathy in the conservative leadership of the Union Party. This created a need for some organized expression of aims among those who wished to move with, rather than against, the revolutionary times. This need appeared particularly critical now that Maryland was approaching such an important election. The League could not stay idle under these circumstances. It was too vital, too strong, and too deeply concerned with the progress of the war. Then there were politicians within the organization who tried to capitalize upon the League to further their ambitions.

On Monday, April 20, 1863, the Union League of Maryland tested political sentiment. The occasion was the second anniversary of the April 19th riots. It was an unpleasant, wet day, but Baltimore bedecked itself with an unprecedented display of American flags and bunting. That night the Union League held a public meeting in the packed hall of the Maryland Institute. At least 5,000 persons sat in the galleries or stood on the main floor. Many were unable to gain admission. Governor Bradford, Archibald Stirling, Jr., Thomas

[15] Union League of America. Maryland Grand League, *Opening, Initiatory, and Closing Ceremonies for Union Leagues* (Baltimore, 1862).

[16] *Baltimore Republican*, July 29, 1862.

[17] *Cecil Whig*, March 21, 1863. Just three days before, an Eastern Shore weekly, *Cambridge Herald*, published an address intent upon gathering the loyal into local leagues.

Swann, Senator Hicks, and Montgomery Blair joined the throng. A military band played and, as usual, the distinguished leaders deluged the multitudes with verbal cloudbursts. Schenck told the audience that if he were a southern sympathizer he would join Jeff Davis "and not sneak about and crawl upon the ground, leaving a slimy path wherever I go, and biting the heels of patriotic men." The crowd loved it and applauded uproariously.

None of this was particularly startling or new. In fact, it fell upon a mere secretary of the meeting to pronounce the most significant words of the occasion. His was the job of reading the resolutions prepared for the rally. Having called slavery "an instrument in the hands of traitors to build an oligarchy . . . on the ruins of republican liberty," he continued:

> *Resolved*, That the safety and interest of . . . Maryland, and especially of her white laboring people, require that Slavery should cease to be recognized by the law of Maryland, and that the aid of the United States, as recommended by the President, ought to be asked and accepted.

Then the secretary repeated it. A little more than a year ago these sentiments, publicly expressed, would have invited a thrashing for the speaker. Now the throng cheered. The resolutions also asked Congress to enact the Emancipation Proclamation into law and urged the President to use "all men, white or black, in the way they can most be useful . . . whether it be to handle a spade or shoulder a musket."[18]

Though Governor Bradford could not concur in all of the resolutions, the more radical wing of the Union Party must have been jubilant. Never before in the war had emancipation sentiments been advanced at a public meeting.

One month later Baltimore Unionists elected delegates to the annual City Union Convention. The year before, this body pioneered the hoisting of the emancipation flag. Now it lashed at traitors and appealed to white laborers. In so doing the delegates copied verbatim the six Union League resolutions of April 20[19] and added a

[18] The quotations and the story of the April 20th meeting are based on reports in the *Baltimore American*, April 21, 1863.

[19] Only one slight change was made in the Union League resolutions. The word "Constitution" was substituted for "law" in "slavery should cease to be recognized by the law of Maryland. . . ." See *Baltimore American*, April 21, 1863, and May 26, 1863, for comparisons of the two sets of resolutions.

specific recommendation calling for a constitutional convention as soon as possible. All of the wards, except the Irish eighth, backed the resolutions.

The parrot-like behavior of the City Union Convention symbolized its subordinate role in the League's newly inaugurated drive toward emancipation. The latter now exerted the real thrust behind this revolutionary movement and even showed a readiness to provide still broader leadership. The Maryland Leagues demonstrated this willingness by urging that a national convention be held in Washington on June 17. The proposal came to naught when a May 20th meeting in Cleveland brought about the formation of a National Union League.[20]

Their appetite no doubt whetted by the April 20 mass meeting, Union League politicians chartered a daring course—capture of the Union Party. Answering the plea of an Allegany County mass meeting,[21] they called a statewide convention for June 16 to nominate candidates for public office and to work for a constitutional convention. Further justification did not much trouble them. They simply claimed possession of the Union Party as its only existing organization and fired a partisan shot at the already rallying conservatives.

The rebuked stood aghast. Members of the Union State Central Committee reportedly were so astonished that they could hardly believe the action was serious. Certainly the question of legitimacy never before entered their minds. In rebuttal they accused the Union Leagues of trying to hinder the regular call for a convention by summoning one of their own.[22]

[20] John Dukehart, president of the Grand League of Maryland, cancelled the proposal on June 1, 1863. *Baltimore American*, June 2, 1863. The Maryland delegates to the first national convention of the Union League numbered nine, all of whom came from Baltimore. They included Montgomery Blair's ally. United States Marshal Washington Bonifant, and Winter Davis' colleague, Judge Hugh L. Bond. See *Proceedings of the National Convention, Union League of America . . . May 20 and 21, 1863. . . .* (Washington, D. C., 1863), p. 5. The National Convention gave leadership of its united front to the Washington league, which had close connections with Radical Republicans but also friendly associations with Lincoln. See Gibson, "Lincoln's League," p. 120.

[21] The Allegany County meeting of Unconditional Unionists was called by the Union League in Cumberland for April 23. Its participants urged not only gradual emancipation but also a state-wide convention of the loyal, irrespective of "old extinct party associations." See *Civilian and Telegraph*, April 30, 1863. The convention proposal was endorsed by the *Cecil Whig* and the *Cambridge Intelligencer.*

[22] "Carroll County" to editors, *Baltimore American*, August 1, 1863.

Conservative Unionists met in Baltimore on May 13 and 14[23] to consider the plight of the divided Party. They gathered at Barnum's Hotel, an establishment deeply suspect in the eyes of many patriots. The participants came from Baltimore and fourteen counties and included Congressmen Crisfield and Calvert. Samuel Snowden Maffit, state comptroller and bête noire of the emancipationists, and Frederick Fickey, Jr., were also there. Fickey, secretary of the Union State Central Committee, was then in bad repute with the officials of the Party in Baltimore because he had run against Mayor Chapman in 1862. Governor Bradford and Senator Hicks declined invitations to attend.

The man picked to preside over the conference was legislator Allen Bowie Davis, who the year before had written Montgomery Blair of his mortification over the government's action upon slavery. Now he placed a proposal before Brantz Mayer, president of the Union State Central Committee, to urge the calling of a state convention. Mayer responded by first convening his city members and then on May 28, his full committee. The latter directed Maryland Unionists to elect delegates to a June 23rd state convention.[24] The call came one day after a similar one by the Union League.

The rival summons forced each Maryland county to resolve the dilemma in its own way. With political ingenuity, Talbot selected a delegation committed to harmonizing the Union League meeting of June 16 with its competitor. If unsuccessful, the Talbot men were to work for the dissolution of both conventions and the calling of a third. Failure to gain either objective meant choosing another alternative, participation in the Union State Convention.[25]

Most counties did not evolve such a complicated plan. Some sent delegates only to the conservative convention of June 23. Others engaged in a factional rivalry that resulted in the dominant group authorizing delegates to one convention and the dissidents sending representatives to the rival gathering. Baltimore County Unionists, however, held together so well that they dispatched the same con-

[23] Frederick Fickey, Jr. to Brantz Mayer, May 13, 1863, with note appended by Mayer, Brantz Mayer Collection, Maryland Historical Society.

[24] Information on the May meetings of the regular Union Party organization can be found in the Brantz Mayer Papers and various Maryland newspapers.

[25] See Harrison Journal, II, June 9, 1863; *Easton Gazette*, June 13, 1863; and *Cambridge Herald*, June 17, 1863, for a report on the Talbot County meeting on June 9.

tingent to both conventions. In the city of Baltimore two separate but equally legitimate meetings picked delegates. Four men were given double duty, being picked for both eleven-member delegations.

Maryland politicians jockeyed for position as the fabric of the Union Party began to split. The schism bothered many loyal Marylanders. The *Cambridge Herald* deplored the uselessness of the struggle.[26] The *Baltimore American* pleaded for harmony. It upheld the legitimacy of the June 23rd affair but admitted that the June 16th meeting had been summoned by men just as zealous.[27]

Montgomery Blair worried too. He urged "one ticket and a common platform."[28] Upon its achievement, he believed, rested the question of whether the Union Party would fall into the hands of the Democrats or support the Administration. Blair feared that the frequenters of political conventions would obstruct his goal. They underrated, he felt, the people's intelligence and reiterated the same phrases their Missouri counterparts parroted last year, i.e., "for the sake of the Union and for the good of the State Slavery should be abolished, but the people are not ready for the question and if it is pressed wd endanger the election[.]"[29] Blair warned that this very attitude caused many an over-cautious Missourian to be defeated.

Blair would have been happy to know that practical steps were being taken to heal the Maryland breach. William L. S. Seabrook, a newspaperman completing his first term as Commissioner of the Land Office, had more reason than most to be appalled at the prospect of a divided party because his office was one of the two state-wide posts on the November ballot. He joined like-minded Unionists in wresting from the League leaders an agreement to discourage nominations and seek instead a conference of representatives from both conventions.

He confronted Henry Winter Davis aboard the steamer plying from Annapolis to Baltimore. The young commissioner frankly told Davis he considered the League action "irregular" and injurious.

[26] *Cambridge Herald,* June 10, 1863.

[27] *Baltimore* American, June 15, 1863.

[28] Undated, unsigned draft or copy of a letter in the handwriting of Montgomery Blair [early June, 1863], Blair Family Papers, Gist Blair Collection, Box 7.

[29] *Ibid.* Blair added, "We may be beaten in battle and yet save the Union if we succeed in putting down slavery in the border states. . . ." The ablest southerners conceded, said Blair, that the Confederacy could not exist without the border States. See also Blair's views as expressed in a letter to Henry W. Hoffman, June 15, 1863, Henry W. Hoffman Papers, Sarasota, Fla.

Davis retorted that the loyalty of those who did not fully embrace Maryland emancipation was questionable, but he agreed not to oppose Seabrook's efforts to reach an accord. If Seabrook's suggestion that Davis originated the League project was correct, this was a notable concession.[30]

Upon convening in Temperance Temple on North Gay Street, the Union League Convention installed as president a former Whig and Know-Nothing of Massachusetts birth, Henry Stockbridge,[31] who often worked with Winter Davis. Extremism vied with a more moderate approach as the meeting got under way. A Davis man, Archibald Stirling, Jr., tried to bind the delegates in advance to whatever decision the convention might make. The delegates from Talbot County, faithful to their conciliatory platform, appealed for no anticipation of the question, but Stirling got his wish. Nonetheless, the forces of amity upheld the really decisive point by seeing to it that no nominations were made. Besides, a five-man committee, headed by Henry W. Hoffman, was appointed to confer with the June 23rd delegates and propose adjourning the two conventions in favor of holding a joint third.

Moderates happily scanned the results of the meeting and breathed a sigh of relief. The growing force of radical Unionists had been cajoled into accepting harmony. With the aggressive faction bridled, it seemed the lesser task to gain concessions from the conservatives. The moderates looked hopefully to June 23.

During the week separating the two meetings, Baltimore anxiously awaited a possible Confederate attack. General Lee was on the move again, and there was no telling whether Baltimore or even Philadelphia might feel the fury of his armed might. Major General Schenck appealed to the Union Leagues, and 6,000 responded. Henry Winter Davis assumed charge of enrolling volunteer companies. Large numbers of Negroes and some suspected rebel sympathizers were conscripted for work upon the entrenchments. Before Sunday was over, the city had been encircled with a defense rim ready for instant occupancy. Barricades of carts, paving stones, and earth blockaded many a street corner.[32]

---

[30] William L. W. Seabrook related the story of his meeting with Davis in *Maryland's Great Part in Saving the Union* (n. p., 1913), p. 8.

[31] *Baltimore American*, June 17, 1863.

[32] *National Intelligencer* (Washington, D. C.), June 23, 1863, and John T. Scharf, *History of Maryland* (Baltimore, 1879), III, 537–39.

Two days later a menaced city faced not the guns of rebel troops but rather a political fight. Men from fifteen counties and Baltimore city assembled for the Union State Convention, surpassing the number at the League gathering. Every jurisdiction represented at the June 16th affair sent delegates, except the special case of Talbot County. No one came to either convention from the black belt of rebel sympathizers in Charles, Calvert, and St. Mary's Counties.[33]

Cecil, on the other hand, had two delegations seeking admittance to the Union State Convention. The latter rejected the selections of an ultraconservative rump group, seating instead a more regularly chosen delegation that included John Angel James Creswell.[34] Born into a family of means and social position in 1828, Creswell achieved success as a lawyer and prominence as a political leader. First a Whig, he switched to the Democrats before winning a seat in the House of Delegates as a Unionist in 1861. Later Creswell became a Republican, United States senator, and member of President Grant's cabinet.[35]

At the Union State Convention Creswell joined the moderates in clashing with the very conservative. After a debate and some quibbling over rival motions by Creswell and Howard County's Thomas Donaldson, the League's offer was referred to a committee to which both of these men were named. When it became apparent that a majority of the appointees favored harmony, an attempt was made to pack the committee. Creswell objected, but the motion was carried by a vote of 36–26. The tally probably revealed fairly accurately the relative strength of the hard shell conservatives and the moderates present.

The addition of four new members fell one short of doubling the size of the committee. Chaired by Donaldson, the group decided to write a "strong, clear" platform acceptable to all loyal Marylanders. Actually it pursued a somewhat different course. In the time-hon-

[33] Compare lists of delegates in *Baltimore American*, June 17, 1863, and June 24, 1863.

[34] *Baltimore American*, June 18, 1963; *Cecil Whig*, June 13, 20, and 27, 1863. The rump group apparently came into being when a majority in the Cecil County Central Committee bolted and called its own county convention. The regulars sent two delegations to Baltimore, one to each state convention.

[35] For information on John A. J. Creswell, who was born in 1828, see *Dictionary of American Biography*, IV, 541–42 and Elizabeth M. Grimes, "John Angel James Creswell, Postmaster General," M. A. thesis, Columbia University, New York.

ored tradition of being all things to all people, the platform featured two mutually contradictory planks. The fourth resolution said, "this Convention ignores all issues, local or national, but those of war, until treason shall succumb."[36] In other words, the question of emancipation should be set aside and silenced. If this seemed unrealistic to more enlightened Unionists, then moderates could point to the fifth resolution. It assigned to the next session of the legislature the obligation of promptly "submitting to the people the question of a call for a Constitutional Convention, and for the assembling of the said Convention." There was no mention of slavery, it was true, but this proposal offered the emancipationists the opportunity they needed to destroy the institution.

When the representatives from the Union State and Union League Conventions got together, Donaldson took the initiative by reading his committee's resolutions. These received the general approval of the League men, though some of them announced they had publicly gone further. But this was not the point of the conference, warned Henry H. Goldsborough. Both conventions must give way to a new one if harmony were to be achieved.

Rebuffing this conciliatory gesture, Donaldson explained that dissension would be intensified if the current meeting were dissolved, for rival factions would fight to control delegates to new county and state conventions. Nor was there any way to know when free elections could be conducted throughout the state, with rebel armies operating in Maryland. Since the League committeemen professed such a great desire for harmony let them "acquiesce in the action of the authoritative organ of their party"and not seek an addition to the platform that would be offensive to many Unionists.

Very clever reasoning and a strong case for the Donaldson committee, but revolutions did not wait for the brilliance of some legal mind. An impasse had been reached. Hopes for a rapprochement shattered against a wall of intransigence.

When the Union State Convention gathered for an evening session, Donaldson reported for his committee. He depicted his group as motivated solely by a desire for accord, but of course this accord could be gained only by the League's surrender. His resolutions were approved despite Creswell's opposition. Nominations being in or-

[36] *Baltimore American* of June 24 and 29, 1863, printed a factual account of the Union League and Union State meetings on June 23, 1863.

der, the convention picked incumbent William L. W. Seabrook as the party's choice for commissioner of the land office. Over slight opposition, Cecil County's Samuel S. Maffit gained the delegate's support for another term as state comptroller. Though afflicted by ill health and soon to die of consumption, Maffit had earned the respect of friend and foe as a highly capable comptroller. A determined Unionist, he nonetheless revolted against linking its cause to that of emancipation.

Back at the Union League Convention, which had reconvened on June 23, Henry W. Hoffman reported the conference impasse and moved that candidates be selected. One delegate deplored any action that might continue the breach, but it was too late. The hour for conciliation had passed. Unable to stomach the pro-slavery stand of Maffit, the delegates chose Henry H. Goldsborough for state comptroller. A member of a well-known Eastern Shore family, he had presided over the Maryland Senate in its last session. The Convention gave the nod to Seabrook to run again for commissioner of the land office. This virtually assured his re-election.

Somewhat obscured by the excitement was the instruction given the president of the convention, Henry Stockbridge, to appoint a state central committee for Baltimore City and each of the counties. That meant the Union League convention planned a statewide political organization capable of battling the older regime on every level of government.

The Union Leaguers proclaimed unconditional support of the Lincoln Administration in suppressing the rebellion and a relentless determination to rid Maryland of slavery. That qualified them for the label "Unconditional Unionists," a term considerably changed in meaning during the past two years. In 1861 it signified simply a determination to preserve the Union under all, not just some, circumstances. The follower of such a platform did not necessarily support the Administration and might have been a devotee of slavery. Now in 1863 the more progressive Unionists expropriated the title to their own use.

Some people called the Goldsborough men radicals and the Maffit supporters pro-slavery, but this was an oversimplification. True, radicals did infest the Union League movement, but there were many moderately disposed people who believed in accepting reality and making the best of it. They could see no sense in carping at an

Administration bent on winning the war or in trying to ignore the doom befalling slavery. There were men sympathetic to this position in the Union State Convention, but their political association with the immovable conservatives kept them in check. It was difficult to see in June, 1863, how emancipation could be achieved any time in the near future if the adherents of the Union State Convention won in November.

Seabrook felt the conservatives weakened their position by arbitrarily refusing to accept any course leading to harmony.[37] They, however, could see no valid reason for risking their power and legitimacy in a third convention. On the other hand, the Unconditional Unionists could not survive if they allowed themselves to be swallowed by their rivals. They now had little choice but to battle the conservatives openly.

In Winter Davis the Unconditional Unionists found a leader. As such, he determined to regain his seat in the House of Representatives. Just two weeks after the Thirty-seventh Congress adjourned, he talked to Lincoln about the upcoming election and procured a statement. Lincoln said that in the new Congress there would be "some members openly opposing the war, some supporting it *unconditionally*, and some supporting it with 'buts' and 'ifs' and 'ands'." The differing views would cause division on the election of a Speaker of the House, an office exercising vast power. The President pleaded that no one be elected who would not caucus with Unconditional Union men to pick a speaker and abide by the result. Let "the friends of the government first save the government, and then administer it to their own liking."[38]

To avoid any misunderstanding, Lincoln put these thoughts in writing and sent them to Davis, with the caution that they were not to be published. A pleased Davis wrote back, "Your favor of the 18th [March] is all that could be desired."[39]

In the late spring Davis went before the voters of the Third Congressional District. No more important congressional primary occurred in Maryland in 1863. Davis' opponent was the redoubtable Thomas Swann, former Know-Nothing mayor of Baltimore and an

[37] Seabrook, *Maryland's Great Part in Saving the Union*, p. 9.
[38] A. Lincoln to H. W. Davis, March 18, 1863, Miscellaneous Collection, Maryland Historical Society; *Lincoln Works*, VI, 140–141.
[39] H. W. Davis to A. Lincoln, March 20, 1863, Lincoln Collection, Vol. 106; *Lincoln Works*, VI, 141.

ex-president of the Baltimore and Ohio Railroad. Although he wrote in 1861 of his declining interest in public life,[40] the fires had now rekindled. He was once again ready to take his place.

Swann's hesitant attitude toward emancipation did not keep him from pointing to a friendship of over thirty years with Secretary of the Treasury Salmon P. Chase.[41] Apparently Swann's friends in the Custom House and the Post Office pushed his candidacy as the Administration's choice, particularly the preference of Blair and Chase. This claim, however, was not enough to win the Davisites or other Unconditional men. They rebelled at the sight of so-called luke-warm Unionists rallying to Swann's cause.[42]

On June 4 the all important primaries took place in the Balti-more wards. The turnout was unusually heavy. A brisk rivalry enliv-ened the meetings, but there was little disorder. Swann managed to pick up twenty delegates, while Davis swept into his fold an over-whelming forty-five.[43] Swann's supporters were disgruntled. When the congressional nominating convention met the next day, only two of them voted. The great majority stayed away to emphasize their protest against the allegedly fraudulent choice of most del-egates. The convention responded by hissing and groaning at the reading of each protestant's name.[44]

Hostility turned to loud applause as R. Stockett Mathews, a Davisite, delivered a "spirited address" as a warm-up to the long acclamation that greeted Winter Davis' appearance. Davis spoke of Maryland politics entering a new era. He welcomed the opportunity to link his name with emancipation and predicted its achievement in the state within three years. This would break forever the political power of slavery in Maryland. Davis, who usually scorned equivoca-tion and halfway measures, assumed the role of a gracious victor. He spoke favorably of Swann's firm principles, praised his management of the city as mayor, and called him entitled to Unionist respect.[45]

[40] Thomas Swann to S. P. Chase, January 28, 1861, S. P. Chase Papers, Historical Society of Pennsylvania.

[41] Thomas Swann to S.P. Chase, November 8, 1860, S. P. Chase Papers, Historical Society of Pennsylvania.

[42] See W. G. Snethen to S. P. Chase, June 5, 1863, S. P. Chase Papers, Library of Congress and Frederick *Examiner*, June 10, 1863.

[43] *Baltimore American*, June 5, 1863.

[44] *Baltimore American*, June 6, 1863.

[45] *Ibid.*, and Baltimore *Sun*, June 6, 1863. At this time Winter Davis still favored $10,000,000 federal compensation for Maryland emancipation.

Swann evidenced no such ingratiating mood. He had apparently gone into the campaign over-confident, for he figured that nearly two-thirds of the recently elected City Union Convention were his friends. Now he reeled beneath the bitter shock of defeat and raged against Davis' nomination and the way it was achieved. He hoped the Union Party could *"hold its own"* despite this *"crushing blow."* Unwilling to support the victor, Swann said that he might still let his name be used as a candidate. All of this Swann expressed in a letter to his friend Salmon P. Chase just a few days after the election, while the sting of his loss still bit deeply.[46]

Chase was in an embarrassing situation. He cherished his friendship with Swann but found Davis a highly prized ally with views more akin to his. To escape the dilemma, Chase thought he had the solution—get Swann elected to the United States Senate when Hicks' appointment ended early in 1864. This, however, failed to account for that idiosyncrasy of Maryland law which required one senator to be from the Eastern Shore.

As the campaign progressed, Swann continued to enjoy a key position. If only he could be prevailed upon to join the Unconditional Unionists, it would assure their victory; at least so thought radical Judge Hugh Lennox Bond in a letter to Secretary Chase.[47] Any hopes that Chase's influence might sway the recalcitrant went unfulfilled. In fact, Chase had to warn his old friend that he could not support him if he decided to run against Davis.[48]

As late as the morning of October 22 Swann was still arousing suspicions,[49] but he did not enter the listings. This doubtlessly pleased Lincoln, for despite Blair's desire to defeat Davis with Swann, the President thought it mean to countenance such action. After all, Davis was the official nominee of the local Union convention and had been recognized as an Administration candidate.[50]

The only other Congressional District that included wards in Bal-

---

[46] Thomas Swann to S. P. Chase, June 8, 1863, S. P. Chase Papers, Historical Society of Pennsylvania.

[47] Hugh L. Bond to S. P. Chase, August 18, 1863, S. P. Chase Papers, Historical Society of Pennsylvania.

[48] Chase conveyed this message to Swann on September 3, 1863, through intermediaries. David Donald, *Chase Diaries* (New York, 1954), p. 184.

[49] See W. P. Smith to [S. P. Chase], October 23, 1863, S. P. Chase Papers, Historical Society of Pennsylvania.

[50] Tyler Dennett (ed.), *Lincoln and the Civil War in the Diaries and Letters of John Hay* (New York, 1939), October 22, 1863, p. 105.

timore City was the Second. It stretched into much of Baltimore County and embraced all of Harford. Several contestants gained attention. Among them were two incumbents, Congressmen Cornelius L. L. Leary and Edwin H. Webster, who were forced to face each other because the 1860 census cost the state one seat in the House. A third candidate entering the race with sizable support was Joseph J. Stewart of Towson, a deputy court clerk and unequivocal emancipationist. Meeting on July 2, the second District Convention gave its blessing to Webster.[51]

His views on Union and slavery followed closely those of Crisfield. On February 28 Webster had accused the Sumners, Lovejoys, Greeleys, and Phillipses of accomplishing more for disunion than if they had sat in Jefferson Davis' cabinet or served in the rebel army.[52] Webster even criticized the conscription of Negro troops. He gave little indication of understanding or sympathy for the Unconditional Unionism of 1863. If, however, he did not assume a more progressive position, there were those who would likely seek another candidate.

But Colonel Webster did alter his position, and what an alteration it proved to be! Writing from the headquarters of 7th Maryland Volunteers on September 25, he addressed the voters of his district, assuring them he would not vote for any man to be Speaker of the House of Representatives who was "hostile to the administration."[53] He now favored emancipation in Maryland and urged the calling of a state constitutional convention. Thus purged, Webster faced his electorate on a platform bearing little resemblance to his actions in the Thirty-seventh Congress.

The shift was not quite as difficult for Francis Thomas, who in the short, third session of that Congress had already begun to edge away from the proponents of slavery. Nevertheless, many of his constituents, who lived in the western counties of Allegany, Washington, Frederick, and Carroll, were suspicious of him. The Allegany County delegation to the Fourth Congressional District Convention was instructed to support Thomas only if he satisfied the Unconditional Union men with an adequate pledge of support to the government.[54]

[51] Information on the proceedings of the Convention can be found in the *Baltimore American*, July 3, 1863, and *Baltimore Daily Gazette*, July 5, 1863.

[52] *Congressional Globe*, 37th Cong., 3rd Sess., Vol. 33, Part 2, p. 1425.

[53] Edwin H. Webster to the Second Congressional District Union Voters, September 25, 1863, Ægis, October 2, 1863.

[54] *Civilian and* Telegraph, July 30, 1863.

A similar qualification was tacked on the actual nomination, which was made in Hagerstown.[55] The victorious Thomas obligingly fulfilled the demand.

Neither Winter Davis, Edwin H. Webster, nor Francis Thomas faced any real opposition in the fall general election. Their major obstacle had been surmounted through victory at the primary and commitments to the 1863 version of Unconditional Unionism. Those three districts contained the bulk of such sentiment within the state. In the remaining two districts lay the stronghold of the proponents of slavery and conservatism, whether it be of the Unionist or southern sympathizing brand. Both districts engaged in congressional fights not to be settled until the general election in November.

Over on the Eastern Shore lay the First District, John W. Crisfield's bailiwick. With ease he swept to victory at the Congressional Convention held in Cambridge on August 11. In that meeting Unionist clashed with Unionist but left Crisfield untrammeled. At least one delegate must have been happy. He regarded any platform binding Crisfield as an embarrassment, "for *what would suit in Cecil might not suit in Somerset.*"[56] Crisfield's letter of acceptance protested any change in the original purpose of the war and warned that new issues distracted and divided the loyal.[57] His views probably reflected those of most Eastern Shoremen. So strong was he politically that even George M. Russum, United States assessor for the First District and a prominent emancipationist, supported him as the party's official choice.[58]

But the Davis faction would not accept the decision. Judge Bond gathered together Crisfield's and Russum's published letters and a list of some of the bills Crisfield had opposed in the last Congress. These he dispatched to Chase, telling him that a candidate would be

---

[55] *Baltimore American*, September 8, 1863.

[56] Cambridge *Intelligencer* as quoted in *Chestertown Transcript*, September 5, 1863. For account of First District Convention see also *Cecil Whig*, August 15 and 29, 1863; *Cecil Democrat*, August 22, 1863; and *Baltimore American*, August 17, 1863.

[57] Crisfield softened his stand by adding that he would cheerfully acquiesce in the judgment of a state constitutional convention "if considerately formed, and fairly expressed. . . ." The qualifications provided a convenient loophole. Letter was dated Princess Anne, Maryland, August 17, 1863, and printed in such papers as *Baltimore American*, August 26, 1863, and *Chestertown Transcript*, September 5, 1863.

[58] Letter of George M. Russum dated August 24, 1863, and published in the *Cecil Whig*, August 29, 1863.

run against the congressman.[59] Winter Davis joined the attack. He bluntly urged firing Russum and replacing him by "My friend Mr. {Levin E.} Straughn," who edited the *Intelligencer* in Cambridge.[60] This involved concocting a charge of official neglect against Russum. To Davis' way of thinking such action would greatly help to defeat Crisfield.[61] The plot failed. Russum held his post but did penance for his letter on behalf of Crisfield.[62]

The man Winter Davis had in mind as Crisfield's opponent was 34-year-old William J. Jones of Elkton, State's Attorney for Cecil County. He declined. A group of Unconditional Unionists from Somerset, Worcester, Dorchester, and Cecil counties thereupon turned to John A. J. Creswell, who accepted.[63] That meant an Unconditional Union candidate in the First, Second, Third, and Fourth Congressional districts.

But what of the Fifth, which covered the seven counties of southern Maryland and reached into six Baltimore County election districts? The Democrats bestirred themselves in this one congressional race. They invited to a District Convention all who opposed Administration policy and wished to organize for state rights.[64] Five of the eight counties responded, but no candidate was formally nominated because three counties were not represented. Instead, the convention simply offered the voters the choice of those present, Benjamin Gwinn Harris, of St. Mary's County.[65]

Born in 1806, Harris graduated from Yale and Harvard Law School. He served a term in the House of Delegates in the 1830s and in 1861 ran unsuccessfully against Calvert for Congress. Beaten, he quickly returned to the hustings for a successful quest of a seat in the state legislature. Now he was ready once again to battle Calvert. The latter had declared his candidacy in July of 1863, when he

[59] Hugh L. Bond to S. P. Chase, September 1, 1863, S. P. Chase Papers, Historical Society of Pennsylvania.

[60] H. Winter Davis to Edward McPherson, September 18, 1863, Edward B. McPherson Papers, Box 7, Library of Congress.

[61] *Ibid.*

[62] George M. Russum to John A. J. Creswell, February 4, 1864, Creswell Papers, V.

[63] *Cecil Whig*, October 10, 1863, and *Baltimore American*, October 5 and 7, 1863.

[64] *Baltimore County Advocate*, August 29, 1863, and *Maryland Republican* (Annapolis, Maryland), September 12, 1863.

[65] *Baltimore County Advocate*, October 3, 1863, and *Maryland Republican* (Annapolis, Maryland), September 26, 1863.

denounced the agitation of slavery by Congress and the Executive as grossly violating border state rights.[66] So displeased was he that at one point, said Montgomery Blair, Calvert nearly joined the opposition. Later elections showed this a mistake as the political pendulum swung back. Thereupon Calvert's friends tried to get together a convention to endorse him, thus dropping the idea of running him as an independent. Their plans went askew as the Fifth District Union Congressional Convention fell into hostile hands. Unable to nominate Calvert, they bolted.[67]

The convention met at Bladensburg, near Washington, on September 8. Its integrity lay shrouded in doubt, for of the eight delegates from Anne Arundel, Baltimore, and St. Mary's counties, not one had reportedly been picked at a public meeting.[68] Furthermore, six of these eight held government jobs through the good graces of the district's provost marshal, who happened to be a leading contender for the nomination. One of the six had come to Bladensburg on other business and went to the convention only after being inveigled into a fraudulent participation. As the only representative present from Anne Arundel County, he won the right to cast its four votes.

Rather than accept this trickery, the Prince George's delegation withdrew from the deliberations.[69] The delegates from Montgomery and Howard counties stayed and gave their six votes to Thomas Donaldson,[70] but that still left an adequate majority to carry the nomination for the provost marshal, John C. Holland. He readily donned the mantle of Unconditional Unionism and preached emancipation, though three and a half months ago he had served as secretary of a Baltimore County Convention that unanimously denounced "side issues."[71]

[66] Calvert's address to his constituents, dated July 9, 1863, *Baltimore County Advocate*, August 15, 1863.

[67] Montgomery Blair to Col. John L. Ashburne (?), October 17, 1863, Blair Family Papers, Gist Blair Collection, Box 6.

[68] Correspondence from "A Voter in the 5th Congressional District," *Baltimore County Advocate*, October 3, 1863; Charles B. Calvert "To the Voters of the 5th Congressional District of Maryland," October 5, 1863, *National Intelligencer*, October 9, 1863.

[69] J. I. D. [Dr. Joseph I. Duvall] to editors of *Baltimore American*, September 15, 1863, printed in its September 29,1863 issue. See also September 3 and 11, 1863 editions and *Annapolis Gazette* as cited in *National Intelligencer*, September 22, 1863.

[70] Thomas Donaldson quickly informed the public that this act had been taken without his permission. *Baltimore American*, September 10, 1863. H. Winter Davis to rear Admiral Samuel F. DuPont, September 19, 1863.

[71] *Baltimore American*, May 22, and September 11, 1863.

Holland went into the political campaign of 1863 with the support of both Montgomery Blair and Winter Davis. The latter claimed that his partisans had thrust Holland into the field and sarcastically poked fun at Blair for hopping on the Holland band wagon.[72] Blair, on the other hand, believed that Winter Davis was seeking Holland's defeat, possibly because of some disagreement over slaveholder compensation.[73] Perhaps only by such rationalization could these two back the same man for a public office in Maryland.

A former Democrat and Know-Nothing, Holland had served as a lieutenant colonel until fever forced him to resign.[74] He was named to the post of provost marshal as a result of the Conscription Bill that became law on March 3, 1863. This act replaced the state operated draft of 1862[75] by a presidentially appointed board of enrollment in each congressional district. The three-member board included a physician and a provost marshal, who presided and held the rank of captain.

While the purpose of the boards was to execute any draft the President might call,[76] the politicians saw in them an opportunity to enhance their own power. Here was a veritable bonanza for office seekers. Provost Marshal General James B. Fry sought Governor Bradford's advice on some appointments, but whether such counsel was often given or heeded cannot be readily ascertained.[77] Congressman Crisfield and Senator Hicks supposedly won Lincoln's approval for giving the First District post to Colonel George R. Howard of Cecil county, but it went instead to John Frazier, Jr., who allegedly sold out to the radicals to get it.[78]

---

[72] H. Winter Davis to Rear Admiral Samuel F. DuPont, September 19, 1863, S. F. DuPont Papers.

[73] Montgomery Blair to Col. John L. Ashburne (?), October 17, 1863, Blair Family Papers, Gist Blair Collection, Box 6.

[74] A biographical sketch of John C. Holland is given in *The Biographical Cyclopedia of Representative Men of Maryland and District of Columbia* (Baltimore, 1879), pp. 173–75. Montgomery Blair recommended Holland for provost marshal. See M. Blair to A. Lincoln, May 1, 1863, Lincoln Collection, Vol. 109.

[75] Under this system there was in each county a state-appointed commissioner of draft and enrollment and a deputy provost marshal.

[76] Every man between the ages of 20 and 45 was liable to service, but he could dodge the draft by paying $300 or by getting some one to substitute for him, a shoddy system that generated many abuses.

[77] See printed forms in Executive Papers.

[78] George Vickers to A. W. Bradford, September 14, 1863, and October 30, 1863,

Each provost marshal appointed deputies for the various counties in his district. The deputies in turn held sway over a number of subordinate enrollers. This enabled the provost marshal to control an organization extending into every election district.[79] The political effectiveness of such a setup was aptly demonstrated in southern Maryland by John C. Holland's grab of the Fifth District Congressional nomination.

The federal appointees to these new offices took charge just in time for the political campaign of 1863. If the relatively conservative state officials had been left in control of recruiting, as in 1862, a different fate would probably have awaited Congressman Crisfield in November of 1863. Ironically, he voted for the legislation that made this denouement possible. Thus did the new conscription law give the Unconditional Unionists a powerful tool in the struggle to overthrow the oligarchy. This weapon proved a mighty adjunct to the vital work of the Union Leagues.

A. W. Bradford Papers. Montgomery Blair apparently knew nothing of such a deal because he also supported Frazier. See M. Blair to A. Lincoln, May 1, 1863, Lincoln Collection, Vol. 109.

[79] In the city of Baltimore two enrolling officers were appointed for each precinct, which meant eight to a ward. See *Baltimore Clipper*, June 16, 1863.

CHAPTER IX

THE FLIGHT AND
ENLISTMENT OF SLAVES

SWEEPING DOWN THE Shenandoah Valley, the rebel army overwhelmed the federal detachment at Front Royal, Virginia, spilling
refugees and troops into nearby Hagerstown.[1] The flight to this
Maryland town included hundreds of Negroes, riding in government wagons driven by white men. The spectacle stirred feelings of
revulsion within conservative Unionists. "These are awful times to
live in," wrote one annoyed lady.[2]

She was disgusted with the federal government and fully aware of
the excitement caused by runaway slaves. No part of Maryland escaped losses, though, of course, the southern counties suffered most.
Many slaves sought refuge in army camps. What to do with the
fugitives created a problem that called for prompt decision. Some
commanders at first refused to allow runaways within their lines. On
the other hand, Major General Benjamin F. Butler would not give
up three slaves at Fortress Monroe, Virginia. As they had worked on
Confederate fortifications, he held them on grounds they were "contraband of war."[3] More "contraband" scurried to the safety of military lines, and it became a popular wartime expression.

Attempts to recover the fugitives from army camps caused much
distress among Maryland slave owners. It was not uncommon to be
greeted with threats and catcalls such as "nigger driver, nigger hunter,
put him out."[4] One supplicant bemoaned to the governor that "a

[1] As a result of the battle, fought on May 23, 1862, prisoners from the First Maryland
Regiment (U.S.A.) fell temporarily into the hands of the First Maryland Regiment
(C.S.A.). Baltimore secessionists exulted over the victory, turning Unionist anguish into
anger. *Cecil Whig,* May 31, 1862.

[2] Kate [Mrs. Norman Bruce Scott] to "My Dear Brother" [Edward B. McPherson],
May 28, 1862, Edward B. McPherson Papers, Box 7.

[3] Benjamin F. Butler, *Butler's Book* (Boston, 1892), pp. 256–58.

[4] *Port Tobacco Times,* February 13, 1862.

little orphan girl" might "be deprived of an education" if a valuable slave were not returned from the military lines at Point Lookout in St. Mary's County. Should this state of affairs continue, there was no knowing what the effect might be upon Union men, "as it comes home to every parent."[5] What a chilling declaration! Children were as precious as motherhood, the Constitution, and the flag in the primer of politics. The Negro, on the other hand, was expendable. He had no vote.

A prominent Charles County Unionist struck at the "unprincipled men" who coaxed Negroes into army camps and thereby violated not only the law but also "every principle of honesty, morality, or fair-dealing." Continuance of these practices would strip the land of labor and leave it desolate. Miller warned that governmental interference in slavery would disband every border state regiment, shatter the Constitution, and prolong and embitter the fighting.[6]

His sentiments echoed those of many other southern Maryland Unionists. These men so bitterly opposed any tampering with slavery that they risked their effectiveness as patriots. As one observer noted, "Prince George's and the bay counties are the 'raw' place in the body politic. Touch that in any way and the whole flesh begins to jerk and creep in violent contortions."[7]

Despite this attitude, a public policy gradually developed favorable to the fugitive slave. New federal laws gave sanction to those soldiers who loathed turning runaways back to their masters. The army could thus more openly give the slaves protection.

One of the favorite Negro havens was Washington, so readily accessible to the black belt in southern Maryland. Groups numbering five to fifty often left for the city.[8] Approaching the Eastern Branch bridge, they separated into small units to avoid suspicion, and once across, rejoined their friends in the capital. Their safety was assured if reports reaching Governor Bradford were correct, for it was said that the local marshal had been directed not to execute warrants for their arrest. United States Attorney General Bates pro-

[5] Dr. J. H. Miles to Governor Bradford, September 18, 1862, Adjutant General Papers, Hall of Records, Annapolis, Maryland.

[6] Thomas A. Millar to editor of *Port Tobacco Times*, March 21, 1862, printed in April 17, 1862 issue.

[7] "B" in *Baltimore American*, cited by *Cecil Whig*, May 3, 1862.

[8] Washington *Star*, cited in *Montgomery County Sentinel*, April 11, 1862.

fessed his innocence of such measures, writing Bradford, "I know nothing of any such order, and do not believe that any such exists."[9] Still complaints reached Bradford.[10] On May 16, 1862, the disgruntled from Anne Arundel, Calvert, and Prince Georges counties visited the governor.[11] He agreed to go to Washington the next day, but his trip was not a fruitful one. Bradford got to see the President only long enough to arrange another meeting.

Irregularities continued. An aroused 300 to 400 Maryland planters swarmed upon the national capital. On May 19 Lincoln listened to a sub-delegation of about fifty complain of their inability to retrieve runaways despite presidential orders to the local marshal, Ward H. Lamon, to execute the Fugitive Slave Law.[12] Blame was placed upon Brigadier General James S. Wadsworth, military governor of Washington. He allegedly had wheedled from Lamon an agreement not to surrender any slave until an investigation could be made.[13] The President, who expressed confidence in Wadsworth's intent to

[9] Governor Augustus W. Bradford to Attorney General Edward Bates, May 9, 1862, Executive Letterbook, 289; Edward Bates to Augustus W. Bradford, May 10, 1862, Executive Papers. The Maryland legislature also protested the presence of slaves within military lines. See John H. Bayne et al. to E. M. Stanton, March 10, 1862, Elon A. Woodward (compiler), "The Negro in the Military Service of the United States," RG 94, Adjutant General's Office (1888), National Archives.

[10] Slave owners denounced the President and Secretary of State for "duplicity, and bad faith on the slave question . . . ," said Major General Anthony Kimmel to Augustus W. Bradford, May 1, 1862, Adjutant General Papers.

[11] Augustus W. Bradford Journal, I, May 16, 1862, Maryland Historical Society; Memorial of sundry citizens of Prince George's, Anne Arundel, and Calvert counties pertaining to the flight of slaves to the District of Columbia [no date], Executive Papers; Executive Letterbook, May, 1862, pp. 293–94. The petitioners protested against the unconstitutional protection of fugitive slaves and asked the governor to call out patrols. Bradford rejected the plan as an invitation to a bloody clash between armed Marylanders and federal troops.

On another occasion he advised the sheriff of Prince George's County to arrest fugitives who may be "quietly" apprehended but not to invoke any police power that might collide with the military. See A. W. Bradford to Peter G. Grimes, June 23, 1863, Executive Letterbook, p. 428.

[12] Baltimore *Republican*, May 20, 1862; *Baltimore American*, May 20, 21, 1862. Congressmen Crisfield, Leary, and Webster joined the sub-delegation. It is also noteworthy that slaves living under military protection in Washington were sometimes abducted by "Negro-catchers," who pocketed between $50 and $100 per slave. Through such help some Maryland rebels got back their property. See *National Republican*, April 2, 9, 1862.

[13] *National Republican*, May 20, 1862.

do justice, assured the delegates their problem would be considered and wrong-doing prevented.[14]

Though hardly an explicit response, the delegation left the conference in good spirits, believing their plea would be supported. About forty of them hustled to the court house to get warrants for reclaiming their slaves. The swashbuckling marshal and his deputies co-operated by scurrying around town for Negroes. His action precipitated a clash with Wadsworth.[15]

News reached the general that Althea Lynch, a mulatto bearing one of his military protections, had been jailed. Now it so happened that Althea Lynch cooked for Wadsworth. There was even the hint that the prospects for breakfast were dark indeed. Besides, the general believed Althea's owner, a southern Maryland lady, to be disloyal. He ordered the Negro's release. The jailor refused. An hour later a second demand, threatening force, collapsed before the same rebuff. Undaunted, Wadsworth dispatched an officer and a detachment of a dozen or so soldiers. Their appearance convinced the jailor that resistance would be futile; so he surrendered the keys. The cook was released. The jailor and a deputy marshal were in turn tossed into a military guardhouse.

When Lamon heard the news, he rushed to the White House but could not reach Lincoln. As an alternative, he gathered a posse of such strength that the military guard at the jail could do nothing but meekly yield and be made prisoners. Not until later in the day was there an exchange of captives between the army and the marshal. Lamon, however, did not regain Althea Lynch.[16] Breakfast was assured for General Wadsworth.

When this comic opera conflict came before Lincoln, he turned to his attorney general. Bates promptly declared that under current conditions the civil authority in the District of Columbia outranked

[14] Reply to Maryland Slaveholders, May 19, 1862, *Lincoln Works*, V, 224; *Baltimore American*, May 21, 1862.

[15] Henry Greenleaf Pearson, *James S. Wadsworth of Genesco, Brevet Major-General of the United States Volunteers* (New York, 1913), pp. 136–37. The slaveholders won another point when three commissioners, just appointed by the circuit court to hear fugitive slave cases, denied their competence to decide on the loyalty of a master. This eliminated any oath of allegiance. See *Baltimore American*, May 23, 1862.

[16] Information on this struggle between Lamon and Wadsworth can be found in Pearson, *Wadsworth*, pp. 138–39; *National Intelligencer*, May 25, 1862; and Ward Hill Lamon, *Recollections of Abraham Lincoln 1847–1865* (Washington, 1911), p. 256.

the military.[17] Then on Wednesday night, June 11, the President got Lamon and Wadsworth together with Senator Orville H. Browning of Illinois. The purpose was to find a way of preventing collisions between military and civil officers in fulfilling the Fugitive Slave Law. Browning proposed that Lamon be allowed to execute all writs presented him, with the understanding that Wadsworth be notified. If the general found the arrested slave to be the property of a rebel and entitled to military protection, the Negro would be turned over to the army. Lamon, Wadsworth, and Lincoln agreed to the plan.[18]

Despite this commitment, all did not go well. In August and September of 1862 Wadsworth arrested some of Lamon's men on the charge of kidnapping. When the general left the post of military governor of the District of Columbia, the civil and military were still at odds.[19]

The constant bickering over enforcing the Fugitive Slave Law greatly harassed the President. On one occasion Blair argued for returning a runaway to slavery, while Chase pleaded that the man be allowed instead to join the service. An embarrassed President turned aside the sharp words with an anecdote. He recalled a debtor back in Illinois who acted crazy every time one particularly annoying and pressing creditor approached him on the subject. Lincoln added, "I have on more than one occasion, in this room, when beset by extremists on this question, been compelled to appear to be very mad. I think none of you will ever dispose of this subject without getting mad."[20]

The renewed efforts at enforcing the Fugitive Slave Law in Washington sent dismayed Negroes hurrying across the Potomac River. In Alexandria and other nearby areas of Virginia under military control they hoped to find safety, but the Maryland slave owners followed their prey. A neighbor of State Senator John H. Bayne, for example, successfully regained legal possession of a runaway after proving his ownership to the Virginia civil authorities. But then, as he tried to take the fugitive through the streets of Alexandria, the army intervened. The provost marshal fashioned a trial, denounced as "a complete mockery," and freed the slave.[21]

---

[17] Lamon, *Recollections*, p. 252.

[18] Theodore Calvin Pease and James G. Randall (eds.), *The Diary of Orville Hickman Browning* (Springfield, Ill., 1925), I, June 11, 1862, 549–50.

[19] Pearson, *Wadsworth*, pp. 139–40.

[20] *Diary of Gideon Welles* (Boston, 1911), I, May 26, 1863, 313.

[21] John H. Bayne recounted the story of his neighbor's difficulties in a letter to

Other members of the armed forces made life just as difficult for the slave owners. On December 29, 1862, Colonel James B. Swain sent a regimental band into Charles County from Chapel Point to Port Tobacco and back. Like the Pied Piper of Hamlin, the soldiers intended their "sweetish music" as more than entertainment. They lured the Negroes to Swain's steamboat and induced them to get aboard for a ride to freedom. Other Negroes found themselves forcibly embarked after being attracted to the wharf by the offer of sugar from a freshly opened barrel.[22]

The colonel denied charges pertaining to his role in these irregularities.[23] Weeks later he steamed back into Port Tobacco "creek" and in vain threatened his accuser with arrest unless he recanted the allegations. The defiance went unpunished.[24] The next morning Swain departed but not empty-handed. At least fifteen slaves accepted his latest bid to freedom. Swain had now gone too far. Prodded by Charles Countians, Governor Bradford worked for the colonel's removal. He succeeded—the news was conveyed in Major General Robert C. Schenck's letter of February 18, 1863, to the governor.[25]

These rumblings over military irregularities and fugitive slaves increased in tempo during 1863. For while slaves ran away largely on their own initiative in 1862, by the summer of the following year the army was pulling them off the farms and putting them into uniform. That meant a merging of two formerly separate issues: a man-hunt to fill the hard-pressed army and the agitation over runaways. Inevitably this further undermined slavery and influenced the political campaign of 1863.

There was great antipathy to putting Negroes in uniform. Edwin H. Webster, congressman and army officer, told the House of Repre-

---

Governor Bradford, June 26, 1862, Executive Papers. Bayne said the provost marshal declared that no Marylander would henceforth be allowed to arrest a fugitive in his department.

[22] Judge George Brent and 35 others to Governor A. W. Bradford. No date was placed on this Charles County statement, but it was apparently filed on January 20, 1863, Executive Papers. See also *Port Tobacco Times*, January 8, 1863, cited in *Cecil Democrat*, January 17, 1863.

[23] Colonel James B. Swain to Assistant Adjutant General, February 12, 1863, Executive Letterbook.

[24] F. B. F. Burgess, James H. [?] Neale, George P. Jenkins, and Peregrine Davis to A. W. Bradford, February 7, 1863, Executive Papers. Swain's new appearance at Chapel Point was on February 2, 1863.

[25] Robert C. Schenck to Governor Bradford, February 18, 1863, Executive Papers.

sentatives in February, 1863, that if the white men could not preserve the Union and their rights and liberty, "it is folly, it is shame,
to imagine that this can be done by the enslaved and degraded Negro."[26] The entire Maryland delegation voted against a bill to enlist
the Negro.[27]

The subject was not a new one to Lincoln. Frederick Douglass
had been urging the use of the "strong black arm" ever since the
first month of the Civil War.[28] Chase warmly advocated it to the
Cabinet in July, 1862, but Lincoln was not yet willing to agree.[29]
He knew the prejudice against the Negro as a soldier and the importance of avoiding any rash step. In his Preliminary Emancipation
Proclamation of September 22 he made no mention of Negro troops
though the final document accepted them into the armed forces for
garrison and sea duty. Meanwhile, Negroes were finding their way
into the service. This action accelerated as Lincoln swung around to
an emphatic endorsement of Negro soldiers.[30]

In June, 1863, Schenck furthered the cause by informing Lincoln that one or two regiments could be raised from the 4,000 Negroes working on the fortifications to defend Baltimore against Lee's
invasion.[31] But he needed Lincoln's authorization. It was not immediately forthcoming. Schenck became impatient. The President replied that the dispatches were not uninteresting, but that an answer
was not quite ready.[32] Finally Schenck got his wish. On July 6 Secretary of War Stanton wired the general that Colonel William Birney

[26] *Congressional Globe*, 37th Cong., 3rd Sess., Part 2, p. 1425. Congressman Crisfield
believed a Negro army would weaken the nation and hinder the return to tranquility.
See his address "To the Voters and People of the First Congressional District of Maryland," October 10, 1863, *National Intelligencer*, October 17, 1863.

[27] *Congressional Globe*, February 2 and 3, 1863, 37th Cong., 3rd Sess., Part 2, pp. 690
and 695.

[28] Dudley Taylor Cornish, *The Sable Arm: Negro Troops in the Union Army, 1861–1865*
(New York, 1956), p. 95.

[29] David Donald (ed.), *Chase Diary* (New York, 1954), July 22, 1862, pp. 99–100.

[30] Cornish, *Negro Troops*, p. 99; James Garfield Randall, *Lincoln the President: Springfield
to Gettysburg*, 2 vols. (New York, 1945), p. 188; and Benjamin P. Thomas and Harold M.
Hyman, *Stanton: The Life and Times of Lincoln's Secretary of War* (New York, 1962), p. 256.

[31] R. C. Schenck to A. Lincoln, June 30, 1863, Lincoln Collection, Vol. 116.

[32] A. Lincoln to R. C. Schenck, July 4, 1863, *Lincoln Works*, VI, 317. See also R. C.
Schenck to A. Lincoln, July 4, 1863, *Official Records*, Series I, Vol. 27, Part 3, p. 528.

had been ordered to report to him for the job of organizing a Negro regiment.[33]

The ambitions of Birney, son of a famous abolitionist, extended beyond his job of recruiting free Negroes. He fretted over not being made a brigadier general but confided to his friend, Secretary of the Treasury Chase, that he felt certain "of striking a heavy blow at the 'institution' in this state."[34] For this purpose he readily found allies among Maryland radicals and a number of army officers.

They included the impetuous Donn Piatt, lieutenant colonel and chief of staff to Schenck. A one-time erratic but brilliant student, he had achieved notoriety for humor and invective, qualities amplified by his legal, journalistic, and political experience.[35] Piatt told Stanton about his emancipationist objectives. An amused expression graced Stanton's face. He said dryly: "You and Schenck had better attend to your own business,"—that of "obeying orders." Piatt did not heed the advice. At one point he was summoned to Washington. The President greeted him, and, if we can accept the colonel's impressions, it was far from a happy welcome. Lincoln "was in a rage" and threatened Piatt with a "shameful dismissal" from the army. Only through the intervention of Chase and Stanton and a reluctance to create a row was Piatt saved from being cashiered.[36]

Eager to further the cause of Birney and the rest was Judge Hugh L. Bond of the Criminal Court in Baltimore. He wanted not only the free Negroes but also the slaves enlisted.[37] These views he put into a letter to Stanton dated August 15, 1863. Its appearance in the public press on September 7 provoked a stormy debate with Governor Bradford.

The harassed governor bristled, particularly at the idea of enlisting slaves without their master's consent. Bradford charged that the

[33] E. M. Stanton to Major General Schenck, July 6, 1863, *Official Records*, Series III, III, 470–71.

[34] William Birney to S. P. Chase, July 21, 1863, Chase Papers, Historical Society of Pennsylvania.

[35] *Dictionary of American Biography*, XIV, 555–56.

[36] Quotations in this paragraph are from Donn Piatt, *Memories of the Men Who Saved the Union* (New York, 1877), pp. 43–48. Piatt's memory seems to have suffered from inaccuracy and exaggeration in recalling this story.

[37] Bond charged that the recruitment of free Negroes hurt the free counties, which depended upon their labor, and tended to increase the value of slaves, most of whose owners were disloyal. Hugh L. Bond to E. M. Stanton, August 15, 1863, *Baltimore American*, September 7, 1863.

judge's plan would "impair public confidence in the Administration." People would interpret it "as an effort to effect by military
means a political object, and to ensure by such means a . . . preemp-
tory emancipation." If only the radicals would let the state alone, the
loyal would soon be practically unanimous in favoring gradual emancipation. But it would be acceptable only through the action of
Marylanders. Bradford was implying that Bond saw a short cut to
emancipation through slave enlistments.[38]

The governor did not address these views directly to the judge
but conveyed them instead through a letter to Congressman Francis
Thomas. It gained wide circulation and drew favorable comments
from influential leaders. Montgomery Blair called it "a judicious
move" and urged Bradford to press on. He advised the calling of a
convention of gradual emancipationists to launch a policy that would
counteract Winter Davis'. If Hicks and Crisfield would join the governor, "we could save the State," said Blair, "from Chase's and
Stanton['s] clutches—otherwise we can not[.]"[39] But Bradford would
not exert the kind of energetic, whole-hearted leadership Blair wanted.
How could he when so much of his time was consumed in defending slaveholders? The initiative rested with his antagonists.

No letter from Bradford could silence Bond. The judge defended
himself against the governor's insinuation that he sought emancipation through means contrary to Maryland law. Then he attacked.
Even if slave enlistments tended to destroy the institution, the masters should not complain, or so he insinuated. After all, slavery had
long held preferential treatment in the tax and criminal laws of Maryland. Bond went further. He reminded the inarticulate thousands
who lacked wealth and servants that each drafted Negro provided
an exemption for a white man.[40]

[38] This paragraph is based on A. W. Bradford to Francis Thomas, September 9, 1863.
The letter can be found in the Bradford Papers, executive Letterbook, pp. 446–50, and
several newspapers. Bradford said Bond's proposal would strip the master of the able-
bodied and leave him the aged and infirm to support.

[39] Mr. Blair to A. W. Bradford, September 12, 1863, Bradford Papers. Exactly two
weeks later an editorial writer on the *Baltimore American* reflected similar sentiments by
asking if the Union State Central Committee and men like Crisfield would not reconsider their position in light of the great changes of the last four to six weeks. Step
forward and direct, rather than follow the movement, the editorial seemed to be implor-
ing these leaders.

[40] Hugh L. Bond to editors of the *American*, September 16, 1863, *Baltimore American*,
September 17, 1863. Bond also said that since the North sent its children into the army,

As the public scanned their papers for the latest in this curious debate between a judge and the governor, events hurtled the issue toward a climax. Birney had already invaded Camlin's slavepen on Pratt Street in Baltimore, freed the Negroes, sixteen of whom were shackled with heavy irons, and got the males to agree to enlist.[41] Later that summer Colonel John P. Creager, acting on Birney's behalf, recruited Negroes in Carroll and Frederick counties. On Sunday, August 16, he entered a Negro church in Frederick and reportedly told the congregation that their political regeneration had begun and would go on until the bonds had been struck from every slave in Maryland.

That afternoon one of Creager's hostile relatives got a writ for his arrest. The sheriff accepted it and sent a posse that overtook the colonel northeast of Frederick. Creager was jailed on the charge of enticing slaves to run away, a crime subject to imprisonment for up to fifteen years.[42]

Doubtlessly encouraged by this act, some persons became obstructionists. Birney warned that these enemies "will be dealt with summarily."[43] He saw Creager's imprisonment as an attempt, which involved persons associated with the state government, to stop Negro enlistments in Maryland. The arrest intimidated Negroes and disheartened whites who were helping Birney to recruit. Nonetheless, the War Department refused to intervene because the prisoner, though using the title of colonel, was actually a civilian, subject to the laws of Maryland. The arrest, however, was not an entirely dismal event to the abolitionists. Judge Bond was said to have urged Creager to

---

certainly "it would not be noble for those who have them to refuse their *slaves*." Bradford rebutted. He claimed the Confiscation Act of 1862 did not give the President power to enlist slaves. Bond, backed by Judge Advocate General Joseph Holt, said it did. On the other hand, Holt accepted the right of loyal claimants to compensation, something Bond rejected. See A. W. Bradford to editors *Ibid.*, September 21, 1863; and J. Holt to E. Stanton, August 26, 1863, *Ibid.*, September 24, 1863.

[41] Col. Wm. Birney to Lt. Col. Wm. H. Chesebrough, July 24, 1863, Frank Moore (ed.), *The Rebellion Record* (New York, 1864), VII, 394–95.

[42] The Creager case was reported, among other places, in *The Maryland Union*, August 20, 1863; *Montgomery County Sentinel*, August 21, 1863; and *Ægis*, August 21, 1863. See also documents in RG 94, Adjutant General's Office, Colored Troops Division, Letters Rec'd, 1863. Creager admitted recruiting slaves, though he claimed he "did not know they were such at the time. . . ." *Ibid.*, J. P. Creager to Wm. Birney, August 19, 1863.

[43] Col. Wm. Birney to L. Straughn, August 27, 1863, *Chestertown Transcript*, September 19, 1863.

recruit slaves and, if interfered with, make an issue between Maryland and federal authority.[44] If nothing else, Creager certainly helped precipitate that clash.

By recruiting slaves while ostensibly enlisting free Negroes, the army struck hard at slavery. On August 27 Birney hinted that a Negro regiment would be sent to the Eastern Shore early in September.[45] He might as well have suggested that John Brown had been resurrected and was leading an invading band of abolitionists. But Captain John Frazier, Jr., provost marshal, liked the idea. A Negro company with local recruits could disprove misrepresentations that pictured the Negro as being enlisted only to be sold into slavery or used as a breastwork for white soldiers.[46]

Toward the end of August, 1863, reports of slave enlistments spurred Bradford into requesting the President to stop the practice. Bradford next went to Stanton, who claimed that the government had the right in an emergency to seize slaves for military purposes, just the same as any other property.[47] Nevertheless, Colonel Birney was ordered to stop using civilians as recruiting agents. This slight rebuff did little to squelch him. On September 2 the desist order was repeated, this time through Major General Schenck. It was accompanied by reference to reports that Birney's agents were causing trouble around Easton.[48]

Near that town lay the steamboat wharf at Miles River Ferry where, on the day before, a vessel prepared to carry off a considerable number of slaves. Some gentlemen boarded the steamer, only to confront the Negroes, huddled in the bow, defiantly raising clubs to resist

[44] William Birney to Adj. Gen. U.S. Army, August 20, 1863; William Birney to C. W. Foster, August 26, 1863; and C. W. Foster to William Birney, September 9, 1863; Woodward, "Negro in the Military Service," *Maryland Union*, August 13, 1863. Apparently Creager was not released from jail until November, 1863. See William Birney to Adj. Gen. U.S.A., November 27, 1863, U.S. Colored Troops, Main Series, Letters Rec'd.

[45] Col. Wm. Birney to L. Straughn, August 27, 1863, *Chestertown Transcript*, September 19, 1863.

[46] Capt. John Frazier, Jr. to Col. William Birney, August 28, 1863 and William A. Harding to Colonel William Birney, August 29, 1863, RG 107, Irregular Book 5, National Archives.

[47] A. W. Bradford to C. C. (?) Magruder and others, October 26, 1863, Executive Letterbooks.

[48] C. W. Foster to R. C. Schenck, September 2, 1863, *Official Records*, Series III, III, 760–61.

any close inspection. Thus thwarted, one of the gentlemen asked the commanding officer for permission to see if his Negro were present so that he might have some proof in case the government paid loyal owners. The request was denied. When the steamer pulled away from the dock, the Negroes "cheered lustily."[49]

This news soon reached the governor as four Talbot Countians bared their woes to him. Bradford was deeply disturbed. He had that very week written his first attack on Judge Bond's proposal. Now he prepared a letter to Montgomery Blair. Probably at no other time during the Civil War did the governor write in such a heated, excitable vein. He pointed to the alarm over what practically seemed as if there was a determination to stir up "something of a Civil War in Maryland." Despite his "earnest conversation" with Lincoln and Stanton a fortnight ago, the enlisting of slaves seemed to be increasing. If "such recruiting is unauthorized!—then why in God's name permit it?" Perplexed and angered, he added, "You can hardly estimate the damage we are suffering." The complaints came from the most loyal men. Bradford warned, "mark my prediction—if such practices are not speedily arrested, we are given over in spite of all we can do, once more to Democratic rule. Nothing but bayonets at the breast of the people—as things are now going—can prevent the result." Bradford asked that at least one request be granted: do not send any Negro troops to the Eastern Shore. The governor quoted "a plain, straight-forward, sensible, loyal farmer" as saying to him, "for God's sake let it [the government] not suffer us to be pillaged by a Regiment of Negroes."[50]

Blair laid Bradford's graphic portrayal of near hysteria before the President, but the Postmaster General did not have time to press the matter as far as he would have liked.[51] Perhaps that was why Lincoln failed to submit the letter to Stanton until September 25.[52] In the

---

[49]For information on this incident at Miles River Ferry see *Easton Gazette*, September 5, 1863; A. W. Bradford to M. Blair, September 11, 1863, Bradford Papers; and *National Intelligencer*, September 14, 1863.

[50]Quotations in this paragraph are from A. W. Bradford to M. Blair, September 11, 1863, Bradford Papers. Hicks wrote Lincoln on September 4, 1863, that at no other period of the year was labor so much in demand by the farmers. The recruiting could not help but influence the upcoming election. *Official records*, Series III, III, 767–68.

[51]M. Blair to Governor Bradford, September 15, 1863, Bradford Papers.

[52]Endorsement by Lincoln on Bradford to Blair, September 11, 1863, *Official Records*, Series III, III, 789.

meantime Crisfield had added his entreaty against the dispatch of colored soldiers to the Eastern Shore. He told Lincoln that many of those who claimed to be his friends in Maryland were neither "the best informed" nor "the safest advisers" of what was best for the Union. In their zeal for one goal, they were blinded to all others. If not restrained, both Maryland and the President would be plunged "into terrible difficulties."[53]

Birney's men ignored such lamentations. While the slave owners and politicians raged, his forces carried out more enlistment raids. A steamer with an officer and armed guard aboard would sail into one of the many rivers that flowed into the Chesapeake Bay.[54] Word was gotten to the slaves on the nearby farms that freedom awaited them. Beguiled, the Negroes slipped away into the night. Once they were aboard the steamer, the officer weighed anchor and headed toward a camp in a different part of the state.

The recruiting officers eschewed discretion. They arbitrarily stripped some neighborhoods and left others alone. Sometimes Union masters suffered, while the neighboring disloyal escaped losses. The unfit were set adrift when the rendezvous for the Negro troops was reached.[55] The disloyal feared to raise much of an outcry, but the clamor from afflicted slaveowners of Union sentiments grew steadily louder through September. George Vickers told Schenck the people were indignant; "*all classes*" had been aroused.[56]

Bradford, who had not heard from Lincoln, sent him another protest on September 28. The practice of which he had complained still continued and, in fact, was increasing. The governor urged the President to proclaim it a public necessity before seizing further "property" and asked that Maryland not be the exclusive area of its operation. This would refute the distasteful impression "that some question of mere local policy had mingled with the motives."[57]

---

[53] J. W. Crisfield to A. Lincoln, September 17, 1863, Lincoln Collection, Vol. 124.

[54] A. W. Bradford to A. Lincoln, September 28, 1863, Executive Letterbook; Lincoln Collection, Vol. 125; and "Documents Accompanying the Governors Message to the Legislature of Md.," pp. 95–100. Maryland *House and Senate Documents January Session 1864.*

[55] "Message of the Governor of Maryland, to the General Assembly," Document A in *Maryland House and Senate Documents 1864.*

[56] Geo. Vickers to Gen. R. C. Schenck, September 23, 1863, RG 98, Middle Dept., Letters Rec'd, 1863.

[57] A. W. Bradford to A. Lincoln, September 28, 1863, "Documents Accompanying

Senators Johnson and Hicks bore this communication to Lincoln on October 1 and added their own arguments.[58] Lincoln at once wired Bradford to meet him in Washington on Saturday the 3rd.[59] At the same time he referred the governor's protest to Stanton and ordered Negro enlistment stopped until further instructions.[60]

The Secretary of War quickly replied to Lincoln. He believed that his last conference with the governor had produced a "harmony of views." Bradford assented, according to Stanton, to the enlisting of free Negroes and slaves who had their owners' permission. If necessity dictated recruiting slaves without that consent, no objection would be raised if compensation were given the loyal who filed deeds of manumission. A general order to this effect had been delayed to await an understanding with Governor Andrew Johnson of Tennessee, for it was desirable to have the same policy apply to both states. Stanton proposed General Orders No. 329[61] to establish Negro recruiting stations in the two states and institute a system similar to that discussed with Bradford. The recruits would be forever free and credited to the quota of the county and state in which they enlisted. A three-man board would pass on the claims of loyal masters and award compensation up to $300 per slave.[62]

This order Lincoln handed to Bradford when the two men con-

---

the Governors Message to the Legislature of Maryland," pp. 95–100, *Maryland House and Senate Documents 1864.*

[58] A. W. Bradford to C. C. (?) Magruder and others, October 26, 1863, Executive Letterbook.

[59] A. Lincoln to Gov. Bradford, October 1, 1863, *Lincoln Works*, VI, 491.

[60] A. Lincoln to Gen. Erastus B. Tyler, October 1, 1863. *Lincoln Works*, VI, 494.

[61] Edwin M. Stanton to A. Lincoln, October 1, 1863, *Official Records*, Series III, III, 855–56.

Lincoln summarized the dispute:

"To recruiting Negroes, no objection.

To recruiting slaves of disloyal owners, no objection.

To recruiting slaves of loyal owners, *with their consent*, no objection.

To recruiting slaves of loyal owners, *without* consent, objection, *unless the necessity is urgent.*

To conducting offensively, while recruiting, and to carrying away slaves not suitable for recruits, objection."

Lincoln Works, V, 338, erroneously estimated the date of this memorandum as July 22, 1862

[62] To be compensated, the owner had to be loyal, take the oath of allegiance, and file a deed of manumission. Colonel Birney was authorized to begin recruiting under General Orders No. 329, dated October 3, 1863, on October 16, 1863. See C. W. Foster to Wm. Birney, October 16, 1863, Woodward, "Negro in Military Service."

ferred on October 3. The governor, far from happy with it, considered the proceedings "impolitic" and "unjust" and called attention to the dangerous drain on farm labor. Stanton, who was becoming impatient with Bradford, agreed to modify his order so that no slaves could be taken involuntarily from loyal owners unless thirty days of recruiting failed to produce enough other Negroes. Stanton assured the governor that no troops, Negro or white, would be necessary to accompany the recruiting officers.[63]

Bradford's hard-earned delay for his beleaguered slaveholding constituents proved short lived. Later in the month a steamboat entered the waters of the Patuxent River and landed armed detachments of Negroes.[64] Southern Maryland erupted with indignation. A delegation from Prince George's County expressed their horror when they heard of Negro soldiers exercising military authority over white people. Lincoln told the aggrieved that *the soldiers must be had*," but he did not want to offend the people in accomplishing this.[65] Their complaint about the use of Negro troops appeared reasonable. Why that force had been sent there he did not know, but he believed he would withdraw them.[66] An order was issued to stop any unauthorized recruiting of Negroes on the Patuxent.[67]

Off went a telegram to Schenck, who hastened to urge Lincoln not to intervene, for it would embolden the secessionists. Only one case of violence had occurred—the killing of a white army lieutenant by John H. Sothoron and son.[68] This was just what Lincoln

---

[63] A. W. Bradford to C. C. (?) Magruder and others, October 26, 1863, Executive Letterbook.

Stanton told the governor that in Missouri, now included in the order, and Tennessee "there seems to be less disposition to embarrass the Government . . . and much greater alacrity in affording the required assistance." E. M. Stanton to A. W. Bradford, October 10, 1863, Edwin M. Stanton Papers, Letterbook 3.1, pp. 35–36, Library of Congress.

[64] Prince George's County Citizens to A. Lincoln, October, 1863, though marked in pencil on back Dec. 1 (?), 1862, Lincoln Collection, Vol. 94.

[65] Magruder and others to A. W. Bradford, October 22, 1863, Executive Letterbook. The delegation, which included Congressman Calvert, visited Lincoln on October 21, 1863.

[66] Lincoln's Reply to Maryland Slaveholders, October 21, 1863, *Lincoln Works*, VI, 529–30.

[67] Gilman Marston to Lt. John Mix, October 21, 1863, *Official records*, Series I, XXIX, Part II, 364.

[68] R. C. Schenck to A. Lincoln, October 21, 1863, Lincoln Collection, Vol. 129. Schenck had sent Birney to find a site for a Negro rendezvous and training camp. During the search Birney dispatched recruiting squads to six places on the Patuxent.

wanted to avoid, and he told Schenck as much. White recruiters seemed preferable to Negro, whose presence caused "homicides on punctilio."[69] Lincoln was understandably annoyed. He referred to the general as "wider across the head in the region of the ears, and loves fight for its own sake, better than I do."[70]

Governor Bradford got drawn into the hassle. He went again to the President's office. Reverdy Johnson walked in while they were talking. Lincoln promised the two Marylanders to arrange some satisfactory plan with Schenck.[71]

Five days later seventeen Negro recruiting stations for Maryland were announced, though all of them did not have to begin enlisting at once. A Board of Claims was established in Baltimore. Its three appointees came from the radical wing of the Union Party. Judge Hugh L. Bond presided over the board; his two colleagues were Levin E. Straughn, editor of the *Cambridge Intelligencer*, and Thomas Timmons, an Eastern Shore politician.[72] In November Judge Bond was replaced by another prominent Unionist, Sebastian F. Streeter.[73]

The week before the November election saw Birney's men still active. The steamer *John Tracey* docked at Snow Hill in Worcester County on October 31. On board was Colonel Birney, a Negro brass band, and some Negro soldiers. They paraded the streets of the town with fixed bayonets, much to the disgust of many white inhabitants and hardly in keeping with Lincoln's intentions or Stanton's agreement.[74]

---

[69] A. Lincoln to R. C. Schenck, October 22, 1863, *Lincoln Works*, VI, 532.

[70] Tyler Dennett (ed.), *Lincoln and the Civil War in the Diaries and Letters of John Hay* (New York, 1939), p. 105. The President instructed Schenck to come to Washington, which he did on October 23, 1863.

[71] Bradford to Magruder and others, October 26, 1863, Executive Letter Book. Bradford was "greatly surprised" on reading that a recruiting officer had been killed, because Stanton had ordered the suspension of such enlistments. On October 28, 1863, Thomas Clagett, Jr. and seven colleagues wrote Reverdy Johnson from Upper Marlboro that Negro troops were "still harassing us, plundering us, abducting our Negroes." This statement William Birney vigorously denied in a detailed memorandum on November 8, 1863. See Woodward, "Negro in the Military Service."

[72] C. W. Foster to Hugh L. Bond, October 27, 1863, RG 98, Middle Dept., Letters Rec'd 1863. Through early October, 1864, only 244 of 2,015 claims had been passed upon. Nine of the 244 were rejected. C. W. Foster to Adj. General U.S. Army, Woodward, "Negro in the Military Service."

[73] Edwin M. Stanton, November 19, 1863, U.S. Colored Troops, Main Series, Register Letters Rec'd.

[74] See *Snow Hill Shield*, November 7, 1863, as quoted in *National Intelligencer*, Novem-

And so it went—Schenck, Piatt, and Birney successfully conspiring to exceed and in some cases disobeying the instructions of Lincoln and the War Department; the President, busy with other matters, was unable to follow every incendiary act of his subordinates. The irregular enlistment of slaves goaded irate slaveholders and conservative Union leaders into a barrage of letters, petitions, and protesting delegations. Governor Bradford deeply sympathized with the harassed masters and tried to help them. Their cause seemingly appealed to him more than emancipation. This frustrated Blair's pleas to Bradford to assume an energetic leadership of the freedom march. Thus, either by design or chance, the issue of slave enlistment, which the more progressive called the "poor man's substitute," kept the governor and a number of other conservative Unionists off balance. This left the real driving force behind the emancipation movement in the hands of Winter Davis and his Unconditional Union allies.

---

ber 12, 1863; *Chestertown Transcript*, November 14, 1863; and *Baltimore Daily Gazette*, November 11, 1863.

CHAPTER X

THE POLITICAL
CAMPAIGN OF 1863

DURING THE SIX months prior to the election of November 4, 1863, political activity swirled through Maryland at an uninterrupted pace. Countless primary meetings in election districts and wards picked delegates to county and city conventions, which in turn nominated candidates for public office. Under this system an aspiring politician who failed to win one nomination could seek another place on the same ticket. Joseph J. Stewart did just that. Beaten for Congress, he aimed at the profitable clerkship of the Circuit Court of Baltimore County.

His supporters arrived for the primary at the Ninth Election District by omnibus and foot. It was a good turnout, speaking well for the occasion, but the election ended in a far less auspicious manner. Into a hat, which served as a ballot box, minors and men from other districts dropped their tickets. Some reportedly changed their coats and hats and voted more than once. Then as the polls closed there was a violent rush into the polling room. Fists flew, feet kicked, and pistols flourished, as a number of antagonists collapsed under the blows of a well aimed billy. During the struggle it was quite possible that tickets were taken from the hat or added to it or both, but at least that memorable headpiece escaped capture. With peace restored and the tally counted, the Stewart forces celebrated a 113–56 victory over the adherents of John H. Longnecker, editor of the *Baltimore County American*. The decision entitled Stewart to five delegates favoring him for clerk at the county convention.[1]

Though another fracas occurred at the First District primary in

[1] The Baltimore County primaries and county convention were reported in the *Baltimore County Advocate*, August 15, 1863, and *Baltimore American*, August 13, 1863.

133

Catonsvile, things were quiet in most of Baltimore County's thirteen election districts, a hopeful sign that the democratic process was generally orderly and fair. The winning delegates' arrival in Towsontown for the August 12th county convention signaled a feverish round of "Button-holing," "log-rolling," and "wire-pulling." Competition was particularly keen because many believed the ticket would be unopposed in the general election.[2]

The county clerkship went to four ballots. Though Stewart led on the first tally, the prize eventually went to Longnecker. Then Stewart tried for state senator, but again victory eluded him. His ambitions apparently did not extend to the eighteen other candidacies filled by the delegates. These offices included county commissioners, judges, and state legislators.

Some of the convention's choices rankled a number of Unionists. They included disappointed office seekers and men who believed the delegates' failure to adopt a "platform of principles" did not meet the needs of the day. This was another way of saying that the convention had not shown itself "radical enough."[3]

These rumblings raised the threat of a rival slate. Apparently to forestall it, the regular Union candidates gathered in Towsontown on September 9 and resolved in favor of a constitutional convention as soon as possible. They simultaneously announced themselves "unconditionally in favor of a maintenance of the Union."[4] The dissidents, however, were not satisfied. In October they brought forth an Unconditional Union ticket. Ten of the nineteen candidates on the regular county-wide ticket won endorsement on the new slate. Meanwhile, independent candidates entered the race for a number of jobs, including those on the district level, where justices of the peace, school commissioners, supervisors of roads, and constables vied for office.[5]

Similar dissension scarred the party ranks in other counties. In Frederick the *Examiner,* spokesman for the more radical element,

---

[2] *Baltimore County Advocate*, August 15, 1863.

[3] *Baltimore County Advocate*, August 29, September 5 and 12, 1863; *Baltimore American*, September 8, 1863.

[4] *Baltimore American*, September 10, 1863; *Baltimore County American*, September 12, 1863.

[5] Each district held a meeting to nominate candidates for its own local offices, such as school commissioners.

sparred vigorously with the conservative but loyal *Maryland Union*.[6] The emancipationists won control, but the losers nevertheless fielded a slate. In Harford County the Union Party held together, but Cecil saw its Union forces ripped apart. The Unconditionals, who controlled the county nominating convention, picked for state senator, Jacob Tome, a wealthy capitalist of humble origins. The conservatives countered with a mass meeting of the supporters of Crisfield and Maffit.[7] They opposed Tome with James Touchstone, a blacksmith who frequented the rostrum and the press.

Appealing to the voters from the army in the field, Touchstone attacked the question of emancipation as "unwise and impolitic" at this time.[8] Nor did he overlook the past record of his opponent. In a letter to Governor Bradford, Touchstone recalled an incident, now three years old, in which Tome sold to a notorious slave dealer a faithful servant. Tome "dragged this poor fellow from his work one morning—*ironed* him and sent him off without giving him the poor privilege of saying farewell to his wife and children! . . . I saw him and can hear his cries for mercy yet. . . . Now Mr. Tome is an *emancipationist!*"[9]

Yet Touchstone was not an emancipationist. Here he could rage at the irony of Tome's position but failed to see the incongruity of his own views. He attacked the cruelty within the system as feelingly as any abolitionist but defended slavery as an institution. He suffered the blindness imposed by a culture that for decades had brooked no opposition.

The conservative Unionists were not the only Cecil Countians rankled by the Unconditional breed. The Democrats showed signs of life, a condition not demonstrated in many northern and eastern

---

[6] Frederick *Examiner*, August 5, 1863. The *Examiner*, in summoning voters to the primaries, said that too often these meetings had been engineered, thereby driving away despairing citizens and leaving the franchise to the party hacks.

[7] *Cecil Whig*, September 5 and 19, 1863.

[8] James Touchstone to "Fellow citizens of Cecil County . . . " appeared in *Cecil Whig*, October 17, 1863. Touchstone said, "Fellow citizens, you are told . . . that 'Gentlemen who adhere with *blind pertinacity* to the opinions of *two years ago, are not the men for these times*'. . . . These opinions were, that the Union, the Constitution and the Laws should be preserved and enforced: Are these opinions not admissible now?" He charged that extremists were seeking power and wished to side with "the *purse* and *sword*" so that they could wrest liberties from the people.

[9] James Touchstone, writing from the Sixth Regiment Maryland Volunteers, to August W. Bradford, September 29, 1863, Bradford Papers.

counties. At a county convention the Democratic delegates over-whelmingly declared in favor of presenting a county ticket.[10] This squeezed the conservative Unionists into an untenable position, caus-ing them to withdraw from the race. In doing so, they repudiated "ultraism of all kinds" and urged support of Maffit and Crisfield.[11] Rival Union slates, however, remained in the listings in most of the First Congressional District counties.

Down in Talbot County the Democrats were not so fortunate as in Cecil when they tried to put together a ticket. Some were arrested, gaining their freedom only upon signing a pledge not to organize for the duration of the war any party antagonistic to the Administra-tion nor to nominate or vote for a Confederate sympathizer.[12]

Southern Maryland presented a slightly different problem. The Union Party attracted fewer supporters than in any other section of the state. The luxury of schism could not be so easily indulged. Rather than become involved in the Goldsborough-Maffit and Holland-Calvert struggles, the Anne Arundel County Union Convention left the loyal-ists untrammeled as to their choices. All four names were printed at the masthead of the local organ of the party, the *Annapolis Gazette*. No such neutrality affected the local offices. The County Convention named a slate that it expected all Unionists to support.[13] They faced strong opposition from the Democrats, who backed men for the legislature who in 1861 had run as "Peace Party Candidates."

The general tone of the locality determined the expressed views of many candidates. Both wings of the Union Party were inclined to be more progressive in the north and west and less so in the south and east. While the Maffit men in the "free" counties seemed ready to accept compensated, gradual emancipation, their colleagues in the black belt often opposed it. The alignments frequently found their origin in ante-bellum alliances.

Although the conservatives liked to think of themselves as the "regular" party organization, they often got stuck with the name "Conditional Unionists" because of their qualified support of the

---

[10] *Cecil Democrat*, October 3 and 17, 1863.

[11] *Ibid.*, October 24, 1863.

[12] *Chestertown Transcript*, October 10, 1863; *Easton Gazette*, October 3, 1863; and other papers. In Kent County the Democrats ran only for local posts in order to avoid offices, such as the legislature, that involved political principles. See *Chestertown Tran-script*, October 31, 1863.

[13] *Annapolis Gazette*, October 22, 1863.

federal administration. In some counties they controlled the regular political machinery, while in other areas they were the seceders. Both factions often endorsed a number of the same men. Organization was frequently quite loose.

In the city of Baltimore Union rivals fought within the framework of one organization. Their struggle seemed endless. Ten elections kept them busy between May and November 4 (see Table B). In May each ward picked delegates to the Baltimore City Union Convention to oversee the party interests for the next twelve months. That body in turn summoned the Union voters to the polls on three more occasions to choose delegates: first, to the Second and Third Congressional District Nominating Conventions, then to the City Union Judicial Convention to pick candidates for judge, etc., and finally to the Union Nominating Legislative Convention.

The latter met in July and selected Archibald Stirling, Jr., for state senator along with ten candidates for the House of Delegates. Though the slate was described by one newspaper correspondent as "thoroughly emancipation,"[14] some proponents of that reform questioned the caliber of a number of the candidates. This prompted the *Baltimore Clipper* to recall that the "great men" sent to Annapolis two years ago "did nothing but talk, and now by way of experiment, we will try a smaller size."[15]

The *Baltimore American* took a different tack, criticizing both the local legislative and judicial tickets. So repugnant were some nominees that it felt enough voters might stay away from the polls on November 4 to endanger Goldsborough's chances.[16] A sufficient number of Unionists shared the journal's sentiments to call an Independent Union City Convention and form a new slate. They pruned the more objectionable names from the regular ticket but accepted a reputable radical like Archibald Stirling, Jr. Goldsborough won the convention's support as well. Now Maryland's leading daily was gratified. It commended the new ticket though the *Clipper* tried to cast doubts on the loyalty of all irregular contestants.

During the summer the Unionists in each ward nominated a city

---

[14] "You must not call it abolition, though, for fear of offending the nerves of timid people!" Cited in *Cecil Democrat*, August 1, 1863 and *Maryland Union*, August 6, 1863.

[15] *Baltimore Clipper*, October 13, 1863.

[16] *Baltimore American*, October 15, 1863. No Democratic slate was fielded in the city.

councilman (First Branch), justice of the peace, and two constables. On that or another occasion the annual election of ward officers took place. Some meetings felt the impact of Baltimoreans who had become soldiers. They went armed to gatherings outside their wards and in sufficient numbers "to intimidate and override the citizens." This violated military orders forbidding officers or men from absenting themselves from their commands after 5 P.M. On September 1 Brigadier General Erastus Barnard Tyler censored such conduct and directed a strict enforcement of the curfew.[17]

TABLE B. LIST OF ELECTIONS IN WHICH BALTIMORE UNIONISTS WERE
ENTITLED TO VOTE, MAY–NOVEMBER, 1863

Description	Date
1. Election of delegates to Baltimore City Union Convention	May 15
2. Election of delegates to Second and Third Congressional District Nominating Conventions	June 4
3. Election of delegates to June 10 City Convention, which picked eleven delegates to Union League Convention	June 8
4. Election of delegates to June 16 City Convention, which picked eleven delegates to Union State Convention	June 15
5. Election of delegates to City Union Judicial Convention	June 24
6. Election of delegates to Union Nominating Legislative Convention	July 16
7. Nomination in each ward of city councilman, justice of the peace, and two constables	August–September
8. Election of party officers for each ward	May–September
9. Councilmanic Election (First Branch)	October 14
10. General Election	November 4

City-wide conventions were composed of five delegates from each of the twenty wards.

Factional and policy differences infected not only the members of the army and office seekers but also those who held federal posts. A meeting of these officials was called by the holder of the top federal plum in Maryland, Henry W. Hoffman, in the summer of 1863. Some of the participants adhered to the Blair-Bradford wing, while many looked to Winter Davis and Chase. There were those who came from a Know-Nothing background and others who had dared to accept the Republican label.[18]

[17] *Baltimore American*, September 3, 1863.
[18] Those known to be present at this meeting were: James L. Ridgely and Peter G.

They gathered in the office of the Collector of Customs for the Port of Baltimore to devise means for helping the government suppress the rebellion. Peter G. Sauerwein, collector of internal revenue of the Third Congressional District, and Hoffman pleaded for emancipation. Make it the leading question, they urged. Maryland was ripe for such action. Not so, said James L. Ridgely, collector for the Second District. He looked forward to the eventual end of slavery but warned that victory in Baltimore County depended upon omitting the issue. District Attorney William Price agreed, but not Francis Corkran. His rebuttal must have had the sympathies of the majority, for they endorsed the bold espousal of emancipation.

Corkran had had enough of the conservative Union leadership in Baltimore county. With this meeting fresh in his mind, he went to the President and unraveled the story of Ridgely's unfitness to be a "representative of the Administration."[19] Corkran got his wish for Ridgely's ouster and succeeded in winning the office for the ever-running Joseph J. Stewart.

This was hardly calculated to please Congressman Webster, who had sponsored Ridgely's bid for the office. He got the news while on active duty with his regiment. No doubt angered as well as surprised, he wrote the President that Ridgely was "thoroughly loyal" and, he believed, "a sincere friend of your Administration." If Ridgely's antagonists were alone recognized as the Administration's friends, then "a spirit of hostility" would be engendered among most Unionists.[20]

Ridgely did some talking for himself. On September 16 he called upon Chase and spoke so convincingly of his support of the Administration that Chase feared an injustice had been committed.[21] The

---

Sauerwein, collectors of internal revenue for the Second and Third Congressional Districts, respectively; William E. Beale, assessor for the Third Congressional District; William Price, United States district attorney; and the following Baltimore Custom House officials: Francis S. Corkran, naval officer; John F. McJilton, surveyor; John F. Meredith, appraiser general; James F. Wagner and William J. Nicholls, appraisers. For the story of this meeting see numerous documents, including many letters to and from James L. Ridgely, in Vols. 135 and 136 of Lincoln Collection.

[19] Francis S. Corkran to Abraham Lincoln, December 19, 1863, Lincoln Collection, Vol. 135.

[20] Edwin H. Webster to Abraham Lincoln, September 12, 1863, Lincoln Collection, Vol. 123.

[21] David Donald (ed.), *Chase Diary* (New York, 1954), September 17, 1863, p. 198. Ridgely said that the complaint against him was his support of Webster for Congress.

Secretary of the Treasury expressed this feeling to Lincoln, who found himself in a dilemma. Both Stewart and Ridgely were responsible, loyal Unionists, each with strong supporters. Stewart was outspoken in stumping for emancipation and had the allegiance of the Davis wing as well as that of some moderates.[22] Ridgely, on the other hand, drew support from those Unionists who tended to drag a bit on emancipation, but they were influential and worthy of recognition. No wonder Lincoln remarked to Montgomery Blair, "My friend Corkran has got me into a scrape."

Lincoln apparently hoped to get out of the mess by encouraging Stewart to resign. Montgomery Blair conveyed these sentiments in a letter to Corkran, who showed it to Stewart. The latter rebelled—resignation, he felt, would be betrayal of his supporters and a personal financial blow.[23]

It is not hard to guess the reaction of the Postmaster General. He had worked to get Corkran the office of naval officer at Baltimore. Now Corkran had struck at Blair's allies by undermining Ridgely. Corkran, sensing his delicate position, tried to head off charges of ingratitude and treachery. He wrote Blair, "*I have not sought the aid of any man*, whom I thought did not wish thee well—Abraham Lincoln and Montgomery Blair have been and *will continue* to be my 'Idols,' to promote their interest has been my chief and only aim."[24]

That seemed rather far fetched, particularly when placed alongside Corkran's letter of two days before. Writing to Salmon P. Chase, he frankly admitted Blair's displeasure and added, "I have not asked his pardon nor shall I do so."[25] Later he told Chase that the turnover

[22] Moderate Charles C. Fulton of the *Baltimore American* supported Stewart, who wrote under various signatures at least fifty communications published in the *American* in a year. Stewart, said Fulton, "was *the first man in the State* to take up the controversy on the side of Emancipation, and the sustaining of your Proclamation. He handled the subject with great ability. . . ." Charles C. Fulton to Abraham, Lincoln, December 22, 1863, Lincoln Collection, Vol. 135.

[23] J. J. Stewart to S. P. Chase, February 3, 1864, Chase Papers, Vol. 87, Library of Congress. See also J. J. Stewart to F. S. Corkran, February 20, 1864, Lincoln Collection, Vol. 743.

[24] F. S. Corkran to M. Blair, December 23, 1863, Blair Family Papers, Gist Blair Collection, Box 6. In this letter Corkran referred to M. Blair as "my *best friend*."

[25] Francis S. Corkran to Salmon P. Chase, December 21, 1863, Chase Papers, Vol. 85, Library of Congress.

in the collector's office was "The best act of my life." Without it Maryland could not have become a free state.[26]

The Ridgely case was important to the Unconditional Unionists because they believed that Lincoln's Maryland office holders too often failed to give adequate backing to emancipation. Bond complained in August about the inaction of governmental officials, and Henry W. Hoffman wrote Chase of the need for Administration support.[27] The latter often helped the more extreme Unionists and kept in close touch with Maryland politics.

On occasion Chase visited Baltimore. Late in September Chase dined at Johns Hopkins' with some of the city's leading local capitalists and merchants. They were "nearly all, if not all, decided Emancipationists," according to an optimistic Chase.[28] Later in the fall Chase returned to Baltimore to speak at an Unconditional Union rally. His address on that occasion conveyed, according to one observer, the impression of a presidential candidate.[29] And of course Mr. Chase was ambitious for that elusive high office.

Early in December, 1863, a state corresponding committee to push Chase for president was established, with Frederick Schley of Frederick, Henry W. Hoffman, and John F. McJilton as its three members.[30] Each of these men held federal appointments. In other words, those who had most loudly proclaimed their support of the Administration and emancipation were ready to sabotage their President and patron. Thus the fight to free the Maryland slaves became entangled with the power struggle over the presidency.

Montgomery Blair feared just such a development. He looked coldly at those who wielded emancipation as a tool for dominating

[26] F. S. Corkran to S. P. Chase, December 24, 1864, Chase Papers, Vol. 94, Library of Congress. Corkran did not get his job back in the next Administration. He had alienated Montgomery Blair and could not expect much help from Chase, for the latter was made Chief Justice of the Supreme Court. Ridgely, on the other hand, was offered another office by Lincoln but declined it. Under Andrew Johnson, Ridgely regained his collector's post in Maryland.

[27] Hugh L. Bond to S. P. Chase, August 16, 1863, Chase Papers, Historical Society of Pennsylvania; Henry W. Hoffman to S. P. Chase, August 24, 1863, Chase Papers, Vol. 79, Library of Congress.

[28] For the story of Chase's September visit see *Chase Diary*, September 26–28, 1863, pp. 204–6.

[29] Adam Gurowski, *Diary 1863–1865* (Washington, 1866), p. 22.

[30] "Organization to make S. P. Chase President Dec. 9, 1863 Important," Chase Papers, Ac 4776A, Library of Congress. Major General Robert C. Schenck on the advisory committee in Washington.

the state's role in presidential convention. He saw them as men who
would trade their votes for patronage in the next Administration.[31]
Blair was considerably hamstrung in fighting these people because
of his inability to get the old Union Party regulars to come up to
Administration standards on the issue of emancipation. Yet he of
necessity relied upon these people for his greatest source of support.
After all, they shared his antagonism for the Davis men.

On August 26 the Union State Central Committee of the party
regulars met. Thomas Swann got the chairmanship. He used the
occasion to demonstrate a delicate balancing of the slavery question,
which, of course, bungled Blair's aims. Resolutions adopted at the
meeting reflected similar views, which were transferred to an address
to the people of Maryland.[32] Published on September 11, it fished
for support among the broadest segment of Unionists. The usual
contradictory statements sought to snare the unsuspecting. For instance, if the necessity of war dictated the fall of slavery, then "let it
go." On the other hand, emancipation should be postponed if its
discussion aroused bitterness. Regardless, there should be no agitation until a Constitutional Convention assembled—an impossible
fantasy, for emancipation was the primary reason for calling it.

The document pointed to its rivals' clamoring for "peremptory
emancipation, without regard to constitutional rights." The conservatives rebelled at such thoughts. They were sticklers for adhering
to strict legality and keeping, political temperatures down. The
message spoke kindly of the radicals' favorite target, the slaveholder,
and lamented that "the advocates of a sound and practical emancipation [such as Montgomery Blair] . . . have been pushed from their
stools by men of a more radical school."[33]

No such moderation muffled the ringing tones of the Unconditional Unionists' memorable address to the people of Maryland. Bold
and forthright, this paper spurned the common cunning of being
all things to all people. It assailed slavery and all its trappings. Un-

---

[31] Undated, unsigned draft or copy of a letter in Montgomery Blair's handwriting.
Date was apparently June, 1863. Blair Family Papers, Gist Blair Collection, Box 7.

[32] For a report on August meeting of the Union State Central Committee, see
Baltimore American, August 27, 1863.

[33] The "Address of the Union State Central Committee to the People of the State of
Maryland," *Baltimore American*, September 11, 1863; *Maryland Union*, September 24,
1863; and *Herald of Freedom and Torch Light*, September 30, 1863.

veiled by Henry W. Hoffman at a meeting of the Unconditional Union State Central Committee on September 9,[34] and published seven days later, its real author could not easily hide his unannounced identity. The phrases were too striking. It was apparent that Henry Winter Davis had forged another mighty weapon.[35]

His message slashed at slavery as "the domination of an interest over free men; of property over people; of aristocratic privilege over republican equality, of a minority over a majority." Though only a fourth of Maryland's whites lived in the slave counties, they controlled the state. This control meant depressed land values, an exclusion of immigration, and the keeping out of investments by entrepreneurs from the free states. A flow of statistics detailed the alleged political and economic woes inflicted by slavery.

The appeal was to the middle class of the north and west and to white laborers and plain farmers throughout Maryland. Hopefully rang the declaration, "The free white men," not the slaveholding interest, will henceforth "dictate the policy of the State." But first the legislators needed "to emancipate themselves from the influence" that had so long dictated their actions.

The message refuted the claim that freeing the slaves would bring the Negro into competition with the white working man; "The very object of emancipation is to end that competition." Dipping into the muck of unabashed self-interest, the question came forth, "What will the competition of the Negroes—freed, divided, ignorant, dependent, without capital, without political influence—be in comparison with the competition of the master owning those Negroes."

The Negro as the poor man's substitute emerged as a potent come-on, but the address did support compensation for loyal masters of enlisted slaves. Lincoln's plan for border state emancipation won praise and the slaveholders a warning that the "choice is between that offer and worse!" for Maryland was under no obligation to the grasping, selfish slave interests.

The charge of being revolutionists was denied. No "short-cut" was advocated. Only the skeleton of slavery remained; the substance

---

[34] *Baltimore American*, September 10, 1863.

[35] H. Winter Davis' authorship was confirmed by Creswell on February 22, 1866. "Oration of Hon. John A. J. Creswell [sic] on the Life and Character of Henry Winter Davis," *Davis Speeches*, XXVII.

had gone. For the good of Maryland and the nation, the skeleton should be removed.[36]

The address gained wide circulation. Appearing in several newspapers and a twenty page pamphlet, it provided a source of political ammunition never before so handily and effectively presented. Throughout the campaign the ideas and statistics appeared and reappeared.

Much of the Unconditional Union attack focused upon the comptrollership, the only state-wide office in dispute. Samuel S. Maffit offered an excellent target. Symbol of the status quo, he rallied those who could not or would not see the great transformation sweeping the state and the nation. Maffit condemned secession and abolition and prided himself on not having "swerved the breadth of a hair" from the Union platform of 1861. He openly stated in June of 1863, "I am opposed to an act of Emancipation, with compensation, at this time, because it is not asked for, by any considerable number of slaveholders holding any considerable number of slaves."[37]

This arrogance, so respectable and so acceptable for so long, neatly meshed with Maffit's belief in a grim financial crisis arising from abolition. As no federal compensation could really be expected, he believed Maryland must grant it. This would saddle the state with a huge debt, the tax basis for which would be drained of millions of dollars of slave property. All for what? To free Negroes to become a further burden upon alms-houses, prisons, and taxpayers.[38] This was excellent campaign material for 1861 but not quite in keeping with the changing temper of 1863. Some of the sheen was disappearing from the slave owners.

And gone was some of the allure of the regular Union Party organization. It suffered as the vulnerable Maffit endured a heavy pommeling from the opposition. Something had to be done. The emancipation movement showed no signs of weakening. To cope with this hapless predicament, Thomas Swann brusquely told Maffit

---

[36] *Address of the Unconditional Union State Central Committee to the People of Maryland, September 16th, 1863* (Baltimore, 1863). It also appeared in the *Baltimore American*, September 16, 1863; *Cecil Whig*, September 26, 1863; and *Civilian and Telegraph*, September 24, 1863.

[37] S. S. Maffit's "A CARD" appeared in such papers as *Cecil Whig*, June 6, 1863; *Maryland Union*, June 11, 1863; and *Baltimore American*, June 8, 1863.

[38] *Ibid.*

that their opponent's sole issue arose from Maffit's supposed aversion to a constitutional convention and emancipation.[39]

Maffit capitulated. Without any attempt to explain his reversal or refute Swann's over-simplification, he wrote simply, "I endorse the resolutions of the State Union Convention, passed June 23rd, including the fifth resolution in reference to taking the sense of the people for a call of a Constitutional Convention."[40]

This shift did not free Maffit from attack. One paper called his statement "a tacit acknowledgment" that he opposed a convention.[41] Rumors circulated that the majority of the Union State Central Committee were abandoning him.[42] The *Baltimore County American* ditched Maffit and put up Goldsborough's name. Its editor, John H. Longnecker, candidate for clerk of the circuit court, joined the rest of the regular county ticket in the switch. That left Maffit without the support of any ticket in Baltimore County or city. Even Governor Bradford's name was used against him, which prompted Maffit to write a letter of inquiry on September 23. The governor reassuringly replied that he would "undoubtedly vote for him."[43]

While many of his supporters deserted him in the closing weeks of the campaign, Maffit fought on. He refuted reports that he had quit his candidacy and charged the Unconditional faction with fomenting discord.[44] He was the regular Union candidate. Even if the voter were an emancipationist and he not, this was no justification for refusing him support, for the state comptroller had no more to do with the issue than the private citizen.[45] He launched his appeals through the public press because ill health prevented him from stumping the state.

Sniffing the political winds, Swann moved further from Maffit and closer to an unequivocal position on emancipation. He publicly claimed his executive committee unanimously favored gradual emancipation and an early convention. At the same time he slyly insinu-

[39] Thomas Swann to S. S. Maffit, September 18, 1863, *Baltimore American*, October 19, 1863.

[40] S. S. Maffit to Thomas Swann, October 3, 1863, *Baltimore American*, October 19, 1863.

[41] *Baltimore American*, October 26, 1863.

[42] *Ibid.*

[43] *Cecil Whig*, September 19, 1863 and S. S. Maffit to Augustus W. Bradford, September 23, 1863, Bradford Papers.

[44] *Cecil Democrat*, October 10, 1863.

[45] *Cecil Whig*, October 31, 1863.

ated that "the Committee of the Grand Leagues" favored illegal action to effect emancipation prior to the proposed convention.[46] Note
that Swann refused to dignify his rivals with the name Unconditional Union and claimed that his executive committee (he did not
say the whole State Central Committee) was as Unconditional Union
as any one anywhere.

As the election approached, the politicians hurried from their conventions and committees to carry their messages directly to the people.
Large rallies mushroomed throughout the state. The number might
seem surprising to us now, but then there were no radio, television,
or movies to compete. In the 1860s the voters submitted to lengthy
oratory and many addresses. It was quite common for one of the
speeches in each big meeting to consume two hours. The fortitude
of our ancestors was astonishing.

Most of the political rallies apparently ran under the Unconditional Union banner. Its state central committee played an active
role in the arrangements, publishing a list of places, dates, and speakers. No section of the state was omitted. Local rallies also sprouted.
For example, the Unconditional Union State Central Committee of
Cecil County announced four meetings between October 24 and 31
and hoped for two more in election districts not yet covered.[47]

Much of the burden of addressing the gatherings fell upon Winter Davis and his close associates, men like R. Stockett Mathews,
Judge Hugh L. Bond, Archibald Stirling, Jr., and Henry Stockbridge.
Out-of-state speakers lent a helping hand. Undoubtedly the most
active was Lt. Col. Donn Piatt, who seemed to prefer stumping the
state on the political circuit to confining himself to his military duties. Nor was General Schenck loath to speak.

On August 24 the Unconditional Unionists opened their canvass
in Cambridge,[48] but the heavy campaigning waited until October.
The first Saturday in that month featured an important rally in
Rockville, some ten miles northwest of the District of Columbia. On
this occasion Montgomery Blair bitterly attacked the menacing "am-

---

[46] Thomas Swann's "A Card," September 24, 1863, *Baltimore Clipper*, September 26,
1863.

[47] *Cecil Whig*, October 17, 24, 31, 1863.

[48] Henry W. Hoffman to Salmon P. Chase, August 24, 1863, Chase Papers, Vol. 79,
Library of Congress.

bition of the ultra-Abolitionists" and said their success would be "fatal to Republican institutions."[49]

His speech created a furore It gave the false impression that Blair was "semi-officially" speaking for Lincoln.[50] The address cemented the determination of many men to oust the Blair family from political power. According to the Blairs' biographer, Montgomery "sealed his fate in his Rockville speech."[51] The presidential election of 1864 merely provided an excuse to remove him from the cabinet.

Montgomery had little anticipation of such dire results as the words of the song, "Rally boys for the old Union," rang out, and the crowd took time to eat. In fact, he hoped the meeting would allay party divisions. After dinner loud cheers greeted Francis Thomas. John C. Holland also spoke. Unlike Montgomery Blair, both these candidates concerned themselves with Maryland emancipation. Holland's remarks reportedly were not too well received. Calvert was strong in this area.[52]

Three days later one of the campaign's most important meetings enlivened Elkton. Citizens from Pennsylvania and Delaware, both of which adjoined Cecil County, swelled the throng as the people made their way to a grove on the east side of town. Henry Winter Davis, Henry H. Goldsborough, and Donn Piatt arrived on the train from Baltimore, to be met by Creswell and the local Union League band. Davis delivered a very able speech. It was in parts skillfully conceived and ingeniously executed. Davis related how he had successfully defied traitors and their tools who sought "to soil and blacken my personal and private character." He flung back at his enemies the cry of "revolutionist," charging them with possessing in slavery "a revolutionary weapon." He no longer contemplated tying emancipation to compensation: "If it can be gotten, let it come; if it can not be gotten, Emancipation will come without it." The interests

[49] Blair's speech appeared in such papers as *National Intelligencer*, October 6, 1863; *Baltimore American*, October 5, 1863; and *Baltimore Clipper*, October 7, 1863.

[50] Adam Gurowski, *Diary, November 18, 1862, to October 18, 1863* (New York, 1864), Entry of October 6, 1863, II, 340; Carl Sandburg, *Abraham Lincoln: The War Years* (New York, 1939), II, 411.

[51] William Ernest Smith, *The Francis Preston Blair Family in Politics* (New York, 1933), II, 228.

[52] *National Intelligencer*, October 9, 1863; *Baltimore American*, October 6, 1863. Absent from the rally were Senator Hicks, who was supposed to come, and Governor Bradford, whom Blair begged to attend. See Montgomery Blair to Governor Bradford, September 24 and 26, 1863, Bradford Papers.

now to be considered were not those of the slaveholders but of Marylanders of all kinds.[53]

The next week Davis, Holland, and Major General Schenck spoke to a "tolerable fair assemblage" in Towson.[54] Eight days later Davis was on the Eastern Shore addressing one of the largest political rallies in Easton since the 1860 meeting for Bell and Everett. Both he and Creswell discussed Crisfield's opposition to slave enlistments and their own advocacy of it. This should "arouse every laboring man," according to Creswell, "to a sense of duty." Judge William D. Kelley, congressman from Pennsylvania, took over the rostrum and denounced Crisfield's attempt to get people to believe that Congress had no intention of paying loyal masters for their slaves. Compensation to slave owners in the District of Columbia belied the charge.[55]

Crisfield, on the other hand, publicly accused Creswell of being the agent for men seeking to destroy the Union Party in the First Congressional District. He attacked not only aspersions upon his loyalty but also the failure to discriminate between the Administration and the national government. The Congressman scornfully added, "I am not one of those versatile or weak kneed gentlemen who must look who goes ahead and who follows before they vote. . . . I follow no one; I think and act for myself." Crisfield admitted he opposed Negro recruiting and saw "no sin in slavery." Nonetheless, he favored its eventual end, which of course he hedged with conditions. Now was not the time to consider it.[56]

On October 27 Davis completed his speaking tour of the Eastern Shore in Snow Hill, a short distance from both Virginia and the Atlantic Ocean. Davis bade farewell to Creswell. Climbing into an open wagon, he traveled through the night across the peninsula, reaching Cambridge by daylight. There he boarded a boat to sail more than sixty miles up the Chesapeake to Baltimore.[57] That night,

---

[53] Davis' speech was reported in *Baltimore American*, October 9, 1863.

[54] *Baltimore Clipper*, October 15, 1863. In his address Schenck disclaimed any interference with local issues but said he intended to exert all lawful means to achieve Maryland emancipation.

[55] *Easton Gazette*, October 24, 1863.

[56] John W. Crisfield "To the Voters and People of the First Congressional District of Maryland," October 10, 1863, *National Intelligencer*, October 17, 1863. In this message Crisfield called talk of $10,000,000 compensation inadequate and a delusion. He said, "It will never be given. . . ."

[57] "Oration of Hon. John A. J. Cresswell [sic] on the Life and Character of Henry Winter Davis," *Davis Speeches*, XXVII.

the evening of October 28, he addressed what was doubtlessly the most spectacular of the many campaign rallies.

The weather was ideal—cool, clear, and calm, and the crowd immense. People overflowed Monument Square and extended along Calvert Street from Baltimore to Saratoga. A battery of well-known speakers assembled. They spoke from a fifty-foot platform that sported six columns topped by gas chandeliers. Along the rear of it extended a scroll proclaiming Union, Emancipation, and Goldsborough. About 8:00 P.M. a procession of ward associations and Union Leagues began arriving. Various groups carried flags and transparencies expressing undying loyalty and support of emancipation. Some of the German associations bore colored lanterns. As each new group arrived, cheers rang out and were answered by shouts from the marchers. Rockets and fireworks, bursting into showers of stars and displays of dazzling colors, formed a pyrotechnic background for the blaring bands.

With this rousing start, the speakers opened their verbal barrage. Davis was one of the leadoff men, making a relatively short address. Referring to his recent trip to the Eastern Shore, he said, "I have just returned from carrying the war into Africa." The crowd roared with laughter. The people, he said, favored "lightening the burden of the white man by allowing the negro to fight for his own emancipation."[58] Then he gave a stirring introduction to Salmon P. Chase, who in a brief speech lavished the words "patriotic, gallant, eloquent, fearless" upon Davis. Chase added that, "Other men might hesitate, but Winter Davis went straight on. (Applause.) Other men might doubt, but Winter Davis never faltered." The crowd roared back, "never, never." Chase underscored the cause of Unconditional Unionism as being *"one and the same throughout the land."*[59]

The longest speech of the evening was Samuel Galloway's of Ohio. He extended Lincoln's regret at not being there, repeating what the President had asked him to tell the rally; "I am with them in heart,

[58] See accounts of the rally in *Baltimore Clipper*, October 29, 1863; *Daily Chronicle* (Washington, D.C.), November 2, 1863; and *Baltimore American*, October 29, 1863. Davis claimed that poor white men had been enlisting, leaving their farms uncultivated and their families unsupported while their secession neighbors sat by with slaves to "reap the fruits of their absence."

[59] Pamphlet of some speeches of S. P. Chase (Washington, 1863), Miscellaneous material, Chase Papers, Library of Congress; *Baltimore American*, October 29, 1863.

in sympathy, in the great cause of Unconditional Union and Emancipation."[60]

The fortitude of the great gathering would have been taxed even more had the invitations to several more national leaders been accepted. The conservative Unionists were conspicuous by their absence, for none addressed the throng. In fact, Senators Johnson and Hicks and Governor Bradford kept aloof from campaign oratory throughout the fall of 1863.

The campaign closed with the Davis forces on the march. The theme of the "poor man's substitute" attracted a large following among the inarticulate multitudes,[61] who saw their old leaders fight against it, fight to make the poor man's burden heavier and the slave owner's lighter. Under these circumstances the old appeals to race prejudice and white solidarity seemed less convincing.

The Davis partisans pushed not only for the recruitment of Negroes but also for postponing the draft until after the election. Radical Judge Hugh L. Bond told Stanton that its implementation before that date would "I fear . . . cost us every congressman but Davis," and cripple the drive for emancipation.[62] The radicals got their wish. The *Baltimore Clipper* announced on October 15 that the draft, scheduled to begin that day, had been postponed, while Negro enlistments were being resumed.

Promises of draft deferments accompanied a fanning of class feeling. One paper wrote of "degenerate sons of the distinguished men of Revolutionary fame" becoming traitors, while "the hardy sons of toil, the bone and sinew of the State" came to the rescue of the Union.[63] Some laboring whites, once such obedient followers of the proponents of slavery, now took pleasure from the master's loss of Negroes.[64] Yet one lady found some compensation. Down to her last two slaves, she proudly noted, "I've learned something new today—

---

[60] *Baltimore American*, October 29, 1863.

[61] Less effectively the Democrats countered with the justifiable charge that the draft law favored the rich. The *Ægis*, April 3, 1863, quoted the *Muscatine Courier*, which said, "We are all soldiers except men who can afford to pay the Government three hundred dollars."

[62] Hugh L. Bond to Edwin M. Stanton, October 12, 1863, *Official Records*, Series III, III, p. 877.

[63] *Baltimore Clipper*, November 2, 1863.

[64] One "low fellow," said Samuel A. Harrison in his Journal (September 25, 1863,

for the first time in my life I've had to work and got along very well."[65]

Occasional voices struck at the injustice perpetrated upon the colored race,[66] but it was self-interest that dominated the radical appeal—whether it be slave enlistments, economic growth, or more equitable representation. These were weapons to be used for over-throwing slavery, the aristocracy, and government by the static, agricultural counties. Personal ambitions rode on the results as did presidential and national politics. The campaign climaxed in one of the most critical, dramatic, and controversial elections in the history of the state.

Part 2, p. 553) exultantly remarked that a large slaveholder in Talbot County had not enough Negroes left "to black his boots."

[65] Diary of Miss Lutie Kealhofer of Hagerstown, Md., cited by Fletcher M. Green, "A People at War: Hagerstown, Maryland, June 15–August 31, 1863," *Maryland Historical Magazine*, XL (1945), 259. Some Eastern Shore landowners began considering the subdivision of their estates for white farmers. See *Easton Gazette*, October 17, 1863.

[66] Joseph J. Stewart attacked the "hellish system" that appealed to man's "two grossest passions . . . lust and avarice. . . ." He told of the acquittal of a slave who raped a free Negro mother. A supposedly amused jury had listened to the defense attorney scoff at applying the idea of family to the Negro, likening such offspring to animal stock (*Baltimore American*, October 28, 1863). Despite this solicitude, Stewart could also play the role of a white racist demagogue (See *Cecil Whig*, May 16, 1863).

PART III

THE WINNING OF EMANCIPATION

CHAPTER XI

ELECTION BY
SWORD AND BALLOT

CONSERVATIVE UNIONISTS WERE worried. The extremists appeared too cocky, too defiant for their numbers. Some "sinister scheme" seemed to be afoot to control the November election.[1] Southern Maryland congressional candidate Benjamin Harris heard the rumors. He petitioned Lincoln to prohibit all federal employees from interfering in the voting.[2] But there is no record of the President's dignifying the request with an answer. Harris' fondness for the South was not likely to arouse a sympathetic hearing.

Over on the Eastern Shore Crisfield listened to similar reports— stories of military action to be brought to bear upon the election. He asked Thomas Swann, chairman of the Union State Central Committee, to call upon Lincoln.[3] Unquestionably loyal and with contacts in high places, Swann could not easily be ignored, even by the President of the United States. The two men conferred in Washington on October 26. The gist of their discussion appeared in an exchange of letters in which Swann asked Lincoln for his views.[4] The President retorted, "I am somewhat mortified that there could be any doubts of my views. . . . I wish all loyal qualified voters . . . to have the undisturbed privilege of voting."[5]

[1] George Vickers to Augustus W. Bradford, September 14, 1863, Bradford Papers.

[2] Benjamin G. Harris to Abraham Lincoln, October 6, 1863, *National Intelligencer*, October 9, 1863.

[3] Maryland House of Delegates, *Report of the Committee on Elections, on Contested Elections in Somerset County, together with the Testimony taken before that Committee* (Annapolis, 1864), p. 24. Cited hereafter as *Elections in Somerset County*.

[4] Thomas Swann to Abraham Lincoln, October 26, 1863, Lincoln Collection, Vol. 129.

[5] Abraham Lincoln to Thomas Swann, October 27, 1863, Lincoln Collection, Vol. 129.

This was soothing news to conservatives, but foolish were they who took much comfort from it. Lincoln's wishes had been disregarded before, and the end was not yet.

The radicals intended to employ every means possible to achieve their purpose. The test oath provided a handy weapon. Out of many counties came the plea for its use. A Harford Countian believed the swearing of every voter would help defeat Unionists opposed to the Administration.[6] Even Hicks asked "a stringent oath" for all of doubtful loyalty.[7]

How strange! Hicks favored Crisfield, and yet here he urged Schenck to act, to intervene in the election. This could only help Creswell. Was Hicks hoping to curry radical favor in the new legislature that would elect or reject him as Senator Pearce's successor? Or was he too naïve to foresee the results? The *Denton Journal* suggested that the motivation sprang from Hicks' desire to help his brother win the clerkship in Dorchester County.[8] Perhaps, but Hicks' contradictory behavior was not easy to fathom. He professed his innocence of any wrong doing, and his allies did not seem to find fault with him.[9]

Test oaths were not the only means for striking at disloyalty. Suspension of the writ of habeas corpus enabled the army to rid the state of undesirables. Some were arrested and released without any charge ever being made. Others, including a number of editors, were shipped South.

Of all the arrests, none achieved greater notoriety than the violent seizure of Judge Richard B. Carmichael while presiding in court.

[6] Lewis T. Pyle to Robert C. Schenck, October 29, 1863, RG 98, Middle Department, Letters Received 1863, p. 332.

[7] Thomas H. Hicks to Robert C. Schenck, October 26, 1863, copy in Bradford Papers.

[8] *Denton* (Md.) *Journal* cited by *Cecil Democrat*, February 6, 1864. Back in 1861 Major General John A. Dix rejected similar proposals for a test oath in the gubernatorial election, but oaths gained in popularity as the Unionists consolidated their hold upon Maryland. For instance, in August of 1862 a newly enacted Baltimore ordinance compelled school teachers and all persons connected with the municipal government to swear allegiance. Trading between the Eastern Shore and elsewhere was restricted to persons who swore to their loyalty. In July of 1862 appeared the ironclad test oath exacted of all United States governmental officers, appointed or elected. It attested to past as well as future loyalty. The oath evolved into a partisan weapon, the Republicans overlooking past sins if the office seeker espoused their cause.

[9] Thomas Hicks to A. W. Bradford, August 10, 1864, Bradford Papers.

Though his loyalty was questionable and his legal actions suspect, he hardly merited a personal assault in such a manner and place. This action by the federal authorities displayed a lamentable contempt for Maryland's civil government.[10]

As the election of 1863 approached, steps were secretly taken to combine the coercive measures of test oaths, arbitrary arrests, and military pressure. These techniques aimed primarily at that stronghold of conservative Unionists—the Eastern Shore. Yet in that region there seemed little justification for federal intervention. No rebel invasion threatened the region nor was it included in the martial law declared in Maryland on June 30, 1863.

The radicals and their allies ignored such considerations. Many of them had come to regard conservative Unionists with as much hostility as rebels. This intolerance swept the more rabid into believing that everyone who did not parrot their views was an enemy of the state.[11] On the Eastern Shore these men sought local and legislative offices and, above all, Crisfield's seat in the House of Representatives. Only with outside help could they hope to succeed. Accordingly, Creswell drew close to Winter Davis. This was mutually advantageous, for Davis wanted as many allies as possible in Maryland and in the Congress. Schenck no doubt shared Davis' desire. After all, the general would also be serving in the new House.

About two weeks before the election, Winter Davis chatted about a military order that would elect Creswell—its announcement was to be delayed as long as possible for fear "that old dotard," Lincoln, might revoke it.[12] The order, dated October 27, was quietly dispatched through the state but kept from public notice. To enforce it, at least ten soldiers were to be sent to every political sub-division

---

[10] On the other hand, Circuit Judge Nicholas Brewer, a Unionist, was attacked by drunken rebels in his Calvert County chambers. Brewer believed he would have been killed if he had not been rescued by some friends. Successful prosecution of the offenders, who were members of prominent families, would have been impossible and therefore was not pursued. N. Brewer to A. W. Bradford, October 5, 1863, Executive Papers.

[11] For example, Levin D. Collier, deputy provost marshal for Somerset County, publicly stated that he did not consider Crisfield loyal. See Proceedings of a Military Commission to Investigate and Report upon Captain Charles C. Moore's Conduct in Carrying out General Orders No. 53, Record Group No. 153, Judge Advocate General's Papers. National Archives. Hereafter cited as Military Commission Report upon Captain Charles C. Moore's Conduct.

[12] *Maryland Union*, March 10, 1864.

that had a polling place. The commanding officer of each detachment was to report for instructions to the local provost marshal.[13] These marshals were directed to help carry out the order and got broad powers to make arrests.[14]

This was an intriguing move. The provost marshals sat on the politically saturated Boards of Enrollment, whose agents reached into every election district of every county. John C. Holland was provost marshal in the Fifth District as well as a congressional candidate. Captain John Frazier, Jr. occupied the same office on the Eastern Shore while doubling as candidate for clerk of the Circuit Court in Kent County. Many others on the radically backed Unconditional Union tickets on the Eastern Shore were closely linked to Davis and would greatly benefit by any intervention.

Information pertaining to troop movements planned for Monday, November 2, reached Governor Bradford on October 31. Believing there was no reason to expect violence, he concluded that the troops would be used for exerting "some control or influence" upon the election.[15] Bradford urged a countermanding order, noting that all candidates were loyal except possibly two or three in one congressional district. This did not justify federal interference. In other states citizens voted freely and in one case for a man so hostile to the government that he had been exiled.

These thoughts Bradford put in a letter, which he turned over to John S. Berry, speaker of the House of Delegates. Berry hurried to Washington and got in touch with Montgomery Blair. The Postmaster General endorsed Bradford's protest and asked Lincoln to see Berry briefly at the White House.[16] The wish was granted. The President suspended Schenck's orders and instructed him to come to Washington.[17]

Schenck wired Stanton that he was taking the next train, leaving

[13] Instructions dated October 31, 1863, Middle Department, 8th Army Corps, General Orders 1863. There is a copy in the Executive Papers in Annapolis.

[14] James B. Fry, Provost Marshal General, to Major Noah L. Jeffries, Acting Provost Marshal in Baltimore, October 31, 1863, copy in Bradford Papers.

[15] Augustus W. Bradford to Abraham Lincoln, October 31, 1863, *Baltimore American*, November 3, 1863.

[16] Montgomery Blair to Abraham Lincoln, November 1, 1863, Lincoln Collection, Vol. 130.

[17] Augustus W. Bradford to Reverdy Johnson, November 1, 1863, Reverdy Johnson Papers.

at 5 P.M. "Can I see you first on arrival . . . ?" he asked, warning that a revocation of his order would lose Maryland.[18] Through this statement Schenck was indirectly admitting that the loss he feared was to conservative adherents of the Union, for not enough secession sympathizers were running to swing the state to the South.

That evening Schenck arrived at the White House with Major General James A. Garfield and Judge William D. Kelley, both of whom had spoken to Maryland audiences on behalf of the Unconditional Unionists. Kelley pulled no punches in addressing Lincoln's secretary, John Hay. The judge bitterly accused Montgomery Blair of working against the party in Maryland.[19] Now he and his two colleagues were here to insist upon an order to keep the disloyal from voting. Schenck told Lincoln violence would almost surely occur unless prevented by "provost-guards." In some places Union men would not be willing to vote or put up a ticket unless assured protection.[20]

It is highly doubtful that Schenck heard these charges from any one but the unreliable Frazier and his associates. The military records at the National Archives disclose numerous requests for troops and test oaths to stop the ballots of the disloyal and the "Copperheads" but express no fear of violence.

Schenck claimed in his order, designated as General Orders No. 53, "that there are many evil disposed persons, now at large in the State of Maryland who have been engaged in rebellion" or who have helped those so engaged. For fear that these individuals might "embarrass the approaching election" or use it "to foist enemies of the United States into power" Schenck decreed "I. That all provost marshals and other military Officers do arrest all such persons found at, or hanging about, or approaching any poll . . . on the 4th of November, 1863. . . . II. . . . [and also] support the judges of election . . . in requiring an oath of allegiance to the United States, as the test of citizenship of any one whose vote may be challenged on the ground that he is not loyal."

The 188-word oath did not catechize one's past acts but pledged

---

[18] Robert C. Schenck to Edwin M. Stanton, November 1, 1863, Lincoln Collection, Vol. 130.

[19] Tyler Dennett (ed.), *Lincoln and the Civil War in the Diaries and Letters of John Hay* (New York, 1939), p. 112.

[20] Abraham Lincoln to Augustus W. Bradford, November 2, 1863, *Lincoln Works*, VI, 556.

future loyalty to the United States. It involved swearing that unless official permission were granted, no communication would be held with anyone in the Confederacy—a considerable hardship to those desiring to hear from relatives in the South. The third and final proviso required reporting to military headquarters any election judge who refused to compel a challenged voter to take the oath of allegiance.[21]

On November 2 Lincoln wired Bradford his decision about this order and followed it with a more detailed letter of the same date. The President accepted his general's version of threatened violence and justified Schenck's prescribing an election oath unknown to the laws of the state. Lincoln believed the oath fair and gave an example: Major General Isaac Ridgeway "Trimble, captured fighting us at Gettysburg, is, without recanting his treason, a legal voter by the laws of Maryland. Even General Schenck's order admits him to vote, if he recants upon oath. I think that is cheap enough."

Lincoln did, however, revoke the first clause of Schenck's order not because it was wrong in principle but because the military as exclusive judges of whom to arrest were liable to abuse the provision. He substituted in its place: "That all provost marshals and other military offers do prevent all disturbance and violence at or about the polls." This was more restrictive than Schenck's wide ranging authorization for the arrest of any one in the polling area thought to be disloyal. Lincoln closed his letter with the assurance that "General Schenck is fully determined, and has my strict orders besides, that all loyal men may vote, and vote for whom they please."[22]

Lincoln undoubtedly did not see the order as a despotic and superfluous exercise of force. He had already assumed vast powers in his struggle to save the Union. That which ordinarily would seem intolerable and unjust no longer stung so deeply. The war had caused the change. Nor could Lincoln easily forget the obstructionist tactics of Crisfield, the many pleas by Bradford on behalf of slave owners, or the fact that Schenck seemed to be on the side of emancipation. The general's future presence in Congress must not be over-

---

[21] Schenck's General Orders No. 53 was printed in numerous places, including the November 7, 1863 issues of *Baltimore County Advocate* and *Chestertown Transcript*.

[22] Quotations in preceding two paragraphs are from Abraham Lincoln to Augustus W. Bradford, November 2, 1863, Lincoln Collection, Vol. 130, or *Lincoln Works*, VI, 556–57.

looked either. Despite these conjectures, it is possible that a more effective and detailed presentation would have won Lincoln to Bradford's side. If so, the radical attempt to prevent disclosure of the orders until the final hour largely succeeded.

Lincoln's statement about the oath-takers being allowed to vote could rightfully have aroused scoffing among Marylanders. For a long time army officers within the state had been ignoring, evading, or disobeying orders pertaining to the slaves. Schenck and his chief of staff, Donn Piatt, mounted many a rostrum to preach their brand of Unconditional Unionism. This hardly displeased their boss, the Secretary of War, for he told Schenck just two days before the election, "Now take Blair, skin him, turn his hide inside out, pickle it, and stretch it on a barn door to dry!!"[23]

And no doubt Blair would have delighted in an equally dire fate for Stanton. It so happened, however, that the Secretary of War and the general were in a far better position in Maryland to make Blair writhe than vice versa. After all, armed troops bore a note of authority unequalled by local postmasters and other assorted office holders.

Governor Bradford met the assault upon the purity of Maryland elections head-on. Parts of Schenck's order he denounced as "outrageous," even worse than rumor had led him to expect.[24] Here a general was dictating orders pertaining to a Maryland election and doing it without consulting the governor.

On November 2 Bradford issued a lengthy proclamation to the citizens of the state, with special attention to the judges of election. Never in the last two years, he said justifiably, could sympathizers with treason have gained control of a single department of the state, even if all of them had voted. He praised Maryland loyalty and reminded his readers that Maryland law forbade the appearance of troops within sight of polls during an election. The power to preserve peace and determine a man's right to vote belonged solely to the election judges, whom the state intended to protect. Bradford trusted the judges would "discharge their duty . . . undeterred by any orders to provost marshals to report them to 'headquarters.'"

After writing this section of his proclamation, Bradford received

[23] Henry Winter Davis to Samuel F. DuPont, November 4, 1863, S. F. DuPont Papers.

[24] Augustus W. Bradford to Reverdy Johnson, November 1, 1863, Reverdy Johnson Papers; Augustus W. Bradford to Abraham Lincoln, November 3, 1863, Lincoln Collection, Vol. 131.

Lincoln's telegram modifying General Orders No. 53. This prompted the governor to append a three paragraph commentary in which he claimed the military were still left the "exclusive Judges" of whom to arrest. The army, he warned, was "as likely to provoke" disturbances "as to subdue such a disposition." Bradford could see no reason for changing his proclamation.[25]

The next day the governor read in the Baltimore morning papers Lincoln's letter of November 2, which he had not yet received. Obviously irked, Bradford tossed a few barbed thrusts at the President but dissipated some of his effectiveness by yielding to his passion for verbosity. He repeated his outcry against interfering with the freedom of elections. The oath he considered the least objectionable of Schenck's three clauses. What Bradford could not abide was the idea of military edict prescribing a new law and making a veiled threat to all judges of election not complying with it.[26]

Caught in the middle were these very judges of election, who gained office as appointees of their county commissioners. The judges faced the dilemma of defying either the state or national authority. Neither Bradford nor the federal government would retreat.

When Schenck heard during the night of November 2 of Bradford's action, he at once stopped the American Telegraph Company and the Independent Line from sending any telegrams pertaining to the governor's proclamation. Similar instructions forbade publication in the Baltimore daily papers.[27] The *Baltimore American* got the order just in time. It had already set Bradford's proclamation in type.[28] To clamp tighter the lid of censorship, Schenck refused to let any vessels leave the harbor for the Eastern Shore and ordered a discreet suppression of any of Bradford's proclamations that might slip through.[29]

Schenck was not yet finished. He wired Lincoln for copies of the

---

[25] The quotations in this and the preceding paragraph are from the governor's proclamation, *"To the Citizens of the State, And More Especially the Judges of Election,"* November 2, 1863, printed in many sources, including *Baltimore American*, November 4, 1863.

[26] Augustus W. Bradford to Abraham Lincoln, November 3, 1863, Lincoln Collection, Vol. 131; Executive Letterbook, pp. 476–77.

[27] *Official Records*, Series III, III, 983.

[28] *Baltimore American*, November 4, 1863.

[29] Harrison Journal, Part 2, p. 591, November 4, 1863; *Message of the Governor of Maryland to the General Assembly. January Session, 1864* (Annapolis, 1864), p. 32; Capt. D. P. Thruston to Lt. Col. C. Carroll Tevis, November 2, 1863, Record Group 98, Middle Department, Letters Sent, Vol. 30 pp. 420–21; copy in Executive Papers.

latter's correspondence with Bradford. The President arose from bed, and clad in an overcoat, walked to his desk. There he fumbled sleepily for the letters. His secretary, John Hay, took them to the telegraph office for dispatch that evening.[30]

The next day Schenck, acting under the sting of Bradford's bold stand, stated his case "To the Loyal People of Maryland." Bradford's proclamation, he charged, encouraged "collision between the military power and the citizens." Therefore he had to restrict "its circulation in those parts of the State to be most affected by it," an obvious reference to the Eastern Shore. Thus did Schenck unintentionally confess his complicity in the radical scheme to win the election there. Yet the general called "unworthy of reply" Bradford's intimation "that my order might have been prompted by some other consideration than patriotic purpose or official duty." He intended only to prevent traitorous people from voting.

In claiming this single-minded and patriotic purpose, Schenck was either lying, indulging in a fantasy, or suffering from the bigoted belief that all who disagreed with him were disloyal. He tried to improve the appearance of his instructions by cautioning the men implementing the orders not to commit or allow "any unlawful violence," nor to discuss politics. The soldiers were to support the judges of election.[31] This last injunction particularly smacked of the equivocal because if the judges did their duty they would almost inevitably conflict with the military.

Having issued this rebuttal, General Schenck lifted the restrictions imposed upon the telegraph lines and the newspapers.[32] Whether by accident or more likely design, this step came too late on election eve, November 3, to allow any significant circulation of Bradford's document outside of Baltimore. No other city in the state published daily papers.

Despite these obstacles, Bradford's proclamation did reach much

[30] Robert C. Schenck to Abraham Lincoln, November 2, 1863, *Official Records*, Series III, III; Dennett, *Diaries John Hay*, p. 115.

[31] For the source of Schenck's quotations, see his statement of November 3, 1863 "To the Loyal People of Maryland," *Official Records*, Series III, III, 988–90.

[32] Capt. (no name), A. A. A. G., to *Baltimore American*, November 3, 1863, Record Group 98, Middle Department, Letters Sent, Vol. 30, 423. Copies were sent to the *Sun, Clipper*, and *Gazette*. See also Capt. (no name), A. A. A. G., to Agent of the Independent Telegraph Line and American Telegraph Line, November 3, 1863, Vol. 30, p. 421.

of the Eastern Shore. Benjamin F. May, a conservative Unionist who held the political appointment of inspector general of grain for Baltimore, rivaled Paul Revere in his race to inform the public. He left Baltimore Monday night, November 2, aboard the 8:30 P.M. express heading north. As the train passed through Elkton in Cecil County, he tossed out a package for Samuel S. Maffit. That was at 11 o'clock. May traveled around the top of the Chesapeake Bay and then moved southward. By 4 P.M. the next afternoon he reached Salisbury in the southern part of the Eastern Shore. There he distributed copies of the proclamation and found a volunteer to supply several other voting places

But May was not done yet. Since Salisbury was at the end of the railroad, he boarded the stage for Princess Anne, county seat of Somerset. Along the way he left copies at various stores, mills, and other places of habitation. He arrived at Princess Anne about 7:30 P.M., twenty-three hours after his departure from Baltimore. Hurrying to Crisfield's office, he found the congressman surrounded by friends.[33]

Crisfield needed all the comfort they could give. Only yesterday he had been in Salisbury addressing a crowd on fair day when a train arrived with two companies of troops sent home to vote. Marching to the vicinity of the speaker's stand, they let loose a cheer for Crisfield's opponent. The congressman continued to talk. As he was finishing, another train pulled into town with an estimated 400 cavalrymen under the command of Captain Charles C. Moore. The officer had with him General Orders No. 53, which he intended to promulgate and enforce.

This news greatly alarmed the people. Crisfield was "amazed" and no wonder. He believed Lincoln's assurances guaranteed there would be no armed force used in the election. But even worse, Moore told Crisfield the next day of his intention to go beyond the letter of Schenck's order, arresting judges of election who failed to obey instructions instead of simply reporting them. As to the test oath, it would not assure the right to vote if there were reasonable doubts of a citizen's loyalty.[34]

[33] Benjamin F. May described his trip in a letter to Augustus W. Bradford, November 5, 1863, Executive Papers.

[34] The incidents in Salisbury are reported in *Elections in Somerset County*, pp. 12, 13, 14. Moore allegedly admitted private instructions to arrest the judges of election if they did

With these gloomy events fresh in his mind, Crisfield took a copy of the governor's proclamation that May had brought and began reading it. The faces of those around him seemed to brighten. Who would go to the different election districts of Worcester and Somerset counties, asked Crisfield. Back came the cry in unison, "I will go. I will go."[35] Before 9 P.M. messengers were heading for all but one of the unsupplied districts. May felt confident that before sunrise of election day both counties had been informed.

But the exhilaration of this joint venture could not overcome the force brought to bear upon the actual election. Captain Moore appeared at the Princess Anne polls. He refused to recognize Lincoln's modification of Schenck's order or Bradford's proclamation because neither had been received officially.[36] This placed the election judges in a difficult position. The chief judge, John V. Pinto, called Moore to one side. Pinto confessed he was troubled; "I feel like I am between two fires." Either he would have to violate his oath or incur the general's "displeasure."

Captain Moore had no words of comfort. He replied, "My dear sir, I do not suppose that you can feel half as unpleasantly as I do. Gladly would I be out of my present position if I could, but here I am. I have my orders and must obey them, peaceably if I can." Nothing gained, Pinto returned to the polls which opened an hour late.[37]

When the judges were sworn in, they called on the sheriff to preserve order. He quite naturally asked how to do it. Someone suggested summoning the bystanders, but another member of the crowd objected. The sheriff had no force capable of resisting Moore's. Soldiers were stationed from the door to where the judges presided, some forty either bestriding the polls or within supporting range.[38]

---

not obey Orders No. 53. See November 4, 1863, statement of Isaac D. Jones, verified by many others, in the Executive Papers and *Documents Accompanying the Governor's Message to the Legislature of Maryland* (Annapolis, 1864), pp. 151–56. See also testimony of William J. Brittingham in the Military Commission Report upon Captain Charles C. Moore's Conduct.

[35] Benjamin F. May to Augustus W. Bradford, November 5, 1863, Executive Papers.

[36] Statement of Isaac D. Jones, verified by many others, Executive papers and *Documents Accompanying the Governor's Message*, pp. 151–56.

[37] See Testimony of John V. Pinto and John W. Crisfield, *Elections in Somerset County*, pp. 19 and 59.

[38] *Ibid*. and testimony of Isaac D. Jones and William J. Brittingham from aforementioned sources.

William J. Brittingham, who had declined the Unconditional nomination for register of wills and was running instead on the Conservative Union legislative ticket, stepped forward as the first man to offer his ballot. Captain Moore challenged him and insisted on the administering of the oath. The judges complied under protest. Brittingham took the oath and cast his ballot. Next came forward Arthur Crisfield, son of the congressman.

Again the challenge of Captain Moore was heard. Learning the voter's name, Moore pulled a paper out of his pocket, examined it, and began interrogating Crisfield. The quizzing in substance followed:

CAPT. MOORE: 'Are you loyal?'

MR. A. CRISFIELD: 'I am.'

CAPT. MOORE: 'Have you ever been in the Rebel service?'

MR. A. CRISFIELD: 'No.'

CAPT MOORE: 'Have you ever sympathized with those in rebellion against the Government?'

MR. A. CRISFIELD: 'I have never given aid, assistance or encouragement to the South.'

And so it continued as the inquisitor pressed Crisfield to see if he supported *every* means for prosecuting the war—the implication doubtlessly was abolition. Crisfield stuck to his broad interpretation of the government's right to employ "all the means recognized by international law and civilized warfare within the limits of the Constitution and the laws of the country." At last Moore relented and ordered the oath administered.

An exasperated Pinto could restrain himself no longer. He told Moore that it was impossible to conduct an election in this manner: "We shall never get through." If the election could not be held in accordance with Maryland law, "we submit to arrest."[39] The refusal of the judges to obey Schenck's order brought just that—arrest by Moore. Some of the crowd cheered the judges' stand. This Moore would not tolerate. Hands upon revolvers, he and his men seemed to expect an attack. A bugle sounded, and a half dozen more soldiers rushed in. The action quickly hushed the gathering, for there was no intention of forcible resistance.[40]

[39] The preceding quotations are from the testimony of Isaac D. Jones, November 4, 1863, Executive Papers and *Documents Accompanying the Governor's Message*, pp. 151–56.

[40] Testimony of John W. Crisfield, *Elections in Somerset county*, p. 20. Before leaving the

The three captive judges went by carriage under an armed guard to Salisbury but were not confined very long. Prompted by Brigadier General Henry Hayes Lockwood, Levin D. Collier, the deputy provost marshal, confessed that he was powerless to hold the prisoners and released them before sundown.[41] But Collier defended Moore. He told a military commission that if the captain had not made his arrests, "the judges would have conducted the election to suit themselves." In other words, they would have abided by the laws of Maryland. According to Collier, this "would have been prejudicial to the good of the Government."[42] By such a distortion of the democratic process, any means could be justified for assuring the success of the Unconditional Union candidates, and Collier was only too happy to employ these means.

Collier gained an unenvied reputation among the conservatives for "petty tyranny." He publicly declared that no "*damned Democrat vote*" would be accepted and threatened to arrest any one who dared run as a candidate of that party.[43] In Salisbury on election day, he hovered near the polls, making himself particularly objectionable to Crisfield's supporters. In the afternoon three "worthless" men, two of whom were "drunk," furthered his cause by intimidating voters who held white ballots—the color of the Conservative Union and Democratic ballots. Some tickets were illegally examined and in a number of cases rejected. Such actions discouraged voters from coming to the polls.[44] Not surprisingly, the Unconditional Union candidates scored handsomely in an understandably small turnout.

Court House, Moore confessed his intention to challenge all voters and interrogate those reported to him as having uttered disloyal remarks. Congressman Crisfield's name was said to be upon Moore's list. See testimony of Isaac D. Jones.

[41] See *Elections in Somerset County* and George W. Parsons to Augustus W. Bradford, November 5, 1863 and John W. Crisfield to Montgomery Blair, November 8, 1863, Lincoln Collection, Vol. 131.

[42] Testimony of Levin D. Collier, Military Commission Report upon Captain Charles C. Moore's Conduct.

[43] Testimony of C. S. Packard, *Elections in Somerset County*, p. 85. The Somerset County Democrats worked secretly. They prepared a slate and sent it to Philadelphia for printing. See testimony of various witnesses in *Elections in Somerset County*, pp. 37, 45, 76, 77, 85, 87, 97, 99.

[44] J. H. Tarr to Augustus W. Bradford, November 12, 1863, and George W. Parsons to Augustus W. Bradford, November 5, 1863, Executive Papers, and *Documents Accompanying the Governor's Message*, pp. 177–79, 189–90. The chief judge of election, Jacob White, sanctioned the proceedings. He was a candidate for judge of the orphans court.

In just two other of the fifteen districts in Somerset did the extremists achieve a respectable showing. Fraudulent practices robbed
both contests of impartiality. At the Deal's Island polls in the Tangier
district, Sergeant Frank Melville held sway. He ordered the election
judges to take the oath prescribed by General Orders No. 53 and
pulled from his pocket a yellow paper, the Unconditional Union ballot: "This," he said, "is the only ticket that shall be voted today."[45]

At Brinckley's election district a different story unfolded. After
ten had voted, the commander of the military detachment began
challenging. He got no further than three names when an armed
band of citizens intervened and told him they must vote even if it
necessitated the shedding of blood. The officer allowed himself to be
driven from the polls, deeming it imprudent to open fire.[46]

In some districts there was little intervention. Voters encountered
no questions in Quantico, though three-fourths of them allegedly
clung to "Southern rights."[47] A comparatively full vote was recorded.
The heavy-handed tactics of Collier and his associates seemed to be
directed at those polls where the Crisfield men should have run the
strongest.[48]

[45] Statement of Cyrus L. Jones, chief judge of election, Creswell Papers, III and
Documents Accompanying the Governor's Message, pp. 171–72. Later word came from neigh-
boring Dame's Quarter that names could be erased and changes made on the yellow
ticket as long as it was the one voted. The news had little effect. See Testimony of Cyrus
L. Jones, *Elections in Somerset County*, p. 31. Additional information can be found in
Melville's testimony in the Military Commission Report upon Captain Charles C. Moore's
Conduct and Statement of radical John Dix, December 7, 1863, Creswell Papers, III.

[46] Testimony of Lieutenant George W. Burnes (or Barnes), Military Commission
Report upon Captain Charles C. Moore's Conduct. See also testimony of Isaac Smith
Lankford and Dr. George R. Dennis, *Elections in Somerset County*, p. 78.

[47] John W. Crisfield to Montgomery Blair, November 8, 1863, Lincoln Collection,
Vol. 131.

[48] In the Hungary Neck district in 1861, Crisfield smothered his opponent by a
110–8 vote. Now in 1863 the sergeant heading the military detachment compelled the
judges to examine each ballot to see if Crisfield's name appeared. If it did, then the voter
faced a challenge.

A new twist appeared at the Tyaskin polls, where John W. Davis represented the
provost marshal. Doubling as a candidate for sheriff, he passed the word that all who
voted for him would suffer no interference. Reports circulated of his making a deal with
the Democrats. If so, Davis was duped. When the tally was made, only ten or eleven
votes appeared for Davis.

For details on the Somerset County election, see documents in the Executive Papers,
Elections in Somerset County, and *Documents Accompanying the Governor's Message*.

Despite the widespread intervention, Crisfield carried the county by 691 to Creswell's 348,[49] but this was not enough. Back in 1861 Crisfield won handsomely, piling up 1,991 ballots.[50] Thus he dropped

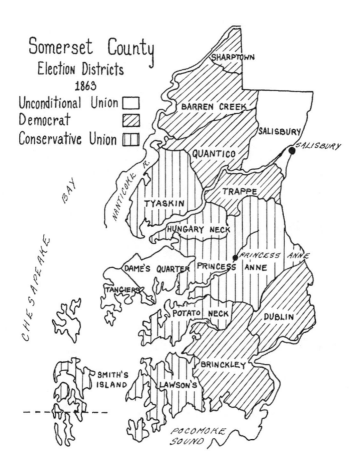

Somerset County
Election Districts
1863
Unconditional Union ☐
Democrat ▨
Conservative Union ⊞

from his previous race 1,300 votes, home county votes that he could ill afford to lose.

[49] *Baltimore American*, November 13, 1863.

[50] A statement in the Executive Papers showed the following total votes for Somerset County:
Congressional Election June 13, 1861—3,178 votes
General Election November, 1861   —2,866 votes.

TABLE C. SOMERSET COUNTY ELECTION RESULTS

District	Cadmus Dashiell (Conserv. Union)	Levin Woolford (Democrat)	Samuel A. Graham (Uncond. Union)	Total	1859 total vote for Comptroller	
		Vote for clerk of Circuit Court November 4, 1863				
1. Barren Creek	85	90	—	175	230	Oath in Order No. 53 correctly applied. Troops not directly at polls.
2. Quantico	52	109	1	162	170	No reports of any questioning or intervention in voting.
3. Tyaskin	126	115	4	245	307	Candidate's "deal" with Democrats.
4. Dame's Quarter	31	7	32	70	137	Only yellow ticket permitted in many cases.
5. Princess Anne	1	—	—	1	331	Arrest of judges of election.
6. Brinckley	56	148	5	209	253	Troops peaceably driven from polls.
7. Trappe	26	111	18	155	189	No reports of intervention in voting.
8. Dublin	30	55	—	85	173	Some Democrats and Unionists challenged Troops 150 yds. from polls.
9. Salisbury	17	—	89	106	257	Numerous fraudulent cases.
10. Hungary Neck	44	20	5	69	114	Illegal examination of ballots. Crisfield supporters forced to take oath.
11. Potato Neck	46	33	13	92	167	After noon, all who wished to vote had to take oath.
12. Smith's Island	27	1	6	34	37	No reports of intervention in voting.
13. Sharptown	34	58	16	108	110	No reports of intervention in voting.
14. Lawson's	213	123	9	345	325	Only yellow ticket permitted.
15. Tangiers	1	1	55	56	138	Troops were apparently at or within a couple of hundred yards of all polls.
Totals	788	871	253	1,912	2,938	

NOTES FOR TABLE C

The total vote for clerk reached 1,912, of which the Union candidates got 1,041. This was practically the same as the 1,039 combined total of Creswell and Crisfield. This indicated that the Democrats remained aloof from the congressional race. No official tally of the congressional contest by election districts could be found. Nor could a breakdown for clerk of the Somerset County Circuit Court be located for 1859. This is why the comptroller tally has been given. The totals should be comparable to the vote for clerk.

Sources. The district votes listed in this table are from:
1. Maryland House of Delegates, *Report of the Committee on Elections, on Contested Elections in Somerset County. Together with Testimony taken before that Committee* (Annapolis, 1864), p. 86.
2. James Wingate, *The Maryland Register, for 1860–61, a Legal, Political, and Business Manual* (Baltimore, 1860), p. 6 (back of book).

If it had not been for the heartening effect of the governor's proclamation, the Crisfield vote would likely have been less. But it was
the Democrats who reaped the greatest benefit from the proclamation. It kept them from withdrawing their ticket. Fortune further
blessed them in their refusal to support Crisfield, for many of their
ballots undoubtedly would have been disallowed if his name had
been on them. The division of the Unionists into two factions also
boosted the cause, enabling the Democrats to sweep the legislative
and county offices with less than a majority vote.

No county in the First Congressional District escaped the charge
of favoritism bestowed upon the Unconditional Union ticket. The
loudest cries of anguish rose from Somerset, Worcester, and Kent.
Even some custom house officials, among whom was Henry W.
Hoffman, spoke of the election as a "mere farce" and admitted that
petty officials "had '*greatly transcended*' their orders."[51]

The election in Kent County told a significant tale. This was the
bailiwick of conservative Unionists George Vickers, future United
States senator, and James B. Ricaud, former congressman. Both these
men had at one time bestowed their favor upon another local resident, John Frazier, Jr. Now Frazier rejected his former patrons and
sought the aid of radical allies in Baltimore. On October 23 he warned
Henry W. Hoffman of the conservatives' plan to elect "the Copper
Head Ticket" by arresting several persons for violating the slave code.

Frazier proposed a counterattack: seize the conspirators and hold
them prisoners until after the election. Those arrested should include Vickers and Ricaud, who was now running for the state senate. As he could not act officially, Frazier asked Hoffman to press the
plan "strongly before the authorities." The arrests would enable the
"Straight-out Ticket" to carry the county and, incidentally, elect
Frazier to its most lucrative office.[52]

General Election November 4, 1863—1,893 votes.
The latter differs slightly with the figure shown in Table C.

[51] J. (?) B. Hopper to Augustus W. Bradford, November 17, 1863, Executive Papers. For
information on election irregularities in Worcester County, see numerous papers in the
Executive Papers; *Documents Accompanying the Governor's Message*; and *Worcester Shield*, November 7, 1863, cited in *National Intelligencer*, November 12, 1863. Some non-resident soldiers
allegedly voted as did rebel sympathizers if they bore the Unconditional Union ticket.

[52] John Frazier, Jr. to Henry W. Hoffman, October 23, 1863, Record Group 98,
Middle Department, Letters Received 1863, F 364.

Benjamin H. Gardner, detective officer, and Eben W. Frazier, provost marshal of
Kent County and brother of John Frazier, Jr., had been indicted for enticing and

Donn Piatt carried out the request by ordering Lieutenant Colonel Charles Carroll Tevis of the Third Maryland Cavalry to make arrests in the course of his election duties on the Eastern Shore. Tevis sailed into Chestertown, Kent County, on Monday morning, November 2, with about 100 cavalrymen. He reported to Provost Marshal John Frazier, Jr., who regaled him with partisan talk of a strong opposition to the Administration, both in relation to the election and to Negro enlistments.[53] Tevis willingly accepted the story that the disaffected would try to grab the polls. As a consequence, he seized the arms of all "suspected persons."[54] Tevis also swallowed the lie that most Kent Countians were as disloyal as any in the rebel states and added a number of names to his proscribed list.

Then came the "pièce de resistance." Frazier wanted to reassure any laborers who were frightened by the conservative opposition. He drafted an order and got Tevis to sign it on grounds that the lieutenant colonel's name would be more effective than his.

The *Kent News* was *"commanded"* to print copies. Fifty were distributed to the five county election districts.[55] The order read:

> Head-Quarters,
> Third Maryland Cavalry,
> Chestertown, November 2nd, 1863
>
> . . . it therefore becomes every truly loyal citizen to . . . [give] a full and ardent support to the whole Government ticket upon the platform adopted by the Union League Convention. None other is recognized by the Federal authority as loyal or worthy of the support of any one who desires the peace and restoration of this Union.
>
> CHARLES CARROLL TEVIS
> LT. COLONEL COMMANDING.[56]

---

abducting slaves. See Benjamin H. Gardner to Donn Piatt, October 31, 1863, copies in Executive Papers and Record Group 94 T261–1863 (from service record of Lt. Col. C. Carroll Tevis, 3rd Maryland Cavalry), National Archives

[53] *National Intelligencer*, November 12, 1863, and C. Carroll Tevis to Donn Piatt, November 6, 1863, copy in Record Group 94, T261-1863 (Tevis). Tevis decided to arrest the two editors of the *Kent News* for publishing an article that purportedly advised resistance to the abduction of Negroes. George Vickers was accused of being the author. See *Ibid.* (Tevis), C. Carroll Tevis to Donn Piatt, November 3 and 6, 1863; Benjamin H. Gardner to C. Carroll Tevis, November 2, 1863; and John Frazier, Jr. to C. C. Tevis, November 3, 1863.

[54] C. Carroll Tevis to Donn Piatt, November 6, 1863, copy in Record Group 94, T261–1863 (Tevis).

[55] *National Intelligencer*, November 12, 1863.

[56] Copy in Executive Papers.

Captain Frazier could not have asked for much more. No wonder he was said to be "strutting about the street."[57] The arrests were particularly gratifying, for they removed from political combat some leading conservative Unionists and intimidated others. Such action tended to keep the vote small, a factor working to the radicals' advantage. Frazier had allegedly said that he would win the clerkship "if he got but ten votes."[58]

The day before the election, Tevis ordered the *Nellie Pentz* to sail for Baltimore with "his caged birds."[59] Originally he intended transporting them on election day, but local sympathy for the prisoners and annoying requests to visit them changed his mind. He advanced the date. This turned into a massive blunder for the Frazier men.

The vessel arrived in Baltimore about nine that evening. The prisoners were taken to General Schenck's headquarters on Calvert Street, to be met by a surprised Donn Piatt. One of the captives, James B. Ricaud, proceeded to read Tevis' order on the "Government ticket." This was too much even for Piatt. Happy as he was to mount the rostrum on behalf of Unconditional Unionists and to apply military pressures on their behalf, he raged at Tevis' presumptuous violation of Lincoln's and Scheneck's orders. Tevis, said the indignant Piatt, was "not much of a politician" even though he rated high as a soldier.[60] Piatt at once issued an order for Tevis to withdraw his decree and to comply with General Orders No. 53 "to the letter." He warned Tevis, "You will play the devil with us."[61]

Piatt agreed to release the prisoners and rush them back home.

[57] George Vickers to Augustus W. Bradford, November 2, 1863, Executive Papers.

[58] *National Intelligencer*, November 12, 1863.

[59] C. Carroll Tevis to Donn Piatt, November 2, 1863, Record Group 98. Middle Department, Letters Received, 1863. George Vickers eluded capture. He called Frazier's malice equal to his lack of principle. See George Vickers to Augustus W. Bradford, November 2, 1863, and C. Carroll Tevis to Donn Piatt, November 3, 1863, Executive Papers.

[60] *National Intelligencer*, November 12, 1863.

[61] Donn Piatt to C. Carroll Tevis, November 3, 1863, Record Group 98, Middle Department, Letters Received, 1863, 389 (copy in Executive papers). Piatt also added, "after the election arrest the editor [*Kent News*] and such others as are complained of for interfering with slave enlistments. These men I return on parole until further orders."

But how were they to get there? The steamer that had brought them to Baltimore lacked enough coal for the return journey. Fortunately, the *Thomas Collyer* was about to head down the bay on its way to New Bern, North Carolina. The Kent Countians got aboard and in less than a four-hour passage disembarked at Chestertown. The time was 5 A.M., Wednesday morning, just four hours before the polls opened.[62] Wherever the news of their arrival reached, it must have greatly relieved anxious and indignant conservatives.

Nevertheless, the vote was only two-thirds that of 1859. For the most part the soldiers behaved well, but officers challenged voters and in one case examined ballots. No one, however, apparently lost the franchise if he took the oath.[63]

Tevis continued his efforts to influence the voting. He allegedly declared that the government would prevent votes for any candidates locked up in Fort McHenry. The implication was that Ricaud and Jesse K. Hines, Frazier's opponent for court clerk, languished within those prison walls, yet Tevis at this very time was carrying a notice of their release.[64] Lt. Colonel Elijah E. Massey of the Second Maryland, Eastern Shore regiment, uncovered the duplicity, announced headquarters' disavowal of Tevis' actions, and proclaimed himself senior officer in command.[65] This angered Tevis, who threatened Massey with a court martial and accused him of working for the "Opposition," namely the Conservative Union ticket.[66]

Then came instructions from Baltimore for the arrest of Tevis and Frazier.[67] What a shock! Their hopes and dreams tumbled before

[62] *National* Intelligencer, November 12, 1863.

[63] See *Baltimore American*, November 12, 1863, and Benjamin F. May to Augustus W. Bradford, November 5, 1863, Executive Papers.

[64] George Vickers to Augustus W. Bradford, November 11, 1863, Bradford Papers

[65] John Frazier, Jr. to Donn Piatt, November 5, 1863, copy in executive Papers; George Vickers to Augustus W. Bradford, November 5, 1863, Bradford papers.

[66] C. Carroll Tevis to Donn Piatt, November 6, 1863, copy in Record Group 94, T261–1863 (Tevis).

[67] Lt. Col. Wm. H. Chesebrough to Lt. Col. C. Carroll Tevis, November 4, 1863, Record Group 98, Middle Department, Letters Sent, Vol. 30, p. 423. Five days later Tevis got back his freedom with only an official rebuke to remind him of his indiscretion. Endorsement of report on Lt. Col. C. Carroll Tevis by Lt. Col. Wm. H. Chesebrough by command of Maj. Gen. Robt. C. Schenck, November 9, 1863, Record Group 94, T261–1863 (Tevis). Frazier was allowed to resume his duties, pending a final decision that became enmeshed in a long political fight.

them. To add to their woe, the Conservative Unionists swept the county, beating the partially filled Democratic ticket and trouncing the Unconditional Unionists. Frazier suffered a particularly crushing defeat.

Elsewhere on the Eastern Shore, Frazier's minions devised a variety of ways for squeezing Unconditional majorities out of a sometimes reluctant populace. His cohorts worked to get friendly servicemen furloughed to vote. In other cases they assured politically helpful draftees they would be replaced in the service by Negroes. This action was vitally important. Thomas Timmons of the Board of Claims said it would give the radicals "character as the poor man's friend.[68]

There were other ways to bargain for votes. George Russum knew of 400 men in Caroline County who could "be reached," an obvious reference to the potency of money. The Unconditional Unionists spent about $2,400 in that county alone.[69] And Frazier was reported to have said that the bayonet could accomplish whatever could not be achieved by "greenbacks."[70]

Particularly helpful to the radicals was the yellow ticket. It made identification of friend and foe quite simple because the Democrats and Conservative Unionists used white paper. Such mockery of the secret ballot was possible because the government did not issue official ballots. Instead, each party or faction printed its own. A citizen picked the one he wanted and voted it. If there were names on the ticket that he did not like, he could cross them out and substitute his preferences. One man bragged that he had erased Crisfield's name from twenty-two tickets and put in Creswell's.[71] Another wrote his own ballot.[72] A straight ticket, however, predominated. That was probably why some political manipulators printed tickets with several regular nominees on them but with other candidates sprinkled in. The purpose was to snare the unsuspecting.

---

[68] Thomas A. Timmons to John A. J. Creswell, November 8, 1863, Creswell Papers, Vol. II. Timmons' pledge must have been redeemed, for on December 7, 1863, he wrote Creswell, "I am greatly relieved with regard to the drafted men. . . ." Creswell Papers, Vol. II.

[69] George Russum to John A. J. Creswell, March 15, 1864, Creswell Papers, Vol. VII.

[70] George Vickers to Augustus W. Bradford, October 22, 1863, Bradford Papers.

[71] J. P. (?) Fieroe to John A. J. Creswell, January 5, 1864, Creswell Papers, Vol. IV.

[72] Testimony of George W. Parson, *Elections in Somerset County*, p. 49.

Maffit, finding no running mates in Cecil County, announced that the tickets of the rival parties would be printed with his name in the comptroller's slot. This was done to save voters the trouble of making changes.[73] Maffit's friends agreed to distribute them in the various election districts.

Ballots in abundance awaited the more than 4,000 Cecil voters. The *Cecil Democrat* alone printed 15,720 tickets in a variety of combinations and then could not fill all the orders.[74] The *Cecil Whig* must also have turned out a goodly number. So ingrained has become the practice of handing out tickets, some of dubious authenticity, that it continues a popular custom at the polls today even though they can no longer be cast as ballots.[75]

Despite the fraudulent practices directed at his candidacy, Crisfield carried half of the counties in the First Congressional District. He lost, however, because his opponent captured 20 to 25 per cent more votes. Crisfield protested to Montgomery Blair the wrongs inflicted upon himself. In a long letter he described the election irregularities but never let the passion of the moment obscure his reason or loyalty. He ended with this forthright declaration, "I am greatly and wantonly injured, but I am an American citizen; and while I indignantly repel all assaults on my rights, and will peril all in their defense; I shall never forget my duty to my country, or hesitate to discharge it."[76]

In the Fifth Congressional District, centered in southern Maryland, the distress calls were few and the drop in votes smaller. Yet this region embraced the largest disloyal area within the state. The biggest outcry raged over an incident at Annapolis. There a number of prominent citizens, including a victorious legislative candidate and ex-Governor Thomas G. Pratt, refused the oath and were in turn denied the ballot. Some of the aggrieved determined to indict the judges of election. The Grand Jury obliged, but the military quickly retaliated, ordering the arrest of Pratt and twelve other oath-

---

[73] *Cecil Democrat*. October 31, 1863.

[74] *Cecil Democrat*, November 7, 1863.

[75] For instance, in 1959 the name of Republican mayoralty candidate, Theodore R. McKeldin, appeared on bogus tickets distributed near Baltimore's polls. All other candidates listed with him were Democrats, yet some of these tickets were marked Republican and others Democratic.

[76] John W. Crisfield to Montgomery Blair, November 8, 1863, Lincoln Collection, Vol. 131.

objectors. The jurymen quickly found reasons for quashing the presentment, whereupon those arrested gained their freedom by taking
an oath. Pratt, however, delayed his release by squabbling over swearing to any pledge. He protested to Bradford, sought Lincoln's inter-
position, and very nearly got sent South.[77]

Much of the Fifth Congressional District lay outside of the Middle
Department. That part adjacent to the capital came under the Department of Washington. Its commander, Major General Christopher Augur, ordered troops to attend various polling places.[78] Schenck's order
was put into effect. When Fendall Marbury, a prominent citizen of
Prince George's County, went to the polls, he was told he would have
to take an oath. Marbury said, "There is nothing in your oath I object
to . . . but I am opposed to taking any oaths. You have no right to
come here and require this oath." The captain in command, a Massachusetts man, sympathized, "I agree with you. . . . We have no right
to put such oaths. But I am a soldier, and it is on my orders."[79]

To the commander of the St. Mary's District Schenck suggested
the use of his Orders No. 53.[80] Soldiers appeared at the various polling places but behaved so well that they won the congratulations of
a local journal.[81] Apparently no oath was required, and the vote fell
just moderately below an average turnout. Only the more timid
were deterred by the presence of the troops.

Because of such relative restraint, Democrat Benjamin G. Harris
was able to capitalize upon the Union split and sweep to victory. He
got 46.9 per cent of the congressional vote, giving him 4,939 votes
to Holland's 3,352 and Calvert's 2,237.[82] Winter Davis believed

[77] For information on the election at Annapolis and the disposition of the cases of ex-
Governor Thomas G. Pratt and others, see the numerous entries (November–December, 1863) in Vols. 131–33 and 135 in the Lincoln Collection. The loyal were also not
above complaining. An enrolling officer, Gassaway H. Laughlin, reported from Anne
Arundel County that he was threatened with being shot while challenging "disloyal
persons" at the polls. Letter of November 6, 1863, Record Group 98, Middle Dept.,
Register Letters Received, Vol. VI.

[78] Copy of Col. L. C. Baker to Maj. Gen. L. Wallace, April 5, 1864, Record Group 98,
Middle Dept., Letters Received, 1864, B190.

[79] Debates of Constitutional Convention of 1864, III, 1736.

[80] Lt. Col. [Donn Piatt], Chief of Staff, to Brig. Gen. Gilman Marston, Comdg. Dept.
of St. Mary's, October 30, 1863, Record Group 98, Middle Dept., Letters Sent, Vol. 30,
p. 416.

[81] St. Mary's Gazette, November 5, 1863, cited in Baltimore Daily Gazette, November
9, 1863.

[82] Baltimore American, November 20, 1863.

Holland would have been victorious had not Lincoln altered Schenck's order and Governor Bradford issued his "foolish proclamation."[83] As it was, the Democrats won the House of Delegates seats for all seven counties of southern Maryland except Howard. Back in 1861 they squeezed a victory out of only three of these counties, but now, be-

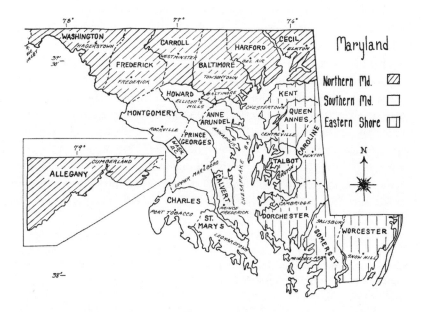

lieved Judge Brewer of Annapolis, southern sympathy was more deeply rooted than ever before in the lower end of the Western Shore.[84]

In the free counties the vote was also off. Harford polled less than half of its November, 1861 totals, but the blame could not be placed just on military orders. The great majority of the regularly nominated Union candidates were unopposed, while the unequal fight for the controllership could hardly be calculated to draw large crowds to the polls. Goldsborough carried the county by a 3 ½ to 1 margin.

[83] H. Winter Davis to Samuel F. DuPont, November 9, 1863, S. F. DuPont Papers. Benjamin Harris, according to intimations heard by Samuel Harrison (his Journal, November 7, 1863, p. 592), was allowed to run in hopes of splitting Calvert's vote. Instead, the Democrats apparently flocked to Harris, while the Unionists divided their votes between Calvert and Holland.

[84] Judge Nicholas Brewer to Abraham Lincoln, November 7, 1863, Lincoln Collection, Vol. 131.

Only in Carroll did Maffit show a winning stance in northern Maryland. He carried it by a comfortable margin, profiting by the division among the so-called Unconditional Union candidates over whom to support for comptroller.[85]

Allegany, Maryland's westernmost county, boasted a voter turnout that was relatively full. Though outside of the Middle Department, Schenck's order was applied wherever it reached in time.[86] No reports of irregularities appeared other than the usual number of citizens who refused the oath and were not allowed to vote.

In Baltimore County the army seized three candidates on the "Independent Ticket" shortly after the polls opened and did not release them until after the balloting stopped.[87] Generally speaking, however, the election went quietly.[88] The same calm prevailed in the city of Baltimore even though the breach between Schenck and Bradford sparked excitement the day before.[89] No effort was made to interfere with the voters as they severely trounced the independent Union slate. John P. Kennedy blamed Winter Davis' unpopularity for the small turnout, asserting that all but Davis' "extreme partisans ab-

[85] The apparent lack of interference in the election in nine of Carroll's eleven districts doubtlessly also helped. The remaining two saw Schenck's order enforced and challenges made. Maffit and the independent candidates did poorly at those polls. *Western Maryland Democrat* (Westminster, Md.), no date (part of issue missing).

[86] *Civilian and Telegraph*, November 12, 1863. According to one observer in Frederick County, those who voted east of the Monocacy River confronted bayonets at the polls, while on the west of the river a man could vote freely. The Monocacy divided the Middle Department from the Department of West Virginia. See Wm. C. Hoffman to A. W. Bradford, September 12, 1864, Executive Papers and Raphael P. Thian (compiler), *Notes Illustrating the Military Geography of the United States* (Washington, 1881), pp. 136–37.

[87] *Baltimore Daily Gazette*, November 5, 1863, and *Baltimore County Advocate*, November 7, 1863. A few persons were also imprisoned in Cecil County until the polls closed. From various counties came other complaints of mistreatment, including a few from Unconditional Unionists.

[88] With the campaign over, the *Advocate* hoped for an era of better feeling, but the victorious John H. Longnecker, editor of the *Baltimore County American*, hardly sounded a conciliatory note. His journal bitterly attacked Winter Davis. See *Baltimore County American* cited in *National American* (Bel Air, Md.), November 20, 1863.

[89] *Baltimore American*, November 4, 5, 1863, and Baltimore *Sun*, November 5, 1863. In Baltimore the army lacked enough soldiers to carry out Schenck's orders; so it called upon the Union Leagues to help. Brig. Gen. Erastus B. Tyler to Lt. Col. William H. Chesebrough, AAG, November 3, 1863, Record Group 98, Middle Dept., Letter Received, 1863.

stained" from voting.[90] Nevertheless, some of Davis' critics yielded
to admiration. The *Clipper*, while admitting his tendencies to be "dic-
tatorial and arbitrary," likened Davis to "a pure, bright spring well-
ing up in the midst of a muddy marsh . . . he is an admirable man."[91]

State-wide, on the average, only 60 per cent as many Marylanders
voted as in the four previous elections. The results sent Davis and
three other Unconditional Unionists to Congress. Only Holland failed.
As for Maryland's legislative body, forty-seven of the seventy-four
seats in the House of Delegates went to the emancipationists, while
another five to eight went to men pledged to a referendum on a
constitutional convention. Twelve of the twenty-two state senate seats
were up for election this year. Of these, nine went to emancipationists, seemingly assuring a workable margin for a convention.[92] These
results deeply interested the Administration in Washington. Hoffman
telegraphed both Lincoln and Chase on November 5, while Secretary Hay expressed relief after an anxious time on election day.[93]

Equally significant was Goldsborough's thumping victory over
Maffit by the margin of 2 ¼ to 1. Goldsborough symbolized Unconditional Unionism and the demand for immediate action on ridding
the state of slavery. Maffit personified those who wished to stand pat
or, at the most, move as slowly as possible. But Maffit also got support from some moderate emancipationists who respected his un-
questioned excellence as comptroller and accepted him as the regular nominee of the Union Party.

The smallness of the vote complicates an analysis of actual sentiment. An untrammeled election would doubtlessly have fattened
Maffit's vote in many areas and carried the Eastern Shore for Crisfield,
but it seems likely that Goldsborough would have won a narrow victory. A more decided majority favored some form of emancipation.

[90] John P. Kennedy's Journal, November 5, 1863, John P. Kennedy Papers. The
belated opposition of Judge Henry Stump, a southern sympathizer masquerading as a
Constitutional Unionist, won only 23 votes. See *Baltimore Daily Gazette*, October 28,
1863, and November 5, 1863.

[91] *Baltimore Clipper*, October 7, 1863. The pro-Davis *Civilian and Telegraph* of November 12, 1863, spoke of the man as presidential timber.

[92] *Baltimore American,* November 12, 1863; *Civilian and Telegraph*, November 19,
1863. On the Eastern Shore the emancipationists swept four counties, the unpledged
Unionists two, and the Democrats one.

[93] Henry W. Hoffman to Abraham Lincoln, November 5, 1863, Lincoln Collection,
Vol. 131: Henry W. Hoffman to Salmon P. Chase, November 5, 1863, *Diaries John Hay*,
November 4, 5, 1863, p. 116.

TABLE D. ELECTION STATISTICS, NOVEMBER 4, 1863

	Senate	House of Delegates	Vote for Comptroller			1859 total vote for Comptroller
			Unconditional Union GOLDSBOROUGH	Union MAFFITT	Total	
Northern Counties						
Allegany	Emancipation	Emancipation	3,162	1,013	4,175	4,508
Baltimore	Pledged to Convention	Emancipation	2,785	474	3,259	6,947
Carroll	Emancipation	Pledged to Convention	1,617	1,912	3,529	4,733
Cecil	Emancipation	Emancipation	2,231	1,556	3,787	4,024
Frederick	For Convention*	Emancipation	3,985	751	4,736	7,422
Harford	Emancipation	Emancipation	1,173	326	1,499	3,738
Washington	Emancipation*	Emancipation	3,362	65	3,427	5,712
Total:			18,315	6,097	24,412	37,084
Southern Counties						
Anne Arundel	Union*	Democrat & Slavery	561	1,141	1,702	2,222
Calvert	Democrat & Slavery*	Democrat & Slavery	86	692	778	908
Charles	Democrat & Slavery*	Democrat & Slavery	41	479	520	1,170
Howard	Emancipation	Union	472	443	915	1,615
Montgomery	Union*	Democrat & Slavery	769	960	1,729	2,516
Prince George's	Union*	Democrat & Slavery	140	1,039	1,179	1,833
St. Mary's	Democrat & Slavery*	Democrat & Slavery	270	737	1,007	1,413
Total:			2,339	5,491	7,830	11,677
Eastern Shore Counties						
Caroline	Union*	Emancipation	868	469	1,337	1,614
Dorchester	Emancipation	Emancipation	773	864	1,637	2,413
Kent	Pledged to Convention	Union	286	785	1,071	1,608
Queen Anne's	Union	Union	328	540	868	1,873
Somerset	Union*	Democrat & Slavery	350	700	1,050	2,938
Talbot	Emancipation	Emancipation	672	39	711	1,696
Worcester	Emancipation	Emancipation	1,267	528	1,795	2,817
Total:			4,544	3,925	8,469	14,959

Baltimore City	Emancipation	Emancipation	Emancipation
10,942	368	11,310	23,453
Grand Total: 36,140	15,881	52,021	87,173

The 1863 comptroller vote as a percentage of the 1859 tally showed:

Eastern Shore	56.6%
Southern Maryland	67.1%
Northern Maryland	65.8%
Baltimore City	48.2%
Average	60.0%

	Senate	House
Emancipation	10	47
Pledged to Convention	2	5
Union, unpledged	6	4
Democrat & Slavery	3	18
Total:	21	74

NOTES FOR TABLE D

* Senate Seats held by virtue of a previous election. Men pledged to a convention were more conservative than immediate emancipationists but could be rallied on to vote for a public referendum on a Constitutional Convention. Without the convention there could be no abolition.

Sources. This legislative break-down is supported by an analysis in *Baltimore American,* November 12, 1863. The Goldsborough-Maffit results are based primarily on the Baltimore *Sun,* November 13, 1863, with reference also to the *Baltimore American* of the same date. As the official totals showed Goldsborough getting 36,360 votes and Maffit 15,984 (announced in *Baltimore American,* November 20, 1863), it is obvious that there are slight discrepancies in the figures listed here. Nonetheless, the relativity of the various tallies, which is the important factor, is clear.

The vote in the 1859 election is recorded in James Wingate, *The Maryland Register for 1860–61* (Baltimore, 1860), p. 8 (back of book).

The stronghold of the slave power thus was shattered, but in the upheaval arbitrary power and corruption had shaken democratic traditions. Without federal interference the Maryland Senate, based on inequitable representation, might have been won by the pro-slavery men. Thus did the election mingle the elements of the lofty and the profane as it heralded a political revolution of great impact upon social and economic life.

Nor can the vital role of the war be forgotten. Had it been brief and less costly in lives and material, the emancipation movement could never have achieved success in that era, either in the nation or in Maryland. Necessity drove men to positions they formerly scorned, forcing people to trample upon their most cherished customs and prejudices.

Lincoln sensed the hand of God in the violence that purchased freedom for all men. Winter Davis thought about it too. Neither man questioned the fury of an Old Testament God. They accepted His awesome majesty and acted their roles as their vision guided them.

CHAPTER XII

THE SHIFTING STRUGGLE FOR POLITICAL POWER

THE ELECTION WAS over but not the tumult. The fundamental right of a democracy—free elections—had been subverted, and conservative Union leaders were not going to let the people forget it. They carried their attack into legislative chambers, executive offices, and courtrooms, striking particularly hard at John Frazier, Jr., and the irregularities in Somerset County.

Off went the interminable delegations to Washington. Montgomery Blair took Crisfield's written report of election abuses to the Executive Mansion and asked Lincoln's prompt consideration.[1] The President complied, saying that any officer who appeared to have violated or exceeded orders would be called to account.[2] But only in the case of Captain Charles C. Moore was a trial ordered.

Brigadier General Daniel Tyler headed the three-man commission that heard the case. John W. Crisfield, Captain Moore, and Levin D. Collier were among those testifying. Crisfield predicted a "whitewashing."[3] From his point of view, he was right. The commission found Moore not guilty of the two charges specified: (1) transcending Orders No. 53 by arresting the election judges and (2) "hindering Arthur Crisfield from voting."[4]

In order to gain more legal evidence to show the legislature and

[1] Montgomery Blair to Abraham Lincoln, November 11, 1863, Lincoln Collection, Vol. 131.

[2] Abraham Lincoln to Montgomery Blair, November 11, 1863, *Lincoln Works*, VII, 9 and Lincoln Collection, Vol. 131.

[3] John W. Crisfield to Governor Bradford, November 30, 1863, Bradford Papers.

[4] See Military Commission Report upon Captain Charles C. Moore's Conduct and Committee on Military Affairs and the Militia, *Report on Military Interference at Elections*, U.S. Senate Rep. No. 14, 38th Cong., 1st Sess. Captain Moore died a prisoner of war on August 31, 1864. *Lincoln Works*, VII, 197.

the public, Crisfield was advised by Montgomery Blair to contest for his seat.[5] Crisfield agreed. He lacked personal desire for the fight but knew more was involved.[6] The dignity of Maryland and the rights of its citizens had been affronted. His memorial to the House of Representatives, however, left that body unmoved. Creswell was not molested. Winter Davis and his allies had threatened to end the Administration majority if any seat were vacated on grounds of military interference.[7]

In the United States Senate the Maryland election got attention from the Committee on Military Affairs and the Militia, which declared it could not find in the First Congressional District the slightest evidence that the military authority exerted "any undue influence." Schenck's Order No. 53 won praise for its honesty of purpose and fairness of execution. As to Governor Bradford's "inflammatory" proclamation, it was likened almost to a declaration of war against federal troops. The governor should have been grateful for "the moderation which arrested its [the proclamation's] circulation instead of its author."[8]

Senator Lazarus W. Powell of Kentucky took an opposite tack. He accused federal officials of violating the Constitution in the loyal border states by prescribing qualifications for voters and candidates. The President shared in the blame. Powell said, "I brush away the trash and come right to the Commander-in-Chief himself, and charge him . . . with trampling under foot the . . . right of free suffrage."[9]

Reverdy Johnson entered the fray by condemning the means employed for Creswell's victory. He did so while admitting a personal preference for Creswell over Crisfield.[10] Johnson later exhorted, "In the name of freedom, . . . save us from the rule of military despotism."[11]

---

[5] Montgomery Blair to Governor Bradford, November 11. 1863, Bradford Papers. Crisfield also asked the opinion of the governor, for without his help he would not contest. See his letters of November 14 and 30, 1863, to the governor (Bradford Papers).

[6] John W. Crisfield to Governor Bradford, November 14, 1863, Bradford Papers.

[7] H. Winter Davis to Samuel F. DuPont, March 5, 1864, S. F. DuPont Papers.

[8] U.S. Senate *Report on Military Interference at Elections*, pp. 22 and 30. The report also considered elections in Kentucky, Missouri, and Delaware.

[9] *Congressional Globe*, 38th Cong., 1st Sess., Vol. 34, Part 4, Appendix, p. 62. See also p. 57. Senator Powell also charged that the army had no legal right to suppress domestic violence at the polls except upon request by the state.

[10] *Ibid.*, p. 90.

[11] *Ibid.*, p. 3193. The southern sympathizing Benjamin G. Harris went further in the

Enough senators shared his feelings to approve a bill prohibiting those in the service of the United States from using troops in an election except "to repel the armed enemies of the United States or to keep peace at the polls."[12] It passed on June 22 by a vote of 19 to 13, with both senators from Maryland in the affirmative. The bill became law early the following year.

Meanwhile Lincoln listened to pleas for ousting John Frazier, Jr. In one delegation was George Vickers, who, though impressed by the President's "frank and honest impulses," complained of his lack of independence and "moral firmness."[13] For why else did Lincoln fail to dismiss Frazier at once?

The radicals agreed to this character judgment because they too mistook Lincoln's agile balancing of opposing political forces as weakness. Winter Davis referred to "Lincoln's half and half constitution"[14] and more than once went to the President on behalf of Frazier.

Davis' and Creswell's persistence helped win a suspension of Lincoln's order to remove Frazier.[15] This did not please all of Creswell's adherents. Many Unconditional Unionists lacked confidence in Frazier. One of them called him "small potatoes" and warned Creswell that identification with the captain would destroy his future locally.[16]

Frazier countered with messages extolling himself and attacking his enemies. He baited one of his pleas to Creswell with the promise of "a private champagne supper" if the congressman got him released.[17]

House of Representatives. He charged "Right after right has been taken from us . . ." and added, "I tell you, sir, we will not stand it much longer. The men who . . . shall further assail that great right, will see ere long the ballot-boxes baptized in blood—a baptism that may be necessary to wash away the foul stains of tyranny and oppression." *Ibid.*, Part 3, p. 2194.

[12] *Ibid.*, Part 4, p. 3192.

[13] George Vickers to Governor Bradford, December 15, 1863, Bradford Papers.

[14] Henry Winter Davis to Rear Admiral Samuel F. DuPont, December 5, 1863, S. F. DuPont Papers. F. DuPont Papers.

[15] Samuel T. Hopkins to John A. J. Creswell, December 10, 1863, Creswell papers, III.

[16] J. H. Emerson to John A. J. Creswell, January 11, 1864, Creswell Papers, IV. Emerson was a newspaperman who held the office of an assistant assessor for United States Internal Revenue.

[17] John Frazier, Jr., to John A. J. Creswell, November 23, 1863, Creswell Papers, III. Frazier also asked that the *Kent News* be suppressed and its editors exiled for printing a "scurrilous" article about him. This action, said Frazier, would kill Copperheadism on the Eastern Shore. See John Frazier, Jr., to Henry Winter Davis, November 30, 1863, Creswell Papers, III.

The enticement failed. On February 15 a presidential order revoked Frazier's appointment.[18] The coveted office then went to William James Leonard, a resident of Salisbury, Somerset County, and recent commander of the Purnell Legion.[19]

A prime political plum, this provost marshal's post provided only one of many jobs at issue after the 1863 election. The patronage struggle was endless, both in military and civilian appointments. Regimental commands more than once became battlegrounds between the radicals and their more conservative opponents.[20] Custom house and deputy provost marshal positions generated quarrels, and of course the Post Office was not above politics. Conflict occurred within factions as well as between them. That old nemesis of Somerset County conservatives, Levin D. Collier, was accused of drunkenness and showing favoritism to the Salisbury area. One of his aides at the November election sought to replace him.[21]

Newspapers too slipped into the ring of patronage seeking. The *Baltimore Clipper* offered to sell Montgomery Blair a two year control of its political sentiment. Five thousand dollars plus government advertising and printing for Maryland was the requested fee along with the salary of the editor and any assistant. In addition, the proposal obligated the Post Office to help increase the circulation of the *Clipper*. The plan never achieved realization, but it created a furor in March, 1864.[22]

Such an offer lent support to Winter Davis' charge that newspapers are "money making machines, not Light Houses for public ben-

---

[18] *Ibid.*, John Frazier, Jr., to John A. J. Creswell, February 19, 1864, VI, and March 12, 1864, VII.

[19] *Baltimore County Advocate*, February 27, 1864.

[20] For example, Lt. Colonel C. C. Tevis not only survived attempts to dismiss him but also won promotion to colonel of a Maryland cavalry regiment. Tevis' glory, however, was short lived. In the summer of 1864 he was discharged for the good of the service. See numerous letters in the Executive Letterbook for November–December, 1863; Adjutant-General Papers (Hall of Records); and A. W. Bradford to R. Johnson, April 2, 1864, Reverdy Johnson papers.

[21] See George Russum to John A. J. Creswell, February 23, 1864, Creswell Papers, VI; Henry C. McCoy to John A. J. Creswell, March 19, 1864, and Henry C. McCoy to John Frazier, Jr., March 19, 1864, *Ibid.*, VII.

[22] The *Clipper's* proposal, dated April 10, 1863, was published on March 18, 1864, in the *Baltimore American*. An indignant *Clipper* attacked Henry W. Hoffman for revealing the letter. On March 21, 1864, it likened him to a jackal and a parasite.

efit. . . . they are mean and selfish and will do nothing for justice."[23] Nor would they, in most cases, do anything for Winter Davis. But then Davis did much for himself.

He advocated Donn Piatt as the man to carry on Schenck's policy as commander of the Middle Department.[24] Judge Bond agreed, but the President refused. He explained, "Schenck and Piatt are good fellows, and if there were any rotten apples in the barrel they'd be sure to hook 'em out. But they run their machine on too high a level for me. They never could understand that I was boss."[25]

The prospect of Piatt's promotion kindled hardly any enthusiasm among those Marylanders still smarting from the excesses of the previous military administration. In fact, many Unionists wanted Piatt ordered out of Baltimore. They eventually got their wish. Piatt was indignant. He offered his resignation. These Maryland people, he said, have "been too much for me. But thank God I do not live by their consent and will survive their efforts."[26]

The strongest candidate among the conservative and moderate Unionists for Schenck's old job seemed to be Brigadier General Erastus Barnard Tyler, but he did not get it. On December 5, 1863, Schenck relinquished command to Brigadier General Henry H. Lockwood, the top ranking officer left in the department. Lockwood promptly announced that his views upon the government agreed with Schenck's and warned that retribution would be exacted for all disloyal acts.[27]

Winter Davis must have doubted his profession, for he privately heaped great scorn upon Lockwood. Deeply annoyed over not getting Piatt the appointment, Davis appeared vengeful. On January 25 he talked at length with Lincoln, again asking for Piatt, or at least Brigadier General William Birney. Davis was in a bad humor and Lincoln more than ordinarily blunt in his refusal.[28] The Presi-

[23] H. Winter Davis to Rear Admiral Samuel F. DuPont, April 27, 1864, S. F. DuPont Papers.

[24] *Ibid.*, H. Winter Davis to Rear Admiral Samuel F. DuPont, December 5, 1863.

[25] Donn Piatt, *Memories of the Men Who Saved the Union* (New York, 1887), p. 46.

[26] Donn Piatt to Joseph Holt, February 26 and March 5, 1864, Joseph Holt Papers, Library of Congress.

[27] General Orders No. 67, Middle Department, 8th Army Corps, December 5, 1863, *Official Records*, Series 1, XXIX, Part II, 548.

[28] Montgomery Blair to Governor Bradford, November 6, 1863, Bradford Papers.

dent said he regarded Maryland affairs as a personal quarrel, in which he would not intervene to help one side vent its spite on the other. Davis at once picked up his hat and walked out. He considered the President's remark of such a nature as to prevent further conversation.

When cousin David Davis, now a Supreme Court justice, came the next day with news that Lincoln wanted to be friendly, Winter Davis replied that he had been insulted. He called the President "thoroughly Blairized" and warned that this helped assure a successful coalition of Blair men and Maryland secessionists. Should this happen, Winter Davis determined that Lincoln would not get Maryland's electoral vote in 1864.[29]

Meanwhile, Montgomery Blair continued prodding Bradford. In November, 1863, he vainly urged the governor to call a special session of the legislature. Such initiative would help deflate "the more ambitious emancipationists,"[30] a particularly desirable result because the radicals were considering their own presidential party to exploit popular sentiment against slavery. They intended using it to convert the war into a struggle to subjugate the South and disfranchise "our people." This, warned Blair, placed the very character of both the Constitution and the government at stake.[31]

Though Bradford failed to heed Blair's plea, he did obeisance to the new era. Early in January, 1864, he announced, "I believe today, as I have done for years, that if we had long ago provided for the gradual emancipation of the slaves of the State, we should now be" far more prosperous. He called for "immediate measures" to remove slavery.[32] One journal sarcastically referred to how carefully these views had been hidden from the public.[33] A Democratic legislator was even less kind. He quoted Bradford's inaugural address in which the governor likened the emancipation movement to treason.[34]

[29] H. Winter Davis to Rear Admiral Samuel F. DuPont, January 28, 1864, S. F. DuPont Papers.

[30] Montgomery Blair to Governor Bradford, November 6, 1863, Bradford Papers.

[31] *Ibid.*, Montgomery Blair to Governor Bradford, November 11, 1863. Though he did not say it directly, Blair obviously saw the quarrel in Maryland as an integral part of the national struggle.

[32] These remarks were made in Governor Bradford's message to the General Assembly in January, 1864. The address was printed, among other places, in *Baltimore American*, January 8, 1864.

[33] *Cambridge Democrat*, January 13, 1864.

[34] Daniel Clarke of Prince George's County was the legislator. See *Baltimore American*, January 29, 1864.

The governor was not the only one forced to make an awkward peace with the rapidly changing political scene. The Union State Central Committee faced a similar problem. It convened on December 16 at Temperance Temple in Baltimore with the city and ten counties represented. Swann talked at length. Public opinion, he said, had decreed an end to slavery. To talk of gradual emancipation was profitless. The master could no longer control his slaves. But Swann did not forget those who were unable to wrench themselves free from the past. For them he softened his position by proposing some system of apprenticeship to guard against too sudden a change in the system of labor. This two-part recommendation Swann embodied in a set of resolutions that included support of federal compensation.[35] The resolutions were approved along with others of an anti-slavery nature offered by John Pendleton Kennedy.

The committee's action surprised a number of conservative Unionists. As one Eastern Shoreman put it, the turn-about "has created quite a fluttering among their friends here."[36] He shrewdly opined that the conservatives were trying to outrace the opposition.

One paper saw the conservatives' "spasmodic jerk" as part of the campaign to elect Hicks to the United States Senate and warned that if the people of Maryland placed their trust in Kennedy, Swann, Hicks, Price, and their ilk, they would be cheated.[37] The *Civilian and Telegraph*, on the other hand, hailed the supposed healing of the Union Party schism and, as if to emphasize harmony, labeled Hicks, Swann, and Kennedy along with Winter Davis as "far-seeing statesmen."[38] Probably no one was more pleased than Montgomery Blair. On December 18 he wrote Lincoln, "You will see by the Balt paper of this morning that our political rear guard in Md. have come out flat footed . . . for immediate Emancipation."[39]

Chase also followed the actions of the Central Committee. He

[35] *Baltimore American*, December 18, 1863; *Proceedings of the Union State Central Committee . . . December 16, 1863* (Baltimore, 1863); *Baltimore Clipper*, December 18, 1863. Former Know-Nothing Swann also repeated the theme about foreign immigrants, now considered desirable, being unwilling to settle in the presence of slavery.

[36] Thomas Timmons to John A. J. Creswell, December 23, 1863, Creswell Papers, IV.

[37] *Cecil Whig*, December 26, 1863.

[38] *Civilian and Telegraph*, December 24, 1863.

[39] Montgomery Blair to Abraham Lincoln, December 18, 1863, Lincoln Collection, Vol. 135.

apparently did not like his friend Swann's apprenticeship proposal. This prompted the ever politic former mayor to temporize. In a letter to Chase on December 27, Swann explained the wisdom of his course. He would have lost influence with the men he wished to win if he had moved initially in a more summary fashion. This might have prolonged the turmoil over slavery.[40]

Swann had a remarkable capacity never to find himself in error. His correspondence hinted at no self-doubt. He exhibited an adeptness at shifting, sidestepping, and straddling any and all issues as political positions changed. Confronting the rapidly brewing storm over emancipation, he shifted his position just in time.

Winter Davis would have none of such tactics. He took a position and damned all who disagreed. Even radical Chase endured criticism. Perhaps Davis knew of Chase's contacts with Swann. Chase might profess well, but, according to Davis, he "practices poorly." Like Lincoln, Chase wanted "to keep in with both sides and play his game for power"; but Davis warned, "They *can't* be friends with me and my enemies at once."[41]

About this time Davis' friends were having troubles. Success allowed an element of disagreement to creep into their camp. Out of crowded Annapolis came word of an impending battle over the General Assembly Speakership between two allies of Davis, William J. Jones of Cecil County and Henry S. Stockbridge of Baltimore City.[42] The rivalry proved disastrous to the radicals.

Thomas H. Kemp, recent Caroline County prosecuting attorney, got the office of Speaker. Though he ran on the Goldsborough ticket, he was basically conservative as was John S. Sellman, who won the presidency of the state senate. The radicals had to settle for the chairmanship of two important committees.[43]

Early in the session the General Assembly picked a United States

[40] Thomas Swann to Salmon P. Chase, December 27, 1863, Chase Papers, Historical Society of Pennsylvania. The Unconditional Union State Central Committee, on the other hand, struck at the apprenticeship provision and blasted its protagonists for cheating on the word "immediate" as applied to emancipation. See *Baltimore American*, January 26, 1864.

[41] H. Winter Davis to Rear Admiral Samuel F. DuPont, December 31, 1863, S. F. DuPont papers.

[42] *Baltimore American*, January 7, 1864.

[43] *Cecil Whig*, January 16, 1864. The House Ways and Means chairmanship went to William J. Jones and the Senate Committee on Finance to Archibald Stirling, Jr.

senator from the Eastern Shore to fill the late Senator Pearce's unexpired term. Judge Thomas A. Spence, an unequivocal Unconditional Unionist, went into the contest with strong newspaper and political support, but his candidacy fizzled in the Union caucus of January 6. The incumbent, Thomas H. Hicks, galloped to victory with 47 votes. The *Baltimore American* tried to explain the lopsided margin as an expression of detestation for Winter Davis,[44] while another journalist saw as an important factor a well-timed letter from Hicks expressing strong support of emancipation.[45] The General Assembly ratified the result on the 8th.

Although most of the legislators were pledged to emancipation, they gave Maryland Unconditional Unionists many an anxious moment. Differences of opinion appeared over the methods and timing of achieving the coveted goal. Some doubt loomed as to how a bill would fare in the Senate. One observer commented that the General Assembly seemed "a little *squeamish* upon the *Nigger* yet."[46]

Obstructionist tactics so hindered progress that at one point it was feared the Constitutional Convention Bill would be lost.[47] A substitute bill was introduced that would have postponed the convention two to four years.[48] These shenanigans goaded the Unconditional Union State Central Committee into publicly attacking the weak-kneed and wavering, some of whom were accused of being distracted by concern for local offices.

Montgomery Blair was equally disturbed by this hesitancy. He pleaded to Bradford, "For gods sake help our friends to get the convention bill through this week and prevent them from dividing." The bill, he added, must include some provision for the prevention of traitors' votes so that the military will have no excuse for intervening. Success would "complete the sweep of Davis & co."[49]

The obstructionists did not readily give ground. One of them

[44] *Baltimore American*, January 9, 1864.

[45] *Baltimore County Advocate*, January 16, 1864.

[46] Daniel Blocksum to John A. J. Creswell, January 22, 1864, Creswell Papers, II.

[47] *Baltimore American*, January 26, 1864, and *Easton Gazette*, February 6, 1864. The Unconditional Union State Central Committee noted that most of the counties ran candidates "not made by us, but adopted at the hands of Conventions which acquiesced in our principles with little earnestness. . . ."

[48] *Baltimore American*, January 20, 1864.

[49] Quotations from Montgomery Blair to Governor Bradford, January 26, 1864, Bradford Papers.

decried striking at private property, for it was "the bulwark of civil liberty"[50]—liberty, that is, for the white master. A legislator from Prince George's county, Daniel Clarke, let it be known that slaveholders cherished their principles too much ever to change them, but he did believe a congressional appropriation of $20,000,000 would win support for a Constitutional Convention. The money, however, must not be regarded as a bribe but rather as a contract for the yielding of property.[51]

In so speaking Clarke demonstrated that the oligarchy had lost none of its twisted and sanctimonious morality. How these men loved to hide their own avarice while pointing to the greed of their northern brethren! If they possessed all of the principle they claimed, certainly they would not have reached for a congressional appropriation once denounced by them as unconstitutional. The real, unstated principle of their creed was to cling tenaciously to all of the power, possessions, and prestige they had so long held. They tried to reject the reality of the revolutionary movement affecting the state and nation. This kept the slave owners so far in the rear of the changing times that they never got close enough to grasp the dollars they wanted.

Speaker Kemp also offered a plan—one more modest than Clarke's. His resolutions denied the right of unrecompensed emancipation and asked for a Congressional appropriation of $10,000,000. The proposals struck Stockbridge as "insulting to the Government."[52] They were defeated by a 37 to 31 vote.

Stockbridge pleaded the cause of the Unconditional Union Convention Bill, which he authored. He pointed to the shackles by which slavery bound white as well as black, shackles that inhibited free discussion and legislative action, shackles that tolerated no challenge to her claim of infallibility. The Baltimorean directed his colleagues' attention to a letter from the son of a former slaveholder. It gave another reason for emancipation—one not often stated. Slavery should be abolished in Maryland because "*it is right*. Right between man and man—right before God."[53]

The Convention Bill passed by a vote of 45 to 17 and a similar one got through the Senate by a 13 to 2 vote on the same day,

[50] *Baltimore American*, January 29, 1864.

[51] *Ibid*. Clarke estimated the value of slaves in Maryland at the beginning of the war at $40,000,000. A more frequent estimate was $30,000,000.

[52] *Ibid*., February 22 and March 1, 1864.

[53] *Ibid.,* January 29, 1864.

January 28. Differences between the two versions went to a conference committee. The new interpretation passed both houses on February 9 by votes similar to those of the preceding month.[54]

In this final form the bill became law. It provided for an election to be held on the first Wednesday in April to decide for or against a Constitutional Convention. To speed its convening, the voters would simultaneously select delegates, the same in numbers as there were seats in the General Assembly. Each of the ninety-six victorious candidates must swear to an iron-bound oath of past and future loyalty before assuming office.[55] Voters, if challenged on grounds of disloyalty, would also have to take an oath, though its wording was not specified.

Some of Bradford's recommendations to the legislature found their way into the law.[56] Ballots had to be on white paper, thereby restoring the secrecy that had been stripped away by the radicals' yellow tickets of November, 1863. Then there was the problem of the governor's inability to withhold certificates of election despite allegations of fraud and military interference. The law forced him to declare elected the persons the county clerks reported with the most votes.[57] The Convention Bill struck at this defect—in keeping with Bradford's suggestions. The new law required judges of election to notify the governor if an uninvited United States armed force appeared at the polls and interfered in the election. In this event the governor must order a new election for the troubled district.

[54] *Ibid.*, January 29 and February 10, 1864; Baltimore *Sun*, January 29, 1864. One senator "felt empowered to say, . . . that the President . . . was ready, so soon as the Legislature showed a disposition to give up Slavery, to take us by the hand . . . in favor of compensation. . . ." *Baltimore American*, January 21, 1864

[55] Among the places where the Convention Bill can be found is *The Debates of the Constitutional Convention of the State of Maryland . . . 1864* (Annapolis, 1864), pp. 22–24.

[56] In his address to the legislature (*Baltimore American*, January 8, 1864), Bradford charged the army with "stifling the freedom of election in a faithful State, intimidating its sworn officers, violating the constitutional rights of its loyal citizens, and obstructing the usual channels of communications between them and their executive." He blamed General Orders No. 53 more on unnamed instigators than on Schenck. After the election Schenck and Bradford endeavored to re-establish rapport. See Charles Findlay to Governor Bradford, November 7, 1863, Bradford Papers.

[57] Reverdy Johnson wrote this opinion to Governor Bradford on November 23, 1863, Executive Papers. In the General Assembly some legislators tried to throw out the election of various Somerset County officials but were stymied by a combination of Democrats and Unconditional Unionists.

Conservative Unionists were pleased about this action against military interference, which would have been omitted if the lower house had had its way. On the other hand, radicals were disappointed by the failure to require a strict oath of allegiance of all voters. Even the *Baltimore American* complained of the bill's wording, seeing in the law "pits and dead-falls" concocted by the manipulators of slavery to catch the unwary.[58]

Further dissatisfaction arose over the failure to pass a law to allow soldiers to vote in the field. Nor did the legislature abolish the Black Code or reapportion seats in the lower house. It did, however, repeal the prohibition against manumission. All these acts and failures to act faded into secondary significance before the important fact that a Convention Bill had been approved that provided the means for rapidly destroying slavery.

[58] *Baltimore American*, March 12, 1864.

CHAPTER XIII

ANOTHER VICTORY
AT THE POLLS

MEN DEBATED PUBLICLY. They also wrestled inwardly over the changing status of the Negro. Old associations and habits of thinking vied with changing circumstances and new insights. The sight of Negro troops generated disgust within a white man on one occasion and stirred respect within that same person on another. Unprecedented events in the life of the Negro were constantly occurring, causing the white man to react.

Take, for instance, an event that appalled Governor Bradford less than a month before the spring, 1864 election. A lieutenant colonel, having heard of some Negroes imprisoned in Prince George's County because they had run away or helped others to do so, ordered their release on condition they would enlist. Upon entering the jail, the officer confronted eight Negroes chained to a staple. Each leg was encased by a manacle, riveted into place with a hammer and anvil while still hot. If the officer's sense of sight was offended, his sense of smell was also. The atmosphere of the place was foul, "the filth and stench . . . utterly inhuman."[1] Many of the slaves, some of whose masters were in the rebel service, had lived in the jail since the outbreak of the war. One woman had a child born there nearly two years before.[2]

Appalled by such conditions, the lieutenant colonel allowed women and boys as well as the males to escape. Their release from a stinking prison seemed just to some, but others called it a jail delivery of criminals, an arbitrary exercise of military power, for among the fu-

[1] Lieutenant Colonel Joseph Perkins to Colonel S. M. Bowman, March 28, 1864, Executive Papers. The jail delivery took place on March 9, 1864.

[2] Lieutenant D. B. Holmes to Colonel S. M. Bowman, April 5, 1864, Executive Papers.

gitives were persons charged with crimes ranging from attempted poisoning and larceny to the abducting of slaves.[3]

The issues of property rights, state-federal relations, and racial antagonisms were involved in this case as in the whole area of slave enlistments. Many feared that the uniform conferred upon the Negro too much citizenship, with its overtones of social and political equality. Yet soldiers must be had, and the slaves provided a large reservoir of manpower. Necessity dictated the suspension of old taboos.

From the Eastern Shore came the call for recruiting squads to induct the local Negroes and make a draft unnecessary. A draft, said politician Thomas Timmons, would "be fatal to our prospects, *particularly when its so easily avoidable.*"[4] The soldiers co-operated, on occasion exceeding their authority.

Charges rumbled across Maryland that the physically unfit were freed along with women and children. In Talbot and Dorchester counties Negro soldiers reportedly forced off farms both free Negroes and slaves. A Negro commanding some of the Talbot marauders gave the orders "to shoot the *white Sons of Bitches.*" He was arrested for this display of exuberance but soon gained his release.[5]

In another case a Negro detachment in Dorchester took a 50-year-old free Negro from the field. He was not allowed to go home for clothing. Plow and horses were left standing. This man left behind five motherless children with no one to provide for them.[6]

The chief of Negro recruiting denied that force was ever used, but his statement directly contradicted an earlier admission that in many cases he had compelled Negroes to volunteer. Less subject to incon-

---

[3] The county sheriff was thwarted and threatened with violence as he unsuccessfully sought to regain the fugitives. Governor Bradford protested to Lincoln, asking for punishment of the transgressors and an order to prevent a recurrence. See Edward W. Belt, States Attorney of Prince Georges County, to Governor Bradford, March 15, 1864, and Governor Bradford to Abraham Lincoln, March 16, 1864, Executive Papers. The day before Bradford wrote this letter, General Orders No. 11 was issued by the Middle Department to enlist all Negroes in "jails, slave-pens, or other places of confinement, . . . if passed by the surgeon . . . ," willing to enlist, and not "held under criminal process." *Official Records*, Series I, Vol. 33, pp. 680–81.

[4] Thomas Timmons to John A. J. Creswell, January 26, 1864, Creswell Papers, V. The draft ordered for March 10 was suspended.

[5] H. M. Nicols to Governor Bradford, March 14, 1864, Executive Papers.

[6] Thomas King Carroll to A. W. Bradford, May 9, 1864, Executive Letterbook. Bradford vouched for Carroll's reliability in a letter to Lincoln, May 12, 1864, Executive Letterbook.

sistency was the assertion that well-dressed and armed Negro troops, accompanied by a band or fife and drum, produced the most successful recruiting. Meanwhile, the strong opposition to Negro soldiers collapsed. In fact Birney claimed that some owners were trying to foist upon him aged, handicapped, and unprofitable slaves.[7]

Loyal owners on occasion encountered difficulties in getting paid. Their problems were complicated by some slaves who posed as free Negroes in order to get a larger bounty. Recruiting also involved hiring substitutes and paying bounties to volunteers so that the quota could be reached. Not only did the state, counties, and Baltimore compete for men, but there were even instances of individual city wards raising money for bounties. Then there were brokers, sometimes arrested, who tried to recruit substitutes for another state.[8]

These problems of enlistments and race harassed the politicians, but they did not forget one of the delights of their trade—composing slates for the April election. In Baltimore County the Union Party was dominated by an element too conservative for the tastes of the more radically disposed. Yet the latter allowed the county ticket to stand unopposed. Resolutions had been passed by the local convention sufficiently unconditional in tone to rob the radicals of any great issue. Of even greater moment was the memory of the radical debacle in November, 1863, and a fear that a split Union vote would give the Copperheads a victory. Archibald Stirling, Jr., told Creswell

[7] William Birney to an unnamed member of the House of Delegates, January 19, 1864, *Annapolis Gazette,* January 28, 1864; William Birney to Adj. Gen. U.S. Army, January 26, 1864 and Colonel S. M. Bowman to Lt. Colonel Lawrence, AAG, April 29, May 11, and June 6, 1864, Elon A. Woodward (compiler), "The Negro in the Military Service of the United States," National Archives. Samuel M. Bowman, Birney's successor in Maryland, wrote Brig. General Lorenzo Thomas on July 23, 1864 (*Ibid,* Woodward) that "we revolutionized the state." He also noted that the troublesome interference with Negro recruiting by prejudiced army officers and white Maryland soldiers had been eliminated.

[8] The newly enacted $4,000,000 Maryland Bounty Bill sought to encourage volunteering by supplementing federal and county grants. A re-enlisting veteran could get $925 from city, state, and U.S. funds if he re-enlisted in Baltimore. A new recruit got less. A slave received $100 from the state. Competition tended to draw men from one area to fill the quota of another. This on occasion created havoc and worried politicians who wanted to be sure their bailiwicks got proper credit for enlistments. Among sources of recruiting information are Baltimore *Sun,* February 8, 1864; *Baltimore American*, February 8 and August 6, 1864; and *Baltimore Clipper,* February 11, 1864. See also Record Group 94, Adjutant General's Office, U.S. Colored Troops, National Archives.

that "our special friends cant carry it alone."[9] Matters here had to be carefully managed, and so they did elsewhere in the state.

Caroline County required money and the vote of its soldiers if victory were to be won. But even $3,000 would not save the emancipationists if the conservatives coalesced and no military intervention or arrests took place.[10] At least so figured George Russum, who perhaps took a dim view in order to loosen the purse strings. Some greenbacks did arrive, but Creswell's agent refused to hand over $1,000 until election eve in order to protect the money against being lent or stolen.[11]

The radicals dominated the Union Party in Caroline, but in a number of areas the conservatives held sway. In some places both factions put up slates. Dorchester County experienced just such a schism. All chances of settling differences looked hopeless until on March 19 the Cambridge *Intelligencer* announced the withdrawal of the two Union tickets. This accompanied the call for a new county convention, which picked two candidates from each of the old slates.[12]

In Kent County the Union split was too great to be bridged. Profiting by it were the Democrats, who tried to rally all persons opposed to "the Abolition party."[13] Victory seemed within their grasp. Radical John Frazier, Jr., did not dread the prospect, for he believed the election results would end division in the Union Party. Some of the conservative leaders would join the Democrats, while the masses would adhere to the Unconditional line.[14]

---

[9] Archibald Stirling, Jr. to John A. J. Creswell, February [no day given], 1864, Creswell Papers, VI.

[10] George M. Russum to John A. J. Creswell, March 15, 1864, Creswell Papers, VII. Russum asked, "Can't we have a few arrests made of sundry gentlemen if it should be necessary?"

[11] A. J. Willis to John A. J. Creswell, April 22, 1864, Creswell Papers, VIII.

[12] Levin E. Straughn to John A. J. Creswell, March 8, 1864, Creswell Papers, VI; *Baltimore American*, March 21 and April 1, 1864. The new Convention was called of "all persons 'in favor of Emancipation and opposed to State Compensation'. . . ."

[13] *Chestertown Transcript*, February 27 and March 5, 1864.

[14] John Frazier, Jr., to John A. J. Creswell, March 21 and March 24, 1864, Creswell papers, VII. In the waning days of the campaign the two Union factions in Somerset County harmonized. See *ibid.,* John Dix to Creswell, March 23, 1864 and Henry C. McCoy to Creswell, March 29, 1864. The Queen Anne's County Unconditional Unionists held a convention but left the field to the Conservative Unionists (*Baltimore American*, March 21, 1864). The exact opposite occurred in Harford County (*Cecil Democrat*, April 2, 1864). In Cecil County both wings of the party endorsed the call for the Union county

Lincoln took a far dimmer view of such differences. He feared that "jealousies, rivalries, and consequent ill-blows" among the emancipationists would defeat their objective.[15] All who favored abolition in any form should co-operate, he believed. Though personally feeling that gradual emancipation would create fewer problems, he willingly yielded to those who sought an immediate end to slavery. Maryland emancipation he considered a question of national importance. It would help end the rebellion.[16]

Resurgent Democrats worked against Lincoln's purposes. In Cecil they gathered in county convention, selected a slate, and urged the Democratic members of the General Assembly to summon a state convention.[17] The legislators did act. They joined with their compatriots from all parts of Maryland and determined to fight a vigorous campaign.[18] A group was formed that eventually merged into a reborn state central committee. Committees were appointed for the counties and Baltimore to awaken the people. Diversity of views, however, paralyzed the one in Baltimore and reduced it to ineffectiveness.[19]

The Democrats did not place a ticket before the public in every political jurisdiction, but they consistently opposed a constitutional convention, believing a fair election impossible under present circumstances. The passions of war rather than the interests of Maryland would be reflected in the convention. Its members, feared the Democrats, would incorporate in the new constitution the political disabilities that had already been imposed by the legislature and the army.[20]

The Democrats used every conceivable argument, valid or fanciful, to attack the Constitutional Convention. While the emancipationists glowingly predicted rising land values that would compen-

---

convention, while in rebel-sympathizing St. Mary's County only one Unionist bothered to run though three seats were available (see results in *Baltimore American*, April 12, 1864).

[15] Abraham Lincoln to John A. J. Creswell, March 7, 1864, Lincoln Collection, Vol. 147.

[16] Abraham Lincoln to John A. J. Creswell, March 17, 1864, Lincoln Collection, Vol. 148.

[17] *Cecil Democrat*, March 5, 1864; *Baltimore American*, March 7, 1864. The purpose of the state convention was to pick an electoral ticket and delegates to the Democratic National Convention.

[18] George Earle to John A. J. Creswell, February 26, 1864, Creswell Papers, VI; A. Leo Knott, *A Biographical Sketch of Hon. A. Leo Knott with a Relation of some Political Transactions in Maryland, 1861–1867* (n.d., n.p.), p. 11.

[19] *The Biographical Cyclopedia of Representative Men of Maryland and District of Columbia* (Baltimore, 1879), p. 259.

[20] Knott, *A Biographical Sketch*, p. 12.

sate many slaveholders and make up for the loss of slavery as a tax source, one clever fellow asked how could the poor man buy property if its worth doubled?[21] Others talked of the expense of holding a convention and predicted sky-rocketing costs for almshouses and jails as suddenly freed Negroes became vicious, idle, and drunk. The simultaneous incitement of the working man's fear of losing his job to a Negro lacked logic but fed the worries of the insecure.[22]

Some southern Marylanders attacked the demagogues controlling public opinion in the populous free counties and worried over the threat of increased representation for that region. Asked one writer, "*Do we desire more railroads, to bring Western produce in competition with our own? Shall we dig more canals, that coal may entirely supersede our cord-wood? Do we wish to be still further taxed, that Northern Maryland may be enriched . . . ?*"[23] The *Täglicher Wecker* scoffingly rejoined that Maryland had its county rights as well as state rights Democrats.[24]

The Democrats blamed outside influence for the emancipation movement, the success of which would bring "ruin, revolution, anarchy."[25] As if this were not enough to attract the wavering, the Democrats tried to picture their rivals as favoring Negro equality. Society, said the immovable, had to have distinctions. In Maryland the Negroes provided a low caste, which was as it should be, for God created the Negro inferior and intended him "to be wisely and tenderly governed and controlled by the white man."[26] This could be achieved only through black slavery.

[21] "H. P.," "Appeal to Workers," *Cecil Democrat*, April 2, 1864.

[22] One journal (*Maryland Union*, April 7, 1864) pointed to a concern in Cincinnati that replaced striking whites with Negroes. Another paper (*Cecil Democrat*, April 2, 1864) implied that emancipation would bring to Maryland the New England industrial system, which ground the laborer "into the very dust."

[23] St. Mary's *Gazette*, cited in *Baltimore American*, March 30, 1864.

[24] *Täglicher Wecker* (Baltimore), March 30, 1864.

[25] *Chestertown Transcript*, April 2, 1864. The *Cecil Democrat* of April 2, 1864 commented, "the Democrats have ever been the true Union party of the country. They have ever been faithful to the Constitution. . . . The leading presses and politicians of the miscalled Union party, tell us that the Union cannot be restored as it was. They are revolutionists, and want a new Union, and a new Constitution. . . ."

[26] Resolution of Democratic Convention of Dorchester County, *Ægis*, April 1, 1864, and *Cecil Democrat*, March 19, 1864. One propagandist tried to frighten workers with the warning, "Poor white men think of your fate, and the fate of your children! . . . There *are* those who fear no equality with the negro; for, *fortune* puts them above it; but what

The Democrats' ultimate weapon was the old appeal to all classes of whites to rally to the cause of race purity. The *Frederick Citizen* rose to new heights of the preposterous in summoning all opponents of amalgamation to defeat the convention. It said, "If you are opposed to free-loveism, communism, agrarianism—*vote against a Convention.*"[27]

The emancipationists countered by reminding Marylanders that slave-breeders and traders in human flesh should be the last even to "*whisper*" about amalgamation."[28] One propagandist told of a master who indulged his sexual desires with his slave woman and later with a daughter by this union, and then sold his children's grandmother.[29]

Another aspect that did not escape public notice was the slave market. The *Baltimore American* said that while most masters possibly did not breed Negroes "deliberately," there were very few who would not sell their surplus or value their slaves by the rates of the Georgia traders. This business was at least as profitable as cattle breeding.[30] No wonder one county convention called slavery "a great *moral wrong*, injurious to both master and slave."[31] The *Cecil Whig* even urged a law to compel former slave owners to support their aged servants on the grounds that the latter had earned their master enough profit during their lives to justify it.[32]

Some Unconditional Unionists seethed at the inequitable assessments and unfair legislation fastened upon Maryland by the slave interests. This had cost the state dearly. Now they fought against state compensation, for it would load the state with a heavy public debt. As counterstrategy, the Democrats sought to convey the idea that state compensation and its financial burden would be inevitable if emancipation were passed.[33]

Perhaps some naïve Unionists fell for the trap, but not if the *Cecil Whig* could help it. To believe the people of the free counties would

---

will be *your* fate?" Reprinted from *Frederick Citizen* by *Chestertown Transcript*, March 26, 1864.

[27] *Frederick Citizen*, cited in *Chestertown Transcript*, March 26, 1864.

[28] To the Voters of Allegany County, March 25, 1864, *Civilian and Telegraph*, March 31, 1864.

[29] *Cecil Whig*, April 9, 1864.

[30] *Baltimore American*, March 28, 1864.

[31] *Ibid.*, March 26, 1864.

[32] *Cecil Whig*, February 6, 1864.

[33] *Cecil Democrat*, November 21, 1863, and March 5, 1864.

pay for worthless property was, said the *Whig*, to assume they were fools.[34] They could easily prevent such a mishap, for Baltimore and the border counties dominated the popular vote by which the new constitution would have to be approved.

The plea for a convention involved a subsidiary goal, that of a general free school system in Maryland. One set of county resolutions plugged for "a free State, free schools, plenty of work and good wages is what we want, and will have."[35]

The usual epithets were tossed around—Democrats and pro-slavery men were attacked as traitors and all emancipationists condemned as abolitionists. Positions were influenced by local conditions. Maryland's conservative Unionists varied from favoring state compensation[36] and taking no position on the convention all the way to supporting immediate emancipation without state compensation. The Unconditional Unionists also responded to local sentiment. Henry H. Goldsborough and his two running mates in Talbot County turned from the party line by supporting apprenticeship and the dying cause of colonization.[37] The more radical Unconditional Unionists rejected these last two propositions, and a number even opposed federal compensation to loyal slave owners.

Davis fell into that group but not Creswell. Although a politician susceptible to equivocation, he emphasized the importance of Eastern Shoremen electing "straightout men" to the Constitutional Convention. Only by so doing could he strengthen his case in appealing for Congressional funds. The election of men opposed to the Administration and hesitant on emancipation would destroy all hope

[34] *Cecil Whig*, March 12, 1864. A number of Unionists claimed, as did the *Baltimore American* on February 2, 1864, "To emancipate is merely to refrain from exercising the power by which slaves are held in bondage."

[35] *Baltimore American*, March 12, 1864, and *National Republican*, April 5, 1864.

[36] For instance, the Union candidates of Anne Arundel County said, " . . . Maryland ought to make provision for compensating owners of slaves and claim reimbursement from the General Government. . . ." *Annapolis Gazette*, March 31, 1864 and Baltimore *Sun*, April 1, 1864.

[37] *Easton Gazette*, March 19, 1864. Loose party organization helped make the label "Unconditional Union" a troublesome one. At least one newspaper (*Baltimore American*, April 12, 1864) applied the term to the Montgomery County Union ticket, which obviously was hostile to the dominant elements in that faction. Francis P. Blair, Sr., for example, ran on the Montgomery ticket.

of federal aid. Thus did Creswell counteract the propaganda that compensation could be had if it were not for radical opposition.[38]

Gradual emancipation practically vanished as an issue. A small majority of Unionists clung to slavery while the rest sought its immediate abolition. Unionists voiced fewer surface rumblings among themselves than during the fall of 1863, but intra-party rivalry still ran deep. It involved the reigns of power and considerable but often unstated differences over how far the revolution should be carried.

Various journalists called this the most important election ever held in Maryland, but large numbers of citizens simply yawned. The insidious idea was reportedly circulated through Baltimore that it was not necessary to vote because the regular Union ticket was unopposed.[39] This overlooked the need for a large popular vote to overcome the opposition in the small counties. Many Union men worried over the apathy, and well they might. If the Democrats won one-third of the seats, they theoretically could destroy the plan for the convention. The law required one more than two-thirds to take their seats before the convention could organize.

The Union League tried to inspire the loyal. Its members were summoned to the work of electing "Uncompromising, unconditional Union men" opposed to apprenticeship and state compensation.[40] The call went forth over the signature of the state president, Sebastian F. Streeter, who on February 22 had presided over the Unconditional Union State Convention.

The political rallies to stir the faithful and win the uncommitted did not achieve the magnitude of the campaign of the previous fall. Some indoor meetings took place in Baltimore, but there were no massive, outdoor rallies. The campaign lacked the color and pageantry of torch light processions with men marching to fife and drum and banners flying. "The old fire," said the *Baltimore American*, seemed "dead within us."[41]

The most important rally in Baltimore took place in the Maryland Institute on April 1. It was neither a boisterous nor vociferous affair nor did the hall fill to capacity as on some past political occasions. Bad weather hurt attendance. The radicals controlled the meet-

[38] *Baltimore American*, April 2, 1864, and see George M. Russum to John A. J. Creswell, March 18, 1864, Creswell Papers, VII.

[39] *Baltimore American*, April 6, 1864.

[40] *Baltimore American*, March 29, 1864.

[41] *Ibid.*, April 4, 1864.

ing and quite naturally gave prominence to Winter Davis. He hit hard, wielding the verbal lash with his usual effectiveness. Its bite dug too deeply for the more pacific tastes of the *Baltimore American*. To such criticism Davis only scoffed. He neither asked nor gave his enemy any quarter.

Davis recalled his efforts to get Maryland slaveholders $10,000,000 in order to save a billion dollars and a year of bloodshed and anarchy. "The year," said Davis, "has gone. . . . The blood that pays the ransom of the Negro is poured out, and the money of the government went with it."

Davis looked to a redistribution of political power as the first fruit of the destruction of slavery. He reminded his listeners that the slave interests "have used their power to take to themselves the lion's share of our political honor, and to cast upon you the ass's share of every political burden." He castigated his antagonists who belatedly championed the cause of emancipation. These people were dragged by popular vote to confess what they did not believe. "If you trust them," said the Congressman, "they will cheat you."

Already they had raised the issue of Negro equality in hopes of deluding the public. Davis exploded this treacherous issue with sacasm and wry humor. He drew great applause when he expressed perfect contentment for Negro equality with his enemies "but not with my friends." Then came laughter as Davis added, "In my judgment, they that are afraid of Negro equality are not much above it now. Do they understand that? (Laughter.) In my judgment, they that are afraid of marrying a Negro woman had better go to the Legislature and petition for a law to punish them if they are guilty of that weakness."[42]

On the Eastern Shore the campaign progressed without the services of Senator Hicks. His right foot had been amputated on March 11.[43] Nonetheless, he let it be known that he favored compensated emancipation but wanted slavery ended even if no money could be had.[44]

On the day before the election a notable event occurred in Wash-

---

[42] Quotations from this address can be found in *Davis Speeches*, pp. 385–86, 389, 391. In now opposing all compensation for slave owners, Davis noted (p. 392) that no money was paid for the great losses caused by tariff changes.

[43] *Baltimore American*, March 12, 1864. The cause of the amputation was said to be erysipelas.

[44] T. H. Hicks to editor Cambridge *Herald*, March 24, 1864; *Baltimore American*, April 1, 1864.

ington. Reverdy Johnson rose before the Senate of the United States and pleaded for an amendment to the federal Constitution to abolish slavery. His action surprised the Senate and pleased the radicals. Union senators heartily congratulated him, while the copperheads reportedly scowled.[45] The action came too late to have any real effect on the election in Maryland, but it must have gratified many of the state's emancipationists.

Bradford meanwhile presented a problem to the radicals. Would he agree to a military order to prevent rebels from voting? That was the question Creswell put to George Earle, clerk of the Court of Appeals of Maryland. Earle admitted no man in Annapolis could answer it, but he made a suggestion—go openly to Bradford and ask him. The governor was "straight forward and reliable" and would discuss the issue fully and freely if approached properly. Failure to consult him in the last election had been a great mistake.[46]

The new commanding officer of the Middle Department would not repeat the slight. He was Major General Lewis Wallace, better known as Lew Wallace. He replaced Brigadier General Lockwood, who reluctantly yielded the post in the latter part of March. A native of Indiana, Wallace was the son of one of its former governors. Although only 37, he had already gained considerable experience in legal, political, and military life. After the war he won renown as an author, particularly for his *Ben Hur*.[47]

Winter Davis was pleased with the change. He believed the national administration now ready to help the emancipation movement but feared it was "too late to be useful."[48] George Vickers regretfully gave another opinion of radical activities. He saw in Lockwood's removal and recent Maryland appointments an indication of "some new and secret movement" directed at the Convention election.[49]

After he received his order to the new post, Wallace talked to Stanton, who warned that the department had been a "grave-yard"

[45] *New York Times* cited in *Chestertown Transcript*, April 9, 1864.

[46] George Earle to John A. J. Creswell, March 8, 1864, Creswell Papers, VI.

[47] A. Lincoln to Brigadier General Henry H. Lockwood, March 21, 1864, *Lincoln Works*, VII, 258 and editor's footnote, 259; *Official Records*, Series I, Vol. 33, p. 717; *Baltimore American*, March 26, 1864; and *Dictionary of American Biography*, Vol. 19, pp. 375–76. Wallace assumed command on March 22, 1864.

[48] H. Winter Davis to Rear Admiral Samuel F. DuPont, March 5, 1864, S. F. DuPont Papers.

[49] George Vickers to Governor Bradford, March 17, 1864, Executive Papers.

for its commanders. He added that Lincoln had his heart set on abolition in Maryland by constitutional means. The President, said Stanton, "don't want it to be said . . . that the bayonet had anything to do with the election. He is a candidate for a second nomination. You understand?"[50] Wallace got the point.

He was in his new office only a few days when he acted upon the case of Elbridge Gerry Kilbourn, a man who earlier in the war spent nearly a year as a federal prisoner. Kilbourn regained his freedom without taking an oath of allegiance. Since then his hostility for the government showed no signs of abatement. Now he was running for the Constitutional Convention as a candidate from Anne Arundel County.[51]

Wallace wanted to know if there were not some way to prevent his election. Off went a letter to the governor, couched in diplomatic expressions of the general's great confidence in Bradford. Back came the reply. The governor said he had no power to prevent Kilbourn's election, but victory at the polls would not assure the candidate a seat. An oath stood in the way. Kilbourn must swear that he had "never either directly or indirectly . . . given any aid, comfort or encouragement to those in rebellion."[52] As speaker of the House of Delegates in 1861, he had voted for a resolution supporting recognition of Confederate independence; it was difficult to see how he could so swear. Kilbourn soon confessed, on being subjected to questioning under Wallace's orders, that he would not take the oath. He then withdrew from the campaign.[53]

---

[50] Lew Wallace, *Lew Wallace: An Autobiography* (New York, 1906), II, 670, 672, 675. Wallace also visited Lincoln and Schenck. The latter claimed that socially, Baltimore "is peculiar. There is more culture to the square block there than in Boston. . . . The . . . war divided the old families, but I was never able to discover the dividing line. Did I put a heavy hand on one of the Secessionists, a delegation of influential Unionists at once hurried to the President, and begged the culprit off." The most unfortunate aspect of the Middle Department was the fact that Baltimore was "only a pleasant morning jaunt by rail from . . . Washington.

[51] Major General Lew Wallace to Governor Augustus W. Bradford, March 24, 1864, RG 98, U.S. Army Commands, Middle Dept., Letters Sent, Vol. 31, pp. 21–22; Executive Letterbook, p. 503.

[52] Augustus W. Bradford to Major General Lew Wallace, March 28, 1864, Executive Letterbook, pp. 503–5.

[53] *Baltimore American*, April 2, 1864. One journalist saw in Kilbourn's candidacy an attempted fraud by which Kilbourn and his colleagues would prevent a quorum by absenting themselves from the Constitutional Convention. See *Baltimore Clipper*, April 4, 1864.

On the day that Bradford wrote Wallace the two men talked face to face.[54] The General prepared an impressive display as a prelude to the conversation. He gathered his staff in full regalia for a trip by special train to Annapolis. On arrival the entourage stirred excitement by marching into the executive office. Bradford and Wallace entered an adjoining room for a private interview.

The General judged the governor "a plain, farmer-like" person, undemonstrative and able to handle "himself well under guard." Wallace placed before the governor petitions asking for soldiers at various election districts down the bay—a request that Wallace knew smacked of "the prohibited bayonet." He asked Bradford what would happen if the petitions were endorsed and forwarded to him. The governor, who was singularly direct, told Wallace to mail them. He would approve all he considered in good faith.[55]

Bradford was pleased that Wallace intended to order soldiers into only those districts where the judges of election requested their help in preserving the peace. Even then the soldiers would not be permitted in view of the polls unless summoned by the judges. The General, much to Bradford's relief, seemed determined to observe the laws of Maryland.[56]

Two days later Wallace wrote again, and the following day Bradford answered. Quite likely these two letters were drafted with publication in mind. They covered much of the ground already discussed and quickly found their way into the newspapers. In his letter Wallace asked if it were not the legislature's purpose to exclude disloyal votes.[57] Bradford's answer expanded his written comments of March 28 into a broad interpretation of the Convention Bill. Not only must the election judges put an oath to any voter challenged on grounds of disloyalty but they also should question the suspect and take testi-

---

[54] Wallace did not date his interview, but Bradford wrote of one occurring on March 28, 1864. It is reasonable to believe that both men were talking about the same occasion. See Augustus W. Bradford to George W. Covington, April 1, 1864, and Augustus W. Bradford to John F. Dent, April 2, 1864, smaller Letterbook in Hall of Records, pp. 31–33 and 36–39.

[55] Quotations in paragraph from *Wallace Autobiography*, II, 681–82.

[56] Augustus W. Bradford to George W. Convington, April 1, 1864, and Augustus W. Bradford to John F. Dent, April 2, 1864, smaller Letterbook, pp. 31–33 and 36–39.

[57] Lew Wallace to Augustus W. Bradford, March 30, 1864, Executive Letterbook, pp. 50–56; April 2, 1864 issues of Baltimore *Sun, Baltimore American*, and *Baltimore Clipper*.

mony from knowledgeable bystanders. Bradford believed that a faithful execution of the laws (he had every reason to expect this) would stop the ballots of all who had aided or comforted the enemy at any time since the rebellion began.[58]

This went beyond Schenck's oath in 1863, which exacted only a pledge of future loyalty. Bradford's action, so different from the preceding year, can perhaps be explained by his desire not to afford the military any excuse for intervention. Wallace's politic behavior undoubtedly eased the way for Bradford's shift.

Judges of elections in some counties stretched Bradford's interpretation by adopting a detailed catechism for questioning the challenged. None drew more attention than the list concocted for Cecil County. A remarkable political document, it is given here in its entirety.

QUESTIONS.

1. *Service in the Rebel Army.*
Have you ever served in the Rebel army?

2. *Aid to those in Armed Rebellion.*
Have you ever given aid to the rebellion?
Have you never given money to those intending to join the rebellion?
Have you never given money to their agents?
Have you never given money, clothing or provisions for the purpose of aiding the emigration of persons from this State to the South?
Have you never sent money, clothing or provisions to persons in the South since the rebellion?

3. *Comfort and Encouragement to the Rebellion.*
NOTE: Comfort or encouragement means advocacy, advice in favor of. We *aid* the Rebellion by giving money, clothing and provisions; we give it *comfort* or *encouragement* by our words. A man

---

[58] Augustus W. Bradford to Lew Wallace, March 31, 1864, Executive Letterbook, pp. 506–8; April 2, 1864 issues of Baltimore *Sun, Baltimore American,* and *Baltimore Clipper.* The judges of election, said Bradford, "would be authorized, and I think required, to test the recollection of the party swearing, by propounding to him particular interrogatories, suggestive of different modes by which this aid, comfort or encouragement may have been given. . . ." In his letter of April 4, 1864, to A. G. Woodward, (smaller Letterbook, pp. 44–45, Hall of Records) Bradford left to the judge's discretion "the character of the questions."

who had advocated the cause of the rebellion, who talked in favor of Maryland going with the South, who rejoiced over the victories of the Rebel army, has given *comfort* and encouragement to the Rebellion.

Have you ever given comfort or encouragement to the Rebellion?

Have you never in conversation, attempted to justify the course of the States in Rebellion?

Have you never expressed a wish for the success of the Rebellion or its army?

Have you never in conversation discouraged the cause of the Federal Government?

Did you rejoice over the downfall of Fort Sumter?

4. *Disloyalty.*

NOTE. If the Judges are satisfied that a man is disloyal to the United States, it is their duty to refuse his vote, for such person is not a 'legal voter' of the State of Maryland.

Are you a loyal citizen of the United States?

Have you been loyal ever since the beginning of the Rebellion?

Have you never rejoiced over the defeat of the Union army?

Have you never rejoiced over the success of the Rebel army?

When the Union army and the Rebel army meet in battle, which do you wish to gain the victory?

NOTE. After interrogating the person offering to vote, the Judges may hear other evidence to approve or disprove his statements, and must be governed by the weight of testimony.[59]

This inquisitory device circulated widely and drew favorable comment from the *Baltimore American*. It believed the questions could be useful everywhere.[60] In fact, a strict adherence would prevent even the proprietors of that paper from voting. The *American*, of course, said nothing to this effect, but the *Clipper* was only too happy to recall its rival's questionable conduct during the riotous times of April, 1861—conduct hardly befitting a Union journal.[61]

The *Examiner* recommended the Cecil catechism for Frederick County.[62] In Talbot County a greatly modified form, involving only

[59] These "'interrogatories' are substantially those which were adopted at a meeting of Judges in Cecil county, for their general guidance. . . ." *Baltimore American*, April 4, 1864.

[60] *Ibid.*

[61] *Baltimore Clipper*, April 1, 1864.

[62] Frederick *Examiner*, April 6, 1864.

three questions, got the approval of a minority of that county's election judges.[63] Somerset county whittled it even further and twisted it to Democratic advantage.

The intent of Somerset Democrats was to circumvent the Convention Bill, Governor Bradford, and Major General Wallace. The Somerset document claimed that one's right to vote could be forfeited only by a court conviction for an offense specified by the Constitution. If a voter were challenged on grounds of disloyalty, he must answer under oath whether he had served in the Confederate army or aided or comforted persons in armed rebellion. But regardless of the answer or lack of one, the judges had to accept his ballot if they considered him a legal voter. This loophole opened the polls to the disloyal wherever the Democrats were in control. The circular concluded by warning the judges to watch for political tricks that would consume time. If each vote took ten minutes, only fifty-four ballots could be cast at any one polling place.[64]

Thus did a battle of circulars replace the war of the proclamations waged in November, 1863. The ultra loyalists of Somerset turned to the army for help. Two hundred soldiers were requested to be stationed throughout the various Somerset election districts.[65] The ostensible purpose of preserving the peace provided a seemingly plausible excuse for a less seemly goal—military intervention in the election.

To facilitate requests for troops, a form was printed. It stated that in a particular district the loyalty oath disqualified a large proportion of the people who would nevertheless attempt to vote and, there was reason to believe, try to disturb the election. Blank spaces were left for the names of the election judges and their county and district as well as the number of soldiers desired. In five days, March 25–29, the judges of six districts in Worcester County, four in Caroline, and one in Frederick signed the forms.[66]

---

[63] Howes Goldsborough to Governor Bradford, March 30, 1864, Letters Received 1864–65, Augustus W. Bradford, Hall of Records. Samuel A. Harrison noted in his Journal, March 31, 1864, Part 2, p. 645, that "certain of the judges who hoped to elect their candidates by the Rebel votes, refused to be bound by the written agreement."

[64] The printed circular was included in the Certified Statement of H. C. McCoy, April 13, 1864, Executive Papers.

[65] Endorsement on a wrapper (letter missing):
Princess Anne, Somerset Co., March 31, 1864. Robert H. Elligood and Henry C. McCoy, etc. RG 98, Middle Dept., L. Rec'd 1864, E 37.

[66] See file No. E 31 and E 38, RG 98, Middle Dept., Letters Received, 1864.

Wallace decided to blanket every election district of every Eastern Shore county south of Cecil,[67] even though troop requests obviously did not come from most election judges in the Democratic counties. His goal, however, failed of fulfillment.

Brigadier General Henry H. Lockwood procured troops to be stationed on the Eastern Shore by steaming into fort McHenry aboard the *Meigs* and taking on six officers and 200 men. Departing at 3 A.M. on April 4, he headed for the Chester River. At various places, including Chestertown, the general put ashore detachments totaling 110 men. Leaving the river, he proceeded down the Chesapeake Bay. Night approached, and the weather became threatening. Lockwood sought a safe harbor at Annapolis.

The next day a raging storm, the "severest" of the year, immobilized the *Meigs* until that night. Lockwood sailed out of the harbor at 2 A.M. on the morning of election day. April 6. He landed men in Talbot County and took the remainder to Cambridge in Dorchester County. They did not reach there until 4 P.M., too late to be of help. Lockwood offered his assistance to the election judges, but they "were little disposed, either to carry out the law of the state, or to desire aid from the Military."[68]

Other troops reached the Eastern Shore by rail from Wilmington, Delaware. Boarding a special train on the morning of April 5, Briga-

---

Worcester conservative Unionists were particularly exasperated by this action, for their ticket, which provided the only local opposition, allegedly posed no danger of disorder. See B. Everett Smith to Governor Bradford, March 30, 1864, Executive Papers. The chairman of the State Democratic Executive and Corresponding Committee asked for a gubernatorial proclamation to quiet fears of illegal interference in the April 6 election. Bradford refused, saying there was no evidence of such a move. See A. W. Bradford to John F. Dent, April 2, 1864, smaller Letterbook, pp. 36–39 and John F. Dent to Governor Bradford, March 31, 1864, Letters Received, 1864–65 (Augustus W. Bradford), Hall of Records.

[67] Major General Lew Wallace to Brig. General H. H. Lockwood, April 3, 1864, RG 98, U.S. Army Commands, Middle Dept., Letters Sent, Vol. 31, p. 44. Wallace, along with other commanding generals in the Maryland area, received orders to furlough soldiers so that they could go home to vote. He instructed the officer in charge to march them unarmed to the polls to vote and afterward to a point at least a mile distant unless the election judges designated a closer place. The commanding officer was not to influence his men in choosing candidates but was to prevent them from committing any aggression against civilians. See Lt. Col. Samuel B. Lawrence to Brig. Gen. H. H. Lockwood, March 29, 1864, *ibid.*, Vol. 31, pp. 32–34.

[68] Brig. Gen. Henry H. Lockwood to Lt. Col. S. B. Lawrence, AAG, April 7, 1864, RG 98, Middle Dept., Letters Received, 1864, L65.

dier General John R. Kenly headed south. He and his men arrived in Salisbury that evening. Kenly contacted "the leading Union citizens" and upon their request dispatched troops to a number of districts in Somerset and Worcester. Apparently many districts were left unsupplied. The detachments of six to eleven men each marched to within one mile of the various polls and notified the election judges of their readiness to render assistance. Only in two instances in Worcester County was it requested. The commanding officer in both cases promptly responded and moved his men forward. They remained until the judges said their presence was no longer needed. All detachments got back to Salisbury by midnight and drew praise from their commander for excellent conduct.[69]

Only one precinct in the seven Eastern Shore counties reported military interference.[70] The vote of the Shore rose over that of the last election and gave the convention opponents an edge. George Vickers wrote from Kent County, "I must do the soldiers justice today, that they generally behaved well. . . . I shall have to change my opinion of Genl. Wallace and commend him for the judicious arrangement of his troops."[71] The local Democratic journal called the conduct of the election similar to those held before soldiers were ordered to the polls—with one exception. At Chestertown the known opponents of the Convention were forced to answer a long interrogation.[72]

[69] John R. Kenly to Lt. Col. S. B. Lawrence, AAG, April 8, 1864, *Official Records*, Series I, Vol. 33, pp. 826–27; RG 98, Middle Dept., Letters Received, 1864, K 35.

[70] The judges of election in Somerset's first district said the intervening force was not called to the polls by civil authority. Levin Woolford, Clerk of the Circuit Court of Somerset, reported it to Governor Bradford (See Letters Received, 1864–5, A. W. Bradford, Hall of Records), who returned the certificate because the judges had not sworn to the facts.

[71] George Vickers to Augustus W. Bradford, April 8, 1864, Bradford Papers.

[72] *Chestertown Transcript*, April 9, 1864. In Talbot County, which the Union Party controlled, some rebels swore falsely, and others got permission to concoct their own oath. The *Easton Gazette* of April 9, 1864 said that some Unionists were too inclined to use rebel votes in an attempt to win office. Democratic-controlled Somerset saw the two Democratic election judges overrule fellow Judge Henry C. McCoy and refuse to force the challenged, some fifteen to twenty in number, to take the oath. This caused the judges' presentment before the Grand Jury for violating their office, a meaningless gesture because the judges had the sympathy of the grand and petty jurymen. See in Executive papers H. C. McCoy to Gov. Bradford, April 7, 1864; Certified Statement of H. C. McCoy, April 13, 1864; and H. C. McCoy to Maj. Gen. Lew Wallace, April 13, 1864. See also RG 98, Middle Dept., Register of Letters Received, 1864, Vol. 8, p. 420.

In southern Maryland a significant event occurred in an area out-side of Wallace's jurisdiction. As the polls were about to open in Rockville, Montgomery County, a captain read an order supposedly emanating from the headquarters of Major General Christopher Co-lon Augur. The judges of election countered with the proposal to conduct the voting in accordance with Maryland law and Governor Bradford's published commentary to Wallace. This did not satisfy the captain. He insisted on reserving to himself the right to decide on a voter's qualifications. Unwilling to agree to such terms, the judges refused to hold an election.[73]

When a somewhat similar incident occurred in the case of Cap-tain Moore the preceding November, there was no recourse. Now the Convention Bill provided for the contingency. The governor ordered a new election for the Fourth District polls.[74]

Bradford received word of uninvited troops at other polling places in Montgomery County but took no action because the report was not affirmed under oath by the election judges.[75] Elsewhere in south-ern Maryland the military did not interfere. In fact, some Unionists complained of bad treatment by rebel sympathizers. At the first dis-trict polls in Prince George's County a man was allowed to vote though he had been heard to say "that he wished all the Federal Soldiers were in hell and the Capitol of the United States burned up."[76]

The seven counties of southern Maryland defeated the Constitu-tional Convention by a larger margin than they had Goldsborough in the preceding election. Only in Howard County was the election close. There the convention lost by seven votes, but all three Uncon-

[73] Nathaniel Clagett and others, statement on Returns of Fourth Election District for Montgomery County, Maryland, April 6, 1864, Executive Papers. Troops were ordered to each election district in Montgomery County. All voters suspected of disloy-alty were to be challenged, questioned, and sworn to the iron bound oath of allegiance prescribed by the Congressional act of July 2, 1862 or not vote. General Orders No. 26, April 6, 1864, by order of Major D. W. C. Thompson, Executive Papers.

[74] Augustus W. Bradford Journal, III, April 12, 1864.

[75] See the Official Returns by five judges of elections from five Montgomery County districts, April 8, 1864, Executive Papers; Augustus W. Bradford to B. Prettyman, Clerk of Circuit Court of Montgomery County, April 12, 1864, smaller Letterbook, pp. 53–54; and three statements on Montgomery County Election, April, 1864, Executive Papers.

[76] James D. Cassard to Brig. General [Erastus B.] Tyler, April 14, 1864, Executive Papers; RG 98, Middle Dept., Register of Letters Received, 1864, Vol. 8, p. 136.

ditional Unionist delegates won. Most of Howard's anti-convention support gravitated toward the Conservative Union ticket rather than the Democratic slate.

In northern Maryland the challenged in Cecil County were well catechized. Some tried to get around the question of which side they preferred to win in battle. As the *Whig* expressed it: "Some didn't care which gained the victory, others wished which ever was the strongest to win, while others, more honest, walked doggedly away from the polls without answering."[77]

The "Cecil County Catechism" was used in Frederick County too. It provoked the *Maryland Union* into calling the document "conceived in sin, born in iniquity and sired by as corrupt a set of political scoundrels as ever disgraced the earth."[78] That paper loved to exercise the hyperbole so popular to the political campaigning of that time. It spewed forth invectives and unleashed its usual ill-defined charges of "frauds and outrages and double voting."[79]

So evil did the *Maryland Union* consider these villainies that it seemed to justify an outbreak in the Jackson District. There a sizable band of armed citizens reached the polls at 2 P.M. and tried to seize the ballot box. The intruders cursed and issued violent threats. Fearing personal attack, the judges closed the polls and promised not to reopen on that day. Word was sent to Frederick immediately. A squad of soldiers pursued the culprits. A number of men were caught and dragged back the next day.[80]

In westernmost Maryland the Democrats ran a ticket in Allegany County and were beaten 2 to 1. Although the Unconditional Union vote dropped 27 per cent from its November showing, while the conservatives registered gains, the *Civilian and Telegraph* was not displeased. It considered the vote surprisingly large. True, the weather overhead was fine, but underfoot the mud, slush, and snow made conditions intolerable. Besides, in the mountains this was an excellent "sugar day," a business that permitted no trifling with time.

More than the usual amount of "falsehood, slander and misrepresentation" spiced the campaign. Men opposed to the convention confused many voters by labeling themselves Unionists. In fact, some

---

[77] *Cecil Whig*, April 9, 1864.
[78] *Maryland Union*, April 14, 1864.
[79] *Ibid.*, April 7, 1864.
[80] Geo. Leatherman to Governor Bradford, April 9, 1864, Executive papers; *Valley Register* (Frederick County), April 8, 1864.

had been elected as such, but the *Civilian and Telegraph* considered their right to the name forfeited.[81]

A spurious circular attempted to sabotage the Allegany County Unconditional Union candidates by describing them as "the real friends of the colored people" and calling for political equality.[82] In denying the validity of the document, the nominees gave assurances that they opposed "Negro equality at the ballot-box, in the jury-box, on the witness-stand, or elsewhere."[83] Yet in another statement these very candidates demonstrated the conflicting standards of the day by criticizing the present constitution for withholding its protection from free Negroes.[84]

In the city of Baltimore the Unconditional Union ticket faced no opposition. This reduced the turnout, and discouraged Democrats did not bother to go to the polls. Not a hint of military interference marred the election. There was peace and perfect order as the voters registered their approval of the convention by a vote of 9,102 to 87.[85]

The state-wide result gave the convention an overwhelming victory—31,593 to 19,524.[86] The total vote fell slightly short of 1863. While the slave counties opposed the convention by nearly 2 to 1, building large majorities in southern Maryland and carrying most of the Eastern Shore, the free counties and Baltimore backed the convention by more than 3 to 1. Thirty-five seats went to the pro-slavery Democrats and 61 to the Unionists. Except for possibly three, all of the latter were pledged to unconditional emancipation.[87]

When Reverdy Johnson heard the outcome of the election, he

---

[81] *Civilian and Telegraph*, April 14, 1864. With "some few honorable exceptions," even the federal office holders were generally hostile or passive to the Unconditional Union men.

[82] *Ibid.*, April 7, 1864.

[83] *Ibid.*

[84] "To the Voters of Allegany County," March 25, 1864, *Ibid.*, March 31, 1864.

[85] April 7, 1864 issues of *Baltimore American, Baltimore Daily Gazette, Baltimore Clipper*, and Baltimore *Sun*. In Baltimore County the Democrats withdrew their ticket just prior to the election but nevertheless received over 600 votes. The convention carried the county by 2,016–811. See *Baltimore American*, April 14, 1864, and *Baltimore County Advocate*, April 9, 1864.

[86] Baltimore *Sun*, April 18, 1864, *Baltimore American*, April 16, 1864. The total vote was 51,314, including 197 blank. One hundred ninety-two votes were cast eleven days later in the new election at Rockville in Montgomery County.

[87] *Baltimore American*, April 11, 1864.

wrote newspaperman Charles C. Fulton that he was delighted.[88] Needless to say, Winter Davis was pleased. He congratulated Major General Wallace, telling him "you managed Bradford to a marvel." Lincoln also praised Wallace, and Stanton added his appreciation by warmly shaking Wallace's hand and saying, "It was well done. They can't say now that *we* used the bayonet in the election. If the governor did, that's a different thing. Nobody will deny his right to use it."[89]

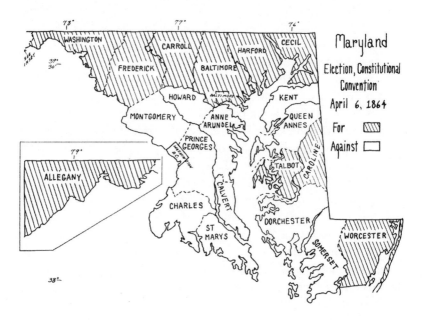

Maryland

Election, Constitutional Convention

April 6, 1864

For

Against

Though the conduct of the election was more peaceful than that of the preceding November, it far from pacified the Democrats. One commentator accused the radicals of using "the Governor's strange construction" for the purpose of getting the election judges to accomplish what the soldiers could not. Bradford's action thereby attempted to legalize an intervention worse than that of the military because it openly degraded the law and dishonored the role of the judges.[90]

[87] *Baltimore American*, April 9, 1864. Johnson's letter, dated April 7, said, "Delighted to hear the result of yesterday's election. A new era is now dawning on our State. Slavery ended, and it will be, as Washington said it would be in the event, 'the garden spot' of the United States."

[89] Quotations from *Wallace Autobiography*, II, 683–65.

[90] *Prince Georgian* cited in the *Chestertown Transcript*, April 16, 1864. The *Cecil Whig*, April 2, 1864, encouraged intimidation by charging that any one voting Democratic

TABLE E. VOTE ON CONSTITUTIONAL CONVENTION, 1864

	For	Against	Total	Total vote for Comptroller 1863	Governor 1861	Comptroller 1859
Southern Maryland						
Anne Arundel	445	1,185	1,630	1,702	2,041	2,222
Calvert	53	458	511	778	812	908
Charles	20	638	658	520	903	1,170
Howard	542	549	1,091	915	1,643	1,615
Montgomery	516	716	1,232	1,729	2,040	2,516
Prince George's	188	1,097	1,285	1,179	1,577	1,833
Saint Mary's	163	763	926	1,007	1,351	1,413
Total:	1,927	5,406	7,333	7,830	10,367	11,677
			70.7%	75.5%	100%	112.6%*
Eastern Shore						
Caroline	630	453	1,083	1,337	1,624	1,614
Dorchester	703	1,105	1,808	1,637	2,115	2,413
Kent	453	991	1,444	1,071	1,758	1,608
Queen Anne's	449	1,631	2,080	868	1,978	1,873
Somerset	813	1,331	2,144	1,050	2,827	2,938
Talbot	570	362	932	711	1,811	1,696
Worcester	890	135	1,025	1,795	2,717	2,817
Total:	4,508	6,008	10,516	8,469	14,830	14,959
			70.9%	51.1%	100%	100.9%
Northern Maryland						
Allegany	2,307	1,135	3,442	4,175	4,322	4,508
Baltimore County	2,016	811	2,827	3,259	6,803	6,947
Carroll	1,898	1,635	3,533	3,529	4,926	4,733
Cecil	2,004	890	2,894	3,787	4,154	4,024
Frederick	3,231	1,957	5,188	4,736	7,649	7,422
Harford	1,302	944	2,246	1,499	3,830	3,738
Washington	3,298	651	3,949	3,427	5,422	5,712
Total:	16,056	8,023	24,079	24,412	37,106	37,084
			64.9%	65.8%	100%	99.9%
Baltimore City	9,102	87	9,189	11,310	21,269	23,453
Total North	25,158	8,110	33,268	35,722	58,375	60,537
			57.0%	61.2%	100%	103.7%
Total South	6,435	11,414	17,849	16,299	25,197	26,636
Grand Total	31,593	19,524	51,117	52,021	83,572	87,173
			61.2%	62.2%	100%	104.3%

* Total votes as a percentage of 1861 tally.
The county totals for the April 6, 1864 election were listed as official in the *Baltimore American* of April 15, 1864. That issue omitted Queen Anne's County. In order to comply with the 31,593 to 19,524 result recorded in Governor Bradford's proclamation, it is necessary to make Queen Anne's tally read 449 to 1,631, a seemingly oversized number but one that is also used by Scharf, *History of Maryland*, III, 581.

But the governor's views were often more honored in the breach than in the observance. The Democrats controlled ten of the four-teen slave counties and appointed their judges of elections. Instruc-tions such as those printed for the judges in Somerset County made Bradford's interpretation meaningless.

The total vote cast in the Democratic counties dropped 21 per cent from 1861. This was not an unreasonable dip, considering the absence of men in the Union and Confederate armies and the lesser appeal of a constitutional issue as opposed to the clash of candidates over the question of preserving the nation. In the four Union-run slave counties,[91] however, the plunge since 1861 was steep—47 per cent. Baltimore dropped almost as far—43 per cent, while the seven northern counties slipped 34 per cent.

A full vote of rebels and Unionists would have carried Baltimore and the free counties for the convention, but whether the margin would have been sufficient to overcome hostile sentiments in the slave counties is debatable. Quite likely the convention would have won a close victory.

---

was giving aid and comfort to the enemy. Such a person should be noted and prevented from receiving pay from the government.

[91] Howard, Talbot, Caroline, and Worcester. Dissatisfaction kept some from the polls. George Vickers wrote Governor Bradford on April 8, 1864 (Bradford papers) that three-fourths of those who did not vote in Kent County were Unionists "dissatisfied with the president's Negro policy. . . ." An examination of the Kent vote will show nearly half of the supporters of the Conservative Union ticket voting against the conven-tion.

CHAPTER XIV

THE CONSTITUTIONAL
CONVENTION OF 1864

ON THE EVE of the third anniversary of the riots against the Massachusetts troops, 30,000 Baltimoreans lined the streets to cheer 3,000 Union troops. It was a festive occasion, this afternoon parade, for in the evening the Maryland State Fair would open. Its proceeds were to benefit the United States Sanitary and Christian Commissions, which provided such things as hospital supplies for the sick and wounded soldiers.

A little after 6 P.M. cannon boomed, announcing the arrival of Abraham Lincoln at Camden Station. A crowd of well wishers cheered the President as he made his way to the carriage that would take him to the residence of William Julian Albert. From there the official party went to the Maryland Institute for the inauguration ceremonies.

As Lincoln entered the hall, the orchestra played "Hail to the Chief." Wild enthusiasm engulfed the throng. Ladies waved handkerchiefs and flags, and gentlemen thrust their hats aloft.[1] But they had to wait through a prayer, hymn, and gubernatorial address before they could hear the President. When he did speak, he talked of liberty. As Lincoln put it, "The shepherd drives the wolf from the sheep's throat, for which the sheep thanks the shepherd as a *liberator*, while the wolf denounces him . . . as destroyer of liberty."[2] Recently, Lincoln happily commented, Maryland had been helping to define "liberty." Lincoln thanked the citizens for these efforts.

On April 27 the Constitutional Convention convened in Annapolis. Eighty of the ninety-six delegates appeared for the first session and elected state comptroller Henry H. Goldsborough as president.[3] The

---

[1] *Baltimore American*, April 19, 1864. William J. Albert shared top office in the fair with the wife of Governor Bradford.

[2] *Lincoln Works*, VII, 302. This speech is better know for Lincoln's remarks on the rebel massacre of Negro and white soldiers at Fort Pillow, Tennessee.

[3] Baltimore *Sun*, April 28, 1864, and *Baltimore American*, April 28, 1864.

absentees, nearly all of whom were from the southern counties, arrived within the next couple of weeks.[4]

The southern delegates bore the names of some of the oldest and best known families in Maryland. They tenaciously opposed all reform and displayed considerable ingenuity in withdrawing from each position as it became untenable.[5] Pushed from their support of slavery, they fought first for state compensation, then federal, and clung at last to Negro apprenticeship, which at least had overtones of the old feudal system.

No man exceeded Daniel Clarke, son-in-law of ex-Governor Thomas Pratt, in his espousal of the old order. An able and articulate leader of the minority, he was frequently on his feet. This did not mean that he was as prominent as some of his colleagues. Ezekiel Forman Chambers, for instance, had fought in the War of 1812 and had been a United States Senator and a judge.[6] Later in the year he would run for governor on the Democratic ticket.

Chambers, like four of the other delegates, had served in Maryland's last Constitutional Convention, that of 1850–51. A much larger group, fourteen, had participated in the 1864 Legislature.[7] Nine of them were Unionists, including such well-known leaders as Henry Stockbridge and Archibald Stirling, Jr. Both of these men achieved prominence in the Convention. In fact, Stirling can be regarded as the leader of the majority.[8]

On the day the convention opened, the Union delegates met in caucus and declared that, in accordance with the popular will, immediate emancipation without compensation must bind their actions. The *Baltimore American* hoped that this declaration would shorten

[4] William Starr Myers, *The Maryland Constitution of 1864* (Baltimore, 1901), p. 36. John F. Dent was an exception. Family illness and domestic matters delayed his taking his seat until July 7.

[5] *Ibid.*, 40.

[6] See *Dictionary of American Biography*, III, 602, for biographical sketch of Ezekiel F. Chambers.

[7] *Baltimore American*, May 3, 1864. According to the *Civilian and Telegraph* of May 12, 1864, those delegates who had served in the last legislature got so many of the better appointments to the various standing committees that the charge of favoritism arose from dissatisfied members.

[8] Myers, *Constitution of 1864*, p. 38. Delegate Edward W. Belt believed many of his colleagues disqualified for service in the Constitutional Convention because of other offices they held. Included were six states attorneys and the comptroller of the treasury, Henry H. Goldsborough. Belt's protest was in vain. See *The Debates of the Constitutional Convention . . . 1864*, II, 1176, 1195–1201.

debate on the subject.[9] Brevity, however, held no allure for the delegates. The "rebels" busied themselves with "long, windy" speeches, thereby adding to the length and expense of the convention.[10] Frequent adjournments and failures to obtain a quorum contributed to what seemed like extremely slow progress. Some devious delegates, who voted against adjournments and for two instead of one daily session, were the first to rush from the State House to catch the steamboat or train leaving Annapolis.[11] Visions of finishing the constitution in two months or less vanished.

The Declaration of Rights alone dominated that two-month period even though this section embodied only three new articles plus the dropping of one and the modifying of two others.[12] Article No. 5 dealt a blow to the advocates of states rights by declaring that every citizen owed "paramount allegiance to the constitution and government of the United States."[13] This statement expressed the philosophy of the new order and attracted wide attention. But none of the forty-five articles in the Declaration of Rights was more applicable to the demands of the time than the 24th. It opposed the strong link between the South and Maryland and upset the political, social, and economic order within the state. The article read:

> Hereafter, in this State, there shall be neither slavery nor involuntary servitude, except in punishment of crime, whereof the party shall have been duly convicted; and all persons held to service or labor, as slaves, are hereby declared free.[14]

The decision on this clause was predetermined and the subject thoroughly exhausted, but the delegates would not let it pass without unleashing a verbal torrent. It was like a theatrical performance. All the players knew the outcome of the drama but eagerly awaited their turn on the stage. As politicians they exercised two advantages over the acting profession. They could write their own lines and make the performance last as long as they wished. Besides, they could glory in the knowledge that their speeches were being re-

[9] *Baltimore American*, April 30, 1864.

[10] *Cecil Whig*, June 4, 1864.

[11] "Romanoff" in *Cecil Whig*, August 13, 1864. See also June 4, 1864 issue of this paper. Delegates continued to draw pay while losing time.

[12] *Baltimore American*, September 13, 1864.

[13] *Debates*, III, 1879.

[14] *Debates*, III, 1880.

corded for posterity. Perhaps this helped create the pleasant social relations that reportedly flourished between opposing members.[15]

The delegates spent one week on the emancipation clause. The arguments largely revolved around the old issues that had long divided Maryland and the nation. One of the questions given most prominence had not, however, been emphasized by Marylanders in recent years. That was the religious issue. Long citations from both Old and New Testaments accompanied extensive commentaries for and against slavery. Perhaps the delegates, impressed by their task, wished to relate their cause to a higher goal than just the more mundane considerations usually heard in the political arena.

Every conceivable argument impinging upon slavery worked its way into the debates. Delegates rattled off reams of statistics on education, population, per capita wealth, and land values to show slavery as having either hindered or advanced the prosperity of Maryland. Even the number of free Negro convicts and insane as compared to the proportion among slaves got proper notice. Fear was expressed that the state would be flooded with free Negroes. This sharply contrasted with the need for Negro labor in Maryland. Jefferson, Washington, and Lincoln also gained attention, as did British emancipation.

Daniel Clarke attacked the newly baptized emancipationists who tried to portray themselves as long-time advocates of the reform. He remarked that dogmas considered treason a year or two before, now provided "the purest test of loyalty." Being an emancipationist, said Clarke, has become "the highroad to political fame" and wealth. He unflatteringly compared the coarse new aristocracy, "fed on fat Government *contracts*," to the slave aristocracy. For that noble minority he tried to salvage some compensation. He proposed that emancipation depend upon congressional appropriation of at least $20,000,000 for Maryland before January 1, 1865.[16]

State compensation, Clarke had political sense enough to know, could not be procured, for it would saddle Maryland with a heavy debt. Yet he voted to let the people decide whether or not the state legislature should

[15] Bernard C. Steiner, *Citizenship and Suffrage in Maryland* (Baltimore, 1893), p. 42.

[16] For Clarke's comments in this paragraph see *Debates*, I, 647–57. Clarke also talked about minority rights. Another minority member, Chapman Billingsley (*Debates*, I, 580) called emancipation "the emanation of a sickly sentimentality, and offspring of a morbid philanthropy. . . ."

be barred, as the new constitution decreed, from granting compensation for the freed slaves. The proposal, a dying gasp coming at the end of the session, suffered overwhelming defeat.[17]

Many Unionists were indifferent to any kind of compensation. Slavery was a nuisance. No one should pay to abate a nuisance. Other Unionists, like John S. Berry of Baltimore County, took a different course. He offered a resolution for the appointment of a committee to see Lincoln and to ask for federal funds for loyal slave owners. It breezed through the convention by a 49 to 24 votes.[18] The effort served no productive purpose, for reimbursement was never obtained.

On June 24 the debate on emancipation ended, and the vote was taken—53 for and 27 against abolition.[19] Several members rose briefly to explain their votes. Fendall Marbury announced, "I consider this robbery, and therefore vote 'no.'" Frederick Schley had the last say. He couched within one sentence his reasons for voting "yea." They included "patriotism, justice, and humanity," Maryland "honor," and popular "welfare."[20]

Thereupon the Convention adjourned until July 6 to give the farm members time to gather their harvests. Such action, or rather lack of action, prompted one journal to call the delegates, with few exceptions, "spiritless donothings [sic] and treasury suckers."[21] Criticism of this nature apparently made its mark. Upon reassembling the delegates voted to limit each person to thirty minutes of debate on any question. This could be extended only by a two-thirds vote of those present.[22]

But progress was now to be slowed by outside intervention. For ten days the convention lacked a quorum as delegates scattered before Major General Jubal Anderson Early's swiftly moving raiders. The Confederates were sweeping into Maryland on their annual invasion. Hagerstown fell on July 6, and Frederick three days later. Both towns felt the brunt of a Confederate attitude that now regarded Maryland as an enemy. Only by gratifying rebel demands for ransom did the two towns escape a holocaust.

Lew Wallace tried to stop Early's troops along the Monocacy River, just east of Frederick. His outnumbered soldiers successfully delayed,

[17] *Debates*, III, 1717–19.
[18] *Debates*, I, 720 and III 1865–66.
[19] *Debates*, I, 742.
[20] *Ibid.*
[21] *Cecil Whig*, June 25, 1864.
[22] *Debates*, II, 749.

but could not turn back, the invaders. The Unionists lost 1,294 men.[23] On toward Washington and Baltimore pressed the rebels, burning bridges, seizing railroad trains, and stirring great excitement in these two cities.

Governor Bradford's home, just north of Baltimore, was set on fire in retaliation for the burning of Governor John Letcher's home in Virginia. Just outside of Washington, Montgomery Blair's home met a similar fate. The rebels spared his father's home but plundered its contents and tarried long enough for a "debauch of gluttony and drinking."[24] Thus did they throw away the opportunity to enter the capital before sizable reinforcements arrived. The marauders soon withdrew to Virginia.

When the Constitutional Convention finally mustered a quorum, some delegates bared their anxiety and hatred. Cushing of Baltimore offered a preamble and resolution that referred to Maryland's being "invaded by bands of robbers and murderers" and called rebel sympathizers "unworthy citizens of Maryland . . . forsaken of God and instigated by the devil."[25] This heated outburst won the convention's approval. Another approved resolution demanded that the United States government imprison or expel all open sympathizers with the recent invasion and all adults who refused to swear allegiance "and obedience to the United States."[26]

Of wider effect was the oath that Stirling successfully included in the elective franchise in the constitution. Voters had to swear both past and future loyalty to the United States,[27] though this was not to be considered conclusive proof of the right to cast a ballot. Standards of loyalty were comparable to those developed for the Cecil County catechism. A person would lose the franchise if he had in any manner given "aid, countenance, or support" to "those in armed

[23] *Official records*, Series I, Vol. 37, Part 1, p. 202. Wallace stated, "I am retreating with a foot-sore, battered, and half-demoralized column." *Ibid.*, Series I, Vol. 37, Part 2, p. 145. The battle took place on July 9, 1864.

[24] Printed excerpts from a letter by F. P. Blair, August 15, 1864, Blair-Lee Papers, Box 4.

[25] *Debates*, II, 787.

[26] *Debates*, II, 830. A resolution by Frederick Schley also passed. It urged the President and his military commanders in Maryland to assess rebel sympathizers for the losses suffered by loyal citizens in order to compensate the latter. *Debates*, II, 800.

[27] By this provision "the judges of election at the first election held under this constitution shall, and at any subsequent election may, administer . . . " the oath. *Debates*, III, 1882.

hostility to the United States." This included sending within enemy lines "money or goods, or letters, or information."[28] Strictly interpreted, the oath would have excluded even those staunch Unionists who wavered during the tumultuous days of April, 1861.

Stirling's proposal stirred the minority to action. Richard H. Edelen of Charles County begged the delegates to look closely. Did they want out of "a spirit of prejudice, or partisan hate" to fix upon the organic law of the state a feature so objectionable? It meant that those who had been granted presidential amnesty would still be outcasts in Maryland. Edelen cried out, "Let bygones be bygones. Let the dead past bury its dead."[29]

Stockbridge retorted. Maryland natives were firing at, robbing, and plundering citizens of their own state. They had left their homes with the intent of returning as conquerors to thrust the Confederate yoke upon the people. Should these men be given the privileges of loyal persons whom they had been seeking to destroy? To do so, said Stockbridge, would be a "gross injustice" and " a wanton outrage."[30]

As to persons who held office under the laws and constitution of the state, they must also take the oath, and it would be required of men henceforth elected or appointed. The constitution further ordered the General Assembly to apply the iron clad oath to such other groups as teachers and lawyers. A particularly controversial clause allowed only those qualified to vote under the new constitution to cast ballots in the election that would reject or put into effect that constitution. On the other hand, the convention extended the ballot to one group never before entitled to vote—soldiers in the field.

All of these measures worked toward assuring political dominance for the Unconditional Unionists. How a state rights advocate like delegate John F. Dent must have longed for the old order! He denounced "blind obedience" to the federal administration; "It stinks in my nostrils as the foul emanation of a tyrant's breath. It is false, it is cruel, it is wicked."[31] Dent dared to support recognition of southern independence. He even told his colleagues he preferred Maryland's joining that confederacy.[32]

The cries of the slavery interests went unheeded as their political power collapsed. The Union majority devised a formula that more

---

[28] *Debates*, II, 1266, 1269 and III, 1882.   [31] *Debates*, II, 1367.

[29] *Debates*, II, 1274.   [32] *Debates*, II, 1368.

[30] *Debates*, II, 1274.

than doubled the number of seats for Baltimore. The city was to be divided into three districts, each to get a state senator and seven delegates. Four northern counties also gained seats, while the southern lost.

Though Baltimore had to settle for six delegates per district, this was basically the plan that won approval. It gave northern Maryland the same proportion of House seats as it had total population. This was the way it worked despite the omission of the Negro from the basis of representation. Such action stirred much debate. A proponent of slavery said the Negroes should be represented. Back came the retort that such representation would be by their enemies. "What justice is there in that?" asked one delegate.[33]

Oliver Miller of Anne Arundel County complained that each Baltimorean's vote could elect six delegates while his could do no better than two.[34] The less gullible would note the fallacy in this argument. Baltimore under the new Constitution could muster only one delegate for 10,251 whites, while Anne Arundel counted one for every 5,852 whites. If Baltimore should achieve an appreciable population growth, the inequity would increase. The approved formula assured that result.

Battered by emancipation and the overthrow of the old system of representation, the Democrats sought solace in apprenticeship. Some Unionists joined them, fearing that society would suffer if helpless Negro minors were freed without provision for them.[35] An article was passed to apprentice minors incapable of being supported by themselves or their parents. Later a loyalty oath was added. In the final days of the convention the delegates changed their minds and discarded apprenticeship.[36] The incumbrance of a loyalty oath made it unpalatable even to many advocates of slavery.

---

[33] Joseph B. Pugh of Cecil County, *Debates*, II, 1052. James T. Briscoe of Calvert County described the rural citizen as a permanent resident while in the city "there is always a floating population. . . ." He warned against Baltimore's absorbing all of Maryland's political power. *Debates*, III, 1660. Another delegate, Eli J. Henkle of Anne Arundel County, asserted that "Property should be . . . taken into consideration in graduating any scale of representation. . . ." *Debates*, II, 1065.

[34] *Debates*, II, 1064.

[35] *Debates*, III, 1581.

[36] *Debates*, III, 1799–1800. Frederick Schley called apprenticeship "nothing more . . . than modified slavery." *Ibid.*, p. 1577.

TABLE F. ALLOCATION OF SEATS IN THE MARYLAND GENERAL ASSEMBLY

| | Constitution of 1851 | | Constitution of 1864 | | |
| | | No. of persons per | | No. of persons per | No. of whites per |
	Delegates	Delegate	Delegates	Delegate	Delegate
Northern Maryland					
Allegany	4	7,087	5	5,670	5,403
Baltimore City	10	21,242	18	11,801	10,251
Baltimore County	6	9,023	6	9,023	7,787
Carroll	3	8,178	5	4,907	4,505
Cecil	3	7,954	4	5,965	4,999
Frederick	6	7,765	6	7,765	6,399
Harford	3	7,805	4	5,854	4,493
Washington	5	6,283	5	6,283	5,661
	40	11,118	53	8,391	7,276
Southern Counties					
Anne Arundel	3	7,967	2	11,950	5,852
Calvert	2	15,224	1	10,447	3,997
Caroline	2	5,565	2	5,565	3,802
Charles	2	8,259	1	16,517	5,796
Dorchester	3	6,820	2	10,231	5,827
Howard	2	6,694	2	6,694	4,541
Kent	2	6,634	2	6,634	3,674
Montgomery	2	9,161	2	9,161	5,675
Prince George's	3	7,776	2	11,664	4,825
Queen Anne's	2	7,981	2	7,981	4,208
St. Mary's	2	7,607	1	15,213	6,798
Somerset	4	6,248	3	8,331	5,111
Talbot	2	7,398	2	7,398	4,053
Worcester	3	6,887	3	6,887	4,481
	34	7,127	27	8,975	4,825
State of Maryland	74	9,284	80	8,588	6,449

| | Constitution of 1851 | | Constitution of 1864 | |
	North	South	North	South
House of Delegates	40	34	53	27
Senate	8	14	10	14
Total	48	48	63	41

An additional provision was the method for registering voters, an innovation for Maryland. Another reform abolished the system by which the governorship had to be rotated between three geographical areas. A new office, that of lieutenant governor, was created. Winning particularly high praise was the provision for a new public school system. These advances improved the organic law of the state[37] even though the restrictions upon the elective franchise marked a step backward.

The constitution was passed by the delegates by a vote of 53 to 26 on September 6.[38] Thus concluded the convention which had assembled in April. Its work now went before the people for approval or rejection.

Their decision would affect more than the status of the Negro. If the constitution failed, then, as one editorial writer observed, Lincoln would lose the state in November.[39] Democratic rule would soon assume control in Maryland. The fortunes of many politicians, of all shades of opinion and on all levels of government, were inextricably linked with the fortunes of the new constitution.

[37] Myers, for instance, said in *Constitution 1864*, p. 88, that "as far as the organic law was concerned, the new Constitution was a decided advance. . . ."

[38] *Debates*, III, 1873.

[39] *Baltimore Clipper*, September 27, 1864.

CHAPTER XV

FUSION OF THE
PRESIDENTIAL AND
CONSTITUTIONAL CAMPAIGNS

PUTTING ASIDE THEIR deliberations, Maryland legislators crowded into the hall of the House of Delegates.[1] They had come on this January day in 1864 to hear three distinguished Unionists: Montgomery Blair, Thomas Hicks, and Thomas Swann. Blair talked at length about the rebellion and in support of Lincoln's Emancipation Proclamations. Maryland matters he avoided. Not so his two colleagues. Hicks in a brief address urged "prompt action" upon emancipation in the state. Swann was even more emphatic on the issue.[2]

When a Creswell supporter heard of plans for the three to talk, he urged the Eastern Shoreman and Winter Davis to attend, "and speak as long and as loud as Messrs. Blair and Hicks."[3] Davis turned a deaf ear to such entreaties. He said "don't expect me to run a race with those creeping things for the honors of humiliation."[4]

He was disgusted with the 1864 legislature and did not change his opinion when the General Assembly endorsed a second term for Lincoln. The resolution was introduced into the Senate by the radical Archibald Stirling, Jr., who was following the dictates of political expediency.

The shift in public opinion toward Lincoln was almost as remarkable as the shift toward emancipation. In 1860 he was able to mus-

---

[1] *Annapolis Gazette*, January 28, 1864.

[2] See *Baltimore American*, January 25, 1864, for account of the addresses.

[3] George Earle to John A. J. Creswell, January 18, 1864, Creswell Papers, IV. Earle feared that the Blair men might try to get the credit for renominating Lincoln.

[4] H. Winter Davis to Rear Admiral Samuel F. DuPont, January 9, 1864, S. F. DuPont Papers.

ter only a few thousand votes in Maryland, yet shortly thereafter he won the sympathies of a large number of Unionists. His growing popularity survived criticism of the Emancipation Proclamations.

Now in 1864 his candidacy became an important element in Maryland politics. The politicians began jockeying for position. A debate arose over who was and who was not a true supporter of Lincoln. The grouping of rival forces troubled the *Baltimore American*, for it feared the effect upon the cause of emancipation.[5]

The first formal political move linking the campaigns for President and for abolition of slavery took place January 21. On that date the Unconditional Union State Central Committee issued a call for a state convention on February 22 to elect delegates to the National Union (Republican) Convention and to take whatever action seemed necessary in the campaign for a new constitution.[6]

What would the rival Union State Central Committee do? The answer was not long in forthcoming. On January 27 its executive committee found no reason for continued division among Unionists and *accepted* the call of the Unconditional faction. One request was made—that the coming convention appoint a new central committee to replace the present competing organizations.[7] Thus the conservatives surrendered far more than they had been asked to yield in June, 1863. This was no fusion. The *Advocate* called it a "going over of the Conservatives to the Radicals."[8]

Some Unconditional Unionists did not welcome their new allies. "Common decency," felt the *Cambridge Intelligencer*, should have made their former foes wait until candidates were chosen rather than have them try "to make our nominations for us."[9] Another observer sensed that the conservatives were attempting to juggle the Unconditional Unionists out of their party.[10] This action by the Swann men, ac-

[5] On February 20, 1864, the *Baltimore American* commented, "We cannot but regard all attempts to couple the great Emancipation movement in this State with the game of President-making or the supremacy of local factions as eminently mischievous."

[6] Invited to attend the primary meetings in the city wards and county election districts were "The supporters of the Unconditional Union nominee for Comptroller at the late election and all such as approve the platform or resolutions of the Convention of 16th June. . . ." *Baltimore American*, January 26, 1864.

[7] *Chestertown Transcript*, February 20, 1864; *Baltimore County Advocate*, February 6, 1864.

[8] *Baltimore County Advocate*, February 6, 1864.

[9] *Cambridge Intelligencer* cited by *Chestertown Transcript*, February 20, 1864.

[10] George M. Russum to John A. J. Creswell, February 4, 1864, Creswell Papers, V.

cording to Baltimore's Postmaster William H. Purnell, surprised and "badly frightened" the "Custom House Party."[11]

If this were so, the latter did not show it publicly. On February 1 Henry W. Hoffman and his associates invited the Swann group to consultations. Swann rejected the offer. He was still smoldering over what he called the Unconditional Central Committee's unprovoked "spirit of bitterness and crimination" directed at him and his committee.[12]

The rejection enraged the Hoffman men who swore "war to the hilt."[13] As part of their strategy, they urged that persons picked by Baltimore's wards to select a delegation to the February 22nd meeting be authorized also to choose the city slate for the Constitutional Convention. Opposing the move was District Attorney William Price, president of the annually elected Union City Convention.[14]

Why the difference on this point?—because, implied the *Clipper*, the Winter Davis faction needed the issue of immediate emancipation to becloud the presidential question.[15] Election of radical delegates uncommitted to Lincoln was no doubt the goal. A look at the Ninth Ward primary seemed to validate this view. There Archibald Stirling, Jr., and four associates breezed to victory on a so-called regular Unconditional Union Ticket calling "For Immediate Emancipation, No State C[o]mpensation, No Negro Apprenticeship."[16] This slogan dealt solely with the state. On the losing side was an "Administration and Unconditional Union Ticket" that indicated by its title a concern with the presidential question and a refusal to submerge it in state issues.

If Davis hoped to circumvent Lincoln by such subterfuge, he partially failed. True, he managed to get many friendly delegates elected, but the ward meetings ordered the voters to support Lincoln. Similar backing for the president appeared when the delegates met in citywide convention and picked their representatives to the state

[11] William H. Purnell to Montgomery Blair, February 3, 1864, Blair Family Papers, Gist Blair Collection, VII.

[12] *Baltimore American*, March 18, 1864. Hoffman was secretary-treasurer of the Unconditional Union State Central Committee on February 1 but became president as a result of the February 22nd convention.

[13] William H. Purnell to Montgomery Blair, February 3, 1864, Blair Family Papers, Gist Blair Collection, VII.

[14] *Baltimore American*, February 13, 1864.

[15] *Baltimore Clipper*, February 20, 1864.

[16] *Baltimore American*, February 15, 1864.

gathering. Later the same city delegates reassembled to choose men for the constitutional slate.[17]

On February 22 the state convention met in Baltimore. The opening session featured competing delegations from the counties of Baltimore,[18] Kent, and Dorchester. Rejected from the first two jurisdictions were men who had assembled under the call of local Conservative Union organizations. On the other hand, both Dorchester delegations gained acceptance as Unconditional Unionists, each receiving half of the county's vote.

Congressman Creswell won the presidency of the convention and the right to appoint a new State Central Committee. He addressed the delegates on behalf of emancipation. Then he said that Maryland wanted Lincoln another four years. Tremendous applause filled the room for about five minutes.

Daniel Blocksom, who had been ousted with John Frazier, Jr., from the Board of Enrollment, offered a resolution stating that Maryland's delegates to the National Convention be instructed to vote for Lincoln, "first, last and all the time." Collier, the controversial figure from Somerset County, opposed, saying that his section of the state was unwilling to pledge its support to any person. Scattered hisses punctuated his remarks.

Stirling entered the debate, calling himself unequivocally a Lincoln man, a statement far removed from the truth. He urged that "earnestly requested" be substituted for Blocksom's "instructed," for he did not want to tie the delegates' hands and thus deprive them of influencing the selection of a Vice President. It was felt by some that Stirling had Winter Davis in mind as Lincoln's running mate.[19]

[17] Each potential candidate for the Constitutional Convention was asked:
"1st. Do you consent to the use of your name as a candidate . . . ? 2nd. Are you for immediate Emancipation in this State? 3d. Are you opposed to State compensation to slave owners? 4th. Are you opposed to 'negro apprenticeship or fixed wages by law? 5th. Are you in favor of representation according to population?"
Baltimore American, March 3, 1864.

[18] William J. Albert headed the local Unconditional Union Central Committee. Its delegation to the state convention was admitted though reportedly this faction held no primaries or county meeting. *Baltimore County Advocate*, February 6, 20, April 9, 1864; *Baltimore American*, February 27, 1864; *Cecil Whig*, March 19, 1864; John S. Berry to Montgomery Blair, February 17, 1864, Lincoln Collection, Vol. 143.

[19] Davis, however, was not anxious for the office. He wrote Samuel F. DuPont on June 4 or 5, 1864 (S. F. DuPont Papers), "Several persons have mentioned the V.P. [Vice Presidency] to me—but I have said I have no ambition for the place."

Blocksom refused to budge; so Stirling shifted, offering to take Blocksom's instructions if Blocksom would take Stirling's resolutions. The latter showered sympathy upon radical emancipationists in other slave states and regretted "that influences in the Cabinet have, in Maryland and those states, depressed the efforts of the radical friends of the Administration and of emancipation, and given prominence to those who are the unwilling advocates of emancipation." In this statement Stirling demonstrated his true feelings— hostility for Montgomery Blair and kinship for those radicals who wished to unseat Lincoln. Both Blocksom's and Stirling's resolutions received the approval of the convention as did resolutions that opposed apprenticeship and state compensation and criticized the legislature for not authorizing a soldier's vote in the field.

The battle over selecting two delegates-at-large from the western shore to the National Convention involved some well-known figures. Francis P. Blair, Sr., of national repute, was entered as a candidate along with William H. Purnell, who believed the "tools" of Winter Davis were "plotting to cheat the people and betray the President." Blair's name sparked a mixed reception—applause and hisses. The more prominent of his two opponents, Henry W. Hoffman, met with a more cheering response. He and his running mate, Albert C. Greene, an Allegany County legislator, overwhelmed Blair and Purnell by about 2 to 1.[20]

Apparently it was Congressman Webster who hastened that evening to Montgomery Blair's home in Washington and told what had happened. Lincoln was there. According to Winter Davis, "the Prest. saw through the mist, and laughed at him and Blair telling them they had plainly been beaten fairly and thoroughly and might as well own it!!"[21]

Creswell and Henry H. Goldsborough were picked for delegates-at-large from the Eastern Shore. The winners from the five congressional districts included such well-known radicals as Levin E.

[20] Reports on the state convention can be found in many papers, including *Baltimore American*, February 23, 1864, and *Civilian and Telegraph*, February 25, 1864. So many office holders were convention delegates that the *Maryland Union*, February 25, 1864, referred to the gathering as "the Abolition Office Holder's State Convention." See also *Baltimore Clipper*, February 29, 1864.

[21] H. Winter Davis to Rear Admiral Samuel F. DuPont, March 5, 1864, S. F. DuPont Papers.

Straughn, Archibald Stirling, Jr., Judge Hugh L. Bond, and Frederick
A. Schley. Yet this delegation was pledged to Lincoln, for he was too
popular in the counties for the convention to act otherwise.

Davis looked upon the results as *"personally"* gratifying. He wrote
a close friend, "I have all the delegates to the Nat. Conv. but two,"
which meant they would follow Davis' lead and desert Lincoln if the
opportunity presented itself. Now Davis began to hope that, "in
spite of the Prests. ill will, we will carry the constitutional conv. for
emancipation."[22]

In other words, he considered Lincoln an obstacle to the achievement of a goal the President held dearly—Maryland emancipation.
Three days after the state convention, Davis proclaimed from the
floor of the House of Representatives that Maryland owed nothing
to Lincoln for the strides it had taken toward emancipation. He even
questioned "whether the hostile influence . . . near the President's
ear will allow Maryland to become a free State."[23] Understandably,
Stirling's resolution of sympathy for the radical emancipationists
found a fitting niche in the speech.

Francis P. Blair, Jr., did not take kindly to some of the things
Davis said. On February 27 he arose in the House of Representatives
and lashed at the "Jacobins" of Maryland and Missouri and their
"desire to glut their vengeance and their lust of spoils." He spot-
lighted the incongruity of the state convention in Maryland supporting Lincoln on the one hand and expressing sympathy for his
enemies on the other. Nor did he overlook what he considered to be
the fraudulent admission to that convention of bogus delegations
from three counties.[24]

The rejected delegates from Baltimore County had already written Francis P. Blair, Jr.'s brother, Montgomery, attacking the legitimacy of the delegates to the national convention and scoring the
resolution sympathizing with the radicals. The Baltimore Countians
suggested that another state convention be called but wished first to

[22] H. Winter Davis to Rear Admiral Samuel F. DuPont, February 29, 1864, S. F.
DuPont Papers. The delegation totaled fourteen members. The two men Davis did not
claim were apparently the Fifth Congressional District representatives, John C. Holland and Wm. L. W. Seabrook.

[23] *Congressional Globe*, 38th Cong., 1st Sess., Vol. 34, Part 4, Appendix, p. 44. The
speech was delivered on February 25, 1864. It can also be found in *Davis Speeches*, pp.
353–67. This volume erroneously dated the speech January 25.

[24] *Congressional Globe*, 38th Cong., 1st Sess., Vol. 34, Part 4, Appendix, pp. 47 and 49.

ascertain the views of the true friends of Lincoln and emancipation.[25] Montgomery Blair quickly replied that they should do nothing despite "this foul dealing." The main objective had been accomplished—the delegates were pledged to Lincoln. As to the resolutions attacking him and giving sympathy to the radicals, Blair wrote them off as a seeming attempt to split the Union Party. He would not accept the bait.[26] The aggrieved Baltimore Countians followed Blair's advice. No action was taken.

During March Lincoln Associations began to appear in Baltimore.[27] A Central Lincoln Association met on April 6 with fifteen wards represented. Through this organization the old conservatives and moderates found a new key to power. Its presidency went to Thomas Swann, who played the demagogue in giving the association what it wanted to hear. For instance, Swann pictured himself as the champion of workingmen, one who did not favor letting the Negro enter Baltimore to compete with white labor and "snatch the bread from the mouths of our mechanics."[28] Thus Maryland entered the political battle of 1864 with Lincoln Associations controlled by the more conservative and moderate elements, while its delegation to the National Union Convention lay under the influence of Winter Davis.

During the spring of that year, the Unionist rivals engaged in two more major tests of strength. One was the Maryland State Electoral Convention. To select delegates, a newly-elected City Union Convention called the usual primary meetings. This accorded with political custom but not with the wishes of the radicals. Unable to control the City Union Convention, they circumvented it by having the State Central Committee issue a competing call for a meeting. Thus two rival delegations sought admission to the State Electoral Convention.

The meeting convened on June 8. Radicals battled vigorously for possession of the chair. On a crucial ballot for president pro tem, radical Levin E. Straughn squeezed through by a one-vote victory. With this narrow margin as a wedge, the radicals tightened their

---

[25] John S. Given and others to Montgomery Blair, February 23, 1864, *Baltimore American*, February 27, 1864; *Baltimore Clipper*, February 27, 1864.

[26] Montgomery Blair to Baltimore County delegates, February 24, 1864, *Baltimore American*, February 27, 1864; *Baltimore Clipper*, February 27, 1864.

[27] *Baltimore American*, March 28, 1864.

[28] *Ibid.*, April 8, 1864. Swann's speech was also reported in *Baltimore Clipper*, April 7 and 8, 1864.

control by admitting friendly delegations from Baltimore City and County while rejecting their opposition from the same jurisdictions.[29]

During the proceedings an announcement was made of Abraham Lincoln's renomination by the National Convention then meeting in Baltimore. The news sparked "vociferous applause" by a large body of delegates.[30] Not to be outdone, another man arose and said that Missouri's radical delegation had won admittance to the National Convention. Now it was the turn of those who reluctantly accepted Lincoln's nomination to cheer. Chosen for the electoral slate were men such as William J. Albert, Henry H. Goldsborough, and R. Stockett Mathews, a strong Davisite.

The second major testing area for divided Unionists revolved around the contest for mayor of Baltimore. The City Union Convention, apparently determined to catch the opposition off balance, gave only one day's notice for the ward meetings which would pick delegates to a nomination convention. Mayor John Lee Chapman benefited by these maneuverings, and was chosen to run again. His supporters emphasized the importance of victory in October. The mayor's defeat, said District Attorney William Price, would dishearten Baltimore's "firm and true men" in the presidential election.[31]

The more radically disposed set up their own convention and selected Archibald Stirling, Jr., for mayor. His forces pinned a variety of charges on the Chapman men:

1. Replacing job holders with new subordinates in order to get into office those most favorable to the mayor's renomination.

2. Hiring unnecessary workers for the city in order "to swell" and corrupt primary meetings.

3. Early forced levy of funds upon city office holders for purposes such as carrying the City Union Convention and acting speedily on the mayoralty.

4. Holding ward meetings at night and having them convene in "poorly ventilated" small rooms, with "a hat for a ballot box."

---

[29] In accordance with custom, a Baltimore County Union Convention had appointed a county executive committee in May, 1863, to conduct local party affairs. Since then the Unconditional Union State Central Committee appointed its own executive committee for Baltimore County. This usurping of local rights angered many Unionists and resulted in rival delegations to state conventions.

[30] *Baltimore American,* June 9, 1864.

[31] William Price to Montgomery Blair, July 30, 1864, Lincoln Collection, Vol. 163.

5. No record of voters' names or the numbers casting a ballot; "no pr[o]vision against sleeve stuffing," which meant shoving into the ballot box votes hidden in one's sleeve.

6. A "muscle" deciding on how many votes to use.[32]

These accusations accompanied a hot debate over whether one or two ballot boxes should be used in the general election. The ballot box issue arose because Baltimoreans would be voting on the same day for a mayor and a new constitution. If the elections were considered separate and distinct, then no oath would be required for casting a ballot for mayor. Such a prospect stirred the wrath of many Stirling men. They saw it as a plot to coax the disloyal into voting for Chapman.

Judges of election and various public officials argued over the issue. It was resolved by authorizing ballot boxes with two compartments, one to hold the votes for municipal offices and the other to receive ballots on the constitution. The judges were to administer the oath to all voters.[33]

Chapman denied any conspiracy to exchange a constitutional defeat for rebel votes on his behalf. He said he had "labored incessantly" for the adoption of the constitution.[34] Counterattacking, Chapman charged the Stirling forces with deliberately arranging for the constitutional and mayoralty election on the same day. Money was the reason—to exploit for Stirling's advantage the funds earmarked for supporting the new constitution.[35]

Nor was this all. The mayor claimed that Winter Davis was assessing both office holders and contractors for Stirling's campaign. Sums ranging from $50 to $2,000 poured out of contractors' purses and into radical coffers. The purpose was to take control of Baltimore in order to employ its patronage for Davis' elevation.[36]

[32] *Baltimore American*, September 17, 1864. An article in the *Baltimore Clipper* of September 28, 1864, signed "PUBLIC GOOD," defended the evening meetings, saying that "regular poll books were kept and each voter's name was recorded."

[33] *Baltimore Daily Gazette*, October 12, 1864; *Täglicher Wecker*, October 7, 1864.

[34] *Baltimore American*, October 7, 1864.

[35] Article signed "ONE WHO KNOWS," *ibid.*, October 10, 1864. The radicals also were accused of trying to gain control of the Baltimore police. On the other hand, Chapman was said to violate his oath of office by forcing city policemen to distribute documents calling for his re-election.

[36] John Lee Chapman to A. Lincoln, November 25, 1864, Lincoln Collection, Vol. 179. Chapman, who did not believe Stirling really wanted the mayoralty, attacked

In the meantime Davis was achieving notoriety in a spectacular clash with the President over plans for governing and reconstructing the rebellious states. Davis got a bill through the House of Representatives that passed the Senate in the final hours of the session. It placed stricter requirements upon accepting Confederate states back into the fold than Lincoln desired. Furthermore, the President opposed the idea that the states in insurrection were out of the Union.

Lincoln neither signed nor vetoed the legislation. He simply pocketed it, a maneuver that killed the bill because the congressional session was at an end. When he heard the news, Davis turned livid, his face "pale with wrath." Standing at his desk, vigorously waving his arms, he denounced Lincoln even though the House had already adjourned.[37]

A few days later the President announced a proclamation that demonstrated a remarkable exercise of executive power. He took what he liked from the congressional bill and rejected the rest. Never, retorted Davis, had "A more studied outrage on the legislative authority of the people . . . been perpetrated."[38] The Maryland congressman called "this rash and fatal act of the President, a blow at the friends of his administration, at the rights of humanity, and at the principles of republican government."[39]

These charges Davis incorporated in a bitter attack known as the Wade-Davis Manifesto. Senator Benjamin Franklin Wade of Ohio was the other signer of the document. Many legislators sympathized with Davis' criticism, but Americans in general sided with the President. *Harper's Weekly* in its August 20th issue denounced the "ill-tempered spirit" of the manifesto.

Nothing daunted, Davis and his cohorts plotted to replace Lincoln with a more suitable candidate. Their prospects brightened as the President's chances for re-election plunged to a low point in August. Dissatisfaction with the lack of military progress, war weariness, and political discontent eroded Lincoln's hopes for victory. James Armitage, president of the Anderson Union League in Baltimore, wrote

---

Stanton's dispensation of War Department patronage to Winter Davis. The latter had allegedly offered army Major Blumenburg a promotion if he would swing the German vote to Stirling. Half of the city's printing purportedly awaited the German newspaper *Correspondent* if it would join the cause. According to Chapman, $30,000 to $50,000 was being used against him.

[37] Noah Brooks, *Washington in Lincoln's Time* (New York, 1895), p. 168.

[38] *Davis Speeches*, p. 422.

[39] *Ibid.*, p. 425.

that the Administration was *"losing ground rapidly"* and that "many of our most reliable men . . . declare that Mr. Lincoln will not get their support unless there is a radical change and that speedily."[40]

The gloom lifted as Atlanta fell to Major General William Tecumseh Sherman on September 2. The movement to replace Lincoln collapsed. Judge Bond told Stanton, "your victory at Atlanta spoiled it all!" to which the Secretary of War commented wryly, "My heavens . . . I knew nothing about it or I would have postponed Atlanta a week!"[41]

Meanwhile, Lincoln had accepted Chase's offer to resign, relieving the President of a strained relationship. The dropping of this radical favorite spurred efforts to reright the balance by ousting Blair. Senator Zachariah Chandler of Michigan convinced a somewhat reluctant President to agree to Blair's dismissal on condition that John C. Frémont, who had been the Republican standard-bearer in 1856, surrender his current presidential ambitions. Frémont thought about it, consulted his friends, and decided to withdraw from the race absolutely.

Chandler had more than he bargained for. In regard to presidential aspirations, he said to Frémont, "But I wish a *conditional one* to get Blair." Frémont reneged, "I will make no conditions—my letter is written and will appear tomorrow." Chandler hurried to Washington to be certain that Lincoln carried out his end of the bargain. Then the President saw Frémont's letter, showed annoyance at the form of it, and seemed tempted to go no further. But Lincoln yielded.[42]

On September 23 Lincoln wrote Montgomery Blair, reminding him of his generous offer to resign whenever this would be a relief to the President. Lincoln added, "The time has come."[43] Exit Mr. Blair!

Winter Davis expressed joy at being "relieved from that galling

[40] James Armitage to James M. Edmunds, July 31, 1864, Lincoln Collection. During the Civil War Edmunds served as Commissioner of the General Land Office and Grand President, Union League of America.

[41] H. Winter Davis to Rear Admiral Samuel F. DuPont, Sept. 23 or 24, 1864, S. F. DuPont Papers.

[42] H. Winter Davis to Samuel F. DuPont, September 28, 1864, S. F. DuPont Papers. This letter sheds additional light on a long debated episode. For a detailed account before the finding of the Davis correspondence, see James G. Randall and Richard N. Current, *Lincoln the President: Last Full Measure* (New York, 1955), pp. 227–31.

[43] A. Lincoln to M. Blair, September 23, 1864, *Lincoln Works*, VII, 18.

humiliation."[44] He and his radical colleagues concealed enough of their distaste for Lincoln to make it possible for them to speak on his behalf during the final stages of the campaign. But Davis did not hide his true feelings for the President. He told an audience at Elkton, Maryland, that neither Lincoln nor his Democratic opponent, Major General George B. McClellan, was a leader equal to the presidency. The important difference between the two candidates revolved around the legislative power. A Union Congress would force Lincoln to wage war and free slaves, while a Democratic Congress would compel McClellan to seek peace.[45] Davis' attitude, according to one associate, was that Lincoln "is neither wise nor honest, good people, but if *I* can vote for him, it would be rediculous [sic] for *you* to be more squeamish."[46]

Nor did Blair sulk. He loyally pleaded the President's case, which he could do unobstructed by any public record of hostility. Lincoln thus managed to rally the discordant elements within the party. It did not mean, however, that he succeeded in getting rival factions to pull together. The struggle for power seemed as fierce as ever. Local elections, as Winter Davis pointed out, complicated the presidential election.[47] And in turn they affected and were affected by the campaign for the new constitution. Lincoln expressed a willingness to lose Maryland in November if the state would only vote for emancipation,[48] but of course Lincoln's chances appeared slim if the constitution failed.

The squabbling over a "wretched mayoralty" and denunciations flung at one another "for being Chase men, or disorganizers, or hypocrites" distracted Unionists.[49] Peter G. Sauerwein, a well-to-do collector of internal revenue, was particularly troubled by Winter Davis'

[44] H. Winter Davis to Samuel F. DuPont, September 28, 1864, S. F. DuPont Papers.
[45] H. Winter Davis to Samuel F. DuPont, September 29?, 1864, S. F. DuPont Papers.
[46] Peter G. Sauerwein to Edward McPherson, October 8, 1864, McPherson Papers.
[47] H. Winter Davis to Samuel F. DuPont, August 18, 1864, S. F. DuPont Papers.
[48] Tyler Dennett (ed.), *Lincoln and the Civil War in the Diaries and Letters of John Hay* (New York, 1939), p. 216.
[49] P. E. [Peter G.] Sauerwein to Edward McPherson, October 8, 1864, McPherson Papers.
[50] *Ibid.*

course. "How the deuce," said Sauerwein, "he hopes to forward the new Constitution by shewing [looks like] up the delinquencies of men whom we have fought and whipped, and who are now working in the same cause—I cannot comprehend." Sauerwein was one of Davis' allies willing to toil with "softs," "pukes," and "skunks" as long as they would support the constitution and Lincoln.[50]

So was Henry W. Hoffman, who confronted a rising clamor for ousting political renegades from the Custom House. The President wired Hoffman on September 25 to meet him in Washington.[51] According to Winter Davis, Lincoln promised Hoffman another four years as collector of customs in Baltimore and sent him back to harmonize the party. To Davis this was equivalent to transferring power to those who had opposed the movement "we are just consummating." He wrote that he was surrounded by "cowardly treachery." The betrayers were "ready to sell Stirling and every body else to secure places."[52]

That Hoffman could stray from the radical fold demonstrated the tenuous nature of political alliances. They could drift apart, break up rapidly, or coalesce under the attraction of expediency. Politics was a shifting sea of complex forces. Self-preservation drove Hoffman to slip away from his master's bidding. The maneuver did not prove successful to Hoffman. Blair called him unreliable, a man who deserted everyone and should be discarded.[53] Hoffman was not reappointed in the next Administration.

While radicals and moderates jostled for position, some of their more conservative members quit the Union Party. Among those leaving the fold was George Vickers. He did so on grounds that Unconditional Unionists had supplanted the original Union Party, making such changes that "I should scarcely recognize my political identity."[54] This separated Vickers from his good friend, Governor

[51] A. Lincoln to Henry W. Hoffman, September 25, 1864, *Lincoln Works*, VIII, 23.

[52] H. Winter Davis to Samuel F. DuPont, September 29, 1864, S. F. DuPont Papers.

[53] Howard K. Beale (ed.), *Diary of Gideon Welles*, 3 vols. (New York, 1960), II, 95.

[54] *National Intelligencer*, October 15, 1864. Vickers accepted a place on the Democratic presidential elector ticket.

Bradford, who earlier in the year had offered the Eastern Shoreman a judgeship.[55]

More surprising was Reverdy Johnson's switch. Elected United States Senator by the Union Legislature of Maryland in 1862, he pleased emancipationists by his speech in favor of a constitutional amendment to abolish slavery. Now Johnson joined Vickers and many other conservative Unionists in opposition to the new Maryland constitution and in support of the Democratic candidate for U.S. President. The two issues became inseparable. Either you were for the constitution and Lincoln or you opposed both.

The Democrats capitalized on this opposition. In the spring of 1864 they had begun to talk about holding a state convention. It convened in Baltimore on June 15, with two-thirds of the counties and the city represented. The membership was well larded with former office holders. By 25 to 21, the delegates voted in favor of sending men to the National Convention.[56] Henry May, Congressman Benjamin G. Harris, and Judge Richard B. Carmichael got three of the places for delegates-at-large. They were called "thorough secession copperheads" by one Union newspaper.[57]

Harris stirred the Chicago Convention with his opposition to Major General George B. McClellan's presidential ambitions. He pointed to the general's role in the arrest of the Maryland legislature in 1861. McClellan, said Harris, was "an assassin of State Rights, an usurper of our liberties." He would not vote for him.[58] Amid wild confusion Harris left the stand. A spectator shouted at him, "You d——d traitor," and got knocked out of his seat by the aroused congressman.[59]

The Democrats tried a marriage of convenience—choosing

---

[55] George Vickers declined in his letter to Governor Bradford of January 21, 1864, Bradford Papers.

[56] For information on Democratic State Convention see *Baltimore Daily Gazette*, June 16, 1864; *Baltimore Clipper*, June 17, 1864; *Baltimore American*, June 16, 1864; and *Chestertown Transcript*, June 18, 1864.

[57] *Baltimore Clipper*, June 17, 1864. Henry May declined the honor and was replaced. See *Baltimore American*, August 20, 1864.

[58] *Baltimore Daily Gazette*, September 1, 1864. Later Harris was quoted as saying that he felt bound to vote for the convention nominee.

[59] *Cecil Democrat*, September 3, 1864. The Democratic platform condemned military interference in elections and warned that "a repetition . . . in the approaching election will be held as revolutionary and resisted with all the means and power under our control."

McClellan, a supporter of the war, for president and adopting a platform calling for peace. A preposterous combination, yet many conservative Maryland Unionists who for more than three years had supported the war allied themselves to men who for a like period had pleaded for peace. These desertions weakened the Union Party at a time when internal dissensions eroded efforts on behalf of Lincoln and the new constitution. Thus did the Unionist enter the fall political campaign in a troubled condition.

CHAPTER XVI

MARYLAND FREE

TILL THE PEOPLE breathe life into the new constitution, "it is as a feather floating upon the breeze of popular opinion,"[1] said George Vickers, who branded as illegal the use of various tests and oaths in the upcoming election. A similar rebuke he accorded the soldiers' vote. These thoughts Vickers incorporated in a letter to the governor, urging him to instruct the judges of election to disregard the restrictions upon voting.

Bradford refused. He said he had no right to assume such a judicial function. If a wrong had been perpetrated, then the courts were the place to seek redress. Besides, the Convention Bill gave the delegates the power to prescribe voter qualifications for the constitutional election.[2]

Vickers disagreed. He summarized his position in six points:

First, That the acts of the convention in respect to a test oath and soldiers voting out of the State, are clearly unconstitutional.

Second, That the execution or enforcement of those acts may inflict a permanent and flagrant wrong upon the people of the State by putting into operation an unconstitutional instrument.

Third, That the consummation of a wrong so great and enormous ought to be avoided.

Fourth, That the power to prevent it is somewhere.

Fifth, That the courts cannot effectually exercise the power; for

---

[1] George Vickers to A. W. Bradford, September 14, 1864, *Debates*, III, 1904. The correspondence of Vickers and Bradford was considered of such importance that it was printed in the official *Debates of the Constitutional Convention.*

[2] A. W. Bradford to George Vickers, September 19, 1864, *Debates*, III, 1905–6. In this letter Bradford also noted that Maryland's first constitution went into operation without ever being ratified by the people and that the Constitution of 1851 was not consummated in accordance with prescribed procedure. The Convention Bill of 1864, it should be noted, failed to specify with exactitude the qualifications that could be required of persons seeking to vote on the constitution.

their redress would succeed and not precede the perpetration of the wrong.

Sixth, That the executive has the appropriate and full power to prevent the wrong, and should exercise it.[3]

Vickers praised Bradford's proclamation in the previous fall's election and concluded that if Schenck's actions were unconstitutional, so were the convention's.

Bradford dissented. He could not see any similarity between the two situations. In one case a military commander concocted an oath and ordered judges of elections to administer it to challenged voters. Then the General threatened to arrest those who refused to comply and sent soldiers to the polls to assure execution of his wishes. These actions conflicted with state law.

Now the people of Maryland had elected delegates to change the constitution. The new document had won a large majority in the convention and was being submitted to the voters in a manner rightfully determined by the delegates. The governor had no authority to intervene.[4]

Bradford announced by circular that the judges of election must verify that all voters took the oath.[5] This appeared in the newspapers as an excerpt from one of Bradford's letters to Vickers. It was followed by long citations from the constitution, particularly from those sections pertaining to voting on the document. Then came a list of eleven questions for catechizing suspicious voters. The interrogation embraced the pattern of April, 1864, being similar in nature and purpose.

This procedure distressed some Unionists as well as Democrats. Reverdy Johnson, though now an emancipationist, spurned the test oath. Neither constitutional nor binding he called it. Voters should take the oath in order to protect their rights. In so doing "no moral

[3] George Vickers to A. W. Bradford, September 27, 1864, *Debates*, III, 1909.

[4] A. W. Bradford to George Vickers, October 3, 1864, *Debates*, III, 1911–14. In 1865 the Maryland Court of Appeals asserted that citizenship and suffrage were not inseparable, that the same power which disfranchised "free colored men in 1801, enabled the Convention of 1864 to disqualify 'all who had been in armed hostility to the United States.'" Nor could the disfranchised protest on grounds that the law was *ex post facto* because that proviso applied only "to penal and criminal proceedings." See Thomas Anderson vs. John W. Baker, George Ernest, and Julian Magruder, *Reports of Cases Argued and Adjudged in the Court of Appeals of Maryland* (Baltimore, 1897), Vol. 23, pp. 619, 622–24. Hereafter cited as *Maryland Reports*.

[5] *Debates*, October 8, 1864, III. 1915.

injunction will be violated."[6] This, of course, was an open invitation to commit perjury and brought bitter denunciation upon Reverdy Johnson.

The Democratic State Convention endorsed the same stand.[7] One Democrat happily announced that he and his compatriots would take any oaths in order to strike at the constitution and help elect McClellan.[8] Another writer rationalized that sending help to a friend or relative in the Confederacy did not violate the oath against giving the rebels aid because the motivation flowed from affection rather than from a desire to overthrow the government. Never to voice the hope for a rebel victory, said the pleader, meant winning the entire war "as a conqueror or victor by arms."[9] In other words, it was all right to express pleasure over an occasional Confederate triumph.

All of this resounded harshly upon the ears of Chief Justice Taney. A vigorous defender of the southern way of life, he nonetheless would not tolerate compromise with what he considered principle. From his deathbed he condemned taking an oath that violated the conscience.[10]

The debate over the constitution stirred the thirty-five minority members of the Constitutional Convention into writing a fiery address, "To the Voters of Maryland." They attacked the power to reach into man's private thoughts, making him swear to his "desires in all previous time." Charging their majority colleagues with "violent partisan measures," they claimed that Negroes were to be instantly turned loose "without the slightest provision for you or them." To perpetuate these outrages, "the fiat has gone forth that no future legislature shall" grant compensation; "the fanatics of 1864 have manacled their hands."[11]

[6] Reverdy Johnson to Messrs. Wm. D. Bowie, C. C. Magruder, John D. Bowling, October 7, 1864, Baltimore *Sun*, October 10, 1864.

[7] *Chestertown Transcript*, October 8, 1864 and *Baltimore Daily Gazette*, September 30, 1864.

[8] "ROMEO" to *Cecil Democrat*, September 12, 1864, *Cecil Democrat*, September 24, 1864.

[9] *Chestertown Transcript*, October 8, 1864. A prominent lawyer, Thomas S. Alexander, argued on October 7 (Baltimore *Sun*, October 11, 1864), "if a person who has committed an overt act of treason cannot be excluded from the rolls until after he shall have been convicted . . . it would be a waste of time to argue that a person may be excluded because of his having indulged speeches, or may have committed acts inconsistent with the duty of a good citizen, but not amounting to treason."

[10] *Daily Morning Chronicle* (Washington, D. C.), October 14, 1864.

[11] The minority address appeared in the *Ægis*, September 16, 1864, and other papers. The address also struck at the reapportionment of the legislature and the disfranchisement of large numbers of citizens.

Many additional arguments of a time-tested nature floated on the political breezes that summer and fall of 1864. The Democrats, immersed in rebel sympathies and imprisoned by a myopia capable only of opposition, staunchly defended the "almost feudatory" system of the old order.[12] As worshipers of state rights, they raised the specter of the new constitution's reducing Maryland to the status of a county or a corporation.[13] The more extreme preached again the divine nature of slavery and asserted that Negroes had never lived so well as they did in bondage in America.[14] If the abolitionists proved successful, then, according to the Democrats, Negro children would go to white schools, and Negroes would be given the ballot in order to keep the radicals in power.

Some citizens shrugged off partisan remarks of an extreme nature. They wanted emancipation but were disturbed by the method of achieving it. The *National Intelligencer*, for instance, did not believe in doing a good thing "in a bad way."[15]

The progressives among the Unionists were not so concerned about method. A German language daily saw the struggle as "the old battle between masses and aristocracy, workers and capital."[16] Another paper, the *Clipper*, championed freedom by rebelling at stigmatizing "labor as a badge of servility" while the ownership of estates was accepted as a mark of social position. It believed adoption of the new constitution would break up these large holdings and create a more populous, wealthier state.[0] Labor would flow into Maryland.

Henry H. Goldsborough viewed "this great social revolution" as

[12] *Baltimore* Clipper, October 8, 1864.

[13] *Denton Journal* cited by *Cecil Democrat*, October 8, 1864. The old theme of increased taxes also came to the fore as did talk of rising cost for higher salaries and new offices.

[14] See "MARYLAND" in *Chestertown Transcript*, August 6, 1864. On April 25, 1864, that paper published an article on "Miscegenation," which claimed that radicals wanted to mix Negro blood with white because the latter was becoming *"effete."* The article then asserted that hybrid animals could not perpetuate themselves. Amalgamation would bring extinction. On the other hand, one emancipationist journal called a vote for the Constitution a vote for "a FREE WHITE MAN'S GOVERNMENT!" because the Negro would no longer be counted for determining legislative apportionment. Frederick *Examiner*, October 12, 1864.

[15] *National Intelligencer*, September 30, 1864.

[16] *Täglicher Wecker* (translated by Betty Adler), October 8, 1864. The *Baltimore American*, September 13, 1864, conveyed the same idea though it did not use the antipodal terminology of the class struggle.

[17] *Baltimore Clipper*, October 8, 1864.

an opportunity for every man, regardless of his color, "to enjoy, as God intended, the fruits of his own personal labor."[17] Rich and poor, said a journalist, would "be treated alike" and children given a free education.[18]

This was not enough to pacify people like the Unionist lady in Hagerstown who longed for the good old days. She was troubled about the servant problem and recalled the past when Negroes were satisfied with the station of life allotted them. Now they seemed to be "the most important race living," one that would eventually gain all the rights of white people. She called the situation "perfectly revolting and disgusting, and my blood boils when I read the papers."[20]

But Negroes were more often treated as pawns than as a favored people. Particularly was this true in the continuing race to recruit troops. Military excesses proved troublesome in other areas as well. This of course affected political reactions. Wallace, whose handling of the April election had won praise, no longer could resist the vast power at his command. He seized the rents, dividends, etc., of all property that belonged to rebels who had gone South.[21] In so doing Wallace usurped the right of the civil government and infringed upon the jurisdiction of Attorney General Bates. The latter requested Wallace not to enforce the order. He refused but obeyed a similar directive instigated by the President.[22]

Wallace must have felt thwarted. Probably he found suitable outlets for his frustrations.[23] On September 30 he stopped the publish-

---

[18] *Debates*, III, 1877.

[19] *Baltimore American*, October 12, 1864.

[20] Kate [Mrs. Norman B. Scott] to "My Dear Brother" [Edward B. McPherson], April 21, 1864, Edward McPherson Papers, Box 8. She would doubtlessly have been even more disgusted if she had heard Essex R. Dorsey's complaints that Negro soldiers stole his hogs and sheep and acted in a threatening manner toward him. See Essex R. Dorsey to Governor Bradford, April 20, 1864, Executive Papers.

[21] General Orders No. 30, April 26, 1864, *Official Records*, Series I, Vol. 33, pp. 989–90.

[22] Edward Bates to Major General Lew Wallace, May 25, 1864, *Official Records*, Series III, IV, 407–8; Major General Lew Wallace to Edward Bates, May 30, 1864, *Ibid.*, pp. 413–15. See also Edwin M. Stanton to Lew Wallace, June 14, 1864, *Ibid.*, p. 431; General Orders No. 45, June 14, 1864, *Ibid.*, Series I, Vol. 37, Part 1, p. 638; and *Bates Diary*, entry of June 13, 1864, pp. 376–77.

[23] Wallace told a postmaster, who complained of rebel sabotage to a loyal flag pole, that on any ensuing occasion to "shoot down the unwashed dogs who desecrate your flag." Lew Wallace to J. [Jonathan] H. Lemmon, August 2, 1864, *Official Records*, Series I, Vol. 37, Part 2, pp. 581–82.

ing of a Democratic journal, *Evening Post*, on the somewhat questionable grounds of preventing violence to the offices of that journal.[24] The *Cambridge Democrat* on the Eastern Shore was suppressed that same month. Senator Hicks had requested it.[25]

Major General David Hunter, commanding in western Maryland, devised his own brand of arbitrariness. He ordered the arrest of all those in Frederick who during the recent raid pointed out property belonging to Unionists and otherwise showed sympathy for the rebels. The males were to be imprisoned, their families sent South, their homes seized for government use, and their furniture sold for the benefit of Unionists who had suffered property loss because of these rebel informers.[26] Less vindictive Unionists protested. Nor were their motives solely humanitarian. They realized the potential destructiveness of retaliatory action should there be another raid.[27]

On the Eastern Shore people were not confronted with the ever present threat of rebel invasion, but they experienced intense feelings born of war tensions, political agitation, and race prejudice. Riding into the village of Trappe on the afternoon of October 8, Dr. Samuel Harrison went to the store of a Mr. Kemp and sat down for a peaceful moment. It did not last long. The quiet dissolved into a roar as an infuriated mob chased a Negro into the store. Shouts of "kill him, kill him!" rattled from the throats of the pursuers. Harrison tried to protect the victim but was unsuccessful. The men yanked the Negro into the street and beat him. He was subsequently arrested, only to be seized again by a group of "enraged men" and taken to the suburbs and whipped. The Negro's alleged offense was impudence to a white man.

[24] Capt. Oliver Matthews, A. A. G., to Editor of *Evening Post*, by command of Maj. Gen. Wallace, September 30, 1864, RG 98, U. S. Army Commands, Middle Dept., Letters Sent, Vol. 34, p. 173.

[25] Thos. H. Hicks, Sept. 7, 1864, Middle Dept., Reg. Letters Received, Vol. 9.

[26] *Cecil Whig*, July 30, 1864. In Frederick all male secessionists and their families were to suffer similarly to the informers.

[27] George R. Dennis wrote Montgomery Blair on July 21, 1864 (Lincoln Collection, Vol. 162) and deplored Hunter's order. He said, "The Rebel Raid was creating a united spirit in the Community. . . ." Some southern sympathizers now were willing to offer armed resistance. Francis Thomas also criticized Hunter's actions in his letter to Blair of August 18 (?), 1864 (Lincoln Collection, Vol. 164). "The arrest of quiet, inoffensive, citizens, who have not, publicly, given, by words, or acts encouragement to the enemy, cannot but be mischievous."

Harrison doubted the charge. Some politicians had just harangued the people, emphasizing race prejudice. The Negro provided a convenient scapegoat. To Harrison's astonishment, some men considered gentlemen defended the crowd's conduct. Little wonder that Harrison wrote, "The sooner we crush this demoralizing system the better will it be for our people."[28]

The Shore resounded not only with the racism of the demagogue but also with the customary political intrigue. Unionist opponents of Creswell talked about running Henry H. Goldsborough against him but dropped the idea when Goldsborough gained consideration as a possible gubernatorial candidate.[29] Mention was then made of the provost marshal of the Fifth District, William J. Leonard. Though Leonard apparently owed his office to Creswell's endorsement, he did not hesitate to criticize the Congressman, calling him "the echo and tool of H. Winter Davis."[30]

Not surprisingly, Stanton ordered Leonard removed from office. Leonard acted as if he were totally innocent of the political uses of the patronage. He snorted and bellowed like a stricken bull and wildly flailed at Creswell's "little, dirty, contemptible act."[31] Comfort for the agitated marshal came from Montgomery Blair, who announced in Salisbury that Lincoln would reappoint the provost marshal.[32]

Blair was touring the Eastern Shore with Swann in an apparent attempt to head off Creswell.[33] Ostensibly though, Swann was traveling in compliance with the request of the executive committee of the Central Association for Lincoln and Johnson. It had asked him on September 13 to go into the counties to encourage the creation

[28] Harrison recounted this incident in Trappe in his Journal, October 8, 1864, II, 726–27.

[29] See, for example, Wm. J. Leonard and Wm. C. Farrow to J. A. J. Creswell, March 30, 1864, Creswell Papers, VII, and John L. Sears to J. A. J. Creswell, September 21, 1864, Creswell Papers, IX.

[30] Wm. J. Leonard "TO THE VOTERS OF THE FIRST CONGRESSIONAL DISTRICT OF MARYLAND," *Baltimore American*, October 3, 1864.

[31] *Ibid.* Leonard, on the other hand, was accused of removing one of his assistants for supporting Creswell's reelection. See John T.(?) Downes to J. A. J. Creswell, September 26, 1864, Creswell Papers, IX.

[32] Jas. W. Clayton to [J. A. J. Creswell], October 7, 1864, Creswell Papers, IX. Leonard also sought help from William H. Purnell and John W. Crisfield as he laid plans for running for Congress. See Wm. J. Leonard to Col. Wm. H. Purnell, September 22, 1864, letter owned by Mrs. A. B. Wills of Towson, Md.

[33] Jas. W. Clayton to [J. A. J. Creswell], October 7, 1864, Creswell Papers, IX.

of auxiliary associations. Meetings were arranged, and various speakers such as Montgomery Blair, Thomas Hicks, William Price, and Francis Thomas were invited to participate. All who favored "Union and Liberty, Lincoln and Johnson, Emancipation and the New Constitution" were asked to attend.[34] During the fortnight prior to the October election, Swann spoke every day.[35]

The more radically disposed were also at work, though weakened by the Wade-Davis Manifesto and Winter Davis' arbitrariness. Their stronghold, the Unconditional Union State Central Committee, announced mass meetings extending from Cumberland in western Maryland to Snow Hill on the lower Eastern Shore. Heading its speakers were the presidential electors for Lincoln and Johnson. The committee expected its county members to arrange successful meetings with local citizens favorable to Lincoln and the new constitution.[36]

On October 7 the Chapman-Lincoln ticket and the Stirling-Lincoln partisans held rival mass meetings near each other in the Old Town section of Baltimore.[37] Crowds passed from one rally to the other, sampling the wares of the various politicos.

Despite the many meetings, things were not going well for the new constitution. Samuel Harrison, arriving in the city, concluded that the mayoralty was badly distracting the Unionists. He feared for the effect upon the constitution.[38] Even Thomas Swann, who earlier had no uncertainty about its success, now hoped "for the best."[39]

Late in September William L. W. Seabrook, Maryland's Commissioner of the Land Office, told Lincoln of his doubts about the constitution's prospects. The President, who had been receiving optimistic reports, exclaimed, "You alarm me sir! you alarm me!"[40] As Seabrook rose to leave, Lincoln stood up, put his hand on the Marylander's shoulder, and said, "I implore you, sir, to go to work

---

[34] *Baltimore Clipper*, September 28, 1864.

[35] Thomas Swann to James H.(?) Orne, October 13, 1864, Society Collection, Historical Society of Pennsylvania.

[36] *Baltimore Clipper*, September 28, 1864.

[37] *Baltimore Daily Gazette*, October 8, 1864.

[38] Harrison Journal, October 8, 1864, Part 2, p. 725.

[39] Thomas Swann to James H.(?) Orne, October 13, 1864, Society Collection, Historical Society of Pennsylvania. Radical Judge Hugh L. Bond admitted, "We are broken down and must be assisted." So he wrote Elihu B. Washburne on October 4, 1864 (Washburne Papers, Vol. 40), in a request for speakers for a big Baltimore rally.

[40] William L. W. Seabrook, *Maryland's Great Part in Saving the Union* (n. p., 1913), p. 55.

... for your Constitution, with all your energy. Try to impress other Unionists with its importance as a war measure, and don't let fail! Don't let it fail."[41] Seabrook assured the President that he was doing everything he could. Then he asked Lincoln's help, urging him to throw his powerful influence behind the cause.

The President did not, however, accept Henry W. Hoffman's invitation to attend a mass meeting in Baltimore for the "Free Constitution" on October 10.[42] Instead, he complied with a request for a letter. The message incorrectly assumed that the only issue provoking "serious controversy" was the one pertaining to emancipation. "I presume," said Lincoln, "it is no secret, that I wish success to this provision. I desire it on every consideration. I wish all men to be free."[43] He called slavery the only thing that could have plunged the nation into civil war and looked forward to the prosperity that he believed would come with its extinction.

Henry W. Hoffman read the letter to the giant rally. The throng responded enthusiastically. So many persons tried to crowd into Monument Square that "thousands" left because of an inability to get close enough to the grandstand to hear. Over the platform extended the slogan, "Lincoln and Johnson—a Free Union—a Free Constitution and Free Labor." A band from Fort McHenry enlivened the occasion, and fireworks dazzled the crowd. The ward processions arrived periodically, bearing Chinese lanterns and entertaining with their own music and fireworks. As prearranged, no demonstration or signs of preference were made on behalf of the mayoralty candidates. Their names were conspicuously absent on the transparencies and box-lights.

Henry W. Hoffman, Thomas Swann, and Senator Henry Wilson of Massachusetts were among those who talked to the gathering. Wilson drew applause as he observed, "The lawyer may forget the cause of popular liberty; the merchant in the counting house may not remember the duty he owes to our common humanity; but the mechanic, the laboring man . . . should ever go for a Free Constitution for Free Labor, and the institutions that elevate the common masses of mankind."[44]

[41] *Ibid.*, p. 56.
[42] See Henry W. Hoffman to A. Lincoln, October 3, 1864, Lincoln Collection, Vol. 172.
[43] A.. Lincoln to Henry W. Hoffman, October 10, 1864, *Lincoln Works*, VIII, 41.
[44] This account of the Baltimore political rally was based on October 11, 1864, issues

Hoffman told Lincoln the rally "was a great success" and predicted that the constitution would be adopted. From current indications he was confident of the 10,000 city majority[45] that some considered necessary to overcome county opposition.

But how would trouble at the polls affect the results? Reports spread that the rapidly approaching election would have an ominous result. A "free vote or free fight" ran one Democratic cry.[46] Threats upon the lives and property of the judges of election in Caroline County were heard. Rumors of resistance from the Eastern Shore counties accompanied requests for military protection.[47] What portion of these pleas arose out of genuine need and what portion out of political motivation cannot be readily ascertained.

One request urged that troops for Caroline County arrive in Denton, the county seat, at 2 P.M., October 11. Why the specific time?—because a "Copperhead meeting" was scheduled for that hour. The petitioner was sure that the soldiers' appearance would disperse the opposition "double quick."[48]

George Vickers believed barroom chatter and hasty talk were going to be used as excuses for military intervention. "Upon my honor," said Vickers, there was not the slightest reason for intercession on the Eastern Shore. He beseeched the governor to prevent it.[49] Apparently spurred by Vickers, some citizens of Kent and Queen Anne's counties joined in similar pleas, stating that their counties were quiet and peaceful, with no disturbance contemplated.[50]

---

of the *Baltimore American*, Baltimore *Sun, Baltimore Clipper*, and *Baltimore Daily Gazette*. See also *Baltimore Clipper*, September 28, 1864.

[45] Henry W. Hoffman to A. Lincoln, October 12, 1864, *Lincoln Works*, VIII, 42.

[46] H. Winter Davis to Rear Admiral Samuel F. DuPont, October 7, 1864, S. F. DuPont Papers and documents in RG 98, U.S. Army Commands, Middle Dept.

[47] See requests of various citizens and judges of elections for troops at the election. RG 98, U.S. Army Commands, Middle Dept., Register of Letters Received, 1864, Vol. 13.

[48] J. H. Emerson to (?), October 3, 1864, RG 98, Middle Dept., Letters Received, 1864.

[49] George Vickers to A. W. Bradford, October 8, 1864, Executive papers. Dr. Samuel A. Harrison, however, wrote in his Journal on October 9, 1864, "A captain or lieutenant called at my house today, and informed me that troops have been brought to the County [Talbot] to protect the voters. . . .I am glad of this, for I have feared that violence would be committed."

[50] Statement of George Vickers and four others, Kent County, October 8, 1864, Executive Papers; petition of twenty-three citizens of Queen Anne's County to Gover-

Bradford would do no more than remind the judges of election that the law required them, as in the April election, to certify that the army had not illegally intervened at the polls.[51] The governor did not expect trouble. Major General Lew Wallace wished to prevent "the slightest demonstration looking to military interference," in Baltimore. On the other hand, he would not hesitate to order troops into any county district where the election judges petitioned for protection. Where loyal citizens but not the judges charged a conspiracy to interfere with voting or challenging, troops should be sent only if there were any to spare. Such action must protect Unionists but not attempt to force a judge to do his duty.[52]

No troops appeared at any of Maryland's polling places except in Caroline and one district each of Talbot, Cecil, and Frederick counties. The judges of election in every case requested military support to help preserve order.[53]

It was a remarkably peaceful election for that era, but the cry of foul play found its accustomed mouthpieces. The charges welled up from both sides. One of the more picayune variety emerged from the pen of the carping editor of the *Maryland Union*, Charles Cole. He complained to the governor that the judges of the northern polls in Frederick permitted a ballot to be cast after the town clock struck five o'clock, the hour for closing the polls.[54]

The *Maryland Union* also claimed that a heavy vote early on October 12 so alarmed the judges that they resorted to "the old Cecil County Catechism." Many "legal voters" therefore refrained from

---

nor Bradford, October 10, 1864, Executive Papers. Only petitions collected by Vickers protested to the Governor against military interference. See A. W. Bradford to George Vickers, November 4, 1864, Executive Letterbook.

[51] *Debates*, III, 1915; Baltimore *Sun*, October 12, 1864; *Baltimore Daily Gazette*, October 11, 1864.

[52] Lew Wallace to Lt. Col. Samuel B. Lawrence, October 4, 1864, *Official Records*, Series I, Vol. 43, Part 2, pp. 279–80. The soldiers were prohibited to talk "to any person unnecessarily, and particularly on politics. . . ." Copies of Wallace's instructions went to the War Department for Stanton's information so that he could make any desired changes. Wallace in the meantime took a leave of absence. See A. A. G. Samuel B. Lawrence to Col. J. A. Hardie, War Dept., October 6, 1864, RG 98, Middle Dept., Letters Sent, 1864, Vol. 34, pp. 217–18.

[53] See election returns documents in Executive Papers.

[54] Charles Cole to Gov. Bradford, October 24, 1864, Executive Papers.

going to the polls.[55] The same catechism saw action in Cecil County. The judges there rejected over "50 legal votes."[56]

The gravest allegations came from Caroline County, where the *Denton Journal* attacked "the contemptible Administration pimps in our midst." The judges in one district reportedly rejected nearly 200 voters willing to take the oath, including one "uncompromising" Unionist who was said to oppose the constitution and Lincoln's re-election. The tally for the district showed only 47 votes against the constitution, despite the fact that 89 men on the poll books certified they cast negative ballots. Five others were known to have voted the same way, making a total of 94.[57]

Apparently legal action was brought against a number of Eastern Shore election judges. They did not suffer alone. Major General Lew Wallace ordered the arrest of those citizens in Caroline and Talbot counties who were brash enough to make the charges.[58]

Perjury was rampant in the state, for the disloyal voter rationalized that the oath was not binding. His ballot was accepted by election judges who lacked the firmness, as one Talbot Countian put it, to reject ballots when challenged. This so discouraged the Unionists in Talbot that they stopped working.[59]

The social influence of slavery still acted as an inhibiting factor upon some people. A neighbor of Dr. Samuel A. Harrison refused to vote, though favoring the constitution, because he feared that his neighbors might "think the less of him."[60] Other Unionists stayed away from the polls because of disgust over the test oath and fear of the Negro. In one incident on election day an emancipationist tried

[55] *Maryland Union*, October 20, 1864. On the other hand, the Frederick *Examiner*, October 19, 1864, said, "The Copperheads were unusually active during the election, and polled almost their entire strength swallowing the test oath. . . ."

[56] *Cecil Democrat*, October 15, 1864.

[57] This Caroline County account is based on the *Denton Journal* as cited in *Chestertown Transcript*, October 29, 1864. Thomas H. Kemp, Speaker of the House of Delegates and a resident of Caroline, wrote Governor Bradford on October 17, 1864 (Executive Papers) of "the frauds and outrages." On the other hand, J. H. Emerson, newspaper editor and chief election judge of Caroline's Second district, defended himself against allegations that he and an associate had robbed the ballot-box. See J. H. Emerson to Governor Bradford, October 21, 1864, Executive Papers.

[58] Oliver Matthews, A. A. G., to Brig. Gen. Lockwood, November 5, 1864, RG 98, Middle Dept., Letters Sent, Vol. 34, pp. 489–90.

[59] James Valliant to Governor Bradford, October 15, 1864, Executive Papers.

[60] Harrison Journal, October 11, 1864, Part 2, pp. 728–29.

to woo five or six voters, only to meet with this retort: "this may be all very well for you; you are a rich man and can afford to send your children from home to school; but we are poor . . . and we do not want to send our children to school with Negroes." So all but two, whom he got to vote, walked away.[61]

The emancipationists in Maryland had, of course, no intention of integrating the schools, yet the issue attained considerable notoriety and influence. No doubt many folk considered it a step toward the great dread—social equality with Negroes. "The lower the rank of the white," said Dr. Harrison, "the greater the fear."[62]

In the Confederate-sympathizing tobacco country, test oaths provided no impediment to voting. A good turn-out rallied against the constitution. The margin was so overwhelming in Charles County that one wonders if the secessionists did not practice their own brand of intimidation. They swamped the constitution by a vote of 978 to 13. Ten per cent more citizens voted than in November, 1861, a remarkable feat, considering the departure of men for the war and the fact that no candidates were running.

The fourteen slave counties voted in larger number than in the two preceding elections. This region crushed the new constitution by a four to one margin. Only disputed Caroline voiced its approval. More startling was the constitution's loss in Harford and Carroll and the tie vote in Cecil, for all three of these counties were in northern Maryland.

In Baltimore the mayoralty race attracted 3,000 more votes than did the constitutional issue. Chapman severely thrashed the radicals by swamping Stirling 11,237 to 3,290. Stirling won only a single precinct.[63] One journal called the peaceful rout "a perfect annihilation of the whole Custom House clique."[64] The victory was less auspicious for the constitution, for it failed to pick up the expected 10,000 majority, the tally showing 9,779 to 2,053.

The comfortable Maryland majorities enjoyed by the emancipationists in the last two elections melted away. The Unconditional Union State Central Committee blamed it on overconfidence and

[61] "MARYLAND" in *Chestertown Transcript*, October 22, 1864.
[62] Harrison Journal, October 21, 1864, Part 2, p. 740.
[63] *Baltimore American*, October 13, 1864. See also the next day's edition.
[64] *Baltimore County American*, October 14, 1864.

the opposition's "desperate rally."[65] Winter Davis pointed to the poor whites, "nearly all of whom voted for Creswell and Negro enlistments" in 1863 but now turned against the new constitution.[66] Secessionists and slaveholders joined them.

Ballots used by the Soldiers in the Constitutional Election of October, 1864.

So close was the contest that the result remained in doubt for several days. First returns appeared from Baltimore's precincts in the October 13th issues of the local papers. At that time the counties

[65] *Baltimore Clipper*, October 21, 1864. Its October 17, 1864, issue condemned the Winter Davis faction for placing the constitution in jeopardy by frittering away energies in an effort to win control of the city government.

[66] H. Winter Davis to Samuel F. DuPont, October 19, 1864, S. F. DuPont Papers. Davis claimed, "The election was absolutely free in fact and appearance."

were still voting, for they were given an extra day in order to provide ample time for swearing in all the voters.

As the complete county returns came in, they went against the constitution, giving the opposition a state-wide lead of nearly 2,000. The official total read: 27,541 for the constitution and 29,536 opposed. The *Maryland Union* jubilantly headlined:

MARYLAND REDEEMED!
THE NEGRO-ROBBING CONSTITUTION DEFEATED!
DEATH KNELL OF ABOLITIONISM!
MARYLAND SAFE FOR McCLELLAN!
HANG YOUR HEADS FOR SHAME—YE SCOUNDRELS![67]

But there were still the soldiers' votes to be counted, which arrived slowly. Most of them were slips of paper simply printed with "For the constitution" or "Against the Constitution." In rare cases "For" was crossed out and "Against" substituted or vice versa. Many ballots were handwritten.[68] The majority of the votes had apparently been cast in Virginia. The soldiers overwhelmingly supported the new constitution. Their 10 to 1 margin breathed new life into the crushed document, balancing the overall tally slightly in favor of approval.

The closeness of the margin spurred efforts to overthrow the verdict. Democratic war drums reverberated with the charge that some 25,000 opponents of the constitution had been prevented from voting.[69] More serious attacks occupied the courts. On October 24 the Superior Court of Baltimore city received an application for a *mandamus* to command Governor Bradford to exclude all votes cast outside

---

[67] *Maryland Union*, October 20, 1864. Lincoln kept informed of election returns by telegrams from Henry W. Hoffman and Charles C. Fulton of the *Baltimore American*. See telegrams in Lincoln Collection, Vols. 173–74; Hoffman's note of October 17, 1864, RG 98, Middle Dept., Letters Received, 1864; and *Lincoln Works*, VIII, 49.

[68] See ballots in Executive Papers. The soldiers' polls could be held up to five days later than the civilian election. Any soldier who was a legal voter but away from home and his company could vote at the nearest polls in the state. See *Debates*, III, 1901 and documents in the Executive Papers.

[69] See address of the Democratic State Central Committee "To the Democratic and Conservative Voters of the State," *Chestertown Transcript*, October 29, 1864, and other papers. The reasons given for not voting were "an unwillingness to sanction the injunction of an illegal oath, or from scruples of conscience."

of Maryland. The petitioner raised various legal points, hoping to find at least one that would carry the day. The plea failed.[70] The same petition went before the Circuit Court of Anne Arundel County and met an identical fate.

A different tactic saw action in Baltimore County. The opposition tried for an injunction against the governor.[71] Again, no success! Again, no surrender! The injunction suit entered the Circuit Court of Anne Arundel and got the same treatment.

All four cases then went to the Court of Appeals, which directed its attention to the request for a *mandamus*. Bradford refused to appear through counsel, but his side was ably represented by two distinguished gentlemen appearing as *amici curiae*, friends of the court. One was Henry Stockbridge, who had chaired the judiciary committee in the Constitutional Convention, and the other was Winter Davis. I. Nevett Steele, William Schley, and Thomas S. Alexander spoke for the appellants.[72] They repeated the now familiar arguments that no actions of the convention had any effect until after ratification of the constitution. As to the remedy, the governor could be reached by a *mandamus* in performing the ministerial function of counting the votes.

Stockbridge and Davis disagreed. So did the Court. The legislative, judicial, and executive powers were separate and distinct. The Court had no power to interfere with the governor's "exercise of judgment and discretion."[73] Upheld was the decision of the lower court.

That ended the judicial battle to beat the constitution. Only one other loophole remained: show Bradford why certain soldiers' ballots should be rejected. The courts were still at work while the governor labored with this problem. William Schley appeared before him on behalf of the opposition, while Archibald Stirling, Jr., spoke for the supporters of the constitution.

Bradford filed an opinion late on October 28th. He threw out

---

[70] *Debates*, III, 1915–17.

[71] The purpose of the injunction was to prevent the governor from counting the votes cast outside of the state and from declaring the new constitution adopted.

[72] The opponents of the constitution sought the exclusion of the soldiers' vote and the inclusion of certain votes that had been rejected. For information on the legal battle before the Court of Appeals, see *Debates*, III, 1917–19 and Samuel G. Miles v. Augustus W. Bradford, decided October 29, 1864, *Maryland Reports*, Vol. 22, pp. 171–86.

[73] *Debates*, III, 1919; *Maryland Reports*, Vol. 22, p. 185.

TABLE G. VOTE ON CONSTITUTION, OCTOBER 12–13, 1864

	For	Against	Total	Consti-tutional Convention April, 1864	Comptroller November 1863	Governor November 1861
					Total Vote	
Northern Maryland						
Allegany	1,839	964	2,803	3,442	4,175	4,322
Baltimore County	2,001	1,869	3,870	2,827	3,259	6,803
Carroll	1,587	1,690	3,277	3,533	3,529	4,926
Cecil	1,611	1,611	3,222	2,894	3,787	4,154
Fredrick ª	2,908	1,916	4,824	5,188	4,736	7,649
Harford ᵇ	1,083	1,671	2,754	2,246	1,499	3,830
Washington	2,441	985	3,426	3,949	3,427	5,422
Total	13,470	10, 706	24, 176	24, 079	24,412	37,106
Baltimore City ᶜ	9,779	2.053	11,832	9,189	11,310	21,269
Total North	23,249	12,759	36,008	33,268	35,722	58,375
Southern Maryland						
Anne Arundel	281	1,360	1,641	1,630	1,702	2,041
Calvert	57	634	691	511	778	812
Charles	13	978	991	658	520	903
Howard ᵈ	462	583	1,045	1,091	915	1,643
Montgomery ᵉ	422	1,367	1,789	1,232	1,729	2,040
Prince George's	149	1,293	1,442	1,285	1,179	1,577
Saint Mary's	99*	1,078	1,177	926	1,007	1,351
Total	1,483	7,293	8,776	7,333	7,850	10,367
Eastern Shore						
Caroline	471	423	894	1,083	1,337	1,624
Dorchester ᶠ	449	1,486	1,935	1,808	1,637	2,115
Kent	289	1,246	1,535	1,444	1,071	1,758
Queen Anne's ᵍ	220	1,577	1,797	2,080	868	1,978
Somerset	464	2,066	2,530	2,144	1,050	2,827
Talbot	430	1,020	1,450	932	711	1,811
Worcester ʰ	486	1,666	2,152	1,025	1,795	2,717
Total	2,809	9,484	12,293	10,516	8,469	14,830
Total South	4,292	16,777	21,069	17,849	16,299	25,197
Total North & South	27,541	29,536	57,077	51,117	52,021	83,572
Soldier's Vote	2,633	263	2,896	—	—	—
Grand Total	30,174	29,799	59,973	51,117	52,021	83,572

*Many of these were probably votes of soldiers away from home. 2nd Lt. J. Emory Gault of Camp Hoffman at Point Lookout in St. Mary's County took twenty-eight voters to the St. Inigoes polls. All twenty-nine voted for the Constitution. He wrote Governor Bradford to this effect on October 13, 1864, Executive Papers.

Debates, III, 1926 furnished the following code:

ª 23 blanks   ᵇ 19 blanks

ᶜ 8 votes (against) not counted, voters refusing oath

ᵈ 15 votes not included in these (given against the constitution by voters who did not take the oath)

ᵉ 14 blanks, and 10 against the constitution not included in those counted—voters refusing to take the oath

ᶠ 2 blanks   ᵍ 2 blanks   ʰ 1 blank

various technicalities raised against votes of the soldiers. This he did by his interpretation of the convention's purpose: the granting of the ballot to every qualified voter in uniform. Bradford intended no favoritism by this action. He recalled having accepted, despite irregularities, the returns of several counties voting heavily against the constitution.

Nonetheless, Bradford rejected 290 soldiers' votes, all but five of which were for the constitution. He excluded the ballots of the First Regiment, infantry, because the men voted at regimental polls instead of their company commanders' headquarters, as legally specified. Two companies of the First Eastern Shore Regiment reopened their polls several days after an initial tally. Since there was no authority for such action, Bradford rejected these ballots as he did the ones cast in a company with which soldiers had no connection. Votes taken at a place set up just for field and staff officers suffered a like fate.[74] That still left enough soldiers' votes to squeeze a 263 majority out of a total of 59,973 votes recorded.

On October 29 Governor Bradford proclaimed the adoption of the new constitution; it was to go into effect three days later.[75] Though emancipationists might have questioned Bradford's earlier meanderings, now they owed him their gratitude. "Badgered and bullied" by the opposition, he had remained steadfast, scholarly, fair, "and sternly conscientious."[76] With dignity and ability, he had guided the constitution to its promulgation, making Maryland the first border state to free all of its slaves.

Off went a telegram to Lincoln to announce the glad tidings.[77] In anticipation of the event, a group of Marylanders residing in the District of Columbia paraded to the White House. On reaching the President's home, the crowd gave three cheers "for free Maryland and America's Liberator."[78] Lincoln appeared and congratulated them,

---

[74] Bradford's opinion was recorded in *Debates*, III, 1919–25. The question was argued before him on October 27 and 28 (Bradford Journal, III, October 28, 1864). See also A. Stirling, Jr., to J. A. J. Creswell, October 28, 1864, Creswell Papers, X.

[75] *Debates*, III, 1925–26.

[76] *Baltimore American*, November 1, 1864. See also *Baltimore Clipper*, October 31, 1864. The *Maryland Union* (November 3, 1864), on the other hand, unchivalrously attacked Bradford as a man "destined to become a by word and a reproach. . . ."

[77] John S. Berry, Adj. Gen., to A. Lincoln, October 29, 1864, Lincoln Collection, Vol. 175.

[78] *National Republican* (D.C.), October 20, 1864.

the state of "Maryland, and the nation, and the world." He regretted, however, the failure to adopt emancipation two years earlier, for
then it "would have saved to the nation more money than would
have met all the private loss incident to the measure."[79] But now he
hoped for the best.

The November 1st *Baltimore American* was optimistic. It wrote of
Maryland's "regeneration" and the "triumph of right." No longer
would the state be bound to the South. Her interests pointed northward, to a "new alliance with Northern progress and prosperity."[80]

The revolution wrought by the new constitution received a louder
though less critical recognition from army cannon. At sunrise on the
morning of November 1 sixty-five guns boomed at Fort McHenry.
Other cannon roared from various emplacements in Baltimore.
Church bells rang an accompaniment, while flags fluttered from ships
in the harbor and waved from the streets. Converting November 1
into a holiday, the Negroes donned their best clothes, gathered socially, and thronged to their churches.[81]

The slaves displayed no rowdy rejoicing and often approached their
new status with hesitancy and attachment for their masters. Some
slaveholders accepted the changed circumstances with forebearance
and kindness. Others erupted with great bitterness even though
slavery had already become practically worthless. Abolition meant
to them the final, irrevocable step, wiping out property valued before the war at a minimum of $30,000,000.

Some slaveholders, hating to surrender, asked the Courts to bind
Negro children to them as apprentices. "There seems to be an ill
defined belief, a vague hope," observed Dr. Harrison, "that . . . slavery will again be resurrected."[82] The movement spurred Major General Wallace into counteraction. He placed all Negroes freed by the
Constitution of 1864 under military protection and created a

---

[79] *Lincoln Works*, October 19, 1864, VIII, 52–53.

[80] *Baltimore American*, November 2, 1864.

[81] Information on the November 1 events can be found in the November 2nd, 1864,
issues of the *Baltimore Clipper* and *Baltimore American*. Celebrations were also held in
Philadelphia and Washington.

[82] Harrison Journal, November 2, 1864, Part 2, pp. 755–56. Venom was hurled at
some emancipationists, the "grossest calumnys" spilling from the mouths of women.
Henry Goldsborough, for instance, bore such slanderous slurs as dishonesty and having
illicit relations with Negro women. *Ibid.*, October 30 and November 13, 1864, Part 2,
pp. 751–52, 766.

freedman's bureau.[83] The system of apprenticing crumbled and received its death blow through a prohibitory clause in the Constitution of 1867.[84]

A new life began not just for the freed slaves but also for many former masters. The old, respectable, and once wealthy family of General Tilghman found itself with "large property, large debts, large pride, large wants." Only a small income remained. Where troops of servants once roamed, there now labored a cook and two white girls, who refused to do "nigger-work." The Tilghman women did menial chores, carrying the chamber pots from the rooms and milking the cows.[85]

Ironically, on the very day (October 12) Marylanders went to the polls to vote on the new constitution, a native son, Chief Justice of the United States Roger B. Taney, died at the age of 87. His death seemed almost symbolic of the overthrow of the old order. Yet a strange twist of events robbed many of the victors of the fruits of their triumph. As Henry Stockbridge expressed it, "Mr. Blair was told the time had arrived, Mr. Davis that he was not wanted in Congress; Mr. Stirling that he was not wanted any where and so on." Into power went men "who had done nothing to bring about the mighty revolution."[86]

Radical Peter Sauerwein blamed Winter Davis. Unionists preferred to strike at him rather than endanger Lincoln. There was irony here, too, for Sauerwein confessed that the radicals "owe everything to D's genius." Davis "created the emancipation party in this state. He *educated* and stimulated *us*. . . ." Truly, this man was "a glorious fellow; but confound him! he ruined us as a party in the very hour of our triumph."[87]

So great was radical demoralization that Winter Davis did not try

[83] General Orders No. 112, November 9, 1864, *Official Records*, Series 1, Vol. 43, Part 2, pp. 587–88.

[84] W. A. Low, "The Freedmen's Bureau and Education in Maryland," *Maryland Historical Magazine*, Vol. 47 (1952), p. 31.

[85] Dr. Harrison related the Tilghman difficulties in his Journal, December 25, 1864, Part 2, pp. 788–90.

[86] Henry Stockbridge to Montgomery Blair, November 29, 1864, Blair Family Papers, Gist Blair Collection. Stockbridge, incidentally, claimed he tried to avoid taking the side of either faction, but certainly he appeared closer to Davis than Blair.

[87] Peter G. Sauerwein to Edward McPherson, October 22, 1864, Edward McPherson Papers, Box 8.

to retain his Congressional seat.[88] Swann won the governorship in November, while Davis' Unionist replacement proved victorious in the Third Congressional District. Creswell lost, but Harris, Webster, and Thomas were re-elected. The Unionists swung a majority in the House of Delegates and eventually gained an edge in the Maryland Senate.[89] Lincoln carried the state by a comfortable margin.

Winter Davis criticized the campaign as being "shamefully conducted" and called it "a vile scuffle between Hoffman and Purnell for the privilege of licking Lincoln's feet."[90] But the radicals still struggled for patronage and sought to sabotage plans for putting Montgomery Blair into the Senate seat of Hicks, who in turn was to replace Hoffman as Collector of Customs in Baltimore.

A combination of events foiled this game of political musical chairs. Death struck down Hicks on February 13, 1865, and the legislature replaced him with Creswell. Winter Davis was elated. He considered Creswell's election a *coup de grace* to his enemies in Maryland.[91] As to the collectorship, Hoffman was now obviously expendable to Davis. To fill the void, Congressman Webster confidentially made application to the radicals.[92] He was playing a double game, for he also sought support from more conservative Unionists.

These appointments occupied Lincoln during part of April 14, 1865. Creswell and Swann, each representing a different wing of the party, presented the President a list of proposed office holders,[93] including Webster for Collector. The choices became academic that

[88] See H. W. Davis to Samuel F. DuPont, October 19, 1864, S. F. DuPont Papers. The new constitution advanced the gubernatorial election to the same date as the presidential election.

[89] The Democratic victor in Dorchester County, W. M. Holland, resigned on November 15. A special election on December 23 went to Unionist Thomas King Carroll. This turned a 13–11 Democratic margin into a 12–12 tie, giving the lieutenant governor, a new office held by Unionist Christopher C. Cox, the deciding vote.

[90] H. W. Davis to S. F. DuPont, November [no day], 1864, S. F. DuPont Papers. A later letter from Davis to DuPont (January [no day], 1865) blamed the "mean hunt for office" on making his "*good friend* . . . Hoffman not intentionally to injure me but to save himself take the advice of his enemies and mine. . . ."

[91] H. W. Davis to S. F. DuPont, March 12, 1865, S. F. DuPont Papers.

[92] H. W. Davis to S. F. DuPont, March 12, 1865, S. F. DuPont Papers.

[93] See *Lincoln Works*, VII, 411. According to Davis, Creswell succeeded in getting Lincoln "to oust all the men who so treacherously smote me last fall at the president's instigation." H. W. Davis to S. F. DuPont, April 15, 1865, S. F. DuPont Papers.

evening when Lincoln attended Ford's Theatre and was felled by an assassin's bullet.

Andrew Johnson's ascension to the presidency changed some of the appointments, but Webster still got the collectorship.[94] Now Davis considered Webster on the other side,[95] a particularly critical factor because Purnell still retained the important patronage office of postmaster of Baltimore.

During the holidays in December, 1865, Winter Davis caught cold, contracted pneumonia, and died on the 30th at the age of 48. Thus was silenced one of the most tempestuous geniuses ever to enter the political arena of Maryland or the nation.[96]

The death of Davis, Hicks, and the martyred President within less than a year did not heal factional wounds. The struggle continued. In 1864 the first wave of Unionists, men like George Vickers and Reverdy Johnson, had gone over to the Democrats. Now in 1866 Blair, Swann, Purnell, and others of their sentiments left the Republican or Union Party and allied themselves with the Democrats.[97] This second wave so stripped the party that its residue lay firmly in radical hands.

The latter found themselves custodians of a new issue, Negro suffrage. Radicals like Peter Sauerwein did not admire the proposal but considered it essential to restoring the nation.[98] This was similar to the old reaction to emancipation, which had attracted many proponents not as an ideal but as a measure of expediency or necessity.

[94] See *United States Official Register* dated September 30, 1865 (Washington, 1866), p. 112.

[95] H. W. Davis to Charles Sumner, July 26, 1865, Sumner Papers, Harvard College Library. Davis said Webster's and Purnell's "power in *nominations* will throw Md. against us:—Unless their confirmation be refused—good bye to radical representatives and Senators from Md."

[96] Congress paid Davis such high tribute that Secretary of the Navy Welles interpreted it as an attempt to belittle Lincoln as much as to exalt his antagonist. Howard K. Beale (ed.), *Diary of Gideon Wells* (New York, 1960), II, 438. See also Lamb's *Biographical Dictionary of the United States*, edited by John Howard Brown (Boston, 1900), p. 371.

[97] William Starr Myers in his *The Self-Reconstruction of Maryland, 1864–1867* (Baltimore, 1909), pp. 52– 53, referred to March 1, 1866, as marking the end of the Union Party in Maryland and the appearance of the Republican Party. Wm. Seabrook in his book on *Maryland's Great Part in Saving the Union*, pp. 50–55 said that some who joined the Democratic-Conservative coalition later returned to the Republican Party.

[98] Peter G. Sauerwein to Edward McPherson, August 1, 1865, Edward McPherson Papers, Box 8.

The Democrats gained control of Maryland and proceeded to re-scind part of the revolution of 1864. They pushed through a new constitution in 1867. This document condemned Lincoln's war policy, increased the political power of the southern counties by in-cluding the Negro population in determining legislative apportion-ment, and canceled progressive provisions for education.[99]

The new constitution stated that slavery should not be revived, although it charged the federal government with responsibility for Maryland emancipation and sought federal compensation. None was forthcoming, even though Lincoln had contemplated it two months before his death.[100]

Thus did Maryland slavery die. In the muck of self interest and the necessities of a bloody war had sprouted the movement to free the Negro. Political spoils had lured the greedy, but all was not dross. There was hope for a better way of life—one where labor was entitled to respect and where no longer the privileged few could rule Maryland as though it were their own patrimony. The seeds of that great conflict germinated a ferment still to be fulfilled, even as it had been the bearer of an earlier ideal "that all men are created equal."

[99] Myers, *Self-Reconstruction,* pp. 120–22 and 123–24.
[100] Lincoln Works, VIII, 260–61.

BIBLIOGRAPHY

MANUSCRIPT COLLECTIONS

A number of descendants of prominent political figures were traced in an effort to find new material. The investigation brought to light a small but helpful collection of the John W. Crisfield Papers plus a more limited selection from several other prominent Unionists.

One of the most rewarding finds of recent years has been the Samuel Francis DuPont Papers. Rear Admiral John D. Hayes, U.S.N. (Ret.) of Annapolis, Maryland, uncovered and is currently editing these papers for publication. They contain the richest known harvest of the Henry Winter Davis letters. The Davis originals are available in the 1850–60 period, but the ones for the Civil War years are copies.

Other essential collections for this study included the Blair Family Papers in the Gist Blair Collection, Augustus W. Bradford Papers, Salmon P. Chase Papers, John A. J. Creswell Papers, John Pendleton Kennedy Papers, Robert Todd Lincoln Collection, Edward B. McPherson Papers, and the Papers of the Middle Department, U.S. Army Commands. The best Maryland diary for my purposes was Dr. Samuel A. Harrison's Journal.

A more complete list of manuscript collections is listed below.

ADJUTANT GENERAL OF MARYLAND PAPERS, Hall of Records, Annapolis, Md.

BAKER-TURNER PAPERS, Adjutant General's Office, Record Group 94, National Archives.

BLAIR FAMILY PAPERS, Gist Blair Collection, Library of Congress.

BLAIR-LEE PAPERS, Princeton University.

BONAPARTE, JEROME, LETTERBROOK, Maryland Historical Society.

BOND (Judge Hugh L. Bond) CIVIL WAR SCRAP BOOK, Maryland Historical Society.

BRADFORD, AUGUSTUS W., JOURNALS OR DIARIES, 1862–65, Maryland Historical Society.

BRADFORD, AUGUSTUS W., PAPERS, Maryland Historical Society.

BRADFORD'S, GOVERNOR AUGUSTUS W., LETTERBOOK, Hall of Records. (A second volume is marked "Letters Received A. W. B. Gov. 1864–65")

BREWSTER, JAMES, COLLECTION, Hall of Records.

BROWN, GEORGE W., SCRAPBOOK, 1862–64, 2 vols., Maryland Historical Society.

CAMERON, SIMON, PAPERS, Library of Congress.

CARROLL, ANNA ELLA, PAPERS, Maryland Historical Society.

CHANDLER, WILLIAM E., LETTERBROOK, New Hampshire Historical Society.

CHANDLER, ZACHARIAH, PAPERS, Library of Congress.

CHASE, SLAMON P., PAPERS, Historical Society of Pennsylvania and the Library of Congress.

COPPET, ANDRE DE, COLLECTION, Princeton University.

CORRESPONDENCE OF THE BRITISH CONSUL AT BALTIMORE, Foreign Office Papers, Public Record Office, London, England.

CRESWELL, JOHN A. J., PAPERS, Library of Congress.

CRISFIELD, JOHN W., PAPERS, Maryland Historical Society.

DAVIS, HENRY WINTER, PAPERS, Maryland Historical Society.

DONALDSON, THOMAS, PAPERS, Mrs. James Mitchell Hemphill (now deceased), of Elkridge, Md.

DORSEY, JAMES L., PAPERS, Maryland Historical Society.

DUPONT, SAMUEL FRANCIS, PAPERS, Eleutherian Mills Historical Library, Wilmington, Delaware.

ENGLEBRECHT, JACOB, DIARY, Maryland Historical Society (microfilm).

EXECUTIVE LETTERBOOK, Hall of Records.

EXECUTIVE PAPERS, Hall of Records.

GARRETT PAPERS, Library of Congress.

GIST FAMILY PAPERS, Hall of Records.

GLENN, WILLIAM W., CIVIL WAR DIARY, Maryland Historical Society.

GRATZ, SIMON, COLLECTION, Historical Society of Pennsylvania.

HARRISON, DR. SAMUEL A., JOURNAL, Maryland Historical Society.

HICKS, GOVERNOR THOMAS H., PAPERS, Maryland Historical Society.

HOFFMAN, HENRY W., PAPERS, Mrs. Theodore Bliss, Sarasota, Florida.

HOLT, JOSEPH, PAPERS, Library of Congress.

IRREGULAR BOOKS, Office of the Secretary of War, Record Group No. 107, National Archives.

JOHNSON, REVERDY, PAPERS, Library of Congress.

KENNEDY, JOHN PENDLETON, PAPERS, Peabody Institute Library.

LINCOLN, ROBERT TODD, COLLECTION OF THE PAPERS OF ABRAHAM LINCOLN, Library of Congress.

MAYER, BRANTZ, PAPERS, Maryland Historical Society.

MCPARLIN, THOMAS A., PAPERS, in possession of Guy Weatherly, Annapolis, Md.

MCPHERSON, EDWARD B., Papers, Library of Congress.

MARYLAND STATE COLONIZATION SOCIETY PAPERS, Maryland Historical Society.

MIDDLE DEPARTMENT, U.S. ARMY COMMANDS, Record Group 98, National Archives. This important collection includes the registers of letters received, the letters received, and the letters sent.

THE NEGRO IN THE MILITARY SERVICE OF THE UNITED STATES, Adjutant General's Office, record Group 94, National Archives. This eight volume compilation of various records by Elon A. Woodward (1888) was put on microfilm in 1963.

NICOLAY, JOHN G., PAPERS, Library of Congress.

PAGE, COLONEL HENRY (1870–1954), grandson of John W. Crisfield, interviewed on April 21, 1953.

PRATT, ENOCH, PAPERS, Enoch Pratt Library, Baltimore, Md.

PROCEEDINGS OF A MILITARY COMMISSION to Investigate and Report upon Captain Charles C. Moore's Conduct in Carrying Out General Orders No. 53. Judge Advocate General's Papers, Record Group 153, National Archives.

PURNELL, WILLIAM HENRY, PAPERS, Mrs. A. B. Wills, Towson, Md.

REGISTERS OF LETTERS AND LETTERS RECEIVED AND SENT, Adjutant General's Office, Record Group No. 94, National Archives.

SERVICE RECORD OF LT. COL. C. CARROLL TEVIS, 3rd Md. Cav., T261-1863. Adjutant General's Office, Record Group No. 94, National Archives.

SOCIETY COLLECTION, Historical Society of Pennsylvania.

STANTON, EDWIN MCMASTERS, PAPERS, Library of Congress.

STEVENS, THADDEUS, PAPERS, Library of Congress.

SUMNER, CHARLES, PAPERS, Harvard College Library.

THOMAS, JOHN L., PAPERS, Maryland Historical Society.

UNION CLUB RECORDS, Maryland Historical Society.

U.S. COLORED TROOPS, Main Series and Recruiting Series, Adjutant General's Office, Record Group No. 94, National Archives. This voluminous collection includes registers of letters in addition to a great number of boxes containing the original papers.

WADE, BENJAMIN F., PAPERS, Library of Congress.

WASHBURNE, ELI B., PAPERS, Library of Congress.

WASHINGTON, DEPARTMENT OF, GENERAL ORDERS, Adjutant General's Office, National Archives.

WEED, THURLOW, PAPERS, Library of Congress.

WELLES, GIDEON, PAPERS, Library of Congress.

WEST VIRGINIA, DEPARTMENT OF, GENERAL ORDERS, Adjutant General's Office, National Archives.

PERIODICALS

Letters were sent to many newspapers in hopes of uncovering Civil War editions hitherto unknown to researchers and librarians. This effort produced one significant finding, a nearly complete set of the *Cecil Democrat* for the period under study. As the *Cecil Whig* was already available in the Enoch Pratt Library in Baltimore, this permitted an examination of politics and issues through the conflicting viewpoints of two bitterly rival journals.

During the Civil War the *Baltimore American* provided the best news coverage of any paper within the state. Like its competitors in that city, the *Baltimore American* published daily. All other Maryland journals that are listed below were printed weekly.

Annapolis Gazette, Anne Arundel County.
Baltimore American.
Baltimore Clipper.
Baltimore Daily Gazette.
Baltimore Republican.
Baltimore *Sun.*
Baltimore Weekly Sun.
Baltimore County Advocate.
Baltimore County American.
The Southern Ægis, and Harford County Intelligencer.
Cambridge Herald, Dorchester County.
Cecil Democrat, Cecil County.
Cecil Whig, Cecil County.
Chestertown Transcript, Kent County.
Civilian and Telegraph, Allegany County.
Daily Morning Chronicle, Washington, D.C.
Daily National Republican, Washington, D.C.
Der Deutsche Correspondent, Baltimore.
Easton Gazette, Talbot County.
Frank Leslie's Illustrated Newspaper, New York.
Frederick *Examiner,* Frederick County.
The Hagerstown Mail, Washington County.
Harper's Weekly, New York.
The Herald and Torch Light, Washington County.
The Illustrated London News, London, England.
Kent News, Kent County.
London *Times,* London, England.
The Maryland News Sheet, Baltimore.
Maryland Republican, Anne Arundel County.

The Maryland Union, Frederick County.
Montgomery County Sentinel.
National American, Harford County.
National Intelligencer, Washington, D.C.
New York Daily Tribune.
Port Tobacco Times and Charles County Advertiser.
The South, Baltimore.
Täglicher Wecker, Baltimore.
The Valley Register, Frederick County.

CONTEMPORARY DOCUMENTS, DIARIES, EYEWITNESS ACCOUNTS, AND PAMPHLETS

Address of the Unconditional Union State Central Committee to the People of Maryland, September 16th, 1863. Baltimore, 1863.
Address of the Union State Central Committee, of Maryland. Baltimore, 1861.
The American Annual Cyclopaedia and Register of Important Events of the Year 1863. New York: D. Appleton & Co., 1868.
BARTLETT, CATHERINE THOM (ed.). *"My Dear Brother"—A Confederate Chronicle.* Richmond: Dietz Press, 1952.
BASLER, ROY P. (ed.). *The Collected Works of Abrahanm Lincoln.* 9 vols. New Brunswick, N.J.: Rutgers University Press, 1953.
BATES, DAVID HOMER. *Lincoln in the Telegraph Office.* New York: Century Co., 1907.
BEALE, HOWARD K. (ed.). *The Diary of Edward Bates: 1859–1866. (The Annual Report of the American Historical Association for the Year 1930, Vol. IV).* Washington: Government Printing Office, 1933. *Diary of Gideon Welles.* 3 vols. New York: W. W. Norton & Co., 1960. An earlier edition, published in 1911, was a revision of the original diary.
BLAIR, MONTGOMERY. *Comments on the Policy Inaugurated by the President, in a Letter and Two Speeches.* New York: n. p., 1863.
Inaugural Address of Hon. Augustus W. Bradford, Governor of Maryland, Delivered in the Senate Chamber, Annapolis, January 8th, 1862. Annapolis, 1862.
Letters to Gov. Bradford, by a Marylander. Baltimore, 1863.
BREWER, NICHOLAS, JR. (state reporter) and PERKINS, WM. H., JR. (revision and annotation). *Reports of Cases Argued and Adjudged in the Court of Appeals of Maryland.* Vols. 22 & 23. Baltimore: M. Curlander, 1897. These volumes extend from December term, 1863 through October term, 1865.
BROOKS, NOAH. *Washington in Licoln's Time.* Edited by Herbert Mitgang. New York: Rinehart & Co., 1958. An earlier edition appeared in 1895.
BUTLER, BENJAMIN F. *Butler's Book.* Boston: A.M. Thayer & Co., 1892.

CARPENTER, FRANCIS B. *Six Months at the White House with Abraham Lincoln,* New York: Hurd & Houghton, 1867.

Constitution of Maryland. Published by the Secretary of State, n. p. n. d.

(DAVIS), *Speeches and Addresses Delivered in the Congress of the United States, and on Several Public Occasions, by Henry Winter Davis of Maryland.* New York: Harper & Brothers, 1867.

DENNETT, TYLER (ed.). *Lincoln and the Civil War in the Diaries and Letters of John Hay.* New York: Dodd Mead & Co., 1939.

DICEY, EDWARD. *Six Months in the Federal States.* London: Macmillan and Co., 1863.

DONALD, DAVID (ed.), *Inside Lincoln's Cabinet: the Civil War Diaries of Salmon P. Chase.* New York: Longman, Green & Co., 1954.

DOUGLASS, FREDERICK, *Life and Times of Frederick Douglass Written by Himself.* Hartford, Conn.: Park Publishing Co., 1883.

ENOCH PRATT LIBRARY, Maryland Dept., Civil War Clippings from *Harper's Weekly, Leslie's Illustrated Newspaper,* etc., 3 Vols., Baltimore, 1940–42.

GILMOR, HARRY. *Four Years in the Saddle.* New York: Harper & Brothers, 1866.

GUROWSKI, ADAM, *Diary.* Vol. I, Boston: Lee & Shepard, 1862; Vol. II, New York: Carleton, 1864; Vol. III, Washington: W. H. & O. H. Morrison, 1866.

HOWARD, FRANK KEY. *Thoughts on the Times.* Baltimore: n.p., 1863.

Immediate Emancipation in Maryland: Proceedings of the Union State Central Committee, at a Meeting Held in Temperance Temple, Baltimore, Wednesday, December 16, 1863. Baltimore, 1863.

Richard H. Jackson to Robert C. Schenck. n.p., 1867.

JOHNSON, REVERDY. *Speech of Hon. Reverdy Johnson, of Maryland, in Support of the Resolution to Amend the Constitution so as to Abolish Slavery.* n.p., 1864.

KENNEDY, JOHN PENDLETON. *Occasional Addresses; and the Letters of Mr. Ambrose on the Rebellion.* New York: G. P. Putnam & Sons, 1872.

———. *Political and Official Papers.* New York: G. P. Putnam & Sons, 1872.

KLEIN, FREDERIC SHRIVER (ed.). *Just South of Gettysburg: Carroll County, Maryland in the Civil War.* Westminster, Md.: Civil War Centennial Committee of the Historical Society of Carroll County, Maryland, 1963.

LAMON, WARD HILL. *Recollections of Abraham Lincoln: 1847–1865.* Washington: 1911. Edited and published by Dorothy Lamon Teillard.

LORD, WALTER (ed.). *The Fremantle Diary.* Boston: Little, Brown & Co., 1954.

MAYER, BRANTZ. *The Emancipation Problem in Maryland.* Baltimore: n.p., 1862.

MOORE, FRANK (ed.). *The Rebellion Record.* 11 vols. New York: G. P. Putnam & Sons, 1861–63, D. Van Nostrand, 1864–68.

NEVINS, ALLAN, and THOMAS, MILTON H. (eds). *The Diary of George Templeton Strong: The Civil War: 1860–1865.* Vol. III. New York: Macmillan Co., 1952.

NOYES, GEORGE F. *The Bivouac and the Battle-Field; or, Campaign Sketches in Virginia and Maryland.* New York: Harper & Brothers, 1864.

PEASE, THEODORE C. and RANDALL, JAMES G. (eds.). *The Diary of Orville Hickman Browning.* Springfield, Illinois: Trustees of Illinois State Historical Library, 1925.

PIATT, DONN. *Memoirs of the Men Who Saved the Union.* New York: n.p., 1887.

POLLARD, EDWARD A. *Observations in the North: Eight Months in Prison and on Parole.* Richmond: E. W. Ayres, 1865.

Proceedings of the National Convention, Union League of America, Held at Cleveland, May 20 and 21, 1863, with Reports. Washington: Published by Order of the Convention, 1863.

RICE, ALLEN THORNDIKE (ed.). *Reminiscences of Abraham Lincoln by Distinguished Men of His Time.* New York: North American Publishing Co., 1886.

RIDDLE, ALBERT GALLATIN. *Recollections of War Times: Reminiscences of Men and Events in Washington 1860–1865.* New York: G. P. Putnam's Sons, 1895.

Ritual, Constitution and By-laws of the National Council, Union League of America. Washington: n.p., 1867.

RUSSELL, WILLIAM HOWARD. *My Diary North and South.* 2 vols. London: Bradbury & Evans, 1863.

SCOTT, OTHO, and M'CULLOUGH, HIRAM. *The Revised Laws of the State of Maryland.* Bel Air, Maryland: n.p., 1859.

Secret Correspondence Illustrating the Condition of Affairs in Maryland. n.p., 1863.

SEWARD, FREDERICK W. *Reminiscences of a War-Time Statesman and Diplomat: 1830–1915.* New York: G. P. Putnam's Sons, 1916.

The 'Southern Rights' and 'Union' Parties in Maryland Contrasted. Baltimore: n.p., 1863.

STODDARD, WILLIAM O. *Inside the White House in War Times.* New York: Charles L. Webster & Co., 1890.

The Works of Charles Sumner. 20 vols. Boston: Lee & Shepard, 1880.

TROLLOPE, ANTHONY. *North America.* 2 vols. London: Chapman & Hall, 1862.

UNCONDITIONAL UNION STATE CENTRAL COMMITTEE, *No State Compensation for Slaves.* n.p., 1864.

UNION LEAGUE OF AMERICA. *Constitution. n.p., n.d.*

UNION LEAGUE OF AMERICA. *Meeting of the Grand National Council.* n.p., June, 1864.

UNION LEAGUE OF AMERICA, MARYLAND GRAND LEAGUE. *Opening, Initiatory and Closing Ceremonies for Union Leagues.* Baltimore: J. Young, 1862.

UNITED STATES CHRISTIAN COMMISSION. *Third Report of the Committee of Maryland.* Baltimore, 1864.

VON BORCKE, HEROS. *Memoirs of the Confederate War for Independence.* Edinburgh: William Blackwood and Sons, 1866.

WALLACE, LEW. *Lew Wallace, on Autobiography*. 2 vols. New York: Harper & Brothers, 1906.

WILLIAMS, BEN AMES (ed.). *A Diary from Dixie by Mary Boykin Chesnut*. Boston: Houghton Mifflin Co., 1949.

WINGATE, JAMES. *The Maryland Register for 1860–61, a Legal, Political, and Business Manual*. Baltimore, 1860.

GOVERNMENT DOCUMENTS

I. *MARYLAND*

The Debates of the Constitutional Convention of the State of Maryland, Assembled at the City of Annapolis, Wednesday, April 27, 1864. Annapolis, 1864.

Documents Accompanying the Governor's Message to the Legislature of Maryland. Annapolis, 1864.

Journal of the Proceedings of the House of Delegates, of the State of Maryland for the 1862 and 1864 sessions. Annapolis: Thomas J. Wilson, 1862 and 1864.

Journal of the Proceedings of the Senate of Maryland, of the State of Maryland 1862 and 1864 sessions. Annapolis: 1862 and 1864. The 1864 *Proceedings* included Document D, *Report by the Committee on Elections, of the Senate of Maryland*. Annapolis, 1864.

Maryland House and Senate Documents: Special Session December 1861, January Session, 1862. Annapolis, 1861 and 1862.

Maryland House and Senate Documents: January Session 1864. Annapolis, 1864. Document J was the useful, 103 page *Report of the Committee on Elections on Contested Elections in Somerset County, Together with the Testimony taken before that Committee*. Annapolis, 1864.

Message of the Governor of Maryland, to the General Assembly. January Session, 1864. Annapolis, 1864.

Proceedings of the State Convention of Maryland to Frame a New Constitution. Annapolis, 1864.

II. *UNITED STATES*

A. Census Reports

A Century of Population Growth from the First Census of the United States to the Twelfth 1790–1900. Washington, D.C., 1909.

Agriculture of the United States in 1860; Compiled from the Original Returns of the Eighth Census. Washington, D.C., 1864.

Manufactures of the United States in 1860; Compiled from the Original Returns of the Eighth Census. Washington, D.C., 1865.

Population of the United States in 1860; Compiled from the Original Returns of the Eighth Census. Washington, D.C., 1864.

Statistics of the United States in 1860; Compiled from the Original Returns of the Eighth Census. Washington, D.C., 1866.

B. Documents and Reports

Documents Relating to Military Interference at Elections, February 12, 1864. (38th Cong., 1st Sess., Senate Reports, no. 14.)

Journal of the Executive Proceedings of the Senate of the United States of America from December 1, 1862, to July 4, 1864, inclusive. Vol. XIII, Washington: Government Printing Office, 1887.

Minority Report on Abolition of Slavery in the District of Columbia, March 12, 1862. Vol. III. (37th Cong., 2nd Sess.; House Reports, No. 58.) Washington, D.C., 1862.

Minority Report on the Repeal of the Fugitive Slave Act, February 29, 1864. (38th Cong., 1st Sess.; Senate Reports, No. 24.)

Report on Emancipated Slaves in the District of Columbia, February 16, 1864. Vol. IX. (38th Cong., 1st Sess.; House Ex. Doc., No. 42.)

Report on the Repeal of the Fugitive Slave Act., February 29, 1864. (38th Cong., 1st Sess.; Senate Reports, No. 24.)

Report on a Police Force in Baltimore, Secretary E. M. Stanton. May 23, 1862. Vol. III. (37th Cong., 2nd Sess.; House Ex. Doc., No. 118.)

Report on Military Interference at Elections, Committee on Military Affairs and the Militia. February 12, 1864. (38th Cong., 1st Sess.; Senate Reports No. 14.)

Report of the Select Committee on Emancipation and Colonization. (37th Cong., 2nd Sess.; H. R. Report, No. 148.) Washington: 1862.

Report on Military Election Orders, Secretary E. M. Stanton. February 3, 1864. Vol. I. (38th Cong., 1st Sess.; Senate Doc., No. 14.) See also Senate Doc., No. 29, dated March 21, 1864.

C. Miscellaneous

The Congressional Globe. 37th Cong., 38th cong. (1st Sess.), 1861–64.

COWLES, CAPT. CALVIN D. (compiler). *Atlas to Accompany the Official Records of the Union and Confederate Armies.* 2 vols. Washington: Government Printing Office, 1891–95.

Journal of the Executive Proceedings of the Senate of the United States of America, from December 1, 1862, to July 4, 1864, inclusive. Washington, 1887.

Letter on Emancipation of Slaves, Governor of Missouri. June 25, 1862. (37th Cong., 2nd Sess.; House Misc. Doc., No. 87.)

Letter on the Colonization Fund, Secretary J. P. Usher. March 7, 1864. Vol. I (38th Cong., 1st Sess.; Senate Misc. Doc., No. 69.)

Letter on Provost-Marshals and Elections, Secretary E. M. Stanton, March 21, 1864. Vol. I. (38th Cong., 1st Sess.; Senate Doc., No. 29.)

THIAN, RAPHAEL P. (compiler). *Notes Illustrating the Military Geography of the United States.* Washington: Government Printing Office, 1881.

United States Official Register for September 30, of 1859, 1861, 1864, and 1865. Washington: Government Printing Office, 1859, 1862, 1864 and 1866.

The War of the Rebellion: A Compilation of the Official Records of the Union and Confederate Armies. 70 vols. Washington: Government Printing Office, 1880–1901.

SECONDARY WORKS

A number of Maryland's counties have been the subject of books, but they did not impinge upon my study and have therefore been omitted from this bibliography.

ADAMS, CHARLES F. *Charles Francis Adams 1835–1915: an Autobiography with a Memorial Address Delivered November 17, 1915, by Henry Cabot Lodge.* Cambridge, Mass.: Houghton Mifflin Company, 1916.

ANGLE, PAUL M. (ed.). *Herndon's Life of Lincoln.* Cleveland: World Publishing Co., 1949.

The Biographical Cyclopedia of Representative Men of Maryland and District of Columbia. Baltimore: National Biographical Publishing Co., 1879.

BLAINE, JAMES G. *Twenty Years of Congress from Lincoln to Garfield with a Review of the Events which Led to the Political Revolution of 1860.* 2 vols. Norwick, Conn.: Henry Bill Publishing Company, 1884.

BOATNER, MARK MAYO, III. *The Civil War Dictionary.* New York: David McKay, 1959.

BOHNER, CHARLES H. *John Pendleton Kennedy: Gentlemen from Baltimore.* Baltimore: The Johns Hopkins Press, 1961.

BRACKETT, JEFFREY R. *The Negro in Maryland: A Study of the Institution of Slavery.* Extra Volume VI, Old Series, *Johns Hopkins University Studies in Historical and Political Science,* edited by Herbert B. Adams. Baltimore: The Johns Hopkins Press, 1889.

BRAND, WILLIAM FRANCIS. *Life of William Rollinson Whittingham.* New York: E. and J. B. Young & Co., 1886.

BROOKS, NOAH. *Abraham Lincoln: The Nation's leader in the Great Struggle through which Was Maintained the Existence of the United States.* New York: G. P. Putnam's Sons, 1888.

BROWN, GEORGE WILLIAM. *Baltimore and the Nineteenth of April, 1861. A Study of the War.* Baltimore: N. Murray, Publication Agent, The Johns Hopkins University, 1887.

BROWN, JOHN HOWARD (ed.). Lamb's *Biographical Dictionary of the United States.* Boston, 1900.

BUCHHOLZ, HEINRICH E. *Governors of Maryland.* Baltimore: Williams & Wilkins Co., 1908.

CAMPER, CHARELS and KIRKLEY, J. W. (compilers). *Historical Record of the First Regiment Maryland Infantry.* (Washington: n.p., 1871.)

CARMAN, HARRY J. and LUTHIN, REINHARD H. *Lincoln and the Patronage.* New York: Columbia University Press, 1943.

CORNISH, DUDLEY TAYLOR. *The Sable Arm: Negro Troops in the Union Army, 1861–1865.* New York: Longman, Green & Co., 1956.

COULTER, E. MERTON. *The Confederate States of America: 1861–1865.* Volume VII of *A History of the South.* Edited by Wendell Holmes Stephenson and E. Merton Coulter. Baton Rouge: Louisiana State University Press, 1950.

CUNZ, DIETER. *The Maryland Germans: A History.* Princeton, N.J.: Princeton University Press, 1948.

DIX, MORGAN (compiler). *Memoirs of John Adams Dix,* 2 vols. New York: Harper & Brothers, 1883.

DUMOND, DWIGHT LOWELL. *Antislavery origins of the Civil War in the United States.* Ann Arbor: University of Michigan Press, 1959.

DYER, FREDERICK H. *A Compendium of the War of the Rebellion.* 3 vols. New York: Thomas Yoseloff, 1959.

FRANKLIN, JOHN H. *From Slavery to Freedom: A History of American Negroes.* New York: Knopf, 1947.

FREEMAN, DOUGLAS SOUTHALL. *R. E. Lee: A Biography.* 4 vols. New York: Charles Scribner's Sons, 1934–35.

GIBSON, GUY JAMES. "Lincoln's League: the Union League Movement during the Civil War." Doctoral Thesis. University of Illinois, 1957. Now available on microfilm.

GRIMES, ELIZABETH M. "John Angel James Creswell, Postmaster-General." M.A. Thesis, Columbia University, 1939.

GUERNSEY, ALFRED H. and ALDEN, HENRY M. *Harper's Pictorial History of the Civil War.* Chicago: Star Publishing Co., 1866–67.

GWATHMEY, EDWARD M. *John Pendleton Kennedy.* New York: Thomas Nelson & Sons, 1931.

HART, ALBERT BUSHNELL. *Salmon Portland Chase.* Volume XXVIII of *American Statesmen.* Boston: Houghton Mifflin & Co., 1899.

HENDRICK, BURTON J. *Lincoln's War Cabinet.* Boston: Little, Brown & Co., 1946.

HESSELTINE, WILLIAM B. *Lincoln and the War Governors.* New York: Alfred A. Knopf, 1948.

HOCHFIELD, GEORGE (ed.). *The Great Secession Winter of 1860–61 and Other Essays by Henry Adams.* New York: Sagamore Press, Inc., 1958.

HYMAN, HAROLD MELVIN. *Era of the Oath: Northern Loyalty Tests During the Civil*

War and Reconstruction. Philadelphia: University of Pennsylvania Press, 1954.

JOHNSON, ALLEN and MALONE, DUMAS (eds.). *Dictionary of American Biography.* 20 vols., index, supplement. New York: Charles Scribner's Sons, 1928–1936, 1937, 1944.

KENT, FRANK R. *The Story of Maryland Politics, 1864–1910.* Baltimore: Thomas and Evans Printing Co., 1911.

KING, WILLARD L. *Lincoln's Manager: David Davis.* Cambridge, Mass.: Harvard University Press, 1960.

KNOTT, ALOYSIUS LEO. *A Biographical Sketch of Hon. A. Leo Knott with a Relation of Some Political Transactions in Maryland, 1861–1867. From History of Baltimore.* S. B. Nelson Publisher.

MCCONVILLE, SISTER MARY ST. PATRICK. *Political Nativism in the State of Maryland: 1830–1860.* Washington: Catholic University of America, 1928.

MCPHERSON, EDWARD B. *The Political History of the United States of America, during the Great Rebellion...* Washington: Philip & Solomons: 1865.

MANAKEE, HAROLD R. *Maryland in the Civil War.* Baltimore: Maryland Historical society, 1961.

MOOS, MALCOLM. *The Republicans: A History of Their Party.* New York: Random House, 1956.

MYERS, WILLIAM STARR. *The Maryland Constitution of 1864.* Series 19, No. 8–9 in *The Johns Hopkins University Studies in Historical and Political Science.* Baltimore: The Johns Hopkins Press, 1901.

———. *The Self-Reconstruction of Maryland, 1864–1867.* Series 27, No. 1–2 in *The Johns Hopkins University Studies in Historical and Political Science.* Baltimore: The Johns Hopkins Press, 1909.

NICHOLS, ROY F. *The Disruption of American Democracy.* New York: Macmillan Co., 1948.

NICOLAY, JOHN G. and HAY, JOHN. *Abraham Lincoln: A History.* 10 vols. New York: Century Co., 1890.

OWENS, HAMILTON. *Baltimore on the Chesapeake.* Garden City, N.Y.: Doubleday, 1941.

PARRISH, WILLIAM E. *Turbulent Partnership: Missouri and the Union: 1861–1865.* Columbia, Mo.: University of Missouri Press, 1963.

PEARSON, HENRY GREENLEAF. *James S. Wadsworth of Genesco, Brevet Major-General of United States Volunteers.* New York: C. Scribner's Sons, 1913.

POOLE, WILLIAM FREDERICK. *Anti-Slavery Opinions before the Year 1800.* Cincinnati: Robert Clarke & Co., 1873.

QUARLES, BENJAMIN. *The Negro in the Civil War.* Boston: Little, Brown & Co., 1953.

RADCLIFFE, GEORGE L. P. *Governor Thomas H. Hicks of Maryland and the Civil*

War. Baltimore: the Johns Hopkins Press, 1901.

RANDALL, JAMES GARFIELD. *Constitutional Problems under Lincoln.* New York: D. Appleton and Co., 1926.

———. *Lincoln the President: Springfield to Gettysburg.* 2 vols. New York: Dodd, Mead & Co., 1945.

———. *Lincoln the President: Midstream.* New York: Dodd, Mead & Co., 1952.

———, and CURRENT, RICHARD N. *Lincoln the President: Last Full Measure.* New York: Dodd, Mead & Co., 1955.

RIDDLE, ALBERT GALLATIN. *The Life of Benjamin F. Wade.* Cleveland: W. W. Williams, 1886.

RILEY, ELIHU SAMUEL. *A History of the General Assembly of Maryland: 1635– 1904.* Baltimore: Nunn & Co., 1905.

SANDBURG, CARL. *Abraham Lincoln: The War Years.* 4 vols. New York: Harcourt, Brace & Co., 1939.

SCHARF, JOHN THOMAS. *The Chronicles of Baltimore.* Baltimore: Turnbull Brothers, 1874.

———. *History of Maryland from the Earliest Period to the Present Day.* 3 vols. Baltimore: John B. Piet, 1879.

SCHMECKEBIER, LAWRENCE FREDERICK. *History of the Know Nothing Party in Maryland.* Series 17. No. 4–5 in *The Johns Hopkins University Studies in Historical and Political Science.* Baltimore: the Johns Hopkins Press 1899.

SEABROOK, WILLIAM L. W. *Maryland's Great Part in Saving the Union.* n.p., 1913.

SEITZ, DON C. *Lincoln the Politician.* New York: Coward, McCann, Inc., 1931.

SELBY, PAUL. *Abraham Lincoln: the Evolution of His Emancipation Policy.* (An address before Chicago Historical Society, at Chicago, Illinois, February 27, 1906.)

SMITH, WILLIAM ERNEST. *The Francis Preston Blair Family in Politics.* 2 vols. New York: Macmillan Co., 1933.

STEINER, BERNARD CHRISTIAN. *Life of Henry Winter Davis.* Baltimore: John Murphy Co., 1916.

———. *Life of Reverdy Johnson.* Baltimore: Norman, Remington Co., 1914.

———. *Citizenship and Suffrage in Maryland.* Baltimore: Cushing & Co., 1895.

SWISHER, CARL BRENT. *Roger B. Taney.* New York: Macmillan Co., 1935.

THOMAS, BENJAMIN P. *Abraham Lincoln.* New York: Alfred A. Knopf, 1952.

———, and HYMAN, HAROLD M. *Stanton: The Life and Times of Lincoln's Secretary of War.* New York: Alfred A. Knopf, 1962.

TUCKERMAN, HENRY T. *The Life of John Pendleton Kennedy.* New York: G. P. Putnam & Sons, 1871.

VAN DUSEN, GLYNDON G. *Thurlow Weed: Wizard of the Lobby.* Boston: Little, Brown & Co., 1947.

WILEY, BELL IRVIN. *Southern Negroes, 1861–1865.* New York: Rinehart, 1953.

WILLIAMS, THOMAS HARRY. *Lincoln and the Radicals.* Madison, Wisc.: The University of Wisconsin Press, 1941.

WILSON, HENRY. *History of the Antislavery Measures of the Thirty-Seventh and Thirty-Eighth United States Congress, 1861–1864.* Boston: Waker, Wise & Co., 1864.

WRIGHT, JAMES M. *The Free Negro in Maryland: 1634–1860.* Vol. XCVII. No. 3. *Studies in History, Economics and Public Law.* Edited by the Faculty of Political Science of Columbia University. New York: Columbia University, 1921.

ZORNOW, WILLIAM FRANK. *Lincoln & the Party Divided.* Norman, Okla.: University of Oklahoma Press, 1954.

ARTICLES

BLASSINGAME, JOHN W. "The Recruitment of Negro Troops in Maryland," *Maryland Historical Magazine,* LVIII, No. 1 (1963), 20–29.

BLAUGH, L. E. "Education and the Maryland Constitutional Convention, 1850–1851," *Maryland Historical Magazine,* XXV (1930), 169–90.

CARROLL, KENNETH L. "Maryland Quakers and Slavery," *Maryland Historical Magazine,* XLV (1950), 215–25.

CLARK, CHARLES B. "Baltimore and the Attack on the Sixth Masachusetts Regiment, April 19, 1861," *Maryland Historical Magazine,* LVI (1961), 39–71.

———. "Politics in Maryland During the Civil War," *Maryland Historical magazine,* XXXVI–XLI (1941–46). (Reprints of these articles have been found in book form, Chestertown, Md., 1952.)

———. "Recruitment of Union Troops in Maryland, 1861–1865," *Maryland Historical Magazine,* LIII (1958), 153–76.

———. "Suppression and Control of Maryland, 1861–1865," *Maryland Historical Magazine,* LIV (1959), 241–71.

COLBURN, DR. HARVEY. "A Family Letter with views on Lincoln, 1862," *Maryland Historical Magazine,* LIII (1958), 75–78.

CUNZ, DIETER. "The Maryland Germans in the Civil War," *Maryland Historical Magazine,* XXXVI (1941), 394–419.

FRASURE, CARL M. "Union Sentiment in Maryland, 1859–1861," *Maryland Historical Magazine,* XXIV (1929), 210–24.

GALLOWAY, GEORGE B. "Development of the Committee System in the House of Representatives," *American Historical Review,* LXV (1959), 17–30.

FIELDING, GEOFFREY W. (ed.). "Gilmor's Field Report of His Raid in Baltimore County," *Maryland Historical Magazine,* XLVII (1952), 234–40.

FINCKH, ALICE H. (ed.). "Baltimore 1861: We Want Rapp," *Twenty-eighth*

Report of the Society for the History of Germans in Maryland, XXVIII (1953), 79–82. This is a letter from William Rapp to his father.

GODDARD, HENRY P. "Some Distinguished Marylanders I Have Known," *Maryland Historical Magazine,* IV (1909), 24–41.

GREEN, FLETCHER M. "A People at War: Hagerstown, Maryland, June 15– August 31, 1863." *Maryland Historical Magazine,* XL (1945), 251–60. Part of this article is the diary of Miss Lutie Kealhofer.

HAMILTON, E. BENTLEY. "The Union League: its Origin and Achievements in the Civil War." *Transactions of the Illinois State Historical Society for the Year 1921,* pp. 110–15.

HASSLER, WARREN W., JR. "The Battle of South Mountain," *Maryland Historical Magazine,* LII (1957), 39–64.

HENNIGHAUSEN, LOUIS P. "Reminiscences of the Political Life of the German-Americans in Baltimore during 1850–1860," *Seventh Annual Report of the Society for the History of the Germans in Maryland* (Baltimore, 1892–1893), pp. 53–59; *Eleventh and Twelfth Annual Reports of the Society for the History of the Germans in Maryland* (Baltimore, 1897–1898), pp. 3–18.

HOLLAND, EUGENIA CALVERT and GARY, LOUISA MACGILL (compilers). "Minatures in the Collection of the Maryland Historical Society," *Maryland Historical Magazine,* LI (1956), 341–54.

KLEIN, FREDERICK SHRIVER. "Union Mills, the Shriver Homestead," *Maryland Historical Magazine,* LII (1957), 290–306.

LOW, W. A. "The Freedmen's Bureau and Education in Maryland," *Maryland Historical Magazine,* XLVII (1952), 29–39.

LUTHIN, REINHARD H. "A Discordant Chapter in Lincoln's Administration: The Davis-Blair Controversy," *Maryland Historical Magazine,* XXXIX (1944), 25–48.

MATTHEWS, SIDNEY T. "Control of the Baltimore Press During the Civil War," *Maryland Historical Magazine,* XXXVI (1941), 150–70.

MYERS, WILLIAM STARR. Governor Bradford's Private List of Union Men of 1861," *Maryland Historical Magazine,* VII (1912), 83–90.

NICHOLS, ROY F. "The Operation of American Democracy, 1861–1865: Some Questions," *The Journal of Southern History,* XXV (Southern Historical Association, 1959), 31–52.

PATTERSON, JERRY E. "Brantz Mayer, Man of Letters," *Maryland Historical Magazine,* LII (1957), 275–89.

RUSS, WILLIAM A., JR. "Disfranchisement in Maryland (1861–67), *Maryland Historical Magazine,* XXVIII (1933), 309–28.

SANDBURG, CARL. "Lincoln, Man of Steel and Velvet," *National Geographic Magazine,* CXVII (1960), 239–41.

STEINBERG, ALFRED. "Fire-Eating Farmer of the Confederacy," *American Heritage,* IX (1957), 22–25, 114–17.

STEINER, BERNARD. "Brantz Mayer," *Maryland Historical Magazine,* V (1910), 1– 22.

———, (ed.). "Correspondence of James Alfred Pearce," *Maryland Historical Magazine,* XVI–XIX (1921–24).

STUMP, WILLIAM. "Maryland Club: A Civilized Centenarian," Baltimore *Sunday Sun Magazine,* May 19, 1957.

TYSON, RAYMOND W. "Henry Winter Davis: Orator for the Union," *Maryland Historical Magazine,* LVIII (1963), 1–19.

WAGANDT, CHARLES L. "The Opinion of Maryland on the Emancipation Proclamation: Bernal to Russell, September 23, 1862," *Maryland Historical Magazine,* LVIII (1963), 250–51.

WILLIAMS, T. HARRY. "Abraham Lincoln—Principle and Pragmatism in Politics: A Review Article," *Mississippi Valley Historical Review,* XL (1953), 89–106.

WOLF, HAZEL C. "An Abolition Martyrdom in Maryland," *Maryland Historical Magazine,* XLVII (1952), 224–33.

WOOSTER, RALPH A. "The Membership of the Maryland Legislature of 1861," *Maryland Historical magazine,* LVI (1961), 94–102.

ZORNOW, WILLIAM FRANK. "The Judicial Modifications of the Maryland Black Code in the District of Columbia," *Maryland Historical Magazine,* XLIV (1949), 18–32.

———. "The Union Party Convention at Baltimore in 1864," *Maryland Historical Magazine,* XLV (1950), 176–200.

INDEX

A

Abolitionists: cast caution aside, 47–48; and Frederick Douglass, 48; to rescue nation, 55; ways of defeating, 67

"Abolition party, the," 200

Administration, the: Democrats antagonistic to, 136, need for support, 141; *See also* Lincoln, Abraham

Advocate: "going over of the Conservatives to the Radicals," 232

Agricultural society: of tidewater counties, v; unchanging in, 1,2

Albert, William Julian: residence of, 221

Alexander, Thomas S.: as candidate for senator, 38; spoke for appellants, 261

Alexandria, Virginia: Davis began practicing law in, 21; and fugitives, 120

Allegany County: mass meeting, 100; voter turnout, 180; Democrats ran a ticket, 216; and sabotage, 217

Allegheny Plateau, 3

American Anti-Slavery Society: auxiliary groups, 6n

American flag: return of, 72

American Party: out of Know-Nothings, 6; splintered, 6

American Revolution: skirmish at Lexington, 11

American Telegraph Company: and Schenck's orders, 162

Anderson Union League, 240

Annapolis: Constitutional Convention in 1, 221; election incident at, 177

Annapolis Gazette: party organ, 136

Anne Arundel County: and Bladensburg convention, 113; and fugitive slaves, 118; and Union Convention, 136

Antietam Creek: struggle erupting around, 72

Anti-slavery association: organized, 5

Anti-Wool conference: four men arrested, 96

Apprenticeship: proposed for freed slaves, 191–92; prohibitory clause, 265

Arbitrary power: exercise of, v

Arkansas: seceded, 10

Armitage, James: and Wool prisoners, 96; Administration "*losing ground*," 240–41

Atlanta: fell, 241

Augur, Christopher Colon: troops at polling places, 178; mentioned, 215

B

Ballots, 176–177

Baltimore: and Maryland geography, 1; foreign commerce, 4; "Mobtown," 7; reports of civilians shot, 11; Union officeholders, 13; free of secession mobs, 13; needed the Union, 15; delegates from, 102; barricades in, 104; Unconditional Union ticket no opposition, 217; and mayoralty race, 258

Baltimore American: government printing orders, 35; Maryland's leading daily, 35n; and General Assembly, 36–37; Lincoln's message to Congress, 56, 80; on President's policy, 61, 62; deals with ward bosses, 88; and Maryland bill, 91; and Union Party schism, 102; and voters, 137; and Schenck's orders, 162; and Hick's victory, 193; Convention Bill wording, 196; and slave market, 203; and Cecil catechism, 211; declaration of Union delegates, 222; and grouping of rival forces, 232; Maryland's "regeneration," 264

Baltimore and free counties: assessed worth of, 4n

Baltimore and Ohio Railroad: trade out of

Baltimore, 5; secession would cripple, 15, 16; and governmental patronage, 95; Swann ex-president of, 108

Baltimoreans: murdered on Pratt Street, 31

Baltimore City Union Convention, 137

Baltimore Clipper: on candidates, 137; and draft postponed, 150; offered to sell political sentiment, 188; and Cecil catechism, 211

Baltimore County: and convention at Bladensburg, 113; election in, 180; slates for April election, 199

Baltimore County American, 133, 145

Baltimore County Convention, 113

Baltimore County Unionists: same contingent to both conventions, 102

Baltimore election: fall of 1862, 88–89; Chapman swamped Fickey, 89; Union rivals fought, 137; soldiers intimidate citizens, 138

Baltimore jobbers: resold goods to South, 4

Baltimore ordinance: and swearing allegiance, 156n

Baltimore police force: military control of, 31; released, 31

Baltimore Unionists: elected delegates, 99

Barnum's Hotel: meeting at, 101

Barricades: in Baltimore, 103

Bates, Edward: and fugitive slaves, 117–18; civil authority outranked military, 119–20; Wallace infringed upon jurisdiction of, 250

Battle of Bull Run: announced, 29; lost, 29; spectators, 29

Bay Line Steamboat Co., 95

Bayne, John H.: and losses in Negroes, 37

Beale, William E., 139

Beauregard, General: and Confederates 29

Bel Air: home of Bradford, 30

Bell, John: and Constitutional Union Party, 9, 22

Belt, Edward W.: and Constitutional Convention, 222n

Ben Hur, 207

Benton, Thomas Hart: Blair protégé of, 24

Bernal, Frederic, 32

Berry, John Summerfield: elected Speaker, 39, 40; from Davis alignment, 39; and resolutions, 86; to Washington, 158; and federal funds for slave owners, 225

Bingham, John A.: and Maryland bill, 91

Birney, William: organizing a negro regiment, 122–23; and Camlin's slave-pen, 125; and Negro recruitment, 126, 199; mentioned, 189

Black belt: and rebel sympathizers, 104

Black Code, 196

Bladensburg: convention at, 113; and trickery, 113

Blair, Francis, Jr.: helped save Missouri for the Union, 24; signed compensation report, 70; and state convention, 236

Blair, Francis P., Sr.: ambitions for sons, 24; confidential adviser to Lincoln, 24; and Emancipation Proclamation, 81

Blair, Montgomery: Postmaster General, 24; and Maryland's Republican Party, 24, 25; offices held, 24–25; before Supreme Court, 25; for emancipation, 25, 84, 93, 94; personal feuding, 26; and Davis, 26, 27, 109; nonslaveholder obstacle to emancipation, 56; at White House, 58; letter to *Baltimore American,* 62; and Emancipation Proclamation, 73–74, 75; and Maryland Institute meeting, 98–99; and Allen Bowie Davis, 101; and Union Party schism, 102; supported Holland, 114; and Fugitive Slave Law, 120; and slave enlistments, 124; Bradford letter to, 127; and power struggle, 141–42; Rockville speech, 146–47; removed from cabinet, 147; endorsed Bradford's protest, 158; and Crisfield report to Lincoln, 185, 186; and *Baltimore Clipper* offer, 188; prodding Bradford, 190; and the Constitutional Convention Bill; 193, home burned, 226; addresses House of Delegates, 231; Webster calls on, 235; and rejected delegates from Baltimore County, 236–37; offer to resign, 241; pleaded President's case, 242; touring Eastern Shore, 252; allied with Democrats, 267; mentioned, 85, 113, 191

Blocksom, Daniel: and delegates, 234
Bloody Lane: mentioned, 72
Board of Claims: established, 131
Boards of Enrollment, 114, 158
Bond, Hugh Lennox: petition from, 90; and Union League, 100; letter to Chase, 109; wanted slaves enlisted, 123, 124; president, Board of Claims, 131; delegate to National Convention, 236
Bonifant, Washington: Blair urged to replace, 27; delegate to Chicago Convention, 27; and Union League, 100
Border state rights: violation of, 113
Bounty: and Negro enlistments, 199
Bradford, Augustus Williamson: and Henry Clay, 30; Clerkship, 30; gubernatorial post, 30; native of Harford County, 30; to Peace Conference, 30; son in Confederate Army, 30n; overwhelmed Howard, 33; inauguration, 35–36; emancipation a "treason," 36; and runaways, 38; and Emancipation Proclamation, 77; and Union State Central Committee, 85; and Hicks appointment, 89; and slavery, 94; welcomed Schenck, 97; and Maryland Institute meeting, 98–99;and Union League resolutions, 99; and meeting at Barnum's Hotel, 101; and slave enlistments, 117–132 passim; letter to Blair, 127; and Rockville rally, 147n; aloof from campaign, 150; and troop movements, 158; and Schenck's order, 161–62; proclamation "inflammatory," 186; obeisance to new era, 190; and Constitutional Convention Bill, 193; and military intervention in the Convention election, 207–10, 213–14; home set on fire, 226; letters to Vickers, 246–47; and judges of election, 256; adoption of new constitution, 263; rejected votes, 263
Breckinridge, John C.: fire-eaters backing, 9; carried eleven states, 9
Brewer, Nicholas: attacked, 157n; on southern sympathy, 179
Brinckley's election district: armed citizens intervened, 168
Brittingham, William J.: took oath, 166
Brown, George William: won mayoralty,

7; and southern sympathizers, 11; apprehension of, 31, 31n. See also Donaldson, Thomas
Brown, John, 8
Browning, Orville H.: and Emancipation Proclamation, 81; and Fugitive Slave Law, 120
Burnside, Ambrose E.: Union troops stormed bridge, 72
Businessmen: and the Confederacy, 17
Butler, Benjamin F.: troops occupied Federal hill, 13; slaves "contraband of war," 116; mentioned 116–32 passim.

C

Calvert, Charles Benedict: Unionist victory, 20; smear tactics, 20n; majority report, 69; and Emancipation Proclamation, 77; on slavery, 94; and meeting at Barnum's Hotel, 101; candidacy of, 112, 113
Calvert County: and Union State Convention, 104; and fugitive slaves, 118
Cambridge Democrat: suppressed, 251
Cambridge Herald, 102
Cambridge Intelligencer, 232
Campbell's private jail, 50
Capitalism: radicals handmaiden of, 40
Carmichael, Richard B.: seizure of, 156–57; Democratic delegate, 244
Caroline County: buying votes, 176; slates for April election, 200; "frauds and outrages," 257
Carpenter, Francis B., 75
Carroll, Anna Ella: and Hicks, 89
Carroll, Charles: estate of, 41
Carroll County: Negroes recruited in, 125; and Maffit, 180; constitution lost in, 258
Catoctin Mountains, 71
Catonsville, 134
Caucasians: Maryland's, 2
Cecil County: location, 2, 2n; two delegations, 104; and Creswell, 112; and Union forces, 135–36; conservative Unionists withdraw, 136; Democratic county ticket, 135–36; meetings, 146; and April elections, 200n; and votes, 257, 258
Cecil County Catechism: and Convention election, 210–12; Maryland Union on,

216; and constitutional election, 256
Cecil Democrat: old issues of, vii; accused
    Cecil Whig, 62; and ballots, 177
Cecil Whig: and General Assembly, 37;
    slanderous charges, 62; and Emanci-
    pation Proclamation, 78; on Wool, 96;
    and Union Leagues, 98; and ballots,
    177; and state compensation, 203–4
Central Association for Lincoln and
    Johnson, 252–53
Central Lincoln Association, 237
Chambers, Richard, 93
Chandler, Zachariah: and dismissal of Blair,
    241
Chapman, John Lee: mayor of Baltimore,
    88, 238–39, 258
Chapman-Lincoln partisans, 253
Charles County: "States Rights" accept-
    able, 30; and Union State Convention,
    104; swamped the constitution, 258
Charleston, South Carolina, 10
Chase, Salmon P.: Secretary of the Trea-
    sury, 11, 26; on freeing slaves, 56;
    welcomed proclamation, 73; and
    Swann, 108–9; Swann and Davis, 109,
    191–92; and Fugitive Slave Law, 120;
    recruitment of Negroes, 123–24; and
    Ridgely Case, 140–41; for president,
    141; and Monument Square rally, 149;
    resigns, 241
Chesapeake and Ohio Canal, 4
Chesapeake Bay, 1, 4
Chestertown, Kent County, 43, 214
Chicago Times: "Negrophobia," 65
Circuit Court of Anne Arundel County:
    and *mandamus,* 261
City convention resolutions, 85–86
City Council candidates: and political
    manipulators, 88
City Union Convention: and Union Party,
    84–85; and mayoralty nominee, 88;
    copied Union League resolutions, 99
City union Judicial Convention, 137
Civil government, Maryland's, 157
Civilian and Telegraph: and Emancipation
    Proclamation, 82; accused Hicks, 90;
    and healing of Union Party schism,
    191; the vote in Allegany County, 216
Civil War: first enemy action, 11; bloodi-
    est day's battle, 72; great changes
    during, 95; and Negro troops, 122,

126, 127, 128, 197. *See also* Negro re-
    cruiting stations; Slaves: enlisted,
    123–32
Clarke, Daniel: clung to old order, 194,
    222, 224
Clay, Henry: campaign of 1844, 30
Clippers, 4
Cole, Charles: editor, *Maryland Union,* 256
Collector of Customs: office of, 139
Collier, Levin D.: "petty tyranny," 167;
    released judges, 167; and Moore trial,
    185
Colonization: of free Negroes, 80–81
Commerce: foreign, 4
Commercial interests: of north and west, v
"Committee of the Grand Leagues, the,"
    146
Committee of the Whole, 91
Committee on Emancipation and Coloni-
    zation, 91
Committee on Military Affairs and the
    Militia, 186
Compensation: eligibility for, 70; and for
    Maryland, 224–25
Compensated emancipation : for
    Delaware's slaves, 56; Lincoln's pro-
    posal for, 56–60; District bill, 64
"Conditional Unionists," 136
Confederacy: counterrevolution of, 2;
    Maryland sentiments and, 11, 13, 16
Confederate fortifications, 116
Confederate recognition: or war, 17
Confederates: at Manassas, Virginia, 29;
    into Maryland, 71, 225; withdrew, 72,
    226; Baltimore awaited attack, 103
Confederate support: Irish swung toward,
    19
Confederate sympathizer: to vote for, 136
Confederate-sympathizing tobacco coun-
    try; and test oaths, 258
Confiscation Act: slaves forfeited, 56, 67
Confiscation Act, second: far-reaching, 67
Congress: in special session, 17; slavery in
    territories, 67; and Unconditional
    Unionists, 181
Congress, the 37th: Maryland delegation
    and, 67n; Lincoln's message to, 79–80
Congressional appropriation: for Maryland
    slave owners, 194
Congressional District, Second: candidates
    in, 109–10

Congressional election, 17, 18
Conkling, Roscoe, 58
Conscription bill, 114–15
Conservatives: Union and slavery, 55
Conservative Unionists: and status quo, 65–67
Conservative Union leaders: attacked election irregularities, 185
Constitution: new in 1851, 5; and security, 87–88; in 1867, 268. See also Constitutional Convention; Constitutional election
Constitutional amendment: Lincoln proposed, 79–80
Constitutional Convention: in Annapolis, 1; referendum on, 181; election for, 195; victory, 215, 217–20; convened, 221; southern delegates, 222; ballot to soldiers, 227; House seats redistributed, 227–28; on registering of voters, 228; governorship and, 230; provision for public school, 230; office of lieutenant governor, 230; passed, 230; city slate for, 233; a minority addresses, 248
Constitutional Convention Bill: and obstructionist tactics, 193–94
Constitutional election: campaign not going well, 253; peaceful 256; results, 258–60; judicial battle, 260–61; soldiers' votes, 260–61, 263; efforts to overthrow verdict, 260–63
Constitutional Union Party, 9, 17
Constitutional Union ticket, 22
Constitution of 1776, 5
"Contraband of war," 116
Convention Bill: and voter qualifications, 246
Cooper Institute Meeting, 25
"Copperheads": stop ballots of, 159; troops requested, 255
Corkran, Francis S.: and President's plan, 84; Ridgely's unfitness, 139; and emancipation, 139; alienated Blair, 141
Councill, William H.: and Easton Gazette, 35
County conventions, 134–36
Court of Appeals: and mandamus, 261
Covey, Edward, 49
Creager, John P.: recruited Negroes, 125–26

Creswell, John A. J.: and equitable representation, 37; to Union State Convention, 104; Unconditional Union candidate, 112; and political rallies, 147, 148; and Crisfield's opposition, 148; close to Winter Davis, 157; and military order, 157; seat contested, 186; and Frazier, 187; and compensation, 204–5; presidency of state convention, 234; to National Convention, 235; replaced Hicks, 266
Crisfield, Arthur: pressed by inquisitor, 166; and Moore trial, 185
Crisfield, John Woodland: and border state delegations, 18–19; Negroes in servitude, 42, 68–69, 94; fought Maryland bill, 58, 59, 91–92; and District bill, 64; defeating abolitionists, 67; author of majority report, 69; and Emancipation Proclamation, 76–77, 81; and Hicks, 89; meeting at Barnum's Hotel, 101; and victory, 111; Davis faction, 111; and Negro regiment, 128; publicly accused Creswell, 148; asked Swann to call upon Lincoln, 155; obstructionist tactics of, 160; received Bradford's proclamation, 164–65; carried Somerset County, 169; and First Congressional District, 177; seat contested, 185–86
Crittenden, John J.: war to preserve Union, 29; and emancipation parties, 59; and Emancipation Proclamation, 81
Cushing of Baltimore: preamble and resolution, 226
"Custom House Party," 233

D

Davis, Allen Bowie, 101
Davis, David, 24, 190
Davis, Henry Winter: early life, 20, 21; Civil War politician, 21–24; and Montgomery Blair, 26, 27; government looking ridiculous, 32; legislature "timid, irresolute," 38; backing of Examiner and Cambridge Herald, 39; and allies, 39; and Emancipation Proclamation, 78, 79; on Hicks, 90; drafted compensation plan, 91; and radical faction, 94; and volunteer companies, 103;

acclamation greeted, 108; and fall election, 111; behind emancipation, 132; forged a mighty weapon, 143; and rallies, 146–50 *passim*; and a military order, 157; and election in southern Maryland, 178–79; unpopular, 180, 193; Administration majority and military interference, 186; on newspapers, 188; and Lincoln, 189–90, 233–46 *passim*; and Chase, 192; and Maryland Institute rally, 205–6; disgusted with legislature, 231; and delegates to National Convention, 236; patronage for Stirling, 239n–40n; as *amici curiae*, 261; ruined party, 265–66; died, 267; mentioned 13, 85, 114

Davis, Jefferson, 10, 91

Davis, John W., 168n

Deal's Island polls, 168

Declaration of Rights: Article No. 5, 223; Article No. 24, 223–25; vote taken on emancipation, 225

Democratic ballots: white, 167

Democratic cry, 255

Democratic organization: collapsed, 17

Democratic Party, 7, 22

Democratic State Convention: endorsed oath taking, 248

Democrats: split their forces, 6, 9; exploiting fears, 21; and Emancipation Proclamation, 74; and fall elections, 79; District Convention, 112; arrested, 136; opposition from, 136; and Bradford's proclamation, 172; ticket partially filled, 176; won southern Maryland, 179; and Union split, 200; attacked Constitutional Convention, 201–3; the true Union party, 202; polls opened to disloyal, 202; sought apprenticeship, 228; state convention, 244; defended old order, 249; gained control of Maryland, 268

Dennis, George R., 251n

Dent, John F., 227

Denton Journal, 156, 257

Department of the South, 65

Department of Washington, 178

District bill: Marylanders petitioned for repeal of, 64; Lincoln's signature, 64; to abolish slavery in District of Columbia, 64

Dix. John A.: and suffrage, 32; and loyalty oath, 32, 156n; and Unionists, 95

Donaldson, Thomas: defence of Brown, 31; for senator, 38; rival motions, 104; and delegate votes, 113

Dorchester County: and Creswell, 112; clerkship in, 156; Union Party schism, 200

Doughoregan Manor, 41

Douglas, Stephen A.: Democrats rallied to, 9; and slavery, 55

Douglass, Frederick: leading abolitionist, 48–49; and "strong black arm," 122

Draft: and Negro recruiting, 198

Dred Scott case, 25

Dunkard Church, 72

E

Earle, George, 207

Early, Jubal Anderson: and raiders, 225

Eastern Shore: farming, 2; industry, 2; slave counties, 2; static life, 3; Crisfield strong, 18; and First District, 111; Negro regiment to, 126, 127, 128; trading restricted, 156n; and radicals, 157; stronghold of conservative Unionists, 157; Bradford proclamation reached, 163–64; action against judges, 257. *See also* Crisfield, John Woodland

Easton: trouble around, 126–27

Easton Gazette: public office urged for editor of, 35

Easton Star, 37, 42, 52

Economic order: outmoded, v

Edelen, Richard H.: and oath, 227

Editors: shipped South, 156

Education: languished, 51

Eighth Ward: stronghold of Irish, 19

Election, November, 1861, 32–34

Election, November, 1863; control of, 155; and writ of habeas corpus, 156; and violence, 156–72 *passim*; Washington interested in, 181; state-wide, 181–84; political revolution, 184; tumult following, 185–86

Election judges: action against, 257

Elective franchise: oath included, 226

Elkton: campaign meeting, 147

Ellicott Mills, 41

Emancipation: immediate, 1; sentiment 6; rejected as impossible, 42; and the federal government, 57; and fear of Negro equality, 70; social revolution, 70; predicted, 108; "unwise and impolitic," 135; gradual, 190; reaction of the people to, 249–50; and Negro equality, 258; mentioned, 135–51 *passim*, 231, 232, 244

Emancipation flag: hoisting of, 99

Emancipationists, southern, 5

Emancipation Proclamation: 73–78; a military necessity, 73, 74; presented to cabinet, 73–75, 81; solidified South, 76; secessionist sympathizers raged, 76; governors approved, 77; and the newspapers, 78; Northerners applauded, 79; and border state congressmen, 81; and Lincoln's signature, 82; response to, 82–83, 231, 232

Equitable representation: bill reported, 37; House seats redistributed, 228

Evans, French S., 28

Evening Post: Wallace stopped publication of, 250–51

Ewing, Wm. Pinkney, 26

Examiner: and Maryland bill, 19; backing Davis, 39; and city convention resolutions, 86; and President, 62–63; equitable representation, 86; and Cecil catechism, 211

Executive mansion, 185

F

Falls, Moore n.: and Wool, 95

Federal Hill: occupied, 13

Federal interference: in the institutions of any state, 36

Federal officials: meeting of, 138–39

Fickey, Frederic, Jr., 88, 101

Fifth Congressional District, 177

Fifth District Union Congressional Convention, 113

Fillmore, Millard, 7

Financial panic: of 1857, 7

First Congressional District, 148, 172

First Congressional District counties: rival Union slates, 136

First District primary: fracas occurred at, 133

Fisher, George P., 56

Fort McHenry: candidates locked in, 175; mentioned, 213, 264

Fortress Monroe, Virginia, 116

Fourth Congressional District Convention, 110–11

Fourth District polls: new election, 215

Fraudulent practices: and voting, 155–84 *passim*

Frazier, John: assistant grain inspector, 34–35; Negro company, 126; provost marshal and candidate for clerk, 158; and Kent County election, 172–75; arrest of, 175; crushing defeat, 176; attacked by conservatives, 185; appointment revoked, 187–88; and division in Union Party, 200

Frederick, Maryland: General Assembly reconvened in, 31; league formed in, 98; fell, 225

Frederick Citizen: and amalgamation, 203

Frederick County: Negroes recruited in, 125

Frederick ovation: inspiration of, 72

"Free Constitution," 254–55

Freedman's bureau: created by Wallace, 265

Free elections: subverted, 185

Frémont, John C., 241

Front Royal, Virginia, 116

Fry, James B., 114

Fugitives: military protection of, 58; and public policy, 117

Fugitive Slave Law, 118, 120

Fulton, Charles Carroll: publisher, *Baltimore American*, 35n; supported Republican Administration, 35n

G

Galloway, Samuel, 149

Garfield, James A., 159

Garrett, Henry, 48

Garrett, John W.: president of railroad, 16, 95

General Assembly: under Democrats, 12; hostility to Washington, 13; reconvened in Frederick, 31; and federal interference, 36; battle over Speakership, 192; endorsed second term for Lincoln, 231

General Orders No. 11: to enlist all Negroes, 198n

General Orders No. 53; quietly dispatched, 157–58; Schenck defends, 158–61; won praise, 186

German political refugees, 6

German-language newspapers: against slavery, 51
Germans: in Baltimore, 3; gave Leary support, 19
Gilmer, John A., 55
Gist, Richard I., 82–83
Goldsborough, Henry M.: President of the Maryland Senate, 40; and convention harmony, 105; for state comptroller, 106, 179–80; election chances, 137; and Elkton meeting, 147; victory over Maffit, 181; president, Constitutional convention, 221; delegate, 235; and social revolution, 249–50
Goldsborough-Maffit struggle, 136
Goldsborough men: called radicals, 106
Grand League of Maryland, 97
Greene, Albert C., 235

H

Hagerstown: refugees, 116; fell 225
Harford County: Union Party, 135, 179; and April elections, 200n; constitution's loss in, 258
Harpers Ferry: seized, 8; surrender of, 72
Harper's Weekly: Maryland and Lincoln's plea, 65; and Republican defeat, 79; and Wade-Davis Manifesto, 240
Harris, Benjamin Gwinn: candidate, 20, 112; petitioned Lincoln, 155; victory, 178; Democratic delegate, 244; opposition to McClellan, 244; re-elected, 266
Harrison, Samuel, 251–52, 253
Hay, John, 81, 159
Henkle, Eli J., 1
Hickman, John: and border states, 68
Hicks, Thomas Holliday: governor, 7, 11, 12; convened General Assembly, 35; senator, 89–90; presented Lennox petition, 90; toward emancipation, 94; and political meetings, 98–99, 101, 147n; aloof from campaign, 150; asked "a stringent oath," 156; elected senator, 193; wanted slavery ended, 206; addresses House of Delegates, 231; requested suppression of Cambridge Democrat, 251; death, 266
Hill, Ambrose P., 72
Hines, Jesse K., 175
Hoffman, Henry W.: and joint conven-

tion, 103; reported impasse, 106; for emancipation, 138–39; Chase for president, 141; unveiled address, 142–43; and Kent County election, 172; Swann rejection, 233; to National Convention, 235; Blair called unreliable, 243; mass meeting for "Free Constitution," 254–55
Holland, John C.: campaign, 113–15; political rallies, 147, 148; provost marshal and congressional candidate, 158
Holland-Calvert struggle, 136
House of Delegates: new membership, 33; John S. Berry, speaker; and November election, 181; Unionists' address, 231
House of Representatives: war to preserve Union, 29; Lincoln's message, 57; Davis seat in, 107
Howard, Benjamin C.: candidate of southern sympathizers, 30, 31
Howard County, 2, 41, 113
Hungary Neck: and Crisfield, 168n
Hunter, David: insubordinate, 65; and arrests, 251

I

Immigrants: shunned tidewater counties, 1, 2; in Baltimore City, 3; prejudice against, 6
Independent Line: and Schenck's orders, 162
Independent Union City Convention, 137
Industrial products: tripled, 4
Intelligencer: and Union tickets, 200
Invasion: of Maryland, 74
Irish: in Baltimore, 3; Confederate support, 19

J

Jackson, Stonewall: rebel column across Potomac, 71; and surrender of Harpers Ferry, 72
Jackson District: outbreak in, 216
Johnson, Andrew: became president, 267
Johnson, Reverdy: and Dred Scott case, 25; political career of, 33, 38, 39–40, 150; and slavery, 47; and District bill, 63, 64; and Creswell victory, 186; amendment to federal constitution, 207; opposition to new constitution, 244; spurned test oath, 247

John Tracey, 131
Jones, William J., 112, 192
Judges of election: and authority, 162

K

Kelley, William D., 148, 159
Kemp, Thomas, H.: as Speaker, 192; and
   Congressional appropriation, 194
Kenly, John R.: dispatched troops, 214
Kennedy, Anthony: successor to, 38–39,
   fanatical, 44; and district bill, 64; sec-
   ond Confiscation Act, 67; defeatist,
   92–93
Kennedy, John Pendleton, 11, 47
Kent County: election in, 172–75; Union
   split, 200; mentioned, 35
Kent News: on Lincoln's proposal, 61–62;
   and resolution, 86; "*commanded*" to print
   Tevis order, 173
Kilbourn, Elbridge Gerry: and oath, 208
Know-Nothings: and American Party, 6;
   "Americanism," 6; local victories, 7;
   Davis joined, 21; mentioned, 97

L

Lamon, Ward H.: and Fugitive Slave Law,
   118, 120; and Althea Lynch, 119
Landed gentry: 41, 94
Land values, 88
Leary, Cornelius L. L.: congressional triumph, 19; signed majority report, 69;
   and Emancipation Proclamation, 77;
   emancipation sentiment, 92; as incumbent, 110
Lee, Robert E.: and Brown insurrection,
   8; proclamation, 71; on the move, 103
Legislation: reactionary, 6
Legislature: special session in Annapolis,
   35
Leonard, William James: replaced Frazier,
   188; and patronage, 252
Lincoln, Abraham: became president, 9,
   10; and Fort Sumter, 10; and writ of
   habeas corpus, 12, 31, 56; and fashionable world, 15; cabinet of, 24; leadership of, 24, 55, 187; and patronage,
   26; attack on Confederates, 29; and
   Maryland prisoners, 34; and Fulton,
   35n; and public opinion, 55; on slavery, 55; to preserve the Union, 55;
   assumed vast powers, 55–56, 160; and

border state conservatives, 55, 59; proposal to Congress for freeing the slaves,
   56–60; newspapers and, 61–62; and
   the District bill, 64; Hunter insubordinate to, 65; and border state delegations, 68, 72; and Emancipation
   Proclamation, 73–83 and colonization,
   80–81; and arrests in Baltimore, 96;
   and new Congress, 107; and Swann,
   109; and enlistment of slaves, 118–32
   passim; and Negro recruitment, 122,
   129; and Ridgely case, 141; and election abuses, 155, 185; and General
   Orders No. 53, 158, 159, 160–61, 162;
   violence and freedom, 184; revoked
   Frazier's appointment, 187–88; and
   Davis, 189–90; and Maryland emancipation, 201; abolition in Maryland,
   208; talked of liberty, 221; and constitutional election, 231–45 *passim*; re-
   election, 231, 232, 238, 240–41, 266;
   and Wade-Davis Manifesto, 240;
   Davis plotted to replace, 240–44
   passim; and Blair's resignation, 241; the
   constitution's prospects, 253–54; letter to mass meeting, 254; and free
   Maryland, 263; assassinated 267;
   mentioned, 18. *See also* Compensated
   emancipation, Emancipation Proclamation
Lincoln Administration: mix slavery and
   government, 17
Lincoln Associations, 237
Lloyd, Edward: Douglass to plantation of,
   48
Lockwood, Henry Hayes: judges released,
   167; replaced Schenck, 189; yielded
   post, 207; troops on Eastern Shore, 213
Longnecker, John H., 133, 134
Lovejoy, Owen, 48
Lynch, Althea, 119

M

McClellan, George B.: and voters, 32; secessionists held, 32; army and fugitive
   slaves, 38; retook Frederick, 72; removed from command, 77; Democratic
   opponent, 242
McDowell, James, 20
McIlvaine, Charles P., 21
McJilton, John F., 139, 141

Maffit, Samuel S.: comptroller, 30, 106, 144–45; at Barnum's Hotel, 101; supporters of, 106; standing pat, 181
Majority report, 69
Mandamus, 260–61
Manufacturing, 4
Manumission: prohibited, 8; prohibition repealed, 196
Marbury, Fendall: oaths, 178; and vote, 225
Marshall, William L., 52
Maryland: political ascendancy and geography, 1; sectionalized, 1, 5, 15; farms, 2–4; industry, 2–5; free counties, 3; impelled into opposition, 11; Union sentiment, 14; and the Union, 15; battle-ground, 16, 74, 105; emancipation, 197–221 *passim*; emancipation of national importance, 201
Maryland Agricultural College, 20
Maryland bill, 91–92
Maryland Bounty Bill, 199n
Maryland Constitutional Convention, of 1850–51, 18
Maryland emancipationists, 85
Marylanders: thrown into federal prisons, 31
Maryland General Assembly: expulsion of slaves, 6; and Lincoln's proposal, 60
Maryland House of Delegates: and slavery in the District of Columbia, 63, 64
Maryland Institute: pro-Union delegates at, 17; Union League meeting in, 98–99; rally in, 205–6
Maryland legislators: Confederate sympathies, 31; immovable, 70
Maryland legislature: acts restricting the Negro, 8; slave counties exercised veto, 46
"Maryland, My Maryland," 71
Maryland secessionists, 71
Maryland State Electoral Convention: rival delegations, 237
Maryland State Fair, 221
Maryland State Union convention: delegates denounced secession, 29
Maryland Union: and county conventions, 135; and "Cecil County Catechism," 216; picayune charges, 256
Massey, Elijah E.: and Tevis, 175
Matthews, R. Stockett, 108, 146

May, Benjamin F., 164–65
May, Henry: Congressman, 20, 21; blocked Maryland bill, 91; Democratic delegate, 244
Mayer, Brantz, 85, 101
Mayor of Baltimore: contest for, 238–39
Meredith, John F., 139
Meigs: and troops, 213
Melville, Frank: and oath, 168
Merryman, John, 31
Middle Department, 95, 178
Miles River Ferry, 126
Miles River neck, 50
Military interference: and elections, 156–172 *passim*, 256; reported, 214
Military protection: of fugitives, 58
Military records, 159
Millar, Thomas A., 117
Minority report, 69
Missouri bill, 91, 92
"Mobtown," 7, 11
"Monster War Meeting," 95
Montgomery County, 113
Monument Square: meetings at, 98, 149–50
Moore, Charles C.: and General Orders No. 53, 164–67; trial ordered, 185

N

National Convention: Maryland delegates to, 235–37
National Democratic ticket, 30, 31n
National Intelligencer, 249
National Union Convention delegation, 237
National Union League: formation of, 100
National Union (Republican) Convention: delegates to, 232
Negro: fear of, 6; and freedom, 43, 84; and equality, 43, 202; labor, 87; expendable, 117; regiment, 126–28; recruiting of, 131, 198–99; status of, 197, 230; suffrage, 267
"Negro-catchers," 118n
Negroes: to colonize, 5, 25; severe losses, 37; at Doughoregan Manor, 41; freed, 42; as property, 44; fleeing to military, 84; conscripted, 103; flight to Hagerstown, 116, in uniform, 121–22; imprisoned, 197–98; and the new Constitution, 264–65

Negroes, free: in tidewater counties, 1, 2; in Maryland by 1860, 8, 9; asylum for, 43; expulsion rejected, 45; neither idle nor vicious, 45; scapegoat for economy, 45; taxed for support of, 45; deportation for, 80n; recruitment of, 123–25

Nellie Pentz, 174

New York times: and cost of Lincoln's proposal, 60

Nicholls, William J., 139

Ninth election District: primary at, 133

North: seeking commercial supremacy, 20n

North Carolina: seceded, 10

North Gay Street, 103

O

Oath *See* Test Oath

Obstructionist tactics: and Constitutional Convention Bill, 193–94

Offices, minor: and devotion to Union, 34

Oligarchy: clung to power, 194

P

Partridge, James R., 27

Patapsco River, I, 4

Patronage, 28, 188

Patuxent River: and armed Negroes, 130

Peace Commission: of 1861, 18

Peace Convention: and the Union, 10

Peace Party candidates: five kinds of tickets, 30–31; 136

Peace Unionists: against Davis, 21

Pearce, James A.: support for Union, 38; report, 45; dead, 89

Perjury: rampant, 257

Phillips, Wendell: abolitionist, 45, 59

Piatt, Donn: emancipationist objectives, 123; and political rallies, 146, 147; ordered arrests, 173; raged at Tevis, 174; ordered out of Baltimore, 189

Political expediency: and support, 93–94

Political prisoners: released, 34n

Pinto, John V.: and General Orders No. 53, 165; arrested, 166

Poor white: and social structure, 44; cautioned, 87; substitute for, 149n, 150

Port Tobacco, 121

Postmaster General: Blair chosen. *See also* Blair, Montgomery

Potomac River, 1, 71

Powell, Lazarus W., 186

Pratt, Thomas G.: refused oath, 177–78

Pratt Street: Baltimoreans murdered on, 31; Campbell's private jail, 50; slave pen, 125

President, the: job seekers harassed, 26; job disputes, 27–28. *See also* Lincoln, Abraham

Preston, William P., 19

Price, William: United States District Attorney, 38; and emancipation,139; and Union City Convention, 233

Prince Georges County: delegation withdrew, 113; and fugitive slaves, 118; oath taking, 178; Negroes imprisoned in, 197–98

Princess Anne: receives Bradford proclamation, 164

Provost marshal: Conscription bill and political power, 114, 115

Public school: provision for, 230; provisions cancelled, 268

Purnell, William H.: postmaster of Baltimore, 26; and Swann men, 233; allied with Democrats, 267

Purnell Legion, 188

R

Railroads: vital, 4, 5; bridges burned, 11; and escaping slaves, 46. *See also* Baltimore and Ohio Railroad

Rallies: mushroomed, 146–50

Rebel army: at Front Royal, 116

Rebel batteries: opened fire, 10

Rebel column: crosses Potomac, 71

Rebel sympathizers: and Lincoln Administration, 31

Rebels: privation of, 71

Recruiting officers: eschewed discretion. *See also* Negroes, free

Republican Party: emerged, 6; composed of, 24; defeated, 79. *See also* Blair, Montgomery; Lincoln, Abraham

Republicans: opposed slavery, 9; and support, 17; convention of, 25; radicals after power, 40

Revolution: throughout America, v; social, political, and economic, 40; control of movement, 94

Ricaud, James B.: conservative, 34; arrested, 172; Kent County election, 172–75; and Tevis order 174

Ridgely, James L., 139, 141
Ridgely Case, 140–41
Ridgeway, Isaac, 160
Rockville: rally in, 146; judges and election, 215
Ruffin, Edmund, 8
Runaways: problem of, 38; compensation for, 46
Russell, William Howard, 15, 41
Russum, George M.: supported Crisfield, 111; and votes, 176; and arrests, 200

S

St. Mary's Beacon, 61
St. Mary's County: and Union State Convention, 104; and Bladensburg convention, 113; and April elections, 201n
St. Mary's District: election in, 178–79
Salisbury: and Bradford proclamation, 164
Sauerwein, Peter G.: for emancipation, 84, 139; and resolutions, 85; and Wool prisoners, 96; and Davis' course, 242–43, and Negro suffrage, 267
Saulsbury, Willard, 59
Schenck, Robert C.: replaced Wool, 96; and Copperheads, 97; and Maryland Institute meeting, 99; and Union Leagues, 103; and Swain's removal, 121; recruitment of Negroes, 121–32 *passim*; and political rallies, 146; 148; and Bradford's proclamation, 162–63; relinquished command, 189
Schley, Frederick: editor, the *Examiner*, 63; and the Administration, 63; Chase for president, 141; and emancipation vote, 225; delegate, 236
Schley, William, 261
Schools: free, 204; integrating of, 258
Seabrook, William L. W.: and League action, 102–3; for commissioner, 106; conservatives weakened, 107; and the constitution's prospects, 253–54
Secession: and Maryland, v; and the socially ambitious, 15
Secessionists: controlled Baltimore, 12; against Davis, 21; and Lincoln's program, 61; ways of defeating, 67
Select committee on emancipation: Lincoln's bill referred to, 70
Sellman, John S., 192
Seminole War, 24

Seward, Mrs. Frederick, 73
Seward, William H., 13, 73, 74
Sharpsburg: savage struggle at, 72
Sherman, William Tecumseh, 241
Sixth Congressional District, 20
Sixth Massachusetts Regiment, 11
Slave: a pawn, 40; owners, 43; uprising of, 81n; power, 184; market, 203; counties, 258
Slaveholders: rights violated, 58; and fugitives, 116; and new Constitution, 264–65
Slavery: pressure to destroy, v, 4, 40, 190; proponents of, v, 1, 52, 87, 111; linked Maryland to southern culture, 5; westward, 6; agitation of, 36n, 117; a benevolent patriarchy, 42–44, 46; ramifications of, 44, 45; laws enacted, 46; vices of, 48–49; demoralizing, 51; and Union League resolution, 99; army struck hard at, 126; and emancipation, 135–51 *passim*; interests and, 227; social influence of, 257–58
Slaves: movement to free, v; in tidewater counties, 1, 2; and Nat Turner's uprising, 6; emancipated, 8; escaping from steamship, 46; sought refuge, 116; flight of protested, 118; enlisted, 123–32; orders concerning, 161; apprenticeship for, 191–92
Slave-trader: debased, 50
Snow Hill: and Negro soldiers, 131
Soldier's Home: Lincoln at, 74
Somerset county: and Creswell, 112;and April election, 200n; and Democrats, 167n; election irregularities in, 185; soldiers requested, 212
Sothoron, John H., 130
South, the, 15, 44, 57
South Carolina: seceded, 9
Southern colors, 32
Southern Maryland: and institutions of, 1; reactionary, 2; and fugitives, 84
South Mountain: battle at, 72
Speaker of the House: division on, 107
Spence, Thomas A., 193
Stanton, Edwin M.: Secretary of War, 25, 73; endorsed proclamation, 75; and recruitment of Negroes, 123–31 *passim*; and Piatt, 161; and Schenck, 161; ordered Leonard removed, 252

Stars and Stripes: flying in Baltimore, 13
State Central Committee, 17
State compensation, 203, 204
State convention, 234–37
State Rights Convention, 20
Steele, I. Nevett, 261
Stevens, Thaddeus, 59
Stewart, Joseph J.: candidate, 110; election of, 133; replaced Ridgely, 139
Stirling, Archibald, Jr.: convention presidency, 85; and Maryland Institute meeting, 98–99; binding delegates, 103; for state senator, 137; and rallies, 146; leader of majority, 222; and oath, 226; and Lincoln 231; and Blair, 235; delegate, 236; for mayor, 238–39; 258; and soldiers' ballots, 261
Stirling-Lincoln partisans, 253
Stockbridge, Henry: convention vice presidency, 85; president, Union League Convention, 103; and rallies, 146; and Speakership, 192; authored bill, 194; and the Constitutional Convention, 222; as *amici curiae*, 261
Straughn, Levin E.: edited *Intelligencer*, 112; and Russum, 112; and Board of Claims, 131; president pro tem, 237–38
Streeter, Sebastian F.: triumphed, 89; and Board of Claims, 131; president, Unconditional Union State Convention, 205
Stump, Henry, 181n
Sumner, Charles: and emancipation, 57, 73
Sun, the Baltimore, 16, 17
Superior court: and *mandamus*, 260
Supreme Court. *See* Dred Scott case; Taney, Roger B.
Swain, James B., 121
Swann, Thomas: fence-straddling, 93; and Institute meeting, 98–99; and congressional primary, 107–9; and campaign, 144, 145, 146; conferred with Lincoln, 155; end to slavery, 191–92; addresses House of Delegates, 231; rejected Hoffman offer, 233; and "Free Constitution" meeting, 254; won governorship, 266; allied with Democrats, 267

T
Täglicher Wecker, 52, 202
Talbot County: delegation, 101, 103; Democrats arrested, 136
Taney, Roger B.: and Dred Scott case, 25; and writ of habeas corpus, 31; and the oath, 248; died, 265
Temperance Temple, 103, 191
Tennessee: seceded, 10
Test oaths, 156
Tevis, Charles Carroll: and election order, 173; arrest of, 175; efforts to influence voting, 175
Thomas Collyer, 175
Thomas, Francis: retirement and, 19–20; signed majority report, 69; and emancipation sentiment, 77, 92, 94; and Maryland bill, 91; and constituents, 110–11; and fall election, 111; letter from Bradford, 124; and Rockville rally, 147; re-elected, 266
Tidewater counties, 1, 2, 86
Timmons, Thomas: and Board of Claims, 131; and draftees, 176; and Negro recruiting, 198
Tobacco crop, 2
Tome, Jacob, 135
Total vote: for Constitutional Convention, 217, 220
Touchstone, James, 135
Towson, 110, 148
Towsontown: county convention, 134
Treason bill, 37
Troops: and voters, 32, 256; bill prohibiting in an election, 187
Tyaskin polls, 168n
Tyler, Daniel, 185
Tyler, Erastus Barnard, 138, 189

U
Unconditional Central Committee, 233
Unconditional Union: political rallies, 146–50; candidates, 167; ballot, 168; Convention Bill, 194–96
Unconditional Unionism: commitments to, 111; and Holland, 113; cause of, 149; and Schenck, 161; and Piatt, 161
Unconditional Unionists: title, 106; Davis leader, 107; to battle conservatives, 107; turned to Creswell, 112; in Cambridge, 146; and votes, 176; sent to

Congress, 181; and inequitable assessments, 203; political dominance for, 227
"Unconditional Union Men": political initiative to, 85
Unconditional Union State Central Committee: address, 142–44; of Cecil County, 146; attacking the wavering, 193; state convention of, 232; mass meetings, 253
Unconditional Union tickets, 158, 172
Union, the: and Maryland, v, 17; needed Baltimore, 13, 15; force to preserve, 16
Union Central Committee, 70, 85
Union City Convention, 98
Unionists: and power, v; faction within, v; a vindictive war, 17; and minor offices, 34; and McClellan, 72; Swann's cause and, 108; divided, 233–45 *passim*
Union League Convention, 103–6
Union Leaguers, 106
Union Leagues, 97–101
Union Nominating Legislative Convention, 137
Union Party: and federal patronage, 28; hostile factions within, 30; in Baltimore, 85; and slavery, 94, 98, 99; schism, 102, and emancipation, 197–222 *passim*
Union State Central Committee: treasurer of, 88; rebuked, 100; state convention of, 101; party regulars met, 142; address, 142; Thomas Swann, chairman, 155; awkward peace, 191; and Unconditional faction, 232
Union State Convention: and Talbot delegation, 101; delegates to, 104; rump group, 104; and Union League Convention, 105
Union Troops: first killed, 11; retreat, 29; stormed bridge, 72
United States Senate, 186

V

Vallandigham, Clement L., 91–92, 96
Vickers, George: and Frazier, 34; and party, 86; immovable on slavery, 94; arrested, 172; and Kent County election, 172–75; and Lincoln, 187; quit Union Party, 243; and voting, 246–

47; letters to Bradford, 246–47; and Eastern Shore, 255
Virginia: seceded, 10

W

Wade, Benjamin Franklin, 240
Wade-Davis manifesto, 240, 253
Wadsworth, James S., 118–20
Wagner, James F., 139
Wallace, Lewis: and Middle Department, 207; and Convention election, 207–10; praised, 218; tried to stop Early, 225; seized property, 250; instructions on election, 256; arrest of citizens, 257; and freed Negroes, 264–65
War Department, 73
Washington: safe, 14; a Negro haven, 117; delegations to, 185
Washington league, 100
Webster, Edwin Hanson: to Washington, 19; for senator, 38; defeating abolitionists, 67; signed majority report, 69; altered position, 110; and Negro troops, 110, 121–22; views on slavery, 110; as incumbent, 110; and fall election, 111; sponsored Ridgely, 139; to Blair's home, 235; re-elected, 266
Wecker. See Täglicher Wecker
Weed, Thurlow, 24
Welles, Gideon, 73
Western Shore, 38
Whigs, 6
White, Albert S., 70, 91
White, Jacob, 167n
White laborers, 43
White settler, 4
Whitsuntide holidays, 43
Wilson, Henry, 92, 254
Winter, Davis faction, 233
Winter Davis partisans, 84
Wiss, Edward, 27
Woodbury, Levi, 25
Wool, John E.: associating with Garrett and Falls, 95; intense hostility, 95; charges of incompetence, 96; President asked to relieve, 96; replaced, 96
Worcester County, 112
Writ of habeas corpus, 56